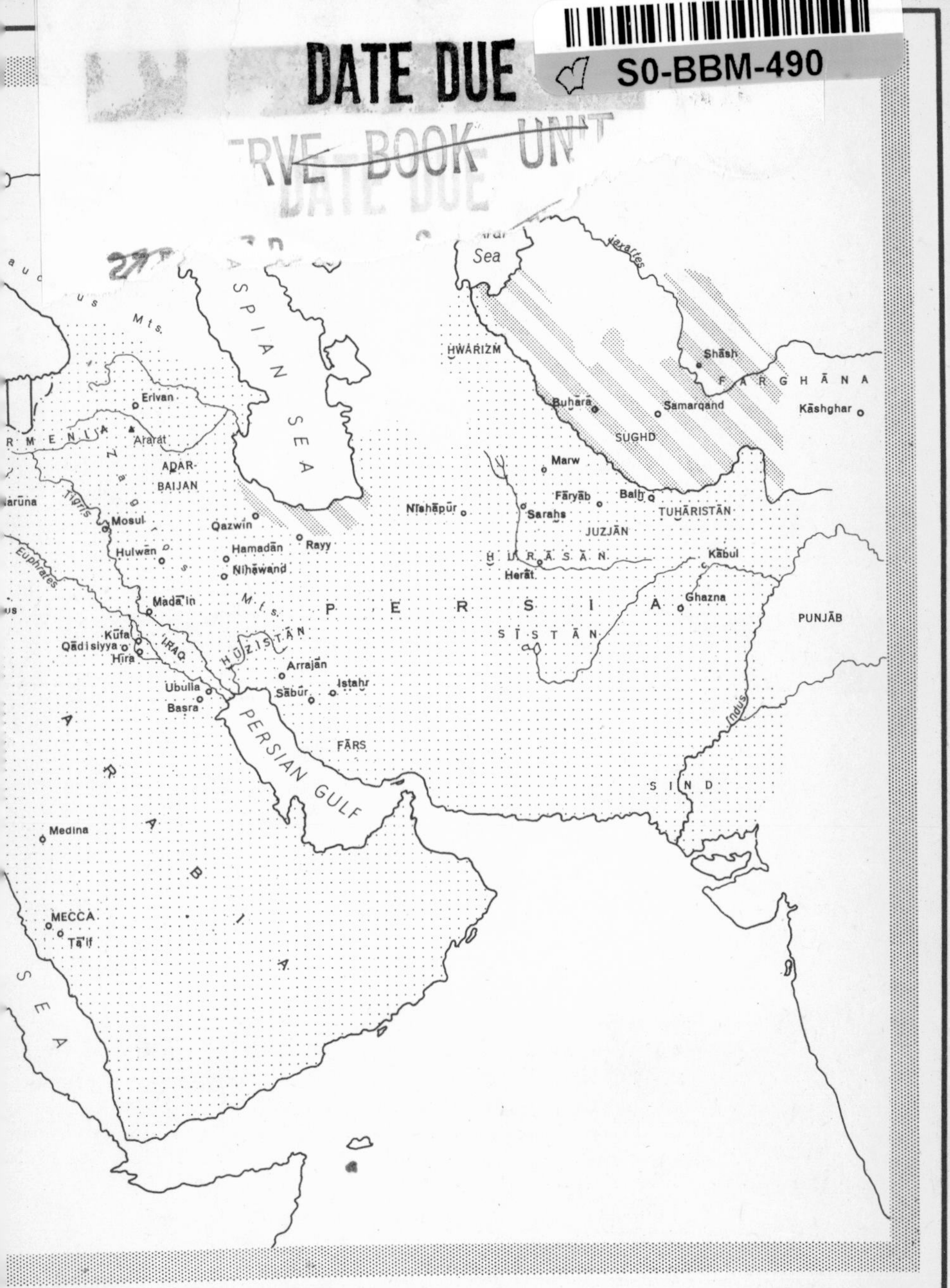
Sea
SPIAN SEA
Jaxartes
Mts.
HWARIZM
Shāsh
FARGHĀNA
Kāshghar
Buhārā
Samarqand
SUGHD
Erivan
Ararat
ADAR-BAIJAN
Marw
Tigris
Mosul
Qazwin
Nīshāpūr
Fāryāb
Balh
TUHĀRISTĀN
Sarahs
JUZJĀN
Hamadān
Rayy
Hulwān
Nihāwand
Euphrates
Herāt
Kābul
Madā'in
Mts.
PERSIA
Ghazna
PUNJĀB
SĪSTĀN
HŪZISTĀN
Kūfa
Qādisiyya
Hīra
'IRĀQ
Arrajān
Ubulla
Sābūr
Istahr
Basra
Indus
PERSIAN GULF
FĀRS
SIND
ARABIA
Medina
MECCA
Tā'if
SEA

ABOUT A.D. 750

MEDIEVAL ISLAM

MEDIEVAL ISLAM

A Study in Cultural Orientation

By

GUSTAVE E. VON GRUNEBAUM

SECOND EDITION

THE UNIVERSITY OF CHICAGO PRESS

CHICAGO · ILLINOIS

AN ORIENTAL INSTITUTE ESSAY

THE UNIVERSITY OF CHICAGO PRESS, CHICAGO 37
Cambridge University Press, London, N.W. 1, England

 Published 1946. Second Edition 1953. Composed and printed by THE UNIVERSITY OF CHICAGO PRESS
Chicago, Illinois, U.S.A.

PREFACE

THIS book has grown out of a series of public lectures delivered in the spring of 1945 in the Division of the Humanities of the University of Chicago. It proposes to outline the cultural orientation of the Muslim Middle Ages, with eastern Islam as the center of attention. It attempts to characterize the medieval Muslim's view of himself and his peculiarly defined universe, the fundamental intellectual and emotional attitudes that governed his works, and the mood in which he lived his life. It strives to explain the structure of his universe in terms of inherited, borrowed, and original elements, the institutional framework within which it functioned, and its place in relation to the contemporary Christian world.

A consideration of the various fields of cultural activity requires an analysis of the dominant interest, the intentions, and, to some extent, the methods of reasoning with which the Muslim approached his special subjects and to which achievement and limitations of achievement are due. Achievements referred to or personalities discussed will never be introduced for their own sake, let alone for the sake of listing the sum total of this civilization's major contributions. They are dealt with rather to evidence the peculiar ways in which the Muslim essayed to understand and to organize his world.

The plan of the book thus rules out the narration of political history beyond the barest skeleton, but it requires the ascertaining of the exact position of Islam in the medieval world and its significance. This plan also excludes a study of Muslim economy, but it leads to an interpretation of the social structure as molded by the prime loyalties cherished by the Muslim.

The Muslim approach to scholarship and literature is investigated, but the individual result attained by the Muslim scholar or writer, however important in the history of science or poetry, is touched upon only inasmuch as it documents a cultural trait not otherwise traced. In this context the structure of thought is regarded as more important than the particular ideas and the limitations of poetical ambition as significant as the successful poem. The Muslim scale of values becomes patent through the analysis of the supreme purpose of his existence rather than through the detailing of individual value-judgments.

As the Muslim lived in a composite civilization, the impulses guiding selection, rejection, and integration of foreign elements will be revealing. An attempt to list borrowed traits, however, would be entirely out of place.

To trace the temper and flavor of the Muslim Middle Ages may then be called the object of this study; with the qualification, however, that the writer considers the fine arts outside his ken.

Except for proper names such as Allah and Mohammed, for which English usage has evolved a familiar spelling, oriental names and terms are presented in the manner of transliteration customary in American orientalist periodicals.

The maps on the end papers are adapted from Reuben Levy, *An Introduction to the Sociology of Islam* (London, 1930–33), by permission of the publishers, The Rationalist Press Association London.

University of Chicago
December 1945

G. E. von Grunebaum

PREFACE TO THE SECOND PRINTING

For the second printing a small amount of additional material has been incorporated in some of the notes.

University of Chicago
June 1947

G. E. von Grunebaum

PREFACE TO THE SECOND EDITION

The opportunity has been seized to correct a number of misprints as well as of errors—some of them ferreted out by helpful reviewers. In a few cases additional information could be incorporated in the body of the book; but most addenda (indicated in the text by asterisks) had to be relegated to a separate section at the end. In either case the newly presented material has been included in the Index.

University of Chicago
January 1953

G. E. von Grunebaum

CONTENTS

CHAPTER ONE

ISLAM IN THE MEDIEVAL WORLD: THE MOOD OF THE TIMES

I

MEDIEVAL history west of India records the growth, decline, and mutual relationship of three political and cultural units—Islam, Greek Christendom, and Latin Christendom. These units represent compact blocs only when set against one another. During their early development each is ruled by a central government, and political theory never ceases to uphold the fiction of unity when actually the territory of each of the three power blocs has been divided among a varying but, on the whole, increasing number of princes. Although out of touch with contemporary reality, this fiction of unity reflects a powerful sentiment of cultural oneness within the area of each bloc and, to a certain extent, retards and obscures its decomposition.

Religion determines the demarcation of the blocs for the most part. Inadequate means of communication and inadequate public finances due to widespread substitution of payment in kind for payment in money make the intervention of the state spotty and jerky The functions of the state are mostly limited to protection of its territory and its faith. Authority is concentrated in the capital or around the person of the ruler and quickly thins when the distance from this center increases. Wars usually involve a small proportion of the population as combatants, and battles between relatively weak forces decide the allegiance of vast expanses of land.

The trend toward political atomization is reversed only toward the end of the period. Throughout most of the Middle Ages man is a Christian or a Muslim first, a native of his own home district and subject of the local lord next, and only last a Frenchman, an Egyptian, or a German.[1] The gradual reversal

[1] Cf. the characteristic statement of the Byzantine scholar and ecclesiastic, George Scholarius Gennadius (d. 1468): "Though I am a Hellene by speech, yet

of the strength of these loyalties marks the close of the Middle Ages.

The crucial problem of the time is the relation between the temporal and the spiritual power. This relation was least troublesome in Islam, where the spiritual power never was formally organized, while the temporal remained satisfied with the role of a *defensor fidei* without arrogating the right of developing or even interpreting the body of religious doctrine. Occasional reversals of this attitude caused no change in the general ideas of function and limitation of the state. In Greek Christianity the solution of the conflict was sought and, in a measure, reached by administrative subjection of the leading cleric to the leading official: the Byzantine emperor appointed the patriarch of Constantinople. In the West, pope and emperor fought each other throughout the period, with the papacy slowly losing out as the age drew to a close. In a sense, every state in the West went through an embittered civil war, while the struggle between church and state went on tenaciously from generation to generation.

All three power blocs were heirs of the Roman Empire. Roman territory formed a considerable proportion of their area. Latin and Greek Christianity claimed legitimate succession to the Rome of the Caesars. In the Byzantine Empire the continuity of Roman law and administration never was broken; the West was careful to conceal the rift. The use of Latin as the language of administration, religion, and education gave substance to the Holy Roman Empire's pretense of perpetuating the glories of the ancient world. By origin Islam had no claim to a share in the Roman tradition. But in taking possession of provinces that either passed directly from Byzantine to Arab authority or had been an integral part of the Western Empire only a few generations before the Muslim invasion, Islam appro-

---

I would never say that I was a Hellene, for I do not believe as the Hellenes believed. I should like to take my name from my faith, and if any one asked me what I am answer 'A Christian.' . . . . Though my father dwelt in Thessaly I do not call myself a Thessalian, but a Byzantine; for I am of Byzantium" (*Disputatio contra Judaeum* 2; quoted by S. Runciman, *Byzantine Civilisation* [London, 1933], p. 29).

priated traditions of law, of administration, of finance, even of philosophy, literature, and architecture; and it was only the transfer of this heritage to the terms and conceits of the Arabic language and its harmonization with koranic requirements that gradually made the Muslims forget that process of borrowing of which in the beginning they had been clearly aware.

Measured against Constantinople and Rome, Islam was the upstart. It had no past, no historical tradition. And so, one feels tempted to say, Islam took unto itself the historical backgrounds of the Roman, the Persian, and the biblical worlds. Islam was born as an Arabian religion. But the memories of the Arabian peninsula were vague and did not reach far back into the past. When Mohammed connected his mission with the teachings of Christians and Jews and when he revealed that the great Arab sanctuary of the Ka^cba in Mecca had been consecrated by Abraham, he gave greater depth to Arab historical consciousness, he prolonged the memories of his people back to the day of Creation, and he gave them a spiritually significant tradition of holy history to supplement their ill-kept records of events of local importance.

The conquest of Persia provided the Arab mind with another set of concepts and memories. The appropriation of biblical history had put the Muslims at the end of one great development; the acquaintance with Persian history made the Muslim state heir of another which, while of slighter religious significance, was of equal imaginative value and whose lesson in statecraft considerably excelled that furnished by the edifying legends of scriptural origin.

And it was from the Greeks and Romans that the Arabs learned abstract thinking and the forming and handling of an abstract terminology.

Despite constant wars and a great many territorial changes, the over-all structure of the medieval world remained surprisingly stable for many a century. The internal upheavals within the areas of the great blocs left their relative situation more or less unaltered. The very speed with which Islam occupied its territory, never to add nor to lose much thereafter, made the distribution of the civilized world definite as early as the middle of the eighth century.

Islam's recession in the extreme West, the loosening of its grip on Spain and Sicily, and the abandoning of its raids on southern France and Italy proceeded as slowly as did the gradual submergence of the Byzantine Empire under the ever recurring waves of Muslim attack. For eight centuries the Byzantines withstood the onslaught of Asia, and again for eight centuries the Muslims in Spain resisted the Christian resurgence. The battle swayed back and forth over the centuries, and most of the time its numerous reversals blinded the contemporary world to the true direction of the development. The Crusaders came but were repelled or absorbed. Except for the steady encroachment of the East on Byzantium, the power blocs expanded, not against, but away from, each other. Latin Christianity won northern Europe, broke into the regions along the Baltic, and converted the Western Slavs. Greek Christianity evangelized large parts of the Balkans and spread to Russia. Islam won new adherents in India, central Asia, and Africa. But no spectacular change occurred in the westward extension of the Muslim area between 732, when the Franks blocked the Muslim march into central France, and the fourteenth century, when the Turks pushed deep into the Balkan Peninsula.

In exactly one hundred years, between the death of the Prophet in 632 and the Battle of Tours and Poitiers, Islam carved out its dominion. During the last ten years of his life Mohammed had built up a state centered on Medina firmly controlling the Ḥijâz and parts of the Najd and more loosely imposing its authority on other sections of Arabia proper. His death was the signal for the nominally converted Bedouins to revolt. When this centrifugal movement had been crushed, expansion set in with incredible swiftness. Syria was torn from the Byzantines, weak and weary after a bitter struggle with Persia and even more embittered religious controversies within. In 638 Jerusalem fell. Only two years later Egypt was invaded, its conquest sealed when Alexandria surrendered in 647. In the meantime Persia had been overrun, and the Battle of Nihâvand (641) had put an end to effective large-scale resistance, although it took another decade before the power of the last Sassanian ruler was completely eliminated and the king himself assassinated by a disgruntled subject (651).

The chronology of the Arab movement to the West is not entirely clear, but in 670 the soldiers of the caliph had advanced into what is today Tunisia and founded the city of Qairawân. Determined resistance of the native Berbers and of the Byzantine garrisons in various seacoast towns slowed up the Arab advance, but by about 700 the country had been cleared of Greek troops and the Berbers subdued. It seems that a sizable percentage of the Latinized and Hellenized population of the cities emigrated to Spain and Sicily. At any rate, the vestiges of ancient civilization were quickly obliterated.

Only ten years later Africa was sufficiently secure for the Arabs to use it as a base for an attack on Spain. In July, 711, the Visigoth Kingdom collapsed in the defeat of its army at Jerez de la Frontera. A few more years and the Arabs felt strong enough to cross the Pyrenees. But despite temporary successes on French soil, where they maintained themselves for about half a century in the south around Narbonne, their aggressive impulse was spent after they had met defeat at the hands of the Franks.

Some time earlier, in 717, the Arabs had tried for the last time to take Constantinople. Their failure at both ends of their front did not exactly stabilize the borders, yet it did decide the general area within which the history of the three power blocs was to unfold. The relinquishing by the Arabs, some time in the eighth century, of the ambition to build up a considerable navy in the Mediterranean is a telling symptom of the caliphs' acquiescence to the status quo. The reconquest of Crete by the Byzantines in 961 underlined the decline of Muslim sea power.

The Muslim conquests had been directed, at least in name, by one central power whose seat was moved, owing to shifts in the internal situation, from Medina to Iraq, then to Damascus and again back to Iraq. When Baghdad was selected as the new capital (762) and the empire rose toward the peak of its cultural splendor under the early ᶜAbbâsids, the process of disintegration had already set in. In 756 Spain declared itself independent of the central government, and half a century later the caliph's writ was no longer valid in North Africa. Shortly after, the weakness of the ʿAbbâsids became apparent in the East as well. The tendency toward the formation of regional powers operated in Europe, too. In 843 the Treaty of Verdun divided the Western Empire into three parts destined never again to coalesce. But just as the higher unity of the Holy Empire continued in the minds of Latin Christendom, so did the unity of Islam remain unbroken in spite of the fragmentation of the caliphate.

The great innovation of the Islamic state or states was to make the area of Muslim political domination and that of Muslim religion coextensive. Until the reconquest of Spain and the decline of the Turkish power in the seventeenth century, there were no sizable Muslim minorities in Christian lands. Muslim law provided for the accommodation of Christian or Jewish populations within the framework of the Muslim state, but it did not until very late provide for the contingency of a Muslim group living in permanent subjection to an unbelieving prince. Thus during our period the withdrawal of the Muslim army from a district usually entailed a recession of the Muslim faith—one more factor strengthening isolation.

It is true that hardly a year went by without wars between Muslim and Christian princes. It is, of course, equally true that these wars, and to an even greater extent the commercial relations which continued in spite of them, appreciably affected the domestic history of each of the power blocs involved. Nevertheless, the relative self-containedness and self-sufficiency of the three major units remain the outstanding characteristics of medieval history. On the whole, the motivation of their political and cultural development lay within their own confines; their problems—economic, political, religious—were predominantly domestic. And it is clear that their contemporaries thought so, too. Practical politics was mostly confined to the bloc of which the planning statesman controlled some part. There is always something utopian about the Western projects to win back the territories occupied by Islam. Lack of information and the technical inadequacy of the age strengthened the natural isolation of the blocs. The spiritual leaders of each bloc were very sure of the vitality and value of their civilization. They were mildly interested in, perhaps even appreciative or envious of, the neighbor's achievement; but there was no wish to change with him, to imitate him, or to remodel essentials on the basis of his superior performance.

Each civilization was convinced of its spiritual superiority, of possessing the unadulterated truth, of contributing, by and large, the best adjustment to the business of living ever made. Curiosity with all the unspoken self-assurance it implies was probably the dominant trait in medieval intercultural relations. Even the outsider's superiority in one field or another did not shake in any way the quiet conviction that one's own world was that of the elect and that, whatever its weaknesses, it was the best and, at any rate, the only one where life was worth living.

The attitude toward the outside world of Athens in the fifth century B.C. and that of Boston during the fifty years preceding the first World War present a small-scale parallel. What went on abroad was of interest, it was relevant in many ways, and it should be taken notice of, but the native *polis* was a cosmos in miniature, and it was a gallery of fellow-Athenians, fellow-Bostonians, fellow-Muslims, to whom you played wherever you happened to live and whatever the stakes of your play.

II

Medieval history, then, as recorded at the time, appears for the most part confined to events affecting no more than one of the three great power blocs. What is more, to the contemporary mind those events sprang from the conflict of forces peculiar to his own unit. The same factors—distance, relative economic self-sufficiency, difference of language, religion, and everyday habits—make for isolation and also accentuate and perpetuate that keen antagonism between Europe and Islam, Islam and the Eastern Empire, the Eastern Empire and Europe, which is the most salient and the most permanent feature of historical development from the rise of Islam to the downfall of Constantinople.

Man in the Middle Ages made, on the whole, little or no effort to comprehend the outsider whose status as an infidel disqualified him as an object of dispassionate inquiry. Almost every response to the foreign world is colored by an element of political volition, be it propaganda or self-defense. But while medieval history portrays the protagonists' conflict over fundamentals, those fundamentals stand revealed as largely identical as soon as the sameness of problems, principles, methods, and aims is envisaged rather than the disparity of the individual solution, procedure, and style of argument or action.

The Muslim lived in the Ptolemaic universe of the Byzantine and the Byzantine's thought was as theocentric as his own; the Muslim's scale of values and his political ideas did not, in themselves, preclude the Byzantine's understanding, or even his sympathy. The same observation would hold good for the relation of the Latin Christian to both Muslim and Greek. And it is only on account of the comparative dimness of vision with which Islam encompassed the Latin world that the basic kinship of concepts and attitudes is more manifest when Muslims and Greeks are confronted with each other.

The identity, or near-identity, of the fundamental structure of their civilizations may have contributed in no small measure to the acrimony of their rivalry, but it preserved the basic unity of the medieval world, marking off the outsider as a barbarian even as exclusion from Greek culture had marked him off in antiquity. The antagonism of the three blocs was beyond reconciliation, but their struggle was meaningful in the sense that all the combatants fought on the same plane and that, therefore, the slogans and reasoning of one party could be understood by the other. The general trend of medieval history may be described as a tendency toward the disruption of this fundamental unity of Christendom and Islam—the end of the Middle Ages marks the end of both identity of structure and equality of achievement.

A common source or unilateral borrowing can readily be established to explain any agreement on essentials. Such an explanation, however, is hardly relevant in this context, since the contemporaries whose orientation is to be retraced, while aware of intercultural parallels, were outside the sphere of religion, almost completely heedless of the historical interdependence which these parallels imply.

Both Islam and the Byzantine Empire aspired to the domination of the civilized world. To the very end the Byzantines as heirs of the Roman Empire upheld their claim to the countries at one time united under the Roman eagle. Neither the independence of the Western states nor the loss of great parts of the East was ever recognized *de jure*. As late as the twelfth century, Anna Comnena, daughter of one emperor and wife of another, denounces that universal and perpetual conspiracy of the Turks, the Celts (i.e., the French), the Scythians (Russians), the Italians, and the Saracens against the Greek Empire, and she describes those peoples, with a grotesque disregard for actuality, as "slaves, envious of their masters, waiting an opportunity to rebel."[2] Who lives within the Empire belongs to the people of God; who lives outside has not attained to full humanity. Byzantium is the civilized world, the *oikoumene;* the regions beyond are *eremos*, desert.[3]

Islam divides the world into regions under its control, the *dâr al-Islâm,* and regions not subjected as yet, the *dâr al-ḥarb*. Between this "area of warfare" and the Muslim-dominated part of the world there can be no peace. Practical considerations may induce the Muslim leaders to conclude an armistice, but the obligation to conquer and, if possible, convert never lapses. Nor can territory once under Muslim rule be lawfully yielded to the unbeliever. Legal theory has gone so far as to define as *dâr al-Islâm* any area where at least one Muslim custom is still observed.

Thanks to this concept, the waging of war acquires religious merit. The Muslim community is under an obligation to combat the infidel. The believer who loses his life in this struggle enters Paradise as a martyr of the faith. A voluminous literature has

[2] This is the condensed import of *Alexiad*, ed. A. Reifferscheid (Leipzig, 1884), XIV, 7 (II, 251–52); trans. E. A. S. Dawes (London, 1928), p. 380. Cf. also *Alexiad*, VI, 11 (I, 214–15; Dawes, p. 159), where it is said that Alexius Comnenus (1081–1118) labored to regain as much as possible of the Roman Empire, which is described as extending from India to Gibraltar.

[3] Cf. A. Rambaud, *L'Empire grec au dixième siècle* (Paris, 1870), pp. 297–302.

developed to formalize the rules pertaining to the *jihâd*, the Holy War. The faithful is told that the sword is the key to heaven and hell. One drop of blood spilled on the battlefield, one night spent under arms, will count for more than two months of fasting or prayer. In the same spirit Nicephorus Phocas (963–69) asked the Greek clergy to honor as martyrs the Christian soldiers killed in the war against the Muslims. Both sides are convinced that they are fulfilling a mission; both sides feel that they are fighting their enemies for their ultimate good.[4]

Unceasing border warfare gives rise to the same social development in both states. From the seventh century onward large parts of the frontier districts are given in fief to a hereditary caste of professional warriors. Islam and the Byzantine Empire know feudalism outside the border provinces, too, but its political importance was greatest where a permanent state of alertness obtained to ward off the incursions of enemy raiders. Muslim and Byzantine feudalism are much alike. Both differ from occidental feudalism principally in maintaining direct dependence of the fiefholder on his sovereign, while the Western vassal formed part of a hierarchy of fiefholders who could give the land bestowed on them by their immediate overlord in fief to others who thus became the vassals of vassals, etc.

Both the Muslim and the Greek empires were ruled by autocrats. The power of the officeholder was unlimited, as it had been in Rome. The outgoing or the fallen official might be asked to account for his administration. But legal theory knew of no restriction of the prince's or governor's authority except such as was expressly imposed by a superior. In the case of both caliph and emperor this meant unrestricted absolutism. Both in Baghdad and in Constantinople two principles interlocked in determining succession to the throne. Theory upheld election, and practice worked in favor of heredity; by somewhat stretch-

[4] Cf. E. Nys, *Revue de droit international et de législation comparée*, XXVI (1894), 467 and 477. It deserves notice that the patriarch Polyeuctes refused Nicephorus' demand on the basis of the thirteenth canon of St. Basil's (d. 379) *First Canonical Epistle* that excludes from communion for three years any Christian who sheds blood, even in war (*Ep.* CLXXXVIII, Can. XIII; cf. also G. Buckler, *Anna Comnena* [London, 1929], p. 99).*

ing the concept of election, Muslim theory succeeded in harmonizing both.[5]

Although Christianity precluded their deification, the Byzantine emperors "came to regard themselves rather as vicegerents of God than as rulers set up by their people." Basil I (867–86) tells his son, "You received the Empire from God."[6] As early as 656 Ḥassân b. T̲âbit eulogizes the murdered ᶜUt̲mân as the "Caliph of God."[7] And despite the protest of many a theologian who urged that "only one who is dead or absent can have a successor" or vicegerent, the designation recurs at various times in regions as widely apart as India and Turkey.[8]

In both countries bodily integrity is included among the indispensable qualifications of the sovereign,[9] and in both countries this requirement leads to mutilation, usually blinding, of deposed rulers and potential or unsuccessful pretenders.

There was, to be sure, this important difference between the caliph and the emperor: the emperor was titular head of the Orthodox Church, while the caliph was nothing but the administrator of the state of the Muslims with no right to add to, or change, or even interpret the corpus of religious law. But to the contemporary world the similarities outweighed the distinctions. And the Latins even went so far as to confuse the merely mundane functions of the caliph with the primarily ecclesiastical position of the pope.[10] Some Muslims reciprocated by calling

[5] Cf., e.g., al-Mâwardî (d. 1058), *al-Aḥkâm as-sulṭâniyya*, ed. M. Enger (Bonn, 1853), pp. 6 ff.; trans. E. Fagnan (Alger, 1915), pp. 9 ff.; for the Byzantine Empire see J. B. Bury, *History of the Later Roman Empire* (*A.D. 395—A.D. 565*) (London, 1923), I, 5–9.

[6] Bury, *op. cit.*, p. 12. For the sacred character of the Western medieval king cf., e.g., M. Bloch, *La Société féodale: Les classes et le gouvernement des hommes* (Paris, 1949), pp. 149–53.

[7] Ed. H. Hirschfeld (London and Leiden, 1910), XX, 9; ed. Tunis, 1281, p. 98, l. 15.

[8] Cf. Sir Th. W. Arnold, *The Caliphate* (Oxford, 1924), pp. 51, 117, 157–58; Mâwardî discusses the problem on pp. 22–23 of the Arabic text, pp. 28–30 of Fagnan's translation.

[9] For their list cf. Mâwardî, pp. 5–6 (trans., pp. 7–8); see also Arnold, *op. cit.*, pp. 71–72.

[10] For this medieval Western misunderstanding cf. Arnold, *op. cit.*, pp. 167–68.

the pope the "Caliph of the Franks";[11] but Ibn Ḫaldûn (d. 1406) correctly uses the "Caliph of the Messiah" (i.e., *vicarius Christi*).[12]

Throughout the Middle Ages religion remained man's primary interest. The Muslim as well as the Latin and the Greek Christian knew himself possessed of the one and only truth. This truth was laid down in a revealed book, to which not a word could be added, from which no syllable could be erased. Thus, in theory at least, man's intellectual effort was mostly expository and interpretative. Cultural and religious border lines coincided. Political power, morally justifiable only as defender of the faith, might conflict with the claims of organized religion but remained coextensive with the area in which the persuasion of the ruler dominated. Arab conquest expanded, Greek or Frankish reconquest shrank, the abode of Islam. Citizenship, if this term is permissible at all, meant affiliation with the world of Islam or of Greek or Latin Christendom rather than with any particular state within those units. While this feeling of unity probably was strongest in Islam, even Western Europe never forgot during its ceaseless internecine strife its unitedness in the Catholic faith against the infidel.

Islam and Christianity differed in most individual doctrines, and for the first three or four centuries of its growth the differences in dogma were sharpened by the theological and philosophical immaturity of Islam. Nevertheless, the Christian world was slow to recognize Islam for what it was, viz., not another outgrowth of the familiar Arian sectarianism but an independent religion of considerable appeal.

The modern heathen when confronted with the Christian mission may refuse to accept the Gospel, but he has no chance and indeed no hope of converting the Christian to his own Weltanschauung. The primitive pagan's arguments will arouse the Christian or Muslim missionary's human or scientific interest, but they will not carry any conviction, as they are inspired by fundamental assumptions and marshaled by means of a

[11] *Ibid.*, pp. 169–70.

[12] Ibn Ḫaldûn, *Prolegomena*, ed. Quatremère (Paris, 1858), I, 420; trans. De Slane (Paris, 1862–68), I, 474.

mechanism of thought which are, to the monotheistic mind, not erroneous but baseless, not defective in their operation but altogether invalid.

Such a deadlock could never have arisen between the medieval Christian and Muslim. Despite the initial inadequacy of Muslim dialectics which secured the Christians some easy controversial victories of little practical consequence, the polemics between the two communities were conducted on the same level of thought. Despite the frequently deliberate misrepresentations of the adversary's opinions, the disputants understood each other perfectly well in that they proceeded from the same basic claim—the possession of the one and only revelation—and that they employed, though with varying skill, the same kind of reasoning. By and large the criteria by which a statement was accepted as truth or rejected as unfounded were the same on both sides. It was because of the political and social implications of apostasy rather than polemical inadequacy that no large-scale conversion to the other faith ever occurred except after territorial changes.

Muslim apologists frequently expressed doubts with respect to the completeness of the Jewish and Christian Scriptures and insinuated both loss and alteration of passages originally contained in them. The Christians and Jews, of course, never accepted the Koran as divine revelation. This attitude did not, however, prevent either party from repeatedly undertaking to demonstrate the truth of their own religion on the strength of the Book of their adversary.

When the Christians found fault with the koranic description of Paradise as a place where the believer was to eat and drink and make merry—by that time they had forgotten that in the fourth century St. Afrêm (d. 373) had pictured the abode of bliss in almost as earthly colors[13]—the Muslims retorted by alleging that the Gospels contained the same joyous promise.[14]

About A.D. 855 the newly converted Muslim, ᶜAlî b. Rabban

[13] Cf. the references in T. Andrae, "Der Ursprung des Islams und das Christentum (Part III)," *Kyrkohistorisk årsskrift*, XXV (1925), 53–54.

[14] Cf. E. Fritsch, *Islam und Christentum im Mittelalter* (Breslau, 1930), pp. 136–38.

aṭ-Ṭabarî, has this to say on that Christian charge: "If somebody reprobates the saying of the Prophet, that in the world to come there is food and drink, the answer would be that the Christ also declared such a thing to his disciples when he drank with them and said to them: 'I will not drink of this fruit of the vine, until I drink it another time with you in the Kingdom of Heaven' (Matt. 26:29). In this he declared that in heaven there is wine and drink; and where drink is found, food and pleasures are not blamed. And Luke declares in his gospel that the Christ said: 'You shall eat and drink at the table of my Father' (Luke 22:30). And John declares that the Christ said: 'There are many mansions and dwellings at my Father's' (John 14:2).

"All these confirm the existence of food and drink in the world to come, and of mansions and pleasures according to what the Most High God said in His Book: 'And gardens shall they have therein and lasting pleasure' (Koran 9:21)."[15]

The Christians, on their part, searched the Koran for statements that seemed to imply the divinity of the Christ.

Ibn Taimiyya (d. 1328) points out that the Christians quote Koran 3:43,[16] where Jesus is presented as saying: "I have come to you with a sign from your Lord (to wit) that I shall create for you from clay the form of a bird and I shall breathe into it and it will become a bird by the permission of Allah,"[17] as proof of his creative power and hence of his divine nature. They opine that, by using the phrase "I shall create," the Koran refers to the Logos that had entered into a *unio hypostatica* with his human nature.[18] Ibn Taimiyya, however, calls the Christians' attention to the fact that nowhere does God speak of Jesus as a creator without qualification—the verse in question merely

[15] *The Book of Religion and Empire*, ed. A. Mingana (Manchester, etc., 1923), pp. 133–34; trans. by the same (Manchester, etc., 1922), p. 157; for the date, cf. trans. Introd., p. xvi.

[16] Koran 5:110 practically duplicates this passage.

[17] Here and later the translation of the Koran by R. Bell (Edinburgh, 1937–39) is used, occasionally with slight changes.

[18] The express designation of Jesus as the *kalimat Allâh* (Koran 4:169), the Word of God, a reflection of the Logos doctrine, caused the Muslims many uncomfortable hours when they had to refute the Christians, who were fond of quoting this verse in support of their theology (cf. Fritsch, *op. cit.*, p. 114).

records that, "by the permission of God," Jesus will demonstrate to the Jews the truth of his mission by means of a miracle.[19]

The Christians adduced, among other passages, Koran 66:12 as a reference to their dogma of incarnation. "And Mary, the daughter of ᶜImrân, who guarded her chastity, so We breathed into her some of Our spirit" (whereupon she gave birth to Jesus). But Ibn Taimiyya quotes in reply Koran 19:17–19, where the Lord relates: "Then We sent to her Our spirit, who took for her the form of a human being, shapely. (18) She said: 'Lo, I take refuge with the Merciful from thee, if thou art pious.' (19) He said: 'I am the messenger of thy Lord, that I may give thee a boy, pure.' " And this passage clearly refutes the specious claim of the Christians.[20]

Not through historical criticism but through the comparison of a koranic passage with biblical information does Nicetas Byzantius (wrote in the second half of the ninth century)[21] uncover erroneous statements of the Muslim Book.

How can it be true that, as the Koran claims, "Abraham raised the foundations of the House (i.e., the Kaᶜba) along with Ismâᶜîl" (Koran 2:121) since the meticulous historian of Gen. 28:18 makes no mention whatever of such a temple being erected by the patriarch?[22]

Ibn Ḥazm (d. 1064), by what would appear to be a deliberately unfair interpretation, obtains these nonsensical or contradictory theses from an analysis of John 1:1–4. The text reads: "In the beginning was the Word, and the Word was with God, and the Word was God. (2) The same was in the beginning with God. (3) All things were made by him; and without him was not anything made that was made. (4) In him was life; . . . ." These verses, Ibn Ḥazm insists, contain the following proposi-

[19] Ibn Taimiyya, *al-Jawâb aṣ-ṣaḥîḥ li-man baddala dîn al-Masîḥ* (Cairo, 1322–23/1905), II, 285–87; cf. Fritsch, *op. cit.*, p. 115.

[20] Ibn Taimiyya, *op. cit.*, II, 137–38; cf. Fritsch, *op. cit.*, p. 115.

[21] Cf. K. Krumbacher, *Geschichte der byzantinischen Literatur* (2d ed.; Munich, 1897), p. 79, and C. Güterbock, *Der Islam im Lichte der byzantinischen Polemik* (Berlin,1912), p. 24.

[22] Nicetas Byzantius, *Refutatio Mohamedis*, in Migne, *Patrologia Graeca*, Vol. CV, chap. 36 (end), col. 720.

tions. (1) The Word is God; the Word is with God. Ergo, God is with God. (2) God is the Word; life is in God; all things, including the Word, are created by God. Ergo, the life of God is created. (3) Since then the life of God is created, God has created accidentia.[23]

No less unfair is Nicetas' reasoning when he concludes from the koranic injunction, "O ye people, eat of what is in the earth as lawful and good and follow not the footsteps of Satan, for he is to you a manifest enemy" (Koran 2:163), that Mohammed "clearly calls Satan the one who sets up the distinction between clean and unclean according to the law." Having established that much, Nicetas turns to his audience with the captious question: "Do ye not see how he openly calls Satan the Lord?"[24]

The Christian Fathers had long argued the legitimacy of the Christ's mission from Old Testament prophecies which they claimed were fulfilled by Jesus' appearance. John of Damascus (d. *ca.* 749) reports that the Muslims, when asked to supply confirmation from the Scriptures of their Prophet's mission, "are put to shame and remain silent."[25] Not much later, however, the Muslims began to interpret those same Old Testament passages as presaging the advent of Mohammed. In addition, they found a number of New Testament verses to strengthen their case.[26]

ᶜAlî aṭ-Ṭabarî informs us that "Simon Cephas, the head of the Apostles, said in the Book of the Acts: 'The time hath come that judgment must begin at the house of God.'[27] The interpretation of this is that the meaning of the house of God mentioned by the apostle is Mecca, and it is there and not at another place that the new judgment began. If somebody says that he meant the judgment of the Jews, the answer is that the Christ had already told them that 'there shall not be left in the temple one stone upon another that shall not be thrown down, and re-

[23] Ibn Ḥazm, *al-Fiṣal fî ᵓl-milal waᵓn-niḥal* (Cairo, 1317–21), II, 61–62; cf. Fritsch, *op. cit.*, pp. 73–74.

[24] Nicetas, *op. cit.*, chap. 38, col. 721.

[25] *De Haeresibus*, chap. 101, in *MPG*, XCIV, 768.

[26] Instances are very numerous; cf. Fritsch, *op. cit.*, pp. 74–96.

[27] Actually I Pet. 4:17.

main in destruction till the Day of Resurrection' (Matt. 24:2)."[28]

Perhaps the most famous instance of a scriptural passage being referred to Mohammed is Isa. 21:5–7: "Let the princes and the leaders rise up to their shields. Let them anoint them with ointment, for thus hath the Lord said unto me: 'Go and set the watchman on the watch, to declare what he seeth.' And what he hath seen was a pair of horsemen, one riding on an ass, and another riding on a camel; and he hath heard great and long speech."[29]

This, too, according to ᶜAlî aṭ-Ṭabarî, "is a clear and obvious prophecy which only the man who deceives himself and throws away his intelligence can reject. As no reasonable man dares feign ignorance and say that there was in the world a rider on an ass more appropriate to this prophecy than the Christ[30] so also no man with sound judgment and intelligence is allowed to say that there was in the world a rider on a camel more appropriate to this prophecy than the Prophet and his nation."[31] It is hardly necessary to add that the "great and long speech" which the watchman heard relates to the Koran.

The Christians, however, were not so easily convinced.

In the so-called *Letter of Leo III to ᶜUmar II*, actually a work of Leontius (Ghevond) dating from *ca.* A.D. 900,[32] the author takes great pains to refute the Muslim interpretation of Isaiah's vision.

"Now it is time for me to explain to you the vision of Isaiah where a rider appears to him mounted on an ass and a camel. The sense is this. The aspect of the maritime desert indicates that it is your desert situated by the side of the sea, a neighbor to and a boundary of Babylonia. Presently the Prophet says

[28] Text, p. 120; trans., p. 142.

[29] According to the Peshiṭtha text.

[30] Because he entered Jerusalem riding on an ass (Matthew, chap. 21).

[31] Text, pp. 82–83; trans., p. 96. This interpretation is adopted also by al-Bêrûnî (d. 1048), *Chronology of Ancient Nations*, trans. E. Sachau (London, 1879), pp. 22–23.

[32] According to A. Jeffery, *Harvard Theological Review*, XXXVII (1944), 275–76.

that he sees two riders mounted the one on an ass and the other on a camel. Those two riders are really one and the same as the Prophet (Isaiah) himself clearly affirms in the passage itself. Under the name of 'ass' the Prophet means the Jewish people, which, although it has read the Law and the prophecies, yet influenced by the teachings of Satan, has refused to submit and accept the Gospel destined to save the universe. . . . . Under the name 'camel,' the Prophet designates the Midianites and the Babylonians, because among them these animals are very common. And the same enemy who led the Jews into error . . . . has made you also fall into idolatry. I have said above that the two riders really represent only one and the same man, as the Prophet lets us know immediately after by saying: 'I saw the same horseman who came mounted on two steeds. Lo, the horseman who appeared two before was only one, and mounted on two horses.'[33] He designates by these two horses the Jews and the pagans dominated by them. Whence then comes this man? What does he say? He comes mounted on two horses, and cries at the top of his voice—'Babylon is fallen, and its works have been overturned' (21:9). It was then the enemy who deplored its desolation, and who, not finding any refuge other than your desert, has led to you the two horses of his iniquity, that is to say, the inconstancy of the Jews and the debauchery of the pagans. . . . ."[34]

The same homogeneity of ideas obtains on that considerably lower plane on which an unnamed spokesman for the Byzantines and the Muslim jurist, al-Qaffâl (d. 976), exchanged their invectives in support of their sovereigns' campaigns in 966–67.

The Christian announces that he will conquer the East and spread the religion of the Cross by way of force:

> And Jesus, His throne is high above the heavens. Who is allied with Him reaches his goal (i.e., salvation) on the Day of Strife (i.e., Judgment Day).
>
> But your companion (i.e., Mohammed), the moisture (of the grave) annihilated him below the ground, and he has turned (a heap of) splinters among those decayed bones.

[33] On this paraphrase of the Septuagint text see *ibid.*, p. 328, n. 35.

[34] Trans. from the Armenian by Jeffery, *ibid.*, pp. 327–28.

The Muslim *shaiḫ* retorts in the same vein:

> Whoever desires the conquest of East and West propagandizing for the belief in a cross is the meanest of all who nourish desires.
> Who serves the crosses and wishes to obtain right guidance through them is an ass with a brand mark on his nose.
> And if the Prophet Mohammed has had to die, he (only) followed the precedent set by every exalted prophet.
> And Jesus, too, met death at a fixed term, when he passed away as do the prophets of Adam's seed.[35]

The Muslim and the Christian alike viewed the history of mankind as leading from Creation to Judgment Day. History culminates in a final revelation of God's will and God's truth. It is for man to accept or reject the message of the Lord and thus to secure for himself salvation or damnation. The historical process will be staged only once. On Judgment Day the book of history is to be closed forever. Any idea of a cyclical return of events would be incompatible with the purpose for which the Lord created the world of man. Thus every moment is unique and irretrievable, and his allotted time is tense with man's anxious struggle to work his salvation ere it is too late. For the individual, then, life in history carries the supreme moral obligation of proving himself in the face of the Lord. Man is on trial. Revelation is his law, the Prophet or the Savior his model and guide, while Satan, prodding his innate sinfulness, seeks to lead him astray. After the final Judgment has acquitted or condemned, Satan will lose his power. Justice has triumphed and history reached its end.

Balʿamî (d. 963) paraphrases in these words the paragraph with which aṭ-Ṭabarî (d. 923) introduces his monumental *Annales:*

"God made the creatures without being under any necessity of creating them. He created them to try them. He ordered them to adore Him so He would know who would and who would not adore Him, who would and who would not execute His commands. His wisdom made Him create them, so their actions would justify what He knew through His foreknowledge.

[35] Ed. trans. by the writer, *Analecta orientalia,* XIV (1937), 41–64, vss. 51–53, 88.89.98.99.

"He said in the Koran (51:56–58), 'I have not created *jinn* and men but that they may serve Me; (57) I desire not any provision from them, nor do I desire that they should feed Me. (58) Verily Allah is the Provider, the Possessor of Strength, the Firm.' This is the meaning of those words: I have made the creatures, men and *jinn*, to have them adore Me and obey My commands. I do not ask of them My daily sustenance, rather it is I Who shall give it them. No advantage accrues to Me from their actions and their conduct, but they receive from Me the reward for what they did. Had I not created them, no harm would have come to Me. Now that I did create them, no harm will come to Me if they trespass and disobey, nor will it profit Me, if they be obedient."[36]

History is compressed into a short period. Ṭabarî suggests seven thousand years as its probable duration, of which rather more than six thousand have elapsed.[37] But much shorter is the time allotted to a nation. And without mercy does the Lord wave those peoples off the stage that reject his warning and spurn his signs.

The unbeliever is stubborn in his blindness. Time and again he scorns God's apostles, and the lesson of the fate of the earlier generations is lost on him. The people of Noah counted his message false—so God drowned them. The people of Hûd disregarded his admonition—so God destroyed them through a roaring wind. The people of Ṣâliḥ made light of his plea—so God smote them with an earthquake.[38]

Mohammed, even as the Christ before him, has brought down to erring man his final chance. Man has no more than a moment to make his decision. While he still hesitates, death will take him away as death has taken away his forebears and the nations that went before them.

What joy of life endures untainted with sorrow?
What glory has remained on earth unshaken?
All earthly things are weaker than shadows, more deceptive than dreams.
One moment—and death receives them all.[39]

[36] Ṭabarî, *Chronique*, trans. H. Zotenberg (Paris, 1867), I, 9–10.

[37] *Annales*, ed. M. J. de Goeje *et al.* (Leiden, 1879–1901), I, 8. Cf. also the computation, *BGA*, VIII, 212.

[38] Cf., e.g., Koran, Suras 26 and 54.

[39] John of Damascus, *MPG*, XCVI, 1368.

Fate may smile on you and extend the term of your choice. But soon there will visit you "he that bids joys be silent and that cuts the ties of friendship, he that destroys the palaces and builds the tombs, he, the reaper for the Day of Resurrection; and you will be as though you had never been."[40]

But death will hold you in his safekeeping until the morn of that terrible time when the sun will rise for the Day of Distinction.

Woe that day to those who count false!
Did We not destroy those of olden time?
Then We cause to follow them those of later times.
Thus We do with the sinners.[41]

Then, a fearful trial will be your lot, O men, your faces will be covered with dust from the reeling of the earth and you will be livid with fright. You will be naked and barefooted as you were on the day you were born. Then the Caller will demand your attention. His look will pierce you through and through. Full of perspiration you will be covered with dust. The earth will tremble with all its burden—mountains will totter and fall and will be swept away by the rising wind. The guilty then will receive their certain doom and even the pure will be in fear and trembling. And the Prophets will bow for fear of the Lord.[42]

The Christian, Helias Syncellus (eighth century),[43] is driven by the same fear not to let slip by the elusive moment.

Why, O my soul, are you asleep?
Why do you contemplate dreams?
Why do you wrestle with shadows?
Why do you move with uncertain step?

Stoop down to the graves,
To those that died long ago,
Look at friends and parents,
Reeking with putrid decay.

Time has slipped from me.
My life has stolen away.
I tarried with trifles,
Prompted by folly.[44]

[40] Slightly changed from *Arabian Nights*, German trans. by E. Littmann (Leipzig, 1921–28), V, 228.

[41] Koran 77:15–18.

[42] Ibn Nubâta (d. 984), quoted by A. Mez, *The Renaissance of Islam* (London, 1937), p. 321.

[43] Cf. Krumbacher, *op. cit.*, p. 712.

[44] W. Christ and M. Paranikas, *Anthologia Graeca Carminum Christianorum* (Leipzig, 1871), pp. 47–48, vss. 13–20.77–80.

History, then, points a moral. It provides inexhaustible subject matter for paraenetic and hortatory literature. The historian need not state the lesson taught by the events he presents. But he should not exclude anything. Creation is the proper starting-point of the Byzantine as well as the Arab annalist.[45] And throughout their journey the heroes of the Christian and of the Muslim writer act their parts on different stages, perhaps, but in the same play.

The common outlook on history as well as the emotional attitudes which this outlook engendered contributed a great deal to the similarity of the moral atmosphere prevailing in Constantinople and Baghdad. To be sure, customs and taboos differed widely, but ethical standards as embodied in paternal recommendation, advice to the inexperienced, or opinions of spiritual leaders would, for the most part, have been equally acceptable on both sides of the denominational border line. Everywhere medieval man was fond of moralizing, everywhere he produced bulky collections of a didactic character, and everywhere the vagaries of fate and the curious complexities of human nature invited the same detached if somewhat inconclusive response.

Again and again Greek and Arab endeavored to picture the terrifying instability of all things human. When the caliph Muᶜâwiya (661–80) said, "What is approved of today, was reproved in the past; what is condemned today, will be approved of in days to come,"[46] he might have drawn the conclusion from the words of Gregory of Nazianz: "There is nothing firm, nothing balanced, nothing durable in human affairs; and nothing remains in its state; rather do our affairs revolve as in a circle; each day, some time each hour, brings change."[47]

[45] Cf., e.g., George Cedrenus (*ca.* 1100), *Synopsis historion*, ed. I. Bekker (Bonn, 1838–39), I, 6; and—aside from Ṭabarî—Masᶜûdî (d. 956), *Murûj aḏ-ḏahab* (Paris, 1861–77), I, 46 ff. Ibn Ḫaldûn calls his history of the world the *Book of Examples, Kitâb al-ᶜibar*, anticipating Bolingbroke's definition of history (1735) as "philosophy teaching by examples" (quoted by D. J. Boorstin, *The Mysterious Science of the Law* [Cambridge, Mass., 1941], p. 31).

[46] Al-Ibshaihî, *Kitâb al-mustaṭraf*, trans. G. Rat (Paris-Toulon, 1899–1902), II, 100.

[47] Quoted by John of Damascus, *Sacra Parallela*, *MPG*, XCV, 1121.

While he deplores the dangerous impiety of envy, John Chrysostom admits, "It is impossible to escape envy while you are prospering."[48] And the Arab who is equally aware of envy's curse exclaims: "I am envied; would that God increase the envy people nourish against me!"[49]

Thus inveighs the Greek Christian against pride and arrogancy. "How can you strive after purity of the soul while in the chains of arrogancy? You proclaim, 'I wish to have a pure heart'—but I find it filled with dust and smoke."[50] And the Arab poet chimes in:

> Tell this fool whose arrogance makes his neck veins swell:
> If you knew the evils pride engenders you no longer were proud.
> Pride corrupts religion, weakens the mind, destroys your reputation—so take heed![51]

And the spirit of hope that moved the Christian saint to exclaim, "Let no one despair of his salvation! . . . . Recognize that you have sinned. This will be the beginning of your correction!"[52] resounds in the koranic exhortation to "turn penitently to Allah," for "He it is who accepteth repentance from His servants, and pardoneth evil deeds."[53]

Scientific interest in the Middle Ages, in the West as well as in the East, was all-inclusive, its goal the *summa* of all attainable knowledge. History and demonology, alchemy and metaphysics, geography and astrology, medicine and erotics—these and many other fields of learning were treated with indiscriminate curiosity although not necessarily with the same respect. The Arabs, it would seem, exhibited greater sobriety and firmer rationalism in the selection of their objects of study.[54] To the

[48] *Ibid.*, XCVI, 420.

[49] *Mustaṭraf*, I, 657.

[50] St. Nilus, *Sacra Parallela*, *MPG*, CXVI, 381.

[51] *Mustaṭraf*, I, 407.

[52] John Chrysostom, *Sacra Parallela*, *MPG*, XCVI, 137–38.

[53] Koran 24:31 and 42:24.

[54] Thus Ibn Sînâ does not believe in demons; cf. D. B. Macdonald, *Encyclopaedia of Islam* (Leiden, 1913–34), I, 1046, where other skeptics are named. Masᶜûdî's introduction to his *Kitâb at-tanbîh waʾl-ishrâf*, trans. Carra de Vaux (Paris, 1896), pp. 1–8, where he enumerates the subjects on which he has written, is characteristic

Byzantines belongs the glory of upholding the primacy of philosophy throughout many a theology-ridden century.[55] But everywhere the common man viewed scientific achievement with the same mixture of awe and distrust and attributed to the outstanding scholars magic practices, or even a covenant with the Evil One: around Albertus Magnus (d. 1280), John the Grammarian (patriarch of Constantinople, 834–43) and Photius (d. 891),[56] and Ibn Sînâ (Avicenna, d. 1037), there clustered the same rumors, suspicions, and legends.

Strong movements of thought or emotion not infrequently gripped both Constantinople and Baghdad. The mood that inspired the Muᶜtazilites in Islam inspired the Iconoclasts across the border.[57] The same problems attracted and exercised the Byzantine and the Arab mind.

In Sura 18:8–25 of the Koran the legend of the Seven Sleepers is narrated, probably with a view to illustrating the plausibility of bodily resurrection. The koranic story reproduces somewhat jerkily a Christian report of seven men who during the persecution under the emperor Decius (249–51) fled to a cave where they were walled in. They fell asleep to awake after 309 years to find their country converted to Christianity. Immediately after their discovery, they died, and a sanctuary was erected over their bodies in their cave near Ephesus.[58]

---

of the clearheadedness of the age. A less critical trend is represented by the Iḫwân aṣ-ṣafâ, Masᶜûdî's contemporaries, who include the science of dreams, portents, etc., and the science of magic, amulets, alchemy, and legerdemain in their studies; cf., e.g., E. G. Browne, *A Literary History of Persia* (Cambridge, 1929), I, 379.

[55] John of Damascus calls philosophy the art of arts and the science of sciences (cf. Rambaud, *op. cit.*, p. 69). Cedrenus, *Synopsis*, II, 326, praises Constantin VII (912–59) for restoring the sciences to their proper place, especially philosophy, "that is superior to them all."

[56] For these cf. J. B. Bury, *A History of the Eastern Roman Empire, 802–867* (London, 1912), pp. 444–45.

[57] Such connection has been plausibly suggested by A. A. Vasiliev, *Byzance et les Arabes* (Bruxelles, 1935), p. 14, where other authorities are named. For an interesting analysis of the motive forces inspiring the iconoclastic movement see Vasiliev, *History of the Byzantine Empire* (Madison, Wis., 1928–29), I, 310–13; cf. also Bury, *Eastern Empire, 802–867*, p. 233.

[58] For details and literature cf. A. J. Wensinck, *EI*, I, 478–79; cf. also J. Horovitz, *Koranische Untersuchungen* (Berlin and Leipzig, 1926), pp. 98–99.

Nicetas takes Mohammed severely to task for telling the story and for telling it as vaguely as he does.[59]

"The seventeenth[60] fable (*mytharion*) of Mohammed is entitled 'The Companions of the Cave.' Here he tells the flight to the cave of the seven saintly youths of Ephesus. The ignorant barbarian mentions them for two reasons, that he should appear learned in many scriptures, and in order to put the miracle vouchsafed them to use in the interest of his own teaching. Since he well knew that they were Christians and that they (i.e., their bodies) were preserved undecayed after death he made pretense of a laudable ignorance (of detail due to the passing of) so many years. . . . . Nevertheless he does not escape censure."

Then Nicetas quotes from the Koran: "One would think them awake as they lay, and We were turning them over right and left, their dog lying with forepaws stretched out on the threshold; if one had observed them he would have turned from them in flight, and been filled because of them with dread. . . . . They said: 'Erect over them a building.' Their Lord knoweth best about them. Those who prevailed in their affair said: 'Assuredly, we shall choose (to build) over them a place of worship.' They will say: 'Three and a dog,' and they will say: 'Four and a dog,' making conjectural statements; and they will say: 'Seven and their dog.' Say: 'My Lord knoweth their number best; there know them only a few.' "[61]

The vagueness of this information as well as the intrinsic interest of the story prompted the caliph al-Wâṯiq (842–47) to send one of his foremost scholars, Muḥammad b. Mûsà al-Ḫwârizmî (d. *ca.* 850), the astronomer,[62] to the land of the Rûm to investigate the cave. The emperor co-operated in the expedition and rendered all possible support. He gave al-Ḫwârizmî a

[59] *Refutatio*, chap. 76, cols. 765–68.

[60] Actually the eighteenth; Nicetas does not count the *Fâtiḥa* when he numbers the suras.

[61] Koran 18:17–20 (part), 21. Nicetas' quotation of the passage is not quite so full.

[62] On him see G. Sarton, *Introduction to the History of Science* (Baltimore, 1927 ff.), I, 563–64, where this incident is, however, not mentioned.

guide. After some days' traveling the group finally arrived at a moderate-sized hill. A subterranean passage led to the People of the Cave. After three hundred paces a portico was reached onto which several chambers opened. One of these whose threshold was exceptionally high was closed by a stone door. Behind this door the bodies were conserved. The guardian, who was assisted by eunuchs of unusual handsomeness, wished to bar the expedition from access to the bodies and from touching them. "To intimidate us," Muḥammad al-H̱wârizmî narrates, "he told us that whoever touches them exposes himself to terrible calamities. The purpose of this lie was to safeguard the profit he derives from these dead." Muḥammad was not to be deterred. The bodies were well preserved, thanks to layers of myrrh, camphor, and aloe. When Muḥammad touched the breast of one of the corpses, he could feel the hair rigidly implanted in the skin. In parting he said to the guardian: We expected you to show us dead who would look like the living, but here we have not seen anything of the kind.

Then al-H̱wârizmî returned to report to the caliph his disappointment.[63]

However much Baghdad and Byzantium might differ in etiquette and style of life, there was enough in common to make each party understand the means of impressing the other. That showiness that was to remain typical of court society almost to our own time was displayed openly and unabashedly in the Middle Ages regardless of the objections of unworldly ecclesiastics. Distinctions existed to be shown. The rich man wore his fur and velvet; the poor man, his rags. The Prophet was quoted as saying that God disliked people to hide the easy circumstances with which he had favored them.[64]

[63] Ibn H̱urdâḏbih, ed. de Goeje, *BGA*, VI (Leiden, 1889), 106–7; trans., *ibid.*, pp. 78–79; Vasiliev (*Byzance*, pp. 8–9) and Rambaud (*op. cit.*, p. 435) accept the historicity of the expedition. Al-Wâṯiq sent Sallâm the Interpreter to explore the wall erected by Alexander the Great against Gog and Magog (*BGA*, VI, 162–70; cf. also al-Muqaddasî, *BGA*, III, 362–65).* More than a century earlier, the Umayyad prince, Maslama b. ᶜAbdalmalik (d. before 743), prepared to visit the Cave of Darkness, *kahf aẓ-ẓulumât*, which Alexander the Great was reported to have entered, but he desisted from his plan when his torches went out (*BGA*, III, 146).

[64] I. Goldziher, *Vorlesungen über den Islam* (Heidelberg, 1910), p. 148.

Since the beginning of the industrial age wealth and social position have developed a tendency toward anonymity: the loud elegance of the parvenu has fallen into disrepute. The medieval Arabs and Greeks felt differently. They wanted the great to display the paraphernalia of his station for all to see. Lavish generosity hardly distinguishable from waste, hordes of servants, golden dishes, splendid garments—these outward signs of power and riches were indispensable to maintain prestige.

Confidence in the effectiveness of ostentatious gestures inspired the ceremonial of international courtesy. It made the Byzantine populace proud to think of the Saracens moved to admiration and wonder when their envoy, the Syncellus John, distributed enormous amounts of money among the courtiers and the crowds of Baghdad. His noble carriage and his generous gifts "struck them dumb."[65] It makes little difference that actually John had gone to Syria to see the caliph on a routine mission and that he probably never reached Baghdad. The people saw his embassy as it ought to have been and as, therefore, it had been.[66] And the historian introduces his report by saying that John was sent "to reveal the grandeur of the empire to the Saracens."[67]

The same apparatus here and there, and the same rather childish means of impressing the foreigner with the grandeur of the sovereign.

In 917, ambassadors from Constantinople arrived in Baghdad to negotiate for peace. Mounted troops, in splendid apparel, lined the streets from the Shammâsiyya Gate to near the palace. The streets were crowded with spectators. "So the Ambassadors, with those who accompanied them, were brought on horseback to the Palace (of the Caliph), entering which, they passed directly into the palace of . . . . the Chamberlain. Here they

[65] P. 97^2: ἐξέπληξε . . . . πάντας. On *ekplexis* cf. this writer, *JAOS*, LXII (1942), 289, where the antecedents are discussed.

[66] Cf. Theophanes Continuatus, ed. I. Bekker (Bonn, 1838), pp. 95–99.

[67] This is the translation given of 95^{20} by Bury, *English Historical Review*, XXIV (1909), 298. H. Grégoire, in Vasiliev, *Byzance*, p. 417, suggests a different interpretation of the passage. The date of the embassy which went to see al-Maʾmûn in Damascus most likely was 831–32.

saw many porticoes and a sight so marvellous to behold that they imagined the Caliph himself must be present, whereby fear and awe entered into them; but they were told that here was only the Chamberlain. Next from this place the Ambassadors were carried on to the palace where lived the vizier . . . . and here the Ambassadors were witnesses of even more splendor than they had seen in the palace of . . . . the Chamberlain, so that they doubted not that this was indeed the Caliph; but it was told them that this was only the vizier. Thence they conducted the Ambassadors and seated them in a hall, with the Tigris on the one hand and gardens on the other; and the hall was hung with curtains, and carpeted all about, and cushions had been placed for them, while all around stood the Eunuchs bearing maces and swords. But after the Ambassadors had been taken through this palace also, they were called for to the presence of Muqtadir the Caliph, whom they found seated with his sons on either side of him, and here the Ambassadors saw a sight that struck them with fear."

The report does not explain what the ambassadors saw, but obviously the right thing for them to do was to exhibit awe and fright.

Next the ambassadors were taken on a tour of the palace grounds to deepen the impression of wonder already provoked. One of their stations on that circuit was the Park of the Wild Beasts. "This was a palace with various kinds of wild animals therein, who entered the same from the Park, herding together and coming up close to the visitors, sniffing them and eating from their hands. Next the Envoys went out to the palace where stood four elephants caparisoned in peacock-silk brocade, and on the back of each were eight men of Sind, and javelin-men with fire, and the sight of these caused much terror to the Greeks. Then they came to a palace where there were one hundred lions, fifty to the right hand and fifty to the left, every lion being held in by the hand of its keeper, and about its head and neck were iron chains."

Later the ambassadors were shown the Palace of the Tree wherein "is a tree, which is standing in the midst of a great circular tank filled with clear water. The tree has eighteen branches, every branch having numerous twigs, on which sit all sorts of gold and silver birds, both large and small. Most of the branches of the tree are of silver, but some are of gold, and they spread into the air carrying leaves of divers colors. The leaves of the tree move as the wind blows, while the birds pipe and sing. On the one side of this palace, to the right of the tank, are the figures of fifteen horsemen, mounted upon their mares, and both men and steeds are clothed and caparisoned in brocade. In their hands the horsemen carry long-poled javelins, and those on the right are all pointed in one direction (it being as though each were attacking his adversary), for on the left-hand side is a like row of horsemen."[68]

When Liutprand, who was to die in 972 as bishop of Cremona, was, in 949, received in audience by Constantin VII as ambassador from Berengar of Ivrea, this is what he saw in the Palace of Magnaura:

"Before the emperor's seat stood a tree, made of bronze gilded over, whose branches were filled with birds, also made of gilded bronze, which uttered different cries, each according to its varying species. The throne itself was so marvellously fashioned that at one moment it seemed of low structure, and at another it rose high into the air. It was of immense size and was guarded by lions, made either of bronze or of wood covered over with gold, who beat the ground with their tails and gave a dreadful roar with open mouth and quivering tongue. Leaning upon the shoulders of two eunuchs I was brought into the emperor's presence. At my approach the lions began to roar and the birds to cry out, each according to its kind; but I was neither terrified nor surprised, for I had previously made enquiry about all these things from people who were well acquainted with them. So after I had three times made obeisance to the emperor,

[68] Al-Ḫaṭîb al-Baghdâdî (d. 1071); trans. from manuscript by G. Le Strange, *JRAS*, 1897, pp. 38–39, 41–42. Another report, also from al-Ḫaṭîb, in G. Salmon, *L'Introduction topographique à l'histoire de Bagdad de ... al-Khatib al-Bagdadi* (Paris, 1904), text, pp. 48–56, trans., pp. 131–41. (I owe this reference to Professor Nabia Abbott.) Somewhat earlier, Ibn al-Muᶜtazz (d. 908), *Dîwân* (Cairo, 1891), I, 138 (=ed. C. Lang, *ZDMG*, XL [1886], 563 ff., vss. 255–59, on p. 582), speaks admiringly of the artificial tree in the garden of the Palace of the Pleiades (*aṯ-Ṯurayyâ*), erected by the caliph al-Muᶜtaḍid (892–902).

I lifted my head, and behold! the man whom just before I had seen sitting on a moderately elevated seat had now changed his raiment and was sitting on the level of the ceiling. How it was done I could not imagine, unless perhaps he was lifted up by some such sort of device as we use for raising the timbers of a wine press. On that occasion he did not address me personally, since even if he had wished to do so the wide distance between us would have rendered conversation unseemly, but by the intermediary of a secretary he enquired about Berengar's doings and asked after his health. I made a fitting reply and then, at a nod from the interpreter, left his presence and retired to my lodging."[69]

Riven asunder by conflicting revelations, uneasily hiding behind dangerous distances and puzzling tongues, East and West when contemplating each other in the medieval world concentrated on what set them apart. Emphasizing through pride and fear and bewilderment what they knew for their own, both Christendom and Islam allowed themselves to forget that they were lauding and damning in subservience to the same values and that their love and hate was born from the same mood.

[69] *Antapodosis*, VI, 5; trans. F. A. Wright, *The Works of Liudprand of Cremona* (London, 1930), pp. 207–8. Similar devices, though on a smaller scale, are recorded in ᶜUmâra b. Ḥamza's (d. 814/15) report of his embassy to Constantinople, which, incidentally, is said to have been responsible for al-Manṣûr's interest in alchemy; cf. Ibn al-Faqîh, *BGA*, V, 137–39.

CHAPTER TWO

ISLAM IN THE MEDIEVAL WORLD

CHRISTENDOM AND ISLAM

I

THE political relationship of the three power blocs did as much as language barriers and religious hostility to conceal their essential kinship of thought and sentiment to the denizens of the individual units. The adventurous, even dramatic, character of some phases in this relationship could not, to the mind of the average Muslim outside the border regions, compensate for their comparative rarity or obscure the obvious fact that hardly ever did international altercations with Byzantium or with the West actually affect his life.

Anti-Byzantine emotion ran high on various occasions down to the late tenth century; popular indignation compelled the Baghdad government to dispatch an ineffective force against the Crusaders at the end of the eleventh—but never once did the Byzantine Empire or Europe threaten the heartland of Islam. Thus, political interference from the West only slightly affected the development of Muslim civilization. The outside danger merely sufficed to fan the flames of hatred; it never constrained the Muslims to rally every cultural and political resource to sustain a fight for survival.[1] This favored position of the Muslim world, coupled with the reminiscence of the stupendous early successes of its arms, tended to color its sense of self-sufficiency with a feeling of superiority which was to lose more and more its justification.

Islam's perennial adversary, the Byzantine Empire, hemmed in on all sides by aggressive neighbors, suffered badly from the constant compulsion of adjusting its organization and its

[1] Only once, in 972, Baghdad was gripped by fear of the Byzantines when John Tzimisces appeared to be advancing unchecked. But John turned back without approaching Baghdad, and the scare quickly subsided.

policies according to the exigencies of the hour. At least three times—in 668, from *ca.* 673–79/80, and in 716–17—the Empire came very near to being obliterated by the Arabs. The Muslim danger was ever present in the thoughts of every Byzantine subject. The very existence of the Muslim power, combined with that of the other unruly nations along her northern and western borders, kept Byzantium in a state of continual and painful alertness.

Byzantine literature clearly reflects this attitude. To be sure, the ceaseless border warfare against the Greeks has left its traces in Arab writings. Not only do poets refer to battles in which their patron played an honorable part,[2] but also events and personalities connected with this ever inconclusive strife entered popular narrative as witnessed by the novel of King ᶜUmar b. an-Nuᶜmân that later came to be incorporated in the *Arabian Nights*. But these testimonials to contemporary interest appear insignificant when compared with the reflection of the same happenings in the popular epic of the Byzantines.[3] Not only does Arab literature lack any work of the type and the merit of the Greek epic centering on that hero of border warfare, Digenis Acritas, but the peculiar atmosphere and manner of life as it must have developed in the frontier districts remains unrepresented in both Arabic prose and poetry. In fact, Arabic literature became increasingly metropolitan in outlook as time wore on. While, three or four centuries after the border conflicts had passed their peak, the Crusades had a more potent effect on literature as well as on popular sentiment in general, it is obvious that they affected European ideas and ideals and also various European literatures much more deeply and lastingly.

Throughout the Middle Ages armed intrusion from the West never touched the core of the Islamic territory. Nor did Islam, once the first rush of expansion had been halted, influence conspicuously the political development of the European West. It

[2] Cf., e.g., M. Canard on Abû Tammâm (d. 846) and al-Buḥturî (d. 897) in Vasiliev, *Byzance*, pp. 397–408; R. Blachère, *Abou 'ṭ-Ṭayyib al-Motanabbî* (Paris, 1935), esp. pp. 144–81, and M. Canard, *Sayf ad Daula* (Algiers, 1934), on Mutanabbî (d. 965); also Abû Firâs (d. 968), *Dîwân*, ed. R. Dvořák (Leiden, 1895), *passim*.

[3] For a good orientation on this subject cf. H. Grégoire and R. Goossens, *ZDMG*, LXXXVIII (1934), 213–32, where literature is listed.

would seem that the disruption of the age-old unity of the Mediterranean world, owing to its passing under the dominion of never less than three antagonistic rulers, considerably accentuated and speeded that reorientation of Europe away from the Mediterranean and toward the North Sea and the Atlantic which, with its weighty economic and cultural consequences, is one of the essential factors in the development of the Western Middle Ages.[4] The loss to Islam of Spain and Sicily for the better part of the period did not influence too much the political growth of the Western world, although it proved stimulating from a cultural point of view. Despite occasional international plotting—the political ties between Charlemagne and Hârûn ar-Rashîd as well as those between Constantinople and the Spanish Umayyads were to prove more picturesque than effective—Islam changed the European scene mostly by representing a constant if somewhat passive threat and by providing the puzzling picture of a different world just near enough to be real.

Since Europe, less self-contained than its adversary, never quite ceased to look south and east, the powerful presence of the Islamic world almost always loomed large in the Western mind. No single fact ever played a bigger part in molding the international relations of the Middle Ages than the existence of a powerful, uncanny, and unpredictable political body on the other side of what the Arabs were fond of calling the "Central Sea."

II

Disregarding the similarities haughtily and naïvely, the Muslim emphasized the differences whenever he bethought himself of the world beyond the pale. Ignorance of the foreign civilization contributed toward the maintenance of his sense of superiority which, at least in the earlier part of the Middle Ages, was not altogether unwarranted.

God in his mercy had placed the center of his empire in the Fourth Climate, the best and noblest of the seven in which, following the Greek tradition, he divided the inhabited quarter of the earth. The center of the Fourth Climate is Iraq, seat of

[4] For a more extreme statement cf. H. Pirenne, *Mohammed and Charlemagne* (New York, 1939), *passim.**

empires from time immemorial. Pappos (*ca.* A.D. 300) had praised this climate for its mean position which allows most readily the realization "of the symmetry obtaining in the phenomena of the globe."[5] The Persians had considered their country the central *kishwar*, or climate, of the world, grouping Arabia, Africa, the Romans, the Turks, China, and India around it.[6] And now the Muslim power emanated from this most temperate and most illustrious of all climates.[7]

There are only four nations whose civilizations count: the Arabs, the Persians, the Indians, and the Byzantines.[8] The remainder are rabble or nearly so. Still the Turks are good at archery and the Chinese at handicraft. But these are natural gifts and not due to cultural achievement.[9] The civilized nations are not on the same level, though. From the point of view of literary accomplishment, for instance, the Indians are disqualified because they have only anonymous books; and the Greeks fall down because, with all their philosophy and logic, they lack oratory (*ḫiṭâba*), which is restricted to Arabs and Persians. The Persians, however, are unable to improvise speeches; they only elaborate what has come down to them from their ancestors, whereas the Arabs possess the gift of extempore speaking. Moreover, while there is no proof of the genuineness of the documents of Persian rhetoric, everybody can easily test for himself the true Arab's power of expression by visiting his

[5] Pappos as quoted by Moses of Khorene, in E. Honigmann, *Die 7 Klimata* . . . . (Heidelberg, 1929), p. 164.

[6] T. H. Weir, *EI*, II, 460–61.

[7] Masᶜûdî, *Tanbîh*, trans., pp. 55–57.

[8] Al-Jâḥiẓ, *Kitâb al-bayân waᵓt-tabyîn* (Cairo, 1351/1932), I, 128. In *ibid.*, I, 294–95, al-Jâḥiẓ criticizes Ḥakîm b. ᶜAyyâsh al-Kalbî for including the Abyssinians instead of the Indians. Al-Iṣṭaḫrî (*fl. ca.* 951), *BGA*, I, 4, after listing the same four nations as leading culturally, indicates his criterion of selection as "the existence in these states of organized religion, civilized mores (*âdâb*), a judicial system, and a set policy." Ibn Ḥauqal (*fl.* 977) again adopts this viewpoint and adds: "I have not described the country of the African blacks and the other peoples of the torrid zone; because, naturally loving wisdom, ingenuity, religion, justice, and regular government, how could I notice such people as these, or magnify them by inserting an account of their countries?" (Ibn Ḥauqal, ed. J. H. Kramers [Leiden, 1938], I, 9–10; trans. in C. R. Beazley, *The Dawn of Modern Geography* [London, 1897–1906], I, 452).

[9] Ḍiyâᵓ ad-Dîn Ibn al-Aṯîr, *al-Maṯal as-sâᵓir* (Cairo, 1312), p. 120.

country.[10] Once the outstanding merit of the Arabs is granted, Persian, Indian, and Greek views on eloquence will be diligently noted[11] and Greek poetry be lauded upon occasion.[12] It is an unparalleled admission when Ibn al-Aṯîr (d. 1239) observes that, despite the inferiority of their language, the Persians have Firdausî's (d. *ca.* 1020) *Shâh-Nâma* ("Book of the Kings"), in sixty thousand couplets, which is, so to speak, their Koran (*wa-huwa Qur'ân al-qaum*) and does not have its like in Arabic literature.[13]

The main source of the Muslim's feeling of superiority, however, was the incontrovertible knowledge that his was the final religion, the one and only truth, and that, while he was traveling the road to salvation and eternal beatitude, the unbelievers sunk in argumentative stubbornness were heedlessly hurrying down to everlasting punishment. Had not God himself assured him that Islam was "the natural religion laid down by Allah which He hath formed the people by nature to follow"?[14] "Verily," the Book told him, "the religion in Allah's sight is Islam."[15] And the Book itself could be relied upon to provide safe guidance. For the Lord had revealed: "(9) Verily this Koran guides to what is straighter, and brings good tidings to the believers, (10) who do the deeds of righteousness, that for them is a great reward, (11) And that for those who do not believe in the Hereafter, We have prepared a punishment painful."[16]

Never ending thanks for his election did the Muslim pour forth "to Allah, Who sent among us the messenger of good news, the warner, the illuminating light that directs toward His approval, calls to His love and leads on to the way to His para-

[10] Al-Jâḥiẓ, *Bayân*, III, 20–22; it is not, of course, suggested that everybody in Muslim lands shared this view, but it seems safe to assume that it represents a fair average of opinion.

[11] E.g., *Bayân*, I, 87, and Ibrâhîm b. al-Mudabbir (d. 892), *ar-Risâlat al-ʿaḏrâʾ*, ed. Z. Mubârak (Cairo, 1931), pp. 44–46.

[12] Sometimes for the wrong reason; e.g., Ibn Rashîq, *ʿUmda* (Cairo, 1353/1934), I, 13, deems it one of the glories of poetry that the Greeks used it for the presentation of scientific topics.

[13] *Al-Maṯal as-sâʾir*, p. 324.

[14] Koran 30:29.

[15] Koran 3:17.

[16] Koran 17:9–11.

dise, opens for us the door of His compassion, and keeps closed before us the door of His anger."[17] With a ring of triumph it is stated that the Muslim community (*al-umma al-Muḥammadiyya*) is the best community (*umma*).[18] Membership in it conveys enthusiasm and lends a lustrous sheen to the lowliest life.

"Praise be to God," exclaims the converted Christian, ᶜAlî aṭ-Ṭabarî. "Praise be to God for the religion of Islam which whoso embraces shall be successful, whoso maintains shall be rightly guided, whoso upholds shall be saved and whoso impugns shall perish. It is by it that the Creator has been made known; it is for it that nations are craving and souls have longed; . . . . it is by it that hope is fulfilled sooner or later, because it is the living light and the crossing to the eternal abode of perfect happiness in which there is no grief nor illusion. God, the Most High, has made us of the number of the people of the Sunna and has caused us to avoid falsehood and the injuries it brings to its adherents; God is indeed to be praised and blessed, and there is no end to His Kingdom, and nobody can change His words. He is the Benefactor and the Wise who has revealed the truth and enlightened it, and has created His servants, sent His Apostle, His Beloved, and His Friend, to those who were in doubt about Him, calling them to the eternal victory and the shining light."[19]

When God revealed his message through his apostle Mohammed, he sent it down as "an Arabic Koran."[20] And God expressly explained to Mohammed: "We have made it (i.e., the Koran) easy in thy tongue in order that thou mayest thereby give good tidings to those who show piety, and warn a contentious people."[21] Many centuries before Mohammed arose to preach, the prophet Zephaniah (3:9) had foretold that the Lord would "renew to the people the chosen language, that all of them may

[17] Ibn Qutaiba (d. 889), *ᶜUyûn al-aḫbâr* (Cairo, 1343–48/1925–30), Introduction, p. 9; trans. J. Horovitz, *Islamic Culture*, IV (1930), 172.

[18] Ibn Kaṯîr (d. 1373), *Tafsîr*, II (Cairo, 1343), p. 213, commenting on Koran 3:106.

[19] *Kitâb ad-daula wa'd-dîn*, p. 5; trans., p. 1.

[20] Koran 20:112 and 42:5.

[21] Koran 19:97.

taste the name of the Lord, and serve Him together with one consent." There could be little doubt but that "the chosen language is the perspicuous Arabic, which is neither unintelligible, nor sophistical (*sûfasṭî*)." It is the language which became common to the Gentiles, who spoke it and were rejuvenated by the new dispensation that it brought to them.

"As to Hebrew, it was already the language of those prophets. As to Syriac, never did it cross the frontiers of the country of Syria; neither did Greek cross the country of the Greeks, nor Persian the city of Îrân-Shahr,[22] but Arabic reached as far as the spot where dust ends, the desert of the Turks, and the countries of Ḫazar and India."[23]

No language can match the dignity of Arabic, the chosen vehicle of God's ultimate message. But it is not only its spiritual rank which transcends the potentialities of the other tongues; its pre-eminence is rooted equally firmly in its objective features—above all, in the unparalleled vastness of its vocabulary. Where Greek frequently has but one word to denote many objects, Arabic offers many words to denote one.[24] Phonetic beauty is added to its staggering richness in synonyms.[25] Precision and concision of expression adorn Arabic speech.[26] While it is true that thoughts can also be rendered in foreign languages, Arabic will render them with greater exactitude and more briefly.[27] Arabic is distinguished by its unrivaled possibilities in the use of figurative speech. Its innuendoes, tropes, and figures of speech lift it far above any other human language. There are many stylistic and grammatical peculiarities in Arabic to which no corresponding features can be discovered elsewhere.[28]

This situation makes satisfactory translation from and into Arabic impossible.[29] The Arabic version of a foreign saying is in-

[22] In northwestern Khorasan.

[23] *Kitâb ad-daula waᵓd-dîn*, pp. 104–5; trans., pp. 121–22.

[24] Ibn Sinân al-Ḫafâjî, *Sirr al-faṣâḥa* (Cairo, 1932), p. 45.

[25] As-Suyûṭî, *al-Muzhir fî ᶜulûm al-lugha* (Cairo, 1282), I, 154; *Sirr*, p. 52.

[26] *Sirr*, pp. 45 and 47.

[27] *Muzhir*, I, 153, quoting Ibn Fâris (d. 1005).

[28] *Muzhir*, I, 157–60; cf. al-Murtaḍâ (d. 1044), *Amâlî* (Cairo, 1325/1907), I, 4.

[29] *Muzhir*, I, 153.

variably shorter than the original.[30] Beautiful Arabic loses when translated into Syriac, but beautiful Syriac gains when translated into Arabic.[31] It is understandable, therefore, that, upon his expulsion from Paradise, Adam was forbidden to talk Arabic and had to take up Syriac instead and that later God acknowledged his repentance by allowing him to resume Arabic.[32] And al-Fârâbî (d. 950) is entirely justified in his praise of Arabic as the idiom of the People of Paradise and as the only language exempt of any shortcoming and exalted above any baseness.[33] Moreover, the natural eloquence of the Arab is remarkable.[34]

Nevertheless, Arabic is too rich to be mastered completely by anyone but a prophet.[35] Thus, while the most excellent of all discourse is that of the eloquent, intelligent, and learned speakers of Arabic,[36] it is necessary to study that language incessantly to attain to understanding of the Holy Book. Already the caliph ᶜUmar I (634–44) noted that the Koran can be read only by one thoroughly familiar with the Arabic language, and the consensus has adopted this view.[37] The duty of comprehending the koranic text involved that of language study. Poetry, not too favorably acclaimed by many of the early believers, is vindicated as a legitimate pursuit because it constitutes a treasure trove of rare expressions and acts as the guardian of good Arabic style. An unnamed rhymer sings:

> To preserve rare expressions is for us a duty like that of prayer.
> Religion cannot be comprehended unless through preservation of rare terms.[38]

The study of poetry becomes thus to many "the greatest of the Arab sciences."[39] This rating reflects the deep pride the

[30] *Sirr*, p. 45.

[31] Abû Dâ'ûd al-Maṭrân, quoted in *Sirr*, pp. 45–46.

[32] *Muzhir*, I, 17.

[33] *Ibid.*, p. 162.

[34] Nafṭawaihi (d. 935) wrote a book, "that the Arabs speak well by nature not through training"; cf. Yâqût, *Irshâd al-arîb*, ed. D. S. Margoliouth (London, 1923–31), I, 308.

[35] Ash-Shâfiᶜî (d. 819), quoted in *Muzhir*, I, 34; cf. also A. Jeffery, *The Foreign Vocabulary of the Qur'ân* (Baroda, 1938), pp. 7–8.

[36] *Bayân*, I, 133.

[37] *Muzhir*, II, 157.

[38] *Ibid.*, I, 157.

[39] ᶜ*Umda*, I, 4.

Arabs have taken in their poetry ever since they emerged into the light of history. The beauty of the language culminates in its verse. The Prophet's attack on the poets: "(224) And the poets—them follow the beguiled, (225) Seest thou not that in every valley they are raving,[40] (226) And that they say what they do not do?" had to be qualified by himself by means of this addition: "(227) Except those who have believed and wrought the works of righteousness, and made mention of Allah frequently."[41] And it was easy (and perhaps not too far from the truth) to interpret the hostile lines as referring solely to those unbelieving poets who had taunted the Prophet with venomous satire.[42] To this day their poetry has remained one of the principal foundations of the Arabs' national pride.

Nations divide into such as do and such as do not cultivate science. Only eight peoples dedicated themselves to the quest of knowledge: the Indians, the Persians, the Babylonians, the Jews, the Greeks, the Byzantines, the Egyptians, and the Arabs. This group of nations constitutes the élite and the essential part of God's creatures. The others, of which the Chinese and the Turks are, comparatively speaking, the best, resemble animals rather than men, having never used their minds properly by striving for wisdom and philosophy.[43]

While thus an important factor in his self-estimate, his scientific achievement does not seem to have loomed as large in the average Muslim's consciousness as his pre-eminence in the field of literature. Although more and more branches of knowledge were appropriated by Muslim scholarship, and although for centuries the Muslim contribution to the several disciplines easily surpassed that of the other cultural groups, the sciences never did slough off entirely the twofold stigma of alien origin and of potential godlessness. In the eighth century there was for a moment the danger that the non-Arabic origin and the precarious social position of many of the early scholars would

[40] Bell has: "fall madly in love."

[41] Koran 26:224–27.

[42] Cf. ᶜ*Umda*, I, 18.

[43] Ṣâᶜid al-Andalusî (d. 1070), *Ṭabaqât al-umam*, ed. L. Cheikho (Beirut, 1912), pp. 7–10; trans. R. Blachère (Paris, 1935), pp. 35–39.

bar occupation with scientific subjects from polite society.[44] Never very great, this danger was eliminated by the end of the eighth century.

The widening of range and scope of scholarship in the ninth century is reflected in the various classifications of the sciences attempted in the tenth. The one encyclopedic summary of scientific information that has come down to us from the ninth century, the *Kitâb al-maᶜârif* ("Book of the Sciences") by Ibn Qutaiba (d. 889), contains hardly anything beyond historical, and biographical knowledge. Not much later, such restriction of scope would no longer have been feasible. During the fruitful period of Arabic research no final and authoritative division of sciences was reached or accepted. But every classification of the period tended to maintain consciousness of the distinction between indigenous and foreign sciences

Muḥammad b. Yûsuf al-Ḫwârizmî's *Mafâtîḥ al-ᶜulûm* ("Keys of the Sciences"), written in 976, which is perhaps best described as a dictionary of technical terms and names, enumerates six sciences as indigenous: jurisprudence, scholastic philosophy (or perhaps, scholastic theology; here the author includes the study of sects and creeds), grammar, *kitâba* (the art of the secretary including the terminology of government administration), prosody and the art of poetry, and history. Nine sciences are considered foreign: philosophy, logic, medicine, arithmetic, geometry, astronomy and astrology, music, mechanics, and alchemy.

The classification proffered by that curious group of tenth-century encyclopedists, the Iḫwân aṣ-Ṣafâ ("Sincere Friends") of Baṣra,* while not explicit on the subject of their origin, does very little to obscure the attribution of the various fields to the categories of indigenous and exotic sciences. They arrange their studies in three groups: mundane, religious, and philosophic. Here the philosophic group corresponds to Ḫwârizmî's foreign group, and when arithmetic, magic, and alchemy are omitted from the mundane studies, these together with the

[44] Cf., e.g., the stories told by al-Mubarrad (d. 898), *al-Kâmil*, ed. W. Wright (Leipzig, 1864–92), pp. 263–64.

religious studies cover about the same ground as the indigenous sciences in al-Ḫwârizmî's scheme.

Muḥammad an-Nadîm's *Fihrist*, written in 987—a catalogue of all the books of which this widely traveled bookseller had obtained information—without formally proposing any classification, agrees with his contemporaries by first treating what they considered indigenous sciences and then taking up the exotic such as philosophy and what he calls the "ancient" sciences: geometry, arithmetic, music, astronomy, mechanics, etc., and also medicine, magic, and alchemy.[45]

His contemporary, Aḥmad b. Fâris (d. 1005), again dwells on the Arabic sciences, grammar, poetry—traditionally considered not only the chief art but also the main record of the early Arabs—prosody, and genealogy, which, according to him, no other nation cultivates as studiously as his compatriots.[46] The commonplace opinion which Ibn Fâris expresses deserves attention only because, by and large, the Muslim world felt more intensely about its literary than about its scientific achievement. Lexicography, grammar, rhetoric, and literature proper remain if not the key disciplines, at any rate, the favorite fields of study. They are deemed indispensable for the jurisprudents who are compelled to arrive at a correct understanding of Koran and Tradition, and they are equally indispensable for the interpretation of the sacred texts themselves.[47]

Ibn Rashîq (d. 1064 or 1070) tells[48] how Abû ʾl-ʿAbbâs an-Nâshî (d. 975) succeeded by a trick in placing poetry in the highest category of knowledge. According to this authority, the philosophers distinguish three classes of knowledge: the highest, attainable by reason only and apparently meant to in-

[45] He treats, however, "Sects and Creeds" between "Magic" and "Alchemy." For these classifications cf. also E. G. Browne, *A Literary History of Persia*, I, 378–88, and R. A. Nicholson, *A Literary History of the Arabs* (London, 1914), pp. 282–83.

[46] *Muzhir*, I, 155–56.

[47] So very emphatically Ibn Ḫaldûn, *Prolegomena*, III, 278–79; trans., III, 307–8.

[48] *ʿUmda*, I, 12–13. Ibn Rashîq refers to the dialectician and poet an-Nâshî al-Aṣghar; on him cf. Blachère, *op. cit.*, p. 34, n. 1; also *Irshâd* III, 119, and V, 37. He belonged to Saif ad-Daula's circle.

clude metaphysics and (esoteric) theology; the middle, treating of concepts deduced by reason from natural objects as, e.g., numbers, geometry, astronomy, and music;[49] and, finally, the lowest, the knowledge of particulars and of the objects of sense perception. By emphasizing the abstract character of both the subject matter and the tools of poetry, an-Nâshî, himself a poet, arrives at the conclusion that poetry forms part of the highest category of knowledge.[50] This result obviously flies in the face of his authorities' intention, and Ibn Rashîq prudently refrains from indorsing it.

Evidence of this kind suggests that the indigenous literary sciences were those that made the educated layman proudest of his cultural background. Of course, his reverence for the study of Koran and Tradition never slackened, but, had he had to account for the motives of his superior attitude toward other cultural units, pride in his language and literature and pride in his scientific mastery of both would have followed very closely the certainty of having been vouchsafed the true faith.

III

The Christian world devoted more attention to Islam than it received. Hatred, fear, admiration, and the attraction of the unknown seem to have coexisted in Christendom throughout the Middle Ages, events determining the paramount emotion of the moment. The foreignness of the Muslim world was keen-

49 Literally, "the science of harmony," *ṣinâ‘at al-luḥûn.*

50 The philosopher (or philosophers) whose scheme an-Nâshî used was clearly influenced by the Iḫwân aṣ-ṣafâ; his second category coincides with the first class of the Iḫwân's "Philosophic Studies"; for these cf. Browne, *op. cit.*, p. 380, and F. Dieterici, *Die Propädeutik der Araber im 10. Jahrhundert* (Berlin, 1865), *passim* (the *Propädeutik* is Part VI of Dieterici's *Die Philosophie der Araber im 9. und 10. Jahrhundert*). The Iḫwân discussed "Prosody" and the "Poetic Art" as the fourth class of mundane studies. The possibility cannot be excluded that an-Nâshî's three categories of knowledge go back, in the last analysis, to the Iḫwân's religious, philosophic, and mundane studies, respectively. Should this prove to be the case, then the motive force that drove an-Nâshî to change the Brethren's scheme solely with respect to the position of poetry would stand revealed even more patently as the desire to obtain philosophical justification for that intense appreciation of literature which is so characteristic of the Muslim Middle Ages.

ly felt and the enigma never solved to satisfaction why so large a part of mankind would cling so staunchly to the manifest errors of its faith.

The Christian knew himself possessed of the perfect and of the whole truth. He reacted with disgust, at best with compassion, when confronted with the crude distortion of this truth by means of which the Evil One had ensnared so many souls that might have been saved. When the Christian looked upon Islam, his primary task was not to study this phenomenon of an alien faith that seemed both akin to and apart from his own but rather to explain the unexplainable, to wit, the artful machinations by which Mohammed had won over his people to the acceptance of his absurd confabulations. There is always, even in the most aggressive and contemptuous discussions of Islam, an element of apologetic self-defense in the utterances of the Christian writers, almost a touch of propaganda for the home front. It is as if only the most derogatory presentation of the despicable but powerful enemy could allay the secret suspicion that his case be stronger than it was wise to admit. It is not surprising, then, that Christianity, Eastern and Western alike, got off to a wrong start in their approach to Islam and its founder.

Popular interest concentrated on Mohammed's personality. John of Damascus, who treats Islam as a Christian heresy, tells how in the days of the emperor Heraclius a false prophet (*pseudo-prophetes*) arose among the Arabs. His name was Maméd. He became acquainted with the Old and New Testaments and later, after discoursing with an Arian monk, "established his own sect." By feigning piety, he won the hearts of his people. Later he claimed that a scripture had been sent down to him from heaven. The ridiculous ordinances which he had put into that book he presented to them as their holy doctrine (*to sebas*).[51]

The first Byzantine historian to deal with Mohammed was Theophanes Confessor (d. 817), whose life of the Prophet was destined to be widely used by later writers.[52] Unfortunately,

[51] *De Haeresibus*, chap. 101, beginning, in *MPG*, XCIV, 764–65.

[52] Cf. W. Eichner, *Islam*, XXIII (1936), 134 and 143.

Theophanes does not indicate his authorities. This is what he has to tell.[53]

"In this year (*Anno Mundi* 6122 = A.D. 632) Mohammed (*Mouámed*) the ruler and false prophet of the Saracens, died, after appointing his kinsman, Abû Bakr (*Aboubácharon*) to succeed him. At the same time his repute was bruited about and all were gripped by fear. At the beginning of his public appearance (*parousia*) the misguided Hebrews thought that he was the Messiah (*Christos*) who(se coming) they expected. So some of their chief men[54] joined him, accepted his religion and forsook that of Moses who had seen God (*theoptes*, God-seeing). Those who did thus were ten in number and they stuck with him until he met his bloody end (*sphage*). When they saw him partake of camel flesh they realized that he was not whom they had thought him to be. They did not know what to do. Afraid to forsake his religion the poor wretches brought charges of unlawful conduct against us Christians, and continued to side with him."

After a brief excursus on the internal relationship of the Arab tribes, Theophanes continues. "Since the aforementioned Mohammed was poor and an orphan to boot he decided to attach himself to a wealthy woman, a relative of his, Ḫadîja (*Chadíga*) by name, in the capacity of an agent hired to take charge of her camels and to do business for her in Egypt and Palestine. Shortly thereafter having won the woman, who was a widow, by his open ways he took her for his wife and thus obtained possession of her camels and other property. In Palestine he mixed with Jews and Christians. Through them he got hold of some scriptures. He also contracted the ailment of epilepsy.

"When his wife became aware of his condition she was sorely grieved that she, a woman of noble birth, was now tied to one who not only was poor but an epileptic. He undertook to placate her by saying: 'I am having the vision of an angel, Gabriel by

[53] Slightly abridged from his *Chronographia*, ed. C. de Boor (Leipzig, 1883–85), I, 333–34; W. Gass, *Gennadius und Pletho* (Breslau, 1844), I, 116–17, translates a small portion of the passage; Anastasius' *Historia tripartita*, II, 208–10, has a Latin version; cf. also Cedrenus, *op. cit.*, I, 738–45.

[54] Anastasius: "those who had listened to him."

name, and as I cannot stand his sight I lose my strength[55] and fall to the ground.' But she had for her lover a monk who lived in these parts having been exiled for miscreancy. She told him all and also the name of the angel. And (this monk) wishing to convince her fully said to her: 'He has spoken the truth. For it is this angel who is sent out to all the prophets.' Accepting the word of the false abbot she believed him and announced to the other women of her clan that (her husband) was a prophet.

"And thus the report spread from the women to the men, reaching first Abû Bakr, whom he later made his successor. In the end his sect (or: heresy) forcibly (lit., through war) gained control of the territory of Yaṯrib (*ta mere tes Ethríbou*). For first he had spent ten years (spreading his message) in secret, then again ten years (spreading it) by war, finally he professed it openly (and ruled) for nine years. He taught his adherents that he who killed an enemy or was killed by an enemy would enter paradise. He described Paradise as a place of carnal (joys), carousing, drinking and embracing of women. There would be a river of wine and honey and milk, and there would be women other than those they now had whose embrace would be long-lasting and of enduring pleasure. And he alleged other fables, immoral and foolish. They should, however, support one another and help the wronged."

Any increase in information about the Prophet that time would bring was counteracted by the mounting hatred fanned by the perpetual wars. In the great tradition of ancient oratory but with a voice made coarse and strident by passion, Bartholomew of Edessa rebukes his Muslim adversary in the thirteenth century.[56]

"Why then do you call him a prophet and a messenger of God, who was but a voluptuary, defiled to the very core, a brigand, a profligate, a murderer and a robber? Tell me, pray, what do you mean by prophecy and by apostle! God knows you would not be able to tell had you not been taught by the Christian! O you unblushingly shameless creature! You allege that

[55] ὀλιγωρῶ; Gass, *op. cit.*, p. 116: "I swoon."

[56] On his date, see Eichner, *loc. cit.*, pp. 137–38.*

for 32 years your Mohammed (*Mouchámet*) neither was, nor spake the words of a prophet, that he was neither an apostle nor a teacher or even a pious man, that he did not pray to, nor know of the Lord, but that after this time he did know Him. But if you so earnestly deny that anything did happen through Mohammed those first 32 years, how should not I, the Christian, deny the happenings of those later 15 years? But tell me first, I beseech you, how he came to know God and in what manner. If you assert that God despatched His angel to him and taught him the knowledge of God, then the angel is God's messenger to him and to the people, and he nothing but a liar, a deceiver. Since you call him a prophet show me what he foretold and in what words, what it is he commands and what sign and wonder he wrought. I have read all your books and I have found out for myself. If he was a prophet as you claim why, when he was about to fall off the horse he rode and to hurt his side and to lose his upper and lower teeth and to suffer bruises owing to the cropper, why did not he foretell, or foresee, the incident?"[57]

Two centuries later, with the collapse of Constantinople at hand, the tune has not changed yet.

When the lecherous former monk noticed the gullibility of the people, "he thought he should give them a creed and a law after the fashion of Arianism and the other heresies for which he had been excommunicated. So he sat down and wrote a book, the so-called Koran (*Korrán*), which is the law of God, disseminating therein all his impiety. He taught that God had neither *logos* nor *pneuma*, that the Christ was not God but only a great prophet, and put together a great amount of other such nonsense. He then handed it to his pupil, Mohammed (*Môámed*) and announced to those senseless people that this book had come down to Mohammed from heaven where it had been with the angel Gabriel. They believed that the matter was such and so the monk assured the establishment of the new law."[58]

The average Latin Christian disposed of no more accurate in-

[57] Bartholomew of Edessa, *Confutatio Agareni*, in *MPG*, CIV, 1388–89.

[58] Anonymus II, in Gass, *op. cit.*, II, 148–49 (Greek text); on the author cf. Eichner, *loc. cit.*, pp. 143–44.

formation. Eulogius of Cordova, reputedly one of the most learned priests of his day (martyred in 859), states that Mohammed, "when he felt his end approaching, foretold that on the third day after his death angels would come and resuscitate him." Accordingly, after his soul had "descended into Hell," his disciples kept watch diligently beside the body. At the end of the third day, however, since no angels had appeared, the disciples, thinking that their presence near the corpse—which already exhaled the odor of corruption—perhaps kept heavenly visitors at a distance, withdrew. Thereupon, instead of angels, dogs came and began to devour the Prophet's body. All that remained was buried by the Muslims, who, to be revenged upon the dogs, decreed the annual slaughter of a large number of these animals. "And such," cries Eulogius, "are the miracles of the Prophet of Islam!"[59]

What is bewildering about this report is the fact freely admitted by the author that he made no attempt to verify the information supplied him by a chance manuscript in Latin by questioning his Muslim compatriots or glancing at their historical works.

Guibert of Nogent (d. 1124), who again confesses with great readiness to the inadequacy of his exclusively oral and Christian sources, goes Eulogius one better by having Mohammed devoured by pigs while unconscious in one of his epileptic attacks. This unusual incident satisfactorily accounts for the Muslim prejudice against the consumption of pork. Another version substitutes drunkenness for epilepsy and thus explains the prohibition of wine as well.[60] Hildebert of Lemans (d. 1133 as archbishop of Tours) has Mohammed prove his divine mission in the eyes of the people by the apparent miracle that a terrifying bull, secretly tamed and trained by the impostor, kneels before him at his bidding.[61] Andrea Dandolo (d. 1354, doge of Venice, 1343–54) knows of a white dove which had been taught by Mohammed to settle on his shoulder and to pick grains of corn from inside his ear: the people took the dove for the heav-

[59] R. Dozy, *Spanish Islam*, trans. F. G. S. Stokes (London, 1913), p. 270.

[60] H. Prutz, *Kulturgeschichte der Kreuzzüge* (Berlin, 1883), pp. 79–80.

[61] *Ibid.*, p. 81.

enly messenger through whom the Lord would communicate with the self-styled prophet.[62]

Side by side with the concept of Mohammed the heretic or the false prophet, medieval literature in the West cherished the concept of Mohammed the god. In fact, this concept was not renounced completely before the middle of the seventeenth century, when dramatists still occasionally present Muslims as praying to their god Mohammed. The *Chanson de Roland* views the Muslims as true heathen who adore a pantheon, quaintly composed of Mahomet, Apollon, Jupin, and Tervagant. Elsewhere Alkaron (i.e., the Koran) joins the group of gods. These gods, and, above all, Mohammed himself, have images made of gold and silver.[63] They are worshiped with elaborate rites, "and their aid is invoked before battle. After defeat the gods are cursed, insulted, dragged in the dust, or even broken to pieces. Defeat is the usual fate of the Saracen. In the only account of a Saracenic victory, when the Sowdone of Babylone (early fifteenth century) takes Rome, the Saracens burn frankincense before their gods, blow brass horns, drink the blood of beasts, and feast on milk and honey."[64] Despite their gaudy rites, Islam sits lightly on those paynims, and, when captured, they find it easy to change their allegiance and become "true Christians."[65] Piers Plowman relegates Mohammed as demon to the infernal powers, and William Dunbar (d. *ca.* 1520) instals "Mahoun" as master of ceremonies in Hell.[66]

The Crusades did much to advance a more correct picture of the Prophet, but it seems that, outside those who had personal experience of the Muslim world, only a comparatively small group of people were prepared to accept this revised portrait. Prominent in this group are such theological leaders as desired to provide their coreligionists with the most effective weapons

[62] *Ibid.*

[63] For references cf. E. Dreesbach, *Der Orient in der altfranzösischen Kreuzzugsliteratur* (Breslau, 1901), pp. 4–6.

[64] B. P. Smith, *Islam in English Literature* (Beirut, 1939), p. 2, quoting *The Sowdone of Babylone*, ed. E. Hausknecht, ll. 676–90.

[65] P. Martino, *L'Orient dans la littérature française au XVIIe et au XVIIIe siècle* (Paris, 1906), p. 8.

[66] Smith, *op. cit.*, p. 3.

to combat the enemy whose influence on scholastic thinking was just then spreading dangerously.

In 1273 William of Tripolis wrote his *Tractate on the State of the Saracens, Mohammed the False Prophet, Their Law and Their Faith.*[67] Although his picture of Mohammed is far removed from the historical personality, the fabulous elements are reduced, and invective is curtailed to the minimum indispensable to medieval apologetics. William reports that the Saracens believe Gabriel to have transmitted *voluntatem divinam* to the Prophet, whose utterances the believers then wove into a book. The Catholics, however, William goes on to say, hold a different opinion. After Mohammed's death his partisans wished to have doctrine and law treated comprehensively on the basis of his teachings. When it was found that the man to whom the work had been intrusted was unable to execute it properly, converted Jews and Christians were asked to assist him. These then thought it best to cull appropriate passages from the Old and the New Testaments and combine them arbitrarily. Thus the book has in it a great deal of beauty borrowed from the Christian and Jewish Scriptures, but the specifically Muslim contribution is nothing but deformation and distortion.[68]

On an even higher level did Ricoldus de Santa Cruce, a Dominican who visited Baghdad toward the end of the thirteenth century, conduct his controversy with the Saracens. Sometime in the middle of the next century, Demetrius Cydones translated his book, which was to enjoy a certain vogue, into Greek.

The author conceals his zeal behind a sober wording. He disproves the Koran's claim to be the Lord's word by pointing to inconsistencies of the text and the unsatisfactory character of its morality. Only at the end of this disquisition he permits himself the statement that, even according to the learned doctors of the Mohammedan faith, not man but the devil was its first author, who with divine permission wanted to prepare the road for the Anti-Christ. When Satan felt unable to arrest the progress of Christianity in the East and to protect his wards,

[67] The Latin text is printed by Prutz, *op. cit.*, pp. 575–98.

[68] *Tractate* . . . . , chap. 25, p. 590.

the heathen gods, and when he realized that it would be impossible simply to deny the law of Moses and the Gospel of Christ, he decided to deceive the world by inventing a scripture which would, as it were, hold the mean between the Old and the New Testaments. To carry out his plan, he used as his tool "a man of diabolical nature, Mohammed (*Môámeth*) by name, an idolater by religion, of poor means but a keen mind, and a notorious malefactor."[69] Ricoldus' contemporary, Dante (d. 1321), has Mohammed in the ninth pit of Hell, together with other "sowers of scandal and of schism."[70]

Under the influence of Peter of Cluny (d. 1156), the first translation of the Koran had been achieved in 1141. It began to be realized that, to refute the foe, one had first to know him. It was perhaps with a view to strengthen what might be called the counterattack of Christian theology that Thomas Aquinas (d. 1272) undertook to write his *Summa contra Gentiles*. A long tradition of more or less unsuccessful arguments made Thomas painfully aware of the difficulties in the way of a convincing exposition of the truth.

"But it is difficult to refute the errors of each individual, for two reasons. First, because the sacrilegious assertions of each erring individual are not so well known to us that we are able, from what they say, to find arguments to refute their errors. For the Doctors of old used this method in order to confute the errors of the heathens, whose opinions they were able to know, since they either had been heathens themselves or had lived among heathens and were conversant with their teachings. Secondly, because some of them, like the Mohammedans and pagans, do not agree with us as to the authority of any Scripture whereby they may be convinced, in the same way as we are able to dispute with the Jews by means of the Old Testament, and with heretics by means of the New: whereas the former accept neither. Wherefore it is necessary to have recourse to natural reason, to which all are compelled to assent. And yet this is deficient in the things of God."[71]

[69] *Contra Mahometem*, chap. 13, in *MPG*, CLIV, 1116.*

[70] *Inferno* xxviii. 35.

[71] *Summa* i. 2, trans. by the English Dominican Fathers, I (London, 1924), 4.

In agreement with Thomas, "who upheld apologetics and made use of 'necessary reasons' to prove all but a few of the higher truths of Christianity,"[72] the Catalan Ramon Lull, the greatest Christian missionary to Islam of the Middle Ages (and one of the greatest figures of his time and of his people) firmly believed in the efficacy of theological disputation.

Appearing before the Council of Vienne (1311–12), he proposed "three things for the honor and reverence and increase of the holy Catholic faith: first, that there should be builded certain places where certain persons devout and of lofty intelligence should study divers languages to the end that they might preach the holy Gospel to all nations; second, that of all Christian knights there should be made a certain order, which should strive continually for the conquest of the Holy Land; third, that in opposition to the opinion of Averroes, who in many things has endeavored to oppose the Catholic faith, men of learning should compose works refuting these errors aforementioned and all those that hold the same opinion."[73]

The immediate fruit of his first proposal was the Council's decision to found five colleges to teach Hebrew, Arabic, and Chaldean, in Rome, Bologna, Paris, Oxford, and Salamanca—the beginning of regular oriental studies in the West.[74] In those writings of his that are devoted to the refutation of Islam, Lull proves himself surprisingly well informed and, what is more, gentle in his language and fair-minded in his procedure.

In his *Book of the Gentile* (written 1272–73) he puts these words in the mouth of a Saracen sage: " 'Since Mahomet is honored so greatly in the world, and by so many people, it follows that in him justice accords with the charity of God; for were this not so, then would God not suffer him to be honored as he is, and, if He suffered it, wrong and honor would accord with charity, against charity and honor and justice, which is im-

[72] E. A. Peers, *Ramon Lull* (London, 1929), p. 405.

[73] *A Life of Ramon Lull*, written by an unknown hand about 1311, trans. from the Catalan by E. A. Peers (London, 1927), p. 43.

[74] This statement is not refuted by the fact that the first school of oriental studies was founded at Toledo in 1250 by the Order of Preachers (cf. A. Guillaume, in *Legacy of Islam*, p. 272).

possible. Whence it follows that, by reason of the honor wherewith Mahomet is honored by God, Mahomet is a prophet.'

" 'From that which thou sayest,' answered the Gentile, 'it follows that Jesus Christ, Who is so greatly honored in this world, is God; and that His apostles, and the other martyrs, who are so greatly honored likewise, died in the way of truth. For, if God suffered not the dead that died in falsehood to be honored in this world, then that which is said of Christ would of necessity be truth; and, if this were so, then thy law would not be true, neither would Mahomet be worthy of honor nor a prophet.' "[75]

In 1307 Ramon Lull crossed to Bugía and preached to the Moors. He was arrested and brought before the chief judge of the town. The judge arranged for a public disputation between Lull and the Muslim doctors, who apparently proved unable to worst him. His biographer tells us that "at his lofty reasoning the Bishop (i.e., the judge) marvelled, and answered never a word, but commanded that he should be thrown forthwith into prison."[76] The people demanded his death. But the Catalans and the Genoese contrived his rescue. But when he returned to Bugía to preach the Gospel once more, he was stoned to death early in 1316. No medieval Latin Christian ever matched his understanding of the Muslims.*

Dislike, fear, and almost deliberate misunderstanding did not, on the part of the Byzantines, preclude respect and even appreciation of the great antagonist. The same Constantin Porphyrogennetus who indorses the conventional slanders about the Prophet in one passage[77] makes it quite clear in another that he reserves his highest esteem for the Saracens of the East. Exquisite politeness characterizes the formulas with which the caliph's emissaries are to be greeted; and with tactful acceptance of the guests' prejudices no questions will be asked with

[75] Trans. E. A. Peers, *Ramon Lull*, p. 95.

[76] *Life*, p. 36.

[77] *De administrando imperio*, chap. 14, ed. I. Bekker in *Works of Constantin VII*, III (Bonn, 1840), pp. 90–92; Gass, *op. cit.*, I, 117, refers to this passage.

respect to the health of the female members of the caliph's household.[78] At the imperial table the "Agarene friends" are seated above all other foreign "friends," and among the Agarenes themselves the Eastern are given higher rank than the Western.[79] The Empire of Baghdad had succeeded to the position once held in the Byzantine mind by Sassanian Persia.

In the face of constant and bitter hostilities, Byzantines and Persians had always considered each other equals.[80] The ceremonial for the reception of the Persian envoy made the emperor ask for the state of health of his brother, the Persian king, and the envoy would respond by announcing the gifts his brother had sent.[81] Theophylactus of Simocatta (*fl.* under Heraclius, *ca.* 610–40) makes the Persian king Khosrau write to the emperor Mauricius: "There are two eyes to which divinity confided the task of illuminating the world: these are the powerful monarchy of the Romans and the wisely governed commonwealth of the Persians. By these two great empires the barbarous and war-loving[82] nations are kept in check, and mankind given better and safer government throughout."[83] Now that the Arabs have taken the place of the Persians, it is they in conjunction with the Byzantines who constitute the pillars of civilization. Aside from the Indians, only their nations are lettered; only they keep aloof from the brutish desires of the barbarians, such as the Turks and the Chinese.[84]

The rise of the Muslim power gave a new impetus to Byzan-

[78] *De caeremoniis*, ed. J. H. Leichius and J. J. Reiske (Leipzig, 1751–54), Book II, chap. 47, pp. 394–96.

[79] *Ibid.*, chap. 52, pp. 428–29.

[80] Cf. Th. Nöldeke, *Geschichte der Perser und Araber zur Zeit der Sasaniden* (Leiden, 1879), p. 454.

[81] *De caeremoniis*, Book I, chap. 89, p. 236.

[82] In another context Khosrau calls himself a "war-hating king," *misopolemos basileus*, Theophylactus Simocattes, *Historiae*, ed. C. de Boor (Leipzig, 1887), IV, 8, 5.

[83] *Ibid.*, IV, 11, 2–3; cf. also Rambaud, *op. cit.*, p. 434.

[84] Cf. Rambaud, *op. cit.*, pp. 434–35, who quotes Barhebraeus; on the Indians, see, e.g., Ṣâᶜid al-Andalusî, *op. cit.*, pp. 12–15; trans., pp. 43–48. Al-Iṣṭaḫrî, *BGA*, I, 4, observes that Persia used to be the principal and the best state in the world and that the Muslim Empire is treading in her footsteps.

tine civilization.[85] And it is curious to observe how Arab prestige rose in Constantinople at the same time that the prestige of Greek science was reaching its peak in Baghdad.

Al-Maʾmûn saw Aristotle in a dream, who told him that the Good per se was what appeared such to reason and that the Good in lawgiving was what appeared such to the community. This experience determined the caliph to ask the emperor for books. The emperor granted the request after some procrastination. Thereupon Maʾmûn sent scholars to Constantinople to procure the manuscripts.[86] Among others he sent Salm, the director of the House of Wisdom (*dâr al-ḥikma*), which he had established in the capital.[87] Private individuals followed the caliph's example.

The three Banû Mûsà were extreme in their search for ancient sciences, expended fortunes on them, and wearied themselves out for them. "They sent to the land of Greece people who would procure scientific works for them and brought translators from various countries at great expense, and so brought to light the marvels of wisdom. The chief subjects with which they occupied themselves were geometry, mechanics, the movements of the heavenly bodies, music and astronomy, but these were the least of their activities."[88]

Greek philosophy had sufficiently penetrated educated circles in Baghdad *ca.* 800 to enable the scholars whom the Barmakid vizier, Yaḥyà b. Ḫâlid (disgraced 803), interrogated on love to expound a variety of classical theories on the subject.[89] Not very long after the Arab physicians had begun their training on

[85] For evidence cf. Bury, *A History of the Eastern Roman Empire, 802–867*, pp. 434–35.

[86] *Fihrist*, ed. G. Flügel (Leipzig, 1871–72), p. 243; cf. also Nicholson, *op. cit.*, p. 359.

[87] Cf. P. Kraus, *Rivista degli studi orientali*, XIV (1934), 11. The *dâr al-ḥikma* was primarily intended as a school for translators; cf. M. Meyerhof, *SBBA* (Phil.-Hist. Kl., 1930), pp. 402 and 403.

[88] *Fihrist*, p. 271; trans. in R. Levy, *A Baghdad Chronicle* (Cambridge, 1929), pp. 87–88. For the import of manuscripts from Constantinople cf. also Honigmann, *op. cit.*, p. 122.*

[89] Masʿûdî, *Murûj*, VI, 368–86. *Irshâd*, V, 280–81, records a similar discussion under Maʾmûn; cf. also F. Rosenthal, *Islamic Culture*, XIV (1940), 421.

Greek authorities, the Byzantine doctors fell back on Arab medicine.[90]

The prestige enjoyed by each civilization in the territory of the other is well reflected in the career of Leon the Mathematician. Outstanding in his philosophical and mathematical learning, Leon buried himself in poor quarters in Constantinople eking out a meager living by teaching. One of his students in geometry was captured by the Arabs and by a curious concatenation of events was admitted into the presence of al-Maʾmûn and confronted with the most renowned geometers. The youth found them failing in their comprehension of geometrical reasoning and impressed the court by demonstrating correct methods. Asked whether his teacher was still alive, he explained that Leon lived in straitened circumstances and was known only to a small circle. Al-Maʾmûn instantly wrote a letter to the scholar, inviting him to Baghdad, and promised the student his freedom if he would deliver the message. The philosopher prudently showed the caliph's invitation to a high official who, in turn, communicated the matter to the emperor. Thus the letter brought Leon's scholarly accomplishments to the attention of the public. The emperor immediately appointed him as a public teacher at the Church of the Forty Martyrs. When al-Maʾmûn realized Leon's reluctance to come to Baghdad, he entered into a correspondence with the scholar, submitting to him a number of geometrical and astronomical problems. The sagacious solutions offered by Leon and the forecasts of future events which he added "in order to astound" made the caliph ever more desirous of attracting him to his court. He turned to the emperor himself and asked him to send Leon to Baghdad for a short while, offering the most splendid compensation. But the emperor, not deeming it wise to give up his own treasure to others and to make precious knowledge accessible to the foreigner, declined. Instead, he raised Leon to the archbishopric of Thessalonica (*ca.* 840).[91]

[90] Cf. Krumbacher, *op. cit.*, pp. 614–15.

[91] Theophanes Continuatus, ed. I. Bekker (Bonn, 1838), pp. 185–92; Cedrenus, *op. cit.*, II, 165–70; Bury, *op. cit.*, pp. 436–38. In the middle of the eleventh century,

The same relationship transpires in the reports that connect the advice of Greek envoys to al-Manṣûr (754–75) with various features in the layout of Baghdad.[92] These reports are matched by the statement that an ambassador returning from Baghdad persuaded the emperor Theophilos (829–42) to build his new palace at Bryas in the guise of the palace of the Saracens, "differing in nothing from their style in shape and decoration."[93]

There is nothing to show whether the Arabs were aware that Constantinople outranked Baghdad in size and in splendor.[94] At any rate, Constantinople retained its attraction and, more or less, its grandeur throughout the Middle Ages, and the admiration evoked by its sight in Ibn Baṭṭûṭa, who visited the city *ca.* 1330, is as evident in his account of it as is his disappointment at the state of Baghdad, where he finds nothing to praise except the construction and organization of the bathhouses.[95]

Muslim civilization attracted the non-Muslims far beyond the spell usually cast by ideas and habits of a dominating group on groups of lesser standing and influence. Not only were the contemporaries conscious of the higher standard of living of the Muslim world and its material superiority in general which, incidentally, merely means the perpetuation of the unequal distribution of wealth between East and West in the

Michael Psellus boasted several Arabs among his pupils, and in the thirteenth and fourteenth centuries Persian-trained Greeks added to the fame of the school of Trebizond (cf. Runciman, *op. cit.*, pp. 230 and 292).

[92] Cf. G. Le Strange, *Baghdad during the Abbasid Caliphate* (Oxford, 1924), pp. 142–44. The Greeks rendered the Arabic designation of the city, *madînat as-salâm*, Abode of Peace, by Eirenopolis (cf. Levy, *op. cit.*, p. 8). The Christian Quarter in Baghdad came to be known as *dâr ar-Rûm* (cf. Le Strange, *op. cit.*, p. 207); this name, however, also applied specifically to a caravanserai near the home of the bishop (cf. Levy, *op. cit.*, p. 67). There was also a *dâr ar-Rûmiyyîn* in Kûfa, Ṭabarî, *Annales*, II, 256–57 (reference owed to Professor Nabia Abbott), and al-Balâḏurî, *Futûḥ al-buldân*, ed. M. J. de Goeje (Leiden, 1865–66), p. 281.

[93] Theoph. Cont., p. 98; cf. Bury, *op. cit.*, p. 133.

[94] For this appraisal of Constantinople cf. Bury, *op. cit.*, p. 238.

[95] Cf. Ibn Baṭṭûṭa, *Travels*, trans. H. A. R. Gibb (London, 1929), pp. 99–100 on Baghdad, and pp. 159–63 on Constantinople.*

last centuries of antiquity;[96] but those that did come in contact with Arab thought and Arab manner often responded with reluctant admiration and not infrequently found themselves imitating Muslim ways.

The splendor of Cordova dazzled the eyes and stirred the imagination of the Latin world. The nun Hrosvitha of Gandersheim (d. *ca.* 1002) thus sets the stage for her *Passion of Saint Pelagius,* martyred during the reign of ᶜAbdarraḥmân III (912–61; the execution of the saint occurred early in the twenties): "In the western parts of the globe, there shone forth a fair ornament, a venerable city, haughty because of its unwonted might in war, a city well cultured, which the Spanish race held in possession, rich and known by the famous name Cordova, illustrious because of its charms and also renowned for all resources, especially abounding in the seven streams of knowledge, and ever famous for continual victories."[97]

The Spanish Christians of the ninth century neglected their classical tradition in favor of Arabic. The Christian zealot and writer, Alvaro, in 854 bitterly deplores this attitude.

"My fellow-Christians delight in the poems and romances of the Arabs; they study the works of Mohammedan theologians and philosophers, not in order to refute them, but to acquire a correct and elegant Arabic style. Where today can a layman be found who reads the Latin commentaries on Holy Scriptures? Who is there that studies the Gospels, the Prophets, the Apostles? Alas! the young Christians who are most conspicuous for their talents have no knowledge of any literature or language save the Arabic; they read and study with avidity Arabian books; they amass whole libraries of them at a vast cost, and they everywhere sing the praises of Arabian lore. On the other hand, at the mention of Christian books they disdain-

[96] On the situation in the early centuries of our era cf. G. Sarton, *Osiris,* III (1936–37), 429; Sarton quotes F. Cumont's corroborative statement, *Les Religions orientales* (4th ed.; Paris, 1929), p. 7.

[97] *Passio S. Pelagii,* vss. 12–18, ed. trans. Sister M. Gonsalva Wiegand, *The Non-dramatic Works of Hrosvitha* (St. Louis, 1936), p. 129; *Works,* ed. K. Strecker (Leipzig, 1930), p. 54. For tenth-century Cordova cf., e.g., R. Altamira, *A History of Spanish Civilization* (London, 1930), p. 54.

fully protest that such works are unworthy of their notice. The pity of it! Christians have forgotten their own tongue and scarce one in a thousand can be found able to compose in fair Latin a letter to a friend! But when it comes to writing Arabic, how many there are who can express themselves in that language with the greatest elegance, and even compose verses which surpass in formal correctness those of the Arabs themselves."[98]

The Franks who settled in the East in the wake of the Crusades accepted a good many customs of their Muslim neighbors. Bowdoin of Edessa, king of Jerusalem (1100–1118), exchanged Western for Eastern dress, grew a long beard, and dined off a carpet, squatting on the ground. Tancred of Antioch (d. 1112) went so far as to mint coins that showed him in Arab attire.[99] The celebrated Usâma b. Munqiḏ (d. 1188) relates the story of one of his men who found himself invited to the house of a Frankish knight. "The knight presented an excellent table, with food extraordinarily clean and delicious. Seeing me abstaining from food, he said, 'Eat, be of good cheer! I never eat Frankish dishes, but I have Egyptian women cooks and never eat except their cooking. Besides, pork never enters my house.' I ate, but guardedly, and after that we departed."[100]

Conversion to Islam of a Christian subject of the caliph naturally was of frequent occurrence, and hardly less frequent was the Christianization of Muslims whom the vicissitudes of war had brought under the emperor's sway. Baptized Arabs were settled as military colons in the border regions and received a subsidy from the state to start the farms on which they were to subsist.[101] Prisoners, exiles, and fugitives of one sort or another would be prepared to switch their allegiance. But that case is of the rarest where a man leaves his civilization without compulsion or without a political motive to live abroad.

Jabala b. al-Aiham, the last of the Ghassanid princes in Syria,

98 Alvaro, *Indiculus luminosus*, chap. 35, in *MPL*, CXXI, 554–56; trans. Dozy, *op. cit.*, p. 268.

99 Prutz, *op. cit.*, p. 62.

100 *Memoirs*, trans. P. K. Hitti (New York, 1929), pp. 169–70.

101 Rambaud, *op. cit.*, pp. 248–49.

realized during the reign of ᶜUmar I (634–44) that his temperament was incompatible with the leveling tendencies of early Islam and forsook Medina for the Byzantine Empire. Attempts to win him back failed.[102] Early in the next century, al-Wâbiṣî, of the Qurashî clan of Maḫzûm, reputedly because he had been punished for drinking wine, went into Byzantine territory, where he became a Christian and married. He experienced bitter attacks of nostalgia but, although invited to return, preferred to stay and died on Greek soil.[103] For fifteen years, *ca.* 895–910, a Saracen, Samonas, was the favorite of Leon VI (886–912). It is uncertain whether he underwent baptism; at any rate, he appears to have planned to return ultimately to his people, and at least once he attempted to break away from the Byzantine court. But he never could quite tear himself away and seems to have died in a Byzantine dungeon.[104]

Perhaps the most profound difference in the outlook of East and West toward each other in the Middle Ages stems from the irrepressible urge of the Occidental to localize in the East his dreams, his hopes, his marvels. The Oriental did not hesitate to accept fables about Western lands, but never did the West become to him the stage of mythical wonders. In fact, when the Muslim narrator of the Middle Ages wishes to find a definite geographical background for his yarn, he usually, unless compelled by tradition to look north, selects a country or an isle believed to lie somewhere in the farther East. The concept of the East as the home of utopian bliss and again as the place where the weirdest fancies of an unbridled imagination would

[102] I. Goldziher, *Muhammedanische Studien* (Halle a/S, 1888–80), I, 75–76, and Th. Nöldeke, *Die ghassânischen Fürsten aus dem Hause Gafna's* (Berlin, 1887), pp. 45–46. Zarr b. Sadûs, of the Ṭayy, likewise refused to submit to the authority of Islam and removed to Christian territory (cf. Goldziher, *op. cit.*, I, 75).*

[103] Abû ᵓl-Faraj al-Iṣfahânî, *Kitâb al-aghânî* (Cairo, 1927 ff.), VI, 116–19 = ed. Bûlâq, 1285, V, 184–86.**

[104] F. W. Bussell, *The Roman Empire* (London, 1910), II, 187–91. According to Rambaud, *op. cit.*, p. 533, Samonas was forced to enter a monastery. We do not know what prompted the conversion to Christianity of the noted translator of Greek mathematical works, al-Baᶜlabakkî (d. 835) (cf. Bury, *op. cit.*, p. 438, n. 3). The emperor Nicephorus I (802–11) was believed to be of Arab extraction (cf. *Tanbîh*, pp. 167–68).

live in baffling reality affected the attitude of the medieval Occidental to an extent hardly appreciable today.

From the time of Herodotus the West had reveled in the wonders of the East. The advance of geographical knowledge had, from time to time, forced the wondrous country to recede, but scientific exploration remained sufficiently spotty and vague to protect the cherished dreams behind the dim veils of ignorance. Did not the Bible expressly tell of a paradise in the East? Medieval maps are fond of including in the eastern part of the world a picture of the Terrestrial Paradise, and we are informed with unquestioning assurance that "the first place in the East is Paradise, a garden famous for its delights, where man can never go, for a fiery wall surrounds it and reaches to the sky."[105]

Jerusalem is at the center of the inhabited world. Dante's Inferno has its axis exactly beneath this city. Gervase of Tilbury (*fl.* 1211) believed that Augustus had thought Judea to be the heart of the earth because he had begun a survey of the provinces of the empire there.[106] At any rate, the pre-eminence given the city of Jerusalem in the Scriptures is sufficient evidence of its pivotal location. The exact spot that marks the navel of the earth is variously identified with Mount Zion or Mount Moriah.[107]

China and, even more so, India, the country of Thomas, teemed with marvels. But around 1170, Benjamin of Tudela could report that four of the ten lost tribes of Israel were settled as near as the mountains of Nîshâpûr, in eastern Persia.[108] And not much farther away stretched the powerful realm of the Prester John, the hoped-for ally of the West against the Muslim unbeliever.

This Christian monarch addressed a letter with a description of his country to the pope, and in other versions to the Byzan-

[105] J. K. Wright, *The Geographical Lore of the Time of the Crusades* (New York, 1925), p. 261, quoting from Honorius Inclusus (or, Honorius of Autun, d. before 1150), *De Imagine mundi*, I, 8; on the authorship of this work cf. Wright, *op. cit.*, p. 403, n. 73.

[106] Cf. Wright, *op. cit.*, p. 259.

[107] *Ibid.*, p. 260.

[108] *The Itinerary of Benjamin of Tudela*, ed. M. N. Adler (London, 1907), p. 59 of the translation.

tine emperor, Manuel Comnenus (1143–90), and again to Frederick Barbarossa (1152–90).[109] Seventy-two kings are his tributaries.[110] He rules the three Indies, and his realm reaches through the Babylonian Desert to the Tower of Babel.[111] The ten lost tribes, too, are under his suzerainty.[112] His states are extremely rich. There is not a single poor man in his dominions. Thieves and robbers are unknown. His subjects have no equals in their wealth except that they possess only a few horses and these of a vile breed.[113] No one knows how to lie nor is any vice practiced among them.[114] But their clemency does not make them unwarlike. On the contrary, they even extended their rule over Amazons and Brahmins.[115] The Prester's palace, which is described in great detail, is of overwhelming splendor. The letter concludes with the statement: "Only if you could count the stars of the heaven and the sands of the sea would you be able to form an estimate of our dominion and our power."[116]

On September 27, 1177, Pope Alexander III wrote to Prester John, "his devout son in Christ, the illustrious and magnificent King of the Indians."[117] The pope seems somewhat worried about the orthodoxy of John and proposes to send him a certain Master Philip, papal physician, to expound to him the tenets of the true Catholic creed. Acceptance of doctrine and ethos of Roman Christianity would raise his repute even higher and would, on the other hand, deflate his pride in his riches and his power.[118]

This passage is proof that the pope was acquainted with Prester John's missive and that he had himself fallen prey to this most curious example of wishful thinking which history presents.[119]

109 Ed. F. Zarncke, *Kgl. Sächs. Ges. d. Wiss., Abhandl., Philol.-hist. Kl.*, VII (1879), 909–24.

110 *Letter*, sec. 9.

111 *Letter*, sec. 12.

112 *Letter*, sec. 41.

113 *Letter*, secs. 45–46.

114 *Letter*, sec. 52.

115 *Letter*, sec. 55.

116 *Letter*, sec. 100; trans. Wright, *op. cit.*, p. 285.

117 Ed. Zarncke, *loc. cit.*, pp. 941–44, sec. 1.

118 Sec. 13.

119 For the historical background of the legend of Prester John cf. Zarncke, *loc. cit.*, VIII (1883), 1–119.

IV

Early in the Middle Ages the Latin West had come to accept the idea that civilization flows from East to West. But it had derived no hope from the upsurge of the Western world the theory presaged. For it was felt that mankind would meet its final doom when the movement had reached the uttermost limits of the Occident.

As early as the fourth century A.D., Severian of Gabala, best known as opponent of John Chrysostom (d. 407), had explained: "God looked into the future and set the first man in that place (i.e., Paradise, in the East) in order to cause him to understand that, just as the light of heaven moves toward the West, so the human race hastens towards death."[120] More explicitly Hugh of St. Victor (d. 1141) declared that "the course of events has gradually been moving westward, until now it has reached the end of the earth and we must face the fact that we are approaching the end of the ages."[121] Otto of Freising (d. 1158) and Alexander Neckam (d. 1217) trace the procession of learning from Egypt and Babylon to Greeks and Romans, and finally to the West, to wit, Italy, Gaul, and Spain.[122]

The chiliastic anticipation was disappointed, but history confirmed what speculation had predicted: at the end of the medieval period civilization had moved its focal points across the Mediterranean and into Western Europe. The discoveries on the far shores of the Atlantic sealed the gradual decline of Islam.

A thousand years of strife and toil had profoundly changed the political face of the world. The Turkish conquest of Constantinople (1453) had finally eliminated one of the three power blocs around the Mediterranean. Western Europe was cleared of Muslim domination when Granada surrendered to the Castilian queen (1492). Both in East and in West the unity of the power blocs had been shattered by internal developments. Everywhere national states arose, and, although the Ottoman

[120] *De mundi creatione,* chap. 5, quoted by Wright, *op. cit.,* p. 234.

[121] Cf. Wright, *op. cit.,* p. 234.

[122] *Ibid.,* p. 452, n. 117.

Turks nominally united most of the Near and Middle East under their rule, they had to recognize the independence of Persia in the East and of Morocco in the West. The Turks were strong in the eastern Mediterranean and threatened to engulf southwestern Europe. Constantinople became the capital of Islam, while Baghdad continued a melancholy memory.

By 1500 the cultural influence of the East had sunk to comparative insignificance. Europe vaguely realized it had no longer anything essential to learn from its age-old opponent, and in the Muslim world political success engendered a deceptive feeling of cultural security and self-sufficiency. Despite two hundred years of uneasiness about the threat of the Turkish might, Europe kept its face turned north and west. Slowly Russia grew to succeed the Byzantines, if not territorially at least in the claim to championship of Greek Christianity which seemed at once to require and to justify eastward expansion. When in the nineteenth century the backsliding Muslim lands were rudely awakened to reality, they found themselves faced once more by two power blocs, perhaps more readily amenable to internal division but infinitely stronger than their medieval predecessors ever had been. At this moment the East is still struggling to get back on its feet.

And all this while civilization pursued its westbound march.

CHAPTER THREE

THE RELIGIOUS FOUNDATION: REVELATION

I

AT THE time of Mohammed's birth (between A.D. 570 and 580) the political situation of the Middle East was dominated, as it had been for two hundred years, by the antagonism between Persia and the Byzantine Empire. During the rare periods when the two great powers were not at war, they watched each other with distrust and maneuvered for better position against the time when hostilities would again break out.

The Arabian peninsula, while not an attractive prize of conquest, bore close observation. Its shiftless population constituted an ever present menace to the settled border districts. To ward off possible encroachments on the part of the Bedouins, the Persians set up in Iraq the little buffer state of the Laḫmids, with its capital at al-Ḥîra, which had its counterpart in the Ghassanid Kingdom organized under Roman suzerainty in Syria. These outposts of the rival empires guarded the fruit lands against the nomads and the frontier areas against each other.

The very lack of large-scale political organization in the northern and central parts of the peninsula heightened the difficulty of keeping the hungry desert tribes in check. Each tribe pursued its own policy. Alliances between tribes were quick to dissolve. Only once in this period did central Arabia give rise to an organized power. For a few decades early in the sixth century the Kinda chieftains controlled most of the tribes, but after a brief spell of expansion their influence broke. There had been no idea, no common aim, to weld the desert-dwellers into a unified state. One defeat at the hands of the Ḥîran king, and ensuing civil war put an end to the rule of the princes of Kinda. Their fall was as sudden as had been their accession.

The cities in the Ḥijâz, possessed of a certain importance as trading-posts on the caravan route to the Yemen, had attained to some sort of organization. In Mecca, commercial center and site of a sanctuary respected throughout the peninsula, the inhabitants fitted out their caravans as co-operative ventures and enforced public safety to an extent sufficient to render possible fairs and festivals on city territory. The clans or subtribes of the Quraish, the dominating group in Mohammed's time, joined in the deliberation and decision of city affairs. But each clan continued to live in its own quarters and was free to run its own life exactly as it pleased. The exigencies of the all-important trade with pilgrims and in foreign goods from which the town situated on barren ground derived its livelihood imposed the only limits to their autonomy.

Southern Arabia, on the other hand, had an old tradition of organized political life. It had been ruled by Sabaean princes when the Romans made their unsuccessful attempt at conquering the region in 25/24 B.C., and gradually the Ḥimyarites, the Homeritae of the Greeks, had gained the power. In the middle of the fourth century A.D. the Axumite kings of Abyssinia annexed southern Arabia, thus acquiring control over both coasts of the Red Sea and therewith over the India trade. The Abyssinians, who had been evangelized by the Eastern Church, were allies of the Byzantines, who thus obtained an important foothold on the peninsula.

Abyssinian rule was far from popular, and *ca.* A.D. 375 it was overthrown, presumably with Persian help, and southern Arabia became again independent. The reaction against Abyssinian influence was coupled with a reaction against Christianity. The new dynasty turned to Judaism. King D̲û Nuwâs, early in the sixth century, is supposed to have cruelly persecuted his Christian subjects. The resurgence of Abyssinian aggression, prodded by the Byzantines and probably welcomed by the Christian part of the population, may have suggested that desperate measure to the king, who must have known that he was fighting a losing battle. After his death the Abyssinians took over once more, and Christianity pushed Judaism into the background. Abraha, the second Abyssinian viceroy, was a zealous

Christian who introduced a famous inscription with the words: "In the power, help, and mercy of the Merciful (*raḥmân*) and His Messiah, and the Holy Ghost."[1]

In preparation for a renewal of their fight, the Byzantines tried to enlist Abraha's support against the Persians, but Abraha remained neutral (A.D. 540). Perhaps a decade or so later Abraha did, however, set out to fight the Persians, but he did not get any farther than Mecca, which appears to have been in sympathy with them. With a sizable army whose equipment included an elephant, he laid siege to the town, but an epidemic of smallpox forced his retreat. Side by side with the information regarding the epidemic, the Arab historians report a miracle by which God saved his sanctuary. By taking up the legend, the Koran canonized it.

> Hast thou not seen how thy Lord did with the fellows of the elephant?
> Did He not put their scheme awry?
> He sent upon them birds in flocks,
> Which pelted them with stones and baked clay,
> And made them like green blades, eaten down.[2]

Popular imagination later claimed that the Prophet was born in the momentous year of the siege, supposed to be the year 570, but this dramatic coincidence is not borne out by our sources. Abraha returned to the Yemen and was succeeded after a few years by his two sons, who lost their realm to the Persians about 570, when these supported a popular rebellion against the Abyssinian rulers. The Persians administered the country through viceroys but refrained from any expansionist adventures. It was from them that Mohammed took over the Yemen in 631.

Mecca kept its Persian sympathies. When Mohammed's congregation first faced oppression, he arranged for the emigration to Abyssinia of a considerable proportion of his followers. Not only did he consider his preaching closely akin to, indeed basically identical with, Christian doctrine but the antagonism of his countrymen led him to look for support from their political opponents. For the same reasons he sided with the Byzantines

[1] F. Buhl, *Das Leben Muhammads* (Leipzig, 1930), p. 11.

[2] Koran, Sura 105.

when all Mecca rejoiced at their resounding defeat at the hands of the Persians, who, in 614, had captured Jerusalem and were to threaten Constantinople itself in 626. He upheld their cause and, sometime between 611 and 616, predicted their ultimate victory.[3] His prophecy came true in 627, when Heraclius marched deep into Sassanian territory. But it would seem that his forecast had been due to fervent partisanship rather than to a sober estimate of the warring powers, for which it would have been impossible to obtain the necessary data in the seclusion of Mecca.

The political influences from abroad to which the peninsula found itself exposed were strong enough to affect, but not sufficiently strong to change, its age-old way of life. Christianity appears to have been advancing along the fringes of the sown, Judaism settled in southern Arabia and in some semiurban centers in the North winning over one or the other Arabic tribe; but, on the whole, the success of both monotheistic faiths was limited.

Foreign religious ideas must have been known practically everywhere, but the standing of their adherents, for the most part aliens or slaves, added little to their persuasiveness. The Arabian border districts had for centuries been a hotbed of sectarianism, and members of every branch of Eastern Christianity must have been represented among the uninstructed motley crowds that passed through or worked in Mecca. That spiritual unrest, that same dissatisfaction with traditional paganism and its threadbare comforts which had marked the last stage of the Roman Empire, seems to have gripped ever widening strata of the peninsula's population when we first meet with the records of pre-Islamic civilization.

There had never been much of an emotional religious life of native origin and even less theological or philosophical speculation. The physiognomy of most of the many deities whose names have been preserved is indistinct. Nearly all are of local importance only; not one profited by an imaginative effort of his followers. Their nomadism tended to disrupt the relationship of

[3] Koran 30:1–4. Bell, in a note to his translation (II, 392–93), is alone in interpreting the passage as occasioned by a Greek success.

the tribes to a god whose place of worship had for a time been in their territory. The priestly families that attended the sanctuary, frequently an oddly shaped stone or a group of trees with oracular powers, surrounded by a sacred pasture, often did not belong to the tribe in whose midst they officiated. Not even Hubal, whose statue stood in the Kaᶜba at Mecca, perhaps the most venerated spot on the peninsula, spurred the inventiveness of religious minds. The real attraction of the Kaᶜba to the worshiper was a black stone of unfathomable age incased in its walls, whose cult the Prophet felt constrained to adopt into the ritual of Islam where it still lingers as a weird testimonial to Islam's failure to rid itself of the crude associations of its origin.

More than localized validity and a somewhat individualized profile had been attained by three female divinities, referred to by the Koran as "Allah's daughters,"[4] Manât (Fate), al-Lât ("*The* Goddess," probably originally a sun-goddess), and al-ᶜUzzà (the Venus or Morning Star). Although their personalities, too, were rather pale and would hardly have roused any pious fervor, they were so firmly ensconced in the minds of the Meccans that, in a curious swerve from his uncompromising monotheism, Mohammed at one time thought he could, by acknowledging their divine rank and power, induce his compatriots to desist from persecuting his ill-protected congregation.[5] Soon, however, Mohammed repented of his weakness and characterized the goddesses as "nothing but names which you and your fathers have used."[6] And it is precisely because their deities had shrunk to little more than names hedged in by the habit of superstitious awe that the Bedouins nowhere put up a fight for them when the Muslims dethroned and destroyed them.

Objections to conversion are mostly political. They never rest on what we might call theological grounds. There is a certain reluctance to yield what the forebears cherished, but there is no

[4] Koran 37:149 and 53:21. For pre-Islamic religion cf. G. Ryckmans, *Les Religions arabes préislamiques* (2d ed.; Louvain, 1951).

[5] Cf. Koran 53:19–23. Al-ᶜUzzà appears on a papyrus of the first century A.D. as μεγάλη θεά, Great Goddess; cf. F. Cumont, *Syria*, VIII (1927), 368.

[6] Koran 53:23.

truth to be defended against the aggression of another and more powerful truth. His gods might tender him prophetic advice, their strength might afford him magic protection, but they could not soothe his melancholy tremors when he pondered the mysteries of the universe and realized his own helpless insignificance—an experience which, despite its familiarity from time immemorial, had, it would seem, suddenly become painful and wearying sometime in the sixth century.

His religious system provided no resources to draw on. It left him a prey to the whims of fate and promised after death if anything a shadowy existence of doubtful desirability. Except for their effect on fame and social standing, one's actions, good or bad, were inconsequential. The gods demanded little more than subservience to ritual, and this none too stringently. They neither embodied nor stood for moral concepts and had no guidance to offer the groping conscience. The utter emptiness of Arabic paganism forced the dissatisfied thinker, the believer in quest of a god to believe in, to fall back on alien notions and alien sentiments if he wished to express his longings at all. Any documentation of religious growth had to assume traits of Christian or Jewish teaching simply because his own background had left him without any pattern for a life in God. How could the stone idols turn the tormented heart's resignation into hope transcending death? Sings al-Aswad b. Yaᶜfur (*fl. ca.* 600):

> Yea, surely well do I know, and need no lesson from thee, the path I travel was traced for those who bear forth the dead.
> Death and Destruction have climbed atop of cliffs where I wend, and watch my shape as I totter (through the narrowing pass).
> No wealth of mine, whether old or newly got, shall redeem the pledge they hold of me—nought but life itself shall avail.
> What can I hope, when Muḥarriq's house have gone to decay and left their palaces void? what better, after Iyâd?[7]

More than half a century earlier, Imruᵓulqais, the errant king (d. *ca.* 540), had exclaimed:

[7] *Mufaḍḍaliyyât*, ed. Sir C. J. Lyall (Oxford, 1918–21), No. 44.5–8; trans. Lyall, *ibid.*, II, 161.

I see us swiftly approaching uncertain doom while food and drink distract us.
Sparrows are we, and flies, and worms, but bolder than the onrushing wolf.
My roots spread to the roots of the earth, but this death robs me of my youth.
And it will (ere soon) rob me of soul and body, and quickly thrust me in the dust.
I drove my mount through every desert of vast expanse whose mirage fluttered,
And I rode amidst the voracious host to reach out for the glory of greedy dangers.
I aspired after every glorious trait and my merit grew.
And I roamed the horizons until I was satisfied with homecoming rather than booty.
But can I, after there went the king al-Ḥâriṯ b. ᶜAmr and after there went Ḥujr, the excellent lord of the leather tents,
Can I hope for clemency from the vicissitudes of Time who not even overlooks the solid mountains?
Well do I know that ere long I shall be caught on the point of a tooth and a claw
As it befell my father Ḥujr and my grandfather, not to forget him who was killed at al-Kulâb.[8]

With the crumbling of the ancestral beliefs, the decline of the cults, and the growing skepticism with regard to the several deities, the concept of one God, less tangible but more universally potent than the many lesser gods, gained importance. The contact with Christians and Jews, however ill informed, could not but strengthen this trend.

When Mohammed was born, Allah was already known as the Lord of men, and it was realized that his writ went further than that of the idols. Allah enjoyed no cult. It may be that some Meccans held the opinion that the Kaᶜba was Allah's sanctuary, and such apparently was the view of the Christian poet, ᶜAdî b. Zaid (*fl. ca.* 580), who swears by the Lord of the Kaᶜba and the Messiah.[9] The Meccans, advanced beyond the general level of

[8] Ed. W. Ahlwardt in *The Divans of the Six Ancient Arabic Poets* (London, 1870), No. 5.1–13 (omitting vs. 3). There is a partial translation of the poem in J. Wellhausen, *Reste altarabischen Heidentums* (2d ed.; Berlin, 1897), pp. 229–30, and also, T. Andrae, *Kyrkohistorisk årsskrift*, XXIII (1923), 190.

[9] Cf. Buhl, *op. cit.*, p. 96, n. 267.

their countrymen, appear to have been quite ready for a noncommittal acknowledgment of Allah's supremacy, but indifference and conservatism prevented them from carrying this notion to its logical conclusion. Allah might well be the creator of heaven and earth, but this was no argument against the existence of other divine beings.*

The Meccan indifference in religious matters which Mohammed was so bitterly to assail was not shared by all. The attraction of the monotheistic faiths made itself felt. It is recorded that four Meccans withdrew from their community and agreed to set out in a quest for a religion better than that left them by their fathers. One of them went to Byzantium and turned Christian; another became a Christian only after a few years spent as a Muslim; the third felt attracted but not entirely satisfied by Christianity; and the last, disappointed in all religions, developed a monotheistic system of his own.

Asceticism was in the air. Individual *Gottsucher* forbade wine and commended sexual continence. As later in Islam, Christian elements probably outweighed Jewish in the formation of their views and precepts. But the Arab who searched for truth cared little whose doctrines he apprehended; the absence of a native tradition compelled syncretism.

The soothsayer who on occasion achieved direct communication with a deity and revealed the rationally unknowable was an accepted type among the Arabs. Christianity and Judaism as well as classical philosophy of later antiquity recognized the prophet, both as a messenger of divine tidings and as a foreteller of things to come. In the seventh century the first Arabic prophets arose. Simultaneous with Mohammed, and perhaps even preceding him by a short time, the prophet Maslama gathered a wide following in Yamâma. He prescribed fasting, prohibited wine, and restricted sexual liberty. He spoke of the Day of Judgment and of the omniscience of the one God. The style of the few sayings of his that have come down to us is strongly reminiscent of, but appears somewhat inferior to that of, the Koran. The similarity may go back to common roots in the soothsayers' mannerisms, but it may also be due to mischievous invention on the part of the Muslims or even to imitation by

Maslama of his more successful rival. A prophetess, Sajâḥ, achieved some popularity when Mohammed died. And there are indications that there were more burning hearts who felt they had received the call to go out to preach and save.

II

The reasons for Mohammed's success were many and varied, some purely political and some due to unexpected assistance of fortune. But the basic causes of his appeal to his contemporaries without which no political constellation, however favorable, and no stroke of luck, however dazzling, could have stabilized his work would seem to be these:

1. His was the most elaborate and the most consistent religious system ever developed by an Arab.

2. This system contained satisfactory answers to the problems exercising his compatriots and responded to the mood of the times.

3. It lifted the Arabic-speaking world to the level of the other scripturaries.

4. By placing himself at the end of a long line of prophets that included Adam, Abraham, Moses, and Jesus, Mohammed explained and legitimized his own advent, suggested the greater perfection and the finality of his version of the Book of God, and gave the Arab nation metaphysical significance by connecting it at the most honorable and most crucial stage with the great drama of God's self-revelation in history, making them the Lord's tool in the propagation of the ultimate truth.

5. Mohammed greatly increased the Arabs' articulateness.

6. He taught the lesson that a community under God was more meaningful and thus of greater political promise than a community under tribal law.

The impulse which compelled Mohammed, the scion of a noble but impoverished branch of the Quraish, to rise up to warn and teach his people was the overwhelming consciousness of the moral accountability of man and of the Judgment, not far off, when the Lord would hold each soul responsible, to reward or condemn according to its deserts. He was to admonish them before it was too late. Their fate in the hereafter was at stake, their moral laxness their danger, their thoughtless idolatry their most awesome failing.

At the time of his call Mohammed was probably in his thirties. He had married a rich widow and thus, after a rather difficult early life, achieved his independence. As time went by and he was more and more tormented by religious doubt, he followed the example of other seekers after truth in retiring to the solitude of the mountains that surround Mecca, his home town. And there the call of his Lord came to him. Gabriel appeared to him, asking him to read from a silken cloth. After refusing twice, Mohammed asked, "What is it I should recite?" Thereupon Gabriel taught him the lines that were to form the first five verses of the ninety-sixth sura.

> Recite in the name of thy Lord who created,
> Created man from clotted blood.
> Recite, for thy Lord is the most generous,
> Who taught by the pen (i.e., the older scripturaries),[10]
> Taught man what he did not know.

Although informed by Gabriel that he was the Messenger of God, Mohammed doubted the veracity of his vision and feared to be possessed by demons. Finally convinced of its true significance, he was pained by the complete cessation of further revelations. But after some time the spell was broken, and the stream of divine communications never again was interrupted to his death.

In excited, grandiose, disconnected pictures Mohammed tells of the day when the graves will open and trembling man face his Lord to be judged for his deeds. The world will come to an end in an agony of terror, and, gripped by a paroxysm of fear, each soul will be left without helper to account for the burden of sin which he accumulated during the brief span of his earthly life. Repent, repent ere it is too late! The Prophet is frenzied with anguish lest he fail to persuade his people of the imminence of their trial, of the seriousness of their peril.

[10] According to Buhl (*ibid.*, p. 137).

By those that are sent gently (probably: winds),
And those that come with hurricane blast,
By those that scatter abroad,
And those that divide asunder,
And those that drop reminders, ...
Verily, what ye are promised is going to happen.

So when the stars are blotted out,
When the heaven is opened,
When the mountains are reduced to powder,
When the messengers are given their time,
For what day is the appointment made?
For the Day of Distinction.[11]
Verily they think it far off,
But We think it near at hand.
On the day when the heaven will be like molten metal,
And the mountains will be like wool, ...
They will gaze at each other, the sinner wishing that he
might ransom himself from the punishment of that day
by his sons. . . . .[12]

Naught, however, will avail them.

Lo, Gehenna has become an ambush,
For the proud transgressors a place of resort,
In which to remain for ages,
Tasting therein neither coolth nor drink,
Except hot water and tears,
A fitting recompense.[13]

But the pious will go to a place of felicity.

Orchards and vineyards,
And full-breasted ones of equal age,
And a cup overflowing,
In which they will hear neither babble, nor accusation
of falsehood.[14]

Mohammed is grieved and puzzled by the unbelievers' perversity in not heeding the signs that evidence the Lord's oneness and omnipotence. His greatest sign is creation itself.

[11] Koran 77:1–5, 7–13.

[12] Koran, 70:6–9, 11.

[13] Koran 78:21–26.

[14] Koran 78:32–35.

Have We not made the earth a flat expanse
And the mountains as pegs?
We have created you in pairs,
We have appointed your sleep as a rest,
We have appointed the night for a covering,
We have appointed the day for a livelihood.
We have built above you seven (heavens) firm,
And We have set a lamp blazing (i.e., the sun).
We have sent down from the rain-clouds water in torrents,
That We may bring forth thereby grain and vegetation,
And gardens luxuriant.[15]

Averse to dogmatism, afraid of impairing the key position of their town by abnegating their deities, the Meccans asked for more convincing evidence of the Prophet's mission. His mannerisms and the language of his visions—short rhythmical lines mostly rhyming, crowded with rare words and puzzling imagery—suggested to the more skeptical among his audience that he was a soothsayer, a poet, or a madman. But God reassured Mohammed expressly on these points,[16] and, when the resistance of his compatriots to his message hardened into active opposition, he realized that being disbelieved had been the fate of every warner and prophet, and he understood that his sad experience constituted one more proof of the truthfulness of his mission.

Each nation had been sent a warner who was to call them to the service of the one and only Lord beside whom the other deities were but names. Each prophet had met with only limited success. His people had scoffed at his preaching, had neglected his message, had outlawed and persecuted him, and, finally, had been struck down by a quick blow, erased from the face of this earth and consigned to eternal damnation. By and large, all prophets had testified to the same basic truths. By and large, the objections of the obstinate had been the same. Noah had been disbelieved when he summoned his folk to the adoration of Allah and to the belief in the Final Judgment. They called him a madman, but the Lord drowned them, saving only Noah and

[15] Koran 78:6–16.

[16] Koran 68:2, 69:41–42.

his own. Still the later peoples did not take warning. ᶜÂd counted God's message false, and he wiped them out in a roaring wind. Their fate did nothing to change the hearts of the Ṯamûd. When revelation came to them, they said: "(24) One single human being from amongst us shall we follow? In that case we should be in error and madness. (25) Has the Reminder been laid upon him from amongst us (all)? Nay, he is a liar insolent." But the Lord did away with them through a great cry. And he had to punish the people of Lot by a gravel storm, and Pharaoh had to be taught his lesson. "We have made the Koran available for the Reminder, but is there any one who takes heed?"[17]

And now the turn of the Arabs had come. Therefore, God had chosen Mohammed to deliver his message to them "in Arabic speech"[18] to confirm what other messengers had been told to transmit to their peoples. "Thus have We suggested to thee an Arabic Koran in order that thou mayest warn the mother of the towns and those around it."[19] Because "We never sent any messenger but with the speech of his people, that he might make (things) clear to them."[20] Every trait in which Mohammed is made to repeat the destiny of his predecessors is one more documentation of his legitimacy as a messenger from the Lord of the Worlds. Mohammed is commanded to say: "I was no innovation upon the (other) messengers; I do not know what will be done with myself or with you; I only follow what is suggested to me, and I am only a warner clear."[21] He recasts the substance of the teachings given the Jews and the Christians, perfecting and completing them.

The unbelievers clamor for a miracle. They pretend to doubt that God would have selected for his tool a man of mediocre social standing. There is nothing for Mohammed to do but to try to convince the skeptics that the Koran itself is the miracle testifying to his veracity. The Koran is a phenomenon unprecedented in the Arabic tongue. Its verses are not inventions of the Prophet; they are, so to speak, the Arabic version of God's own

[17] Koran, Sura 54, condensed; the last verse, No. 17, is repeated three times in the Sura, recurring as vss. 22, 32, and 40.

[18] Koran 46:11.

[19] Koran 42:5.

[20] Koran 14:4.

[21] Koran 46:8.

word as read by or revealed to Mohammed from the Koran's heavenly prototype, the Mother of the Book. Mohammed cannot add or omit a single word. "This Koran is not such as to have been invented apart from Allah; but it is a confirmation of what is before it, and a distinct setting forth of the Book in which there is no doubt, from the Lord of the Worlds. (39) Or do they say: 'He has invented it?' Say: 'Then produce a sura like it, and call upon whomsoever ye are able (to call) apart from Allah, if ye speak the truth.' "[22] But Mohammed himself, the bearer of this exalted message and the last mouthpiece of revelation to be sent forth by the Lord, is nothing but a mortal man.

Gradually men of position in Mecca joined the community of slaves, derelicts, and foreigners dedicated to the service of the one merciful and omnipotent God. Increasing numbers brought increasing tribulations. Common creed and common suffering welded the group together. Their loyalties went out to their coreligionists rather than to their clansmen. The prayer ritual that set them apart drew them together. The Believers, or Muslims, those who had surrendered themselves to Allah,[23] constituted a cross-section of tribesmen and of people without tribal affiliation. At the same time they formed, as it were, a tribe by themselves. While his kinsmen continued to protect Mohammed in the traditional spirit, he and his followers felt untrammeled by the obligations of tribal fealty. This independence made them strong but disqualified them from the standpoint of the old morality.

Persecution could not disperse the Muslim community, but it did contain it within rather narrow bounds. Mohammed, whose political abilities must have shown at an early time in his career, tried to win a foothold in some other Ḥijâzî town. After a conspicuous setback in Ṭâ᾿if, he found himself invited to come to Yaṯrib, about two hundred miles north of Mecca, and to act as an arbiter between the tribes of Aus and Ḫazraj, whose incessant civil war threatened them both with extinction. Mohammed accepted and, outwitting the vigilance of his countrymen

[22] Koran 10:38–39.

[23] There is also the overtone of "entering into a state of *soteria*, salvation, *Heil.*" Cf. also H. Ringgren, *Islam, ᾿aslama and muslim* (Uppsala, 1949).

who dimly sensed the possible consequences of this migration, arrived at Yaṯrib in September, 622.

In Yaṯrib, which soon came to be known as *Medîna* (*an-nabî*), the City (of the Prophet), Mohammed, supported by his fellow-*émigrés* and a body of local converts, quickly built up a political power whose *raison d'être* was community of creed of the citizens. The Messenger of God directed the state whose laws and major decisions were handed down by the Lord through direct revelation. Divine assistance broke the onslaught of the Meccans at Badr (624), and the Lord's directives guided his flock to greater and greater success until the Prophet reentered Mecca as its master (630) and controlled the greater part of the peninsula. At the time of his death (June, 632) Mohammed may have been ready to carry his faith beyond the borders of his homeland.

The denial of his claims by the Jewish community in Medina forced a profound crisis in Mohammed's thought. Not only did the Jews deny the identity of his teaching with that of the former prophets, but they showed up his ignorance of the Scriptures. The only way of invalidating the obvious conclusion that his message, not being in accord with prior revelation, was not based on genuine revelation at all was the assertion that Jews and Christians had falsified their sacred scriptures and thus fallen away from the Lord. Moses and Jesus had indeed spoken the truth, but their ungrateful peoples had diluted their words with inventions of their own. This left the Koran the sole accurate record of revelation and the Arabs the sole possessors thereof.

This realization made Mohammed adopt the Kaᶜba at Mecca, now declared to have been built by Abraham, the first Muslim,[24] as the geographical center of his religion toward which every believer was to turn when praying. Islam was the resurrected uncontaminated religion of Abraham, which the Jews had deserted. The Christians, by concocting foolish myths about the

[24] W. Thomson (*Moslem World*, XXXIV [1944], 132) calls attention to the fact that "Abraham is the pattern of all true believers in the New Testament, and that for Philo he is the type of the man who abandons home and people for the sake of God."

nature of Jesus, whom from a prophet they turned into a divine personage, had lapsed into the sin of polytheism. The older scripturaries stood high above the pagans, who had no book to substantiate their beliefs; but the Muslims towered above the Christians and Jews, who had wilfully missed their opportunity to build their lives upon the revelations vouchsafed them. Islam was not to repeat their fatal error. Its Arabization, which left Islam the only religion based on an authoritative book with which no human hand had tampered, made it truly significant for the whole world.

Day by day, as the need arose, the Lord told the believers through his messenger how to organize under law, how to act in concrete situations, how to tax themselves, how to deal with unbelievers, what to believe on controversial subjects, and what ritual to perform in order to please him. God's interest in detail, and particularly in detail concerning the Prophet's personal life, occasionally bewildered the faithful; but the principle that the whole existence of man should conform to divine ordinance was never put in doubt.

Mohammed's position as the head of a state and his concern with legislation and administration naturally changed the subjects of his revelations to a considerable extent. His poetical force waned as the years went by, the visionary became a preacher, the prophet a theologian, the somewhat naïve sectarian apostle the lawgiver of a community that just missed attaining international importance. His responsibilities had changed and so had his methods. His Lord was forgiving only to the believer; the ethics of his faith applied only within the community. To make Islam secure, assassination and compulsion, trickery and bribery, were legitimate means.

Mohammed preferred clemency to severity, but his was not a God of compromise. The fundamental demands of the Lord had to be accepted: the monotheistic creed, the recognition of Mohammed as his messenger, the ritual of prayer and fasting, the poor tax, the pilgrimage to Mecca. The word of God cannot be graded more or less important. Whatever is revealed is truth and law. The accusation that he had changed from an apostle into a statesman would have been incomprehensible to Mohammed and to his early followers as well. The legal framework of community life was as much a part of Islam as were the fervent admonitions to escape hell-fire by timely repentance. His personal morality caused the believers some uneasy moments, but Allah supported his Prophet and silenced the critics. The difficulties of the community arose not from the Prophet's failings but from the abrupt drying-up of the source of authoritative teaching, theological and practical, when Mohammed died rather unexpectedly without providing any mechanism to carry on the all-inclusive development of the faith.

III

The Koran has been severely criticized for its stylistic inadequacies. The West has been almost unanimous on this count, and not a few Muslims have intimated their disappointment with its language and imagery.

Some of this criticism is undoubtedly justified. Mohammed was not a writer of Plato's or an enthusiast of Amos' rank. His inspiration could hold its sublime level only for a short while before it was brought down to commonplace by exhaustion of the imaginative power or before it broke up into disconnected paragraphs for lack of logical cogency. But the general charge of staleness, poverty of ideas, and repetitiousness is ill considered.

The Book as we have it is not the Book as Mohammed revealed it. In fact, he never revealed a book; he revealed short visions, injunctions, parables, fables, or doctrinal discourses. It is likely, but cannot be proved, that he intended to collect the several "recitations" and to freeze them, so to speak, into canonical form. His successors naturally did not dare to attempt what the Prophet might have done—to discipline, abridge, and organize the many individual texts into a coherent whole.

The reasons for which the learned readers at the caliph ᶜUṯmân's (644–56) behest arranged what survived of the Prophet's revelations—and it is likely that only an insignificant fraction had been forgotten or lost—in exactly 114 suras of very unequal length can no longer be reconstructed; nor can it be satisfactorily explained in every instance why this and that passage were lumped together to form one sura, or why the redactors decided to put the longer suras first and the shorter ones last, although in most cases the latter contain the older material. Sometimes it is similarity of subject matter, sometimes identity of rhyme, that led to joining originally independent passages.

In any event, it is safe to assume that Mohammed never meant to have political directives, legal provisions, biblical legends, and polemics against the unbelievers united in one chapter of arbitrarily defined dimensions. By stringing a number of prophetical stories together, the redactors upon occasion produced a tiresome impression of monotonous dulness for which the Prophet was in no way responsible. Also it should be borne in mind that Mohammed wished to instruct and to reform. The preacher and the educator are by the very nature of their task constrained to repeat, and to repeat in more or less the same terms. We who do not read the Koran for edification or for our moral betterment approach many a passage in the Book with wrong expectations—in numerous verses, what Mohammed essayed to convey was not intellectual stimulation but confirmation of novel standards of piety and morality. God never tires of repeating himself, a Muslim writer argues in the tenth century, because no one will keep in mind more than a little of the Koran's admonitions and examples at first reading.[25]

The obvious imperfections of Mohammed's presentation appear in an entirely different light when the Koran is given its proper place in Arabic literary history. Before Mohammed, Arab prose had hardly ever been used beyond the preservation of tribal memories of warlike or otherwise curious incidents and the formulation of concise proverbs and rulings of law. Rhymed prose seems to have been confined to the soothsayer's saws. Poetry, richly developed in phraseology and technique, had shied away from the religious theme. There was no accepted style in which to present theological or legal deliberations, no precedent for eschatological verse.

Mohammed never employed any of the traditional meters in the Koran, but he loosened and amplified rhymed prose until it became a suitable vehicle for his weird visions of the agonies

[25] Abû Bakr aṣ-Ṣûlî (d. 946), *Adab al-Kuttâb* (Cairo, 1341), p. 229.*

of the Last Day. And he forced onto an undeveloped and recalcitrant prose the formulation of abstract tenets, of juridical stipulations, of political theory. He was not an artist. When he tells of the prophets of yore, his narrative does not measure up to the dramatic poignancy of the *ayyâm* (battle-day) records, and the Meccans would rather listen to the doughty deeds of the Persian heroes than to the devout reports of frustration and vengeance of the Lord's quaint envoys to foreign peoples. Still those reports did impress the listeners almost as much as did the threatening portrayal of the horrors of the Day of Distinction. Subject matter and imagery stemmed largely from Christian preaching and Jewish legend, but it was Mohammed who found an Arabic form for what had become his most personal experience. The full extent of his achievement in introducing those novel themes into convention-bound Arabic literature will be understood through the failure of the next generations to resume the eminently poetical subjects of Paradise and Hell, Last Day and Judgment, in their verse.

No wonder Mohammed was fond of using sonorous foreign words. He must have been in desperate need of vocabulary. Mostly he employed his new terms without explanation—the disagreement of the commentators testifies to the bewilderment of the audience. Sometimes he defines them. Sura 104 proclaims:

Woe to every maligner and scoffer,
Who gathers wealth and counts it over,
Thinking that his wealth will perpetuate him!
Nay, but he shall be cast into al-Ḥuṭama.

The explanation of the unfamiliar expression follows immediately:

What has let thee know what is al-Ḥuṭama?
The fire of Allah set alight,
Which mounts over the hearts.[26]

In some instances Mohammed borrowed a word while misunderstanding its meaning. Aramaic *millâh*, *melṯâ*, "word," becomes *milla*, "religion"; Hebrew *mâᶜûn*, "dwelling," denotes in the Koran, according to the commentators, either "benefaction,

[26] Koran 104:1–7.

alms," or "utensils."[27] In other instances Mohammed subtilized the meaning of existing terms as when he substituted a higher concept of the "fear of God" for the original idea of *taqwà*, the fear provoked by the physical danger a deity or demon might visit on a human being.[28]

Mohammed had no experience in speculative thinking. Inconsistencies which were to cause great discomfort fifty or a hundred years after his death he probably never perceived. Nor did his contemporaries take exception to statements that, to us, are patently contradictory. When he pronounced himself on doctrine, what he actually did was to rationalize a mood. The logical difficulties resulting from verbalization of conflicting moods did not at once transpire.

Whether Mohammed grasped the problem of determination or freedom in its trenchant bareness may be doubted. When he asserts the arbitrariness with which the Lord guides or leads astray, he wishes neither to discourage moral effort nor to depict Allah as a cruel tyrant. He only endeavors to express his own apprehension of God's absolute and unaccountable power in the strongest possible terms. He revels in the Lord's unfathomable might and takes delight in, and religious strength from, the consciousness of man's insignificance. This is perhaps not the theological but certainly the emotional meaning of the merciless words: "But Allah sendeth astray whomsoever He willeth, and guideth aright whomsoever He willeth; He is the Sublime, the Wise."[29]

Nearly as strong is Mohammed's consciousness of man's responsibility. It is for his own deeds that he shall stand judgment at the end of time. Man decides his own course; it is not the Lord who causes evil to be done. He has permitted Satan to tempt man, but man will resist or succumb according to his own bent. So Allah is shown to realize that, without the voluntary inclination of the soul toward religion, nobody will accept the Prophet's teaching. And Allah recognizes the personal effort. "It is hard for the polytheists, (12) what thou callest them to;

[27] Cf. Th. Nöldeke, *Neue Beiträge zur semitischen Sprachwissenschaft* (Strassburg, 1910), pp. 25–26, 28–29.

[28] Cf. Buhl, *op. cit.*, pp. 90–91, and C. Brockelmann, *Archiv f. Religionswissenschaft*, XXI (1922), 115.

[29] Koran 14:4.

Allah chooseth for it those whom He pleaseth and guideth to it those who turn to Him penitently."[30] And even more explicitly it is stated: "Those who avoid serving Ṭâghût and turn penitently to Allah—for them are the good tidings; so give good tidings to My servants who listen to the declaration and follow the best of it; these are the ones whom Allah hath guided; these are the ones who have intelligence."[31]

But again the Lord's omnipotence comes to mind: When the unbelievers hear the revelation, they are prevented from understanding its import. "Allah hath set a seal upon their hearts, and over their hearing and their sight is a covering; for them is (in store) a punishment mighty."[32]

The intricate apparatus of scholastic theology cannot conceal the simple fact that it justified and systematized the stronger of the two popular moods, viz., that calling for the greatest possible emphasis on the unshackled power of the Lord of the Worlds.

There is a touch of the irresponsible in Mohammed's use of half-understood terms. Echoing Christian reasoning, perhaps ultimately derived from Origen's interpretation of the Trinity,[33] Mohammed declares: "The Messiah, Jesus, son of Mary, is only the messenger of Allah, and His Word (*kalima*) which He cast upon Mary, and a Spirit (*rûḥ*) from Him."[34] What exactly this passage with its juxtaposition of "Word" and "Spirit" meant to his audience it is impossible to ascertain. But no sooner had the Christian theologians become acquainted with it and a companion verse that again refers to Jesus as a Word (*kalima*) from God whose name is the Messiah[35] than they identified *kalima* as *logos*, *rûḥ* as *pneuma*, and demonstrated to the Muslim, as yet unskilled in scholastic disputation, that his

[30] Koran 42:11–12.

[31] Koran 39:19.

[32] Koran 2:6.

[33] Origen has the Logos created from the substance of the Father and the Holy Spirit created from that of the Logos (cf. H. Grimme, *Mohammed* [Münster i.W., 1892–95], II, 52).

[34] Koran 4:169.

[35] Koran 3:40.

own Book taught the Christian dogma of Christ as the Logos of God and even the doctrine of the Trinity.[36]

Nicetas of Byzantium, after quoting the koranic reference to Jesus as Word and Spirit,[37] exclaims: "O senseless fool! If the Word of God is Christ as you state, He will say the truth about everything. Now He says that He is the son of God. You said yourself that He was taught His Gospel by the Lord. So He must be believed. Now if He must be believed your impiety stands revealed through your own testimony. It is a cause for wonder that when (Mohammed) called the Christ the Word of God and has the Spirit go forth from Him he was unable to see that what goes forth from the substance of God and is coexistent with Him will also be consubstantial, wherefore One God is to be adored in Three Persons."[38]

And again did the Muslim find himself in utter confusion when, on the basis of deterministic verses in the Koran, his God is made the author of evil and thus unjust.[39] It is likely that John of Damascus was right in predicting that, when confronted with argumentation of this kind, the Muslim would flee, having nothing to answer.[40]

Had the Prophet ever been made aware of the difficulties in which he was to involve his followers, he might have revised his statements and made them less vulnerable. He believed that Allah would if expedient revoke one or the other verse of the revelation and replace it with a more appropriate one. As the prototype of the Book was with Allah, he was free to "delete what He willeth, or confirm."[41] And assurance was given that "for whatsoever verse We cancel or cause (the messenger) to forget We bring a better or the like."[42] But, while this theory of abrogation was useful in readjusting outdated regulations to a

[36] Cf. John of Damascus, *MPG*, XCIV, 1586–87. The passage is paraphrased by R. Bell, *The Origin of Islam in Its Christian Environment* (London, 1926), pp. 209–10. At greater length does John develop this train of thought in *MPG*, XCVI, 1341 ff. Cf. also C. H. Becker, *Islamstudien* (Leipzig, 1924–32), I, 442.

[37] Koran 4:169.

[38] *MPG*, CV, 736; *Refutatio Mohamedis*, chap. 49.

[39] Cf., e.g., Becker, *op. cit.*, I, 439–40.

[40] *MPG*, XCIV, 1587; chap. 1 (end).

[41] Koran 13:39.

[42] Koran 2:100.

changed situation, there was no authority left at Mohammed's death to overhaul the obsolescent and bring the Book up to date. So the Muslims had to find other means of meeting and overcoming the Christians on their own ground of scholastic theology.

The pagan Arabs possessed a not inconsiderable vocabulary of moral terms but hardly the rudiments of a civil or penal code. When Mohammed laid down the law for his community, he proposed to go beyond deciding individual cases and to formulate general rules, either on the basis of custom or in harmony with his own much subtler sense of equity. The only stylistic precedents which he could follow were sententious generalities as were occasionally inserted in poems and, to a certain extent, rules outlined by implication rather than directly when some personage was praised or blamed by a poet for living up to, or falling short of, some accepted standard of conduct.

When Zuhair lauds a tribe for frustrating the foreign tribesman's quest for blood revenge and for never giving up a clansman who has become embroiled in a blood feud,[43] the rules of correct behavior are depicted quite clearly, but not in a manner to satisfy the lawgiver. Nor will it help him to hear another poet reflect that "revenge is like a debt that will be returned even though the creditor be put off a long time."[44] When Aus b. Ḥajar wishes to shame his opponents, he tells them that his own tribe would respect their rights were they to dwell among them as protected guests,[45] the implication being that those opponents fail to treat their guests as they should. Again the law can be sensed between the lines, but codification is still a long way off. Wisdom literature supplied an attractive store of moral apothegms. "Crime will fell the evildoer, and unhealthy are the pastures of transgression (*ẓulm*)," said the poet.[46] But the Prophet had nowhere to turn when faced with the task of de-

[43] Zuhair, ed. Ahlwardt, No. 16.46.

[44] Th. Nöldeke, *Delectus veterum carminum Arabicorum* (Berlin, 1890), p. 1, vs. 10.

[45] Ed. R. Geyer, *SBAW*, Vol. CXXVI (1892), Abh. 13, poem 38.5.

[46] *Delectus*, p. 1, vs. 11.

fining transgression or stipulating the process of law in civil disputes.

At times he expresses himself after the fashion of the poets. He recognizes blood revenge by saying: "In retaliation is life for you, O ye of insight." And to commend a conciliatory spirit in settling blood disputes he adds: "Mayhap ye will show piety."[47] Elsewhere Mohammed falls back on relating Cain's murder of Abel and making Allah point this moral: "Because of that (incident) We have prescribed (as a law) for the Children of Israel that whoever kills a person otherwise than (in retaliation) for another person, or for causing corruption in the land, shall be as if he had killed the people in a body."[48] The Prophet is averse to retaliation, though willing to admit it under certain circumstances, but he is unable to crystallize his ideas in strictly legal forms: "(38) The recompense of an evil deed is an evil like it, so if anyone pardons and makes peace, it rests with Allah to reward him; verily He loveth not those who do wrong. (39) But surely if any vindicate themselves after wrong done them, then against such there is no way (to punish). (40) There is a way only against such as do wrong to the people, and act oppressively in the land without justification; for such is a punishment painful. (41) But surely if one patiently endures and forgives, that is one of the determining factors of affairs."[49] At another time he considerably improves on this phrasing, condensing his ideas into one instead of four somewhat diffuse paragraphs: "If ye take vengeance, take it only in the measure that vengeance was taken from you; but, assuredly, if ye endure patiently, it is better for those who patiently endure."[50]

In regulating inheritance, Mohammed did gradually achieve the necessary precision. At first he seems to have announced only a general principle. "To the men belongs a portion of what their parents and near relatives leave, and to the women belongs a portion of what their parents and near relatives leave, be it little or much; a (legally) assigned portion."[51] Later he arrives

[47] Koran 2:175.

[48] Koran 5:35.

[49] Koran 42:38–41.

[50] Koran 16:129.

[51] Koran 4:8.

at a specific apportionment. "In regard to your children Allah charges you (as follows): The male receives the portion of two females; if they be women (i.e., if there be no male children), more than two, then they receive two-thirds of what a man has left, but if there be only one, she receives a half; etc."[52] The passage ends with an announcement of rewards and sanctions: "These are the limits laid down by Allah; whoso obeys Allah and His messenger He will cause to enter Gardens through which the rivers flow, to abide therein—that is the great success. (18) But whoso opposes Allah and His messenger and transgresses the limits laid down by Him He will cause to enter a Fire to abide therein, and for him is a punishment humiliating."[53]

The lawgiver and the preacher are never really kept distinct in Mohammed's personality and therefore are likely to merge in his pronunciamentos.[54] But while the Muslims had a great deal to learn about legal language and, of course, about law as such from the neighboring peoples whom they were destined to rule, it remains one of the Prophet's outstanding achievements to have been the first to formulate in Arabic legal propositions claiming general validity—as opposed to decisions of specific cases.

The effect of the literary advance which the Koran marks is heightened by a number of passages of sublime beauty. Many of the lines that seem rather commonplace to us must have been astounding and stirring to the contemporaries. But at all times will this simile of the Lord and the mysterious aloofness of his splendor penetrate to the innermost heart: "Allah is the light of the heavens and the earth; His light is like a niche in which is a lamp, the lamp in glass and the glass like a brilliant star, lit from a blessed tree, an olive neither of the East nor of the West whose oil would almost give light even though no fire did touch it; light upon light. . . . ."[55]

[52] Koran 4:12–16; vs. 15 was later amended through vs. 175.

[53] Koran 4:17–18.

[54] Cf. also Koran 4:36–37, the warning against covetousness in connection with inheritances.

[55] Koran 24:35.

And even as persuasive is the portrayal in the famed "Verse of the Throne" of the Lord in his cool and immovable grandeur: "Allah—there is no god but He, the Living, the Eternal; slumber affects Him not nor sleep; to Him belongs whatever is in the heavens and whatever is in the earth; who is there that will intercede before Him except by His permission? He knoweth what is before them and what is behind them, and they comprehend not anything of His knowledge but what He willeth; His throne extendeth over the heavens and the earth, to guard them wearieth Him not; He is the Exalted, the Mighty "[56]

IV

It is curious to note that the deep impression made by Mohammed's personality and his teachings on his contemporaries, friend or foe, did not usually in their minds produce an accurate picture of either. Like many an innovator, he was frequently loved and hated for the wrong reasons. His closest adherents realized his double role as the authoritative transmitter of the divine will and as a human leader who commanded respect in his own right but remained fallible and could therefore be contradicted. The fundamental tenets and prescriptions of the new faith were accepted and, although somewhat casually, obeyed. He inspired self-sacrificing loyalty among the believers, and a mood of prayerful devotion to the one God became the official sentiment of the community. One might venture to say that, while it had at his advent been Mohammed's chief concern to save his people from hell, his people were, a pious and ascetic wing notwithstanding, as long as he was with them, more concerned with making sure of their place in Paradise—acceptance of Islam had to the majority removed the danger of damnation, an attitude which soon was to change radically. The consciousness of belonging to a divinely favored commonwealth of unprecedented and ever growing strength, a privilege which was paid for by maintaining and spreading certain carelessly worn verities and by complying with certain patterns of behavior, this consciousness was the real prize of conversion. Little wonder that the average contemporary entertained rather

[56] Koran 2:256.

hazy notions regarding the *theologoumena* which the Prophet propounded.

Even his principal poet and spokesman, Ḥassân b. Tâbit (d. 674), does not appear encumbered by religious erudition. "We know that there is no god beside Allah and that the Book of Allah is our guide."[57] "With Allah's permission I bear witness that Mohammed is the messenger of Him Who (thrones) on high above the heavens."[58] It is important evidence of Mohammed's mission that "my Lord sent down His hosts to His Prophet and strengthened (or: confirmed) him with victory at every test (*mashhad*)."[59] Another partisan of Mohammed, Kaᶜb b. Mâlik (d. 670 or 673), gives vent to pride that he and his were offered and accepted the revelation, but he does not seem too much interested in its detail.

> (We have been vouchsafed) admonitions from our Lord by which we are guided, in resplendent (*azhar*) language, (full of) good reward;
> They were offered us, and we were eager to listen, after they had been offered to (other) tribes;
> (They are nothing but) words of wisdom which the unbelievers, benightedly, deemed sinful, while the intelligent understand them aright.[60]

And when Kaᶜb b. Zuhair, in fear for his life, approached Mohammed, he praised him and his followers for their strength and power and had nothing but these noncommittal words for his religious significance.

> The messenger is indeed a light through which enlightenment is gained;[61] he is a drawn Indian sword from amongst the swords of the Lord.[62]

Al-Aᶜshà (d. 629), of Christian background, is better, but not much better, informed in his encomium of the Prophet.

[57] *Dîwân*, ed. H. Hirschfeld (Leiden and London, 1910), No. 19.7.

[58] *Ibid.*, No. 91.1.

[59] *Ibid.*, No. 45.4.

[60] Quoted by Ibn Hishâm, *Sîra*, ed. F. Wüstenfeld (Göttingen, 1859–60), pp. 704–5. Cf. the translation by G. Weil (Stuttgart, 1864), II, 119.

[61] *Yustaḍâʾu bihi;* for parallels see the author, *WZKM*, XLIV (1937), 41.

[62] *Burda*, vs. 51 (*Delectus*, p. 114, vs. 6).

He is a prophet who sees what you do not see and, by my life, his renown has spread over highlands and lowlands.
Did you really fail to hear the ordinance of Mohammed, the Prophet of the Lord, when he gave directives and bore witness (to the faith)?
If you do not travel with provisions of fear of God and then, after your death, meet with people who had been well provided,
You will repent of not having been like them and of not having looked out for what they looked out.
Beware of carrion (fallen cattle) and do not eat it and do not use an iron arrow when killing (cattle).
And do not regard with awe (sacred) stones that have been set up (by men), do not worship the idols, but worship Allah.
Pray in the afternoon and in the morn. Do not praise Satan, but praise Allah.[63]

When the Prophet dies, Ḥassân praises him for his readiness to forgive and for his leadership toward the truth. He helped his followers when they were too weak to bear their burden, and he smoothed their path in his kindheartedness. The angels weep over him and so does the earth. Never before was suffered such a loss nor will ever again anybody be mourned as desperately. His generosity was unmatched. In all the forty-six verses of this elegy the only religious touch comes at the very end, when Ḥassân b. Ṯâbit vows never to end the Prophet's praise.

Mayhap I shall thereby obtain a perpetual abode in the Garden of Eternity,
With the Elect (i.e., Mohammed); I hope thereby to become his neighbor (in Paradise); and I strive and toil to reach that day.[64]

V

Throughout his career Mohammed had been careful to emphasize his human nature. By the undeserved and unaccountable grace of God he has been selected as his messenger, but beyond this distinction there is nothing to set him apart from his fellow-men. His knowledge of the hidden is limited to what God chooses to teach him. Wherever he is not guided by revelation, he may go astray. He has no power to work miracles.

[63] *Dîwân*, ed. R. Geyer (London, 1928), No. 17.14, 16–21; for a fuller translation of the passage by the author see *WZKM*, XLIV (1937), 39–40.*

[64] *Sîra*, p. 1024, ll. 10*b*, 11 (trans. Weil, II, 358). For a more detailed account of Mohammed's position in the contemporary mind see the author, *loc. cit.*, pp. 29–50.

However often his enemies challenge him to prove his assertions by a miracle, he refuses in the face of sneers and skeptical disappointment. His very mission is his sign. "They say: 'Why are not signs from his Lord sent down to him?' Say: 'Signs are with Allah only and I am only a manifest warner.' (50) Hath it not sufficed them that We have sent down to thee the Book to be recited to them? Surely in that is a mercy and a reminder to a people who believe."[65]

He did not deny being a bearer of that charismatic force, *baraka,* which his people as ancient and Eastern peoples in general believed to reside in the extraordinary, the saintly, personage. He had no objection when his companions fought for his spittle or the water with which he had washed and when they gathered up and kept his hair. The Christian pilgrim who returns from Jerusalem,[66] the Christian bishop and even his donkey,[67] the converted slave Bilâl under torture for his faith[68]—all carry this force, and the messenger of God, too, has to be imbued with it. But Mohammed would not do as much as the next *kâhin* (soothsayer) and make rain. The pressure of expectation must have weighed heavily on Mohammed. His rival, Maslama, succumbed and sweetened a brackish spring by spitting into it.[69]

Mohammed's discretion was, however, of no avail. No denial of his could persuade the Arabs that he lacked supranatural insight into the hidden and into the future. And he had been dead only for a short while when popular fancy, overruling the very wording of the revelation as well as the somewhat feeble protests of the more conscientious theologians, retold the Prophet's life as that of a powerful thaumaturge. The naïve desire to magnify one's hero by lifting him as far as possible out of the human sphere combined with the age-old tradition that under-

[65] Koran 29:49–50.

[66] Imruʾulqais (Ahlwardt), No. 31.12. Later the returning Mecca pilgrim is touched for *baraka;* cf., e.g., Ibn Jubair, *Travels* (2d ed.), ed. W. Wright and M. J. de Goeje (London, 1907), p. 286, for the behavior of the Damascenes in A.D. 1185.

[67] Cf. the story of al-Aḫṭal and his wife, *Aghânî* (3d ed.), VIII, 310.

[68] *Ibid.*, III, 120–21.

[69] T. Andrae, *Die Person Muhammeds in Lehre und Glauben seiner Gemeinde* (Stockholm, 1918), p. 14, quoting Ṭabarî, *Annales*, I, 1935.

lined the significance of the extraordinary personality by ascribing to him the co-operation or even the submission of the nonhuman cosmos. The great man's life possessed of a stronger spark of the divine than his frail kin is meaningful to the universe as a whole; his mission marks a stage in the drama of the world. The forces he unchains will serve him. The major phases of his stay on earth will be hailed or mirrored by the universe whose course he affects by his very presence. Unaware that this supranatural machinery detracts from the human triumph of the hero, the untutored heart strings incidents of a miraculous kind around the life of the *theios aner*.

Perhaps a hundred years after Mohammed's demise the faithful knew of the portentous details surrounding his birth. Ḥassân b. Ṯâbit himself has heard a Jew mounted on a rooftop in Medina warn his coreligionists of the rise of the star under which Aḥmad (i.e., Mohammed) was to be born. While he was born, a light emanated from his mother that made visible the castles of Bostra in Syria. A calf on being sacrificed to an idol prophetically announces the advent of him who will teach that there is no god but Allah. When Abû Jahl wishes to throw stones at the Prophet, his hands dry up. A handful of pebbles thrust against his enemies decide the Battle of Badr. Mohammed gives a believer a piece of wood, and it changes into a sword. With an insignificant quantity of food he feeds and satisfies huge crowds. The bone of a sheep tells him that its meat is poisoned. He dies of his own choice when presented with the keys of eternal life on this earth and those of Paradise.[70]

Christian, Zoroastrian, Hellenistic, and Buddhist miracle tales are freely attached to the person of the Prophet. The craving to glorify the Apostle of God by dehumanizing him is directed into definite channels by the desire, already powerful in Mohammed himself, to demonstrate his being true to type. Whatever evidenced the claims of prior messengers will be retold of Mohammed. It is not enough to have his deeds and his message testify for him; belief in his mission has to be justified by showing him at least as powerful as those other awe-inspiring

[70] All instances are taken from Ibn Hishâm, *Sîra*. Cf. J. Horovitz, *Islam*, V (1914), 45–48.

figures conformity to whom constitutes his real proof.[71] It is likely that those legends were at first confined to the unlearned and that the professional storyteller was primarily responsible for shaping and spreading them. But it did not take too long before the respectable theologians stepped in to collect systematically those *dalâ᾽il an-nubuwwa*, signs of prophethood.[72]

The theologians had been under a twofold pressure. Popular imagination insisted on changing the Apostle of God to a wonder-working prophet—a change recalling that of Epictetus' ideal cynic who was to be a messenger (*angelos*) from Zeus to men sent "in order to show them that in questions of good and evil they have gone astray, and are seeking the true nature of the good and the evil where it is not, but where it is they never think,"[73] to Philostratus' Apollonius of Tyana, whose moral teachings are heightened by the miraculous paraphernalia of their delivery.

The consensus of the believers in demanding the recognition of miraculous elements in Mohammed's life would by itself have forced the theologians' hands. But the Christian challenge to set forth the supernatural evidence, if any there was, of the Prophet's claims compelled a speedy response. Even when the Christian demand had been lavishly met, the clamor of the Christian polemicists continued with unabated violence. In his usual unrestrained invective Bartholomew of Edessa inquires ironically: "So Mohammed is the equal of the Christ, albeit he never revived the dead, nor like the Christ called back to life Lazarus who had been dead for four days, or opened the eyes of one born blind, or cured every disease and infirmity, or cleaned the lepers. No deaf or mute were healed by him, never did he stay the force of the winds and the furious billows, nor did he

[71] Cf. the writer's article cited in n. 64. A great many miracles of Mohammed and their non-Muslim sources or parallels have been collected by Andrae, *Person*, pp. 26–91.

[72] Samples from Abû Nuᶜaim al-Iṣfahânî's (d. 1038) *Dalâ᾽il an-nubuwwa* (Ḥaidarâbâd, 1320) are quoted by D. S. Margoliouth, *The Early Development of Mohammedanism* (New York, 1914), pp. 241–58. Andrae (*Person*, pp. 57–58) traces the early history of this literary genre.

[73] *Dissertationes*, iii. 22, 23; trans. W. A. Oldfather ("Loeb Classical Library" [1926–28]), II, 139.

ever walk on water as upon dry land. He never entered unto his disciples through closed doors. He was neither impeccable nor immortal nor a just judge. How then can you declare him the Christ's equal, since he did nothing of this kind nor anything like it? He had no share in truth or justice, but exhibited every kind of injustice ordering everybody executed who would deny that he was the Apostle of God. And still you will impudently assert that Mohammed and Jesus Christ were on the same level!"[74]

In struggling with the concept of miracle, the Muslim divines had to ban the misunderstanding that the Prophet had wrought wonders by his own suprahuman power. While the Koran insisted on Mohammed's human frailty, it also told of a number of miracles performed by the former prophets. Referring to them as "signs" (*âyât*) or "proofs" (*burhân*), the text made it plain that those prophets had never acted on their own but had been given more than human power on certain occasions and with the sole view of convincing the skeptics of their veracity. The wording of the Book therefore suggested the collection of the several miraculous stories that had clustered about Mohammed as signs of his prophethood (*aᶜlâm* or *dalâʾil an-nubuwwa*).[75]

The task of the theologian was eased by the Ashᶜarites' refusal to accept the idea of a law of nature. Once this concept of a stringent regularity of all natural processes is discarded and the axiom that like causes will engender like effects is dismissed as an unwarranted restriction of God's omnipotence, a miracle ceases to present too many logical difficulties. Each event is to the Ashᶜarite due to a special creative act of God. Where we are inclined to assume necessary consequences of recurring causes it is actually only *usus*, *ᶜâda*, that makes for regularity and thus a limited predictability of happenings. If God should choose to withhold the accident "hunger" from the substance, no hunger would be felt no matter how empty one's stomach. God is in the habit of creating the same "causal" sequences, but there is

[74] *MPG*, CIV, 1417, in his *Confutatio Agareni*. Cydones (*Contra Mahometem*, chap. 7; *MPG*, CLIV, 1069–72) argues the falsity of the koranic doctrine from its lack of a miraculous confirmation.

[75] Cf. Andrae, *Person*, pp. 93–94.

nothing to prevent him from breaking this habit. And a miracle is exactly such a "break of habit" (*ḫarq al-ᶜâda*).[76]

In due time an elaborate theory of the miracle was developed. It strictly maintained the distinction between *muᶜjiza,* the miracle of a prophet after his call, and the *karâma*, the miracle of a saint. After centuries of discussion, al-Îjî (d. 1355) formulates these (among other) requirements for a *muᶜjiza.*[77]

1. It must be an act of God, or tantamount to an act.
2. It must "break the habit" of the course of nature. Al-Îjî notes, however, that it is a confirmed habit of Allah to work wonders for his prophets.
3. The *muᶜjiza* must be inimitable and uncontrovertible.
4. It must happen at the hands of a man who claims prophethood.
5. It must come off exactly as predicted by the claimant.[78]

An-Nasafî (d. 1142) includes the *muᶜjiza* in his creed: "And He has fortified them (the Apostles) by miracles contradicting the usual course of events."[79] His commentator, at-Taftazânî (d. 1389), explains this statement in the following way: "A thing deviating from the usual course of things, appearing at the hands of him who pretends to be a prophet, as a challenge to those who deny this, of such a nature that it makes it impossible for them to produce the like of it. It is Allah's testimony to the sincerity of His apostles."[80]

The doctrine of the *muᶜjiza* is evidently tailored to fit the Koran as the miraculous proof of Mohammed's mission. The inimitability of the Holy Book, its *iᶜjâz,* is stated in the Book itself. "This Koran is not such as to have been invented apart from Allah."[81] And even more clearly: "Say: 'Verily if man and *jinn* agree to produce the like of this Koran, they will not pro-

[76] It hardly needs mention that those Arab thinkers who followed Greek thought —except Neo-Platonic—bitterly combated this whole train of ideas. The Ashᶜarite view is well set forth by I. Goldziher, *Vorlesungen über den Islam* (Heidelberg, 1910), p. 130.

[77] It may be noted incidentally that neither *muᶜjiza* nor *karâma* are koranic terms.

[78] Andrae, *Person,* pp. 101–2; cf. also A. J. Wensinck, *EI,* III, 624.

[79] *ᶜAqâʾid,* ed. W. Cureton (London, 1843), p. 4.*

[80] Wensinck, *loc. cit.*

[81] Koran 10:38.

duce the like of it though one to the other were backer.' "[82] At various times did the Prophet challenge the critics to "produce a sura like it."[83] And the dogma of the *iʿjâz* came to be based mostly on this challenge, *taḥaddî*, and the Arabs' failure to meet it. The *iʿjâz* seemed to imply stylistic uniqueness as well. But, since the style of the Koran did not suit everybody's taste, thinkers like the Muʿtazilite an-Naẓẓâm (d. between 835 and 845) argued that "if the Arabs were left alone they would have been able to compose pieces like those of the Koran. But they were deterred by God from attempting to rival the Koran and in this lies the miracle."[84] This is the so-called argument of the *ṣarfa* ("turning away"). Aside from the *ṣarfa*, an-Naẓẓâm based the Koran's uniqueness on its prophecies of future events.

Not until late in the ninth century was the insuperability of the koranic style generally accepted. And even later a cautious theologian like al-Bâqillâni (d. 1013) preferred to use the beauty of its presentation only as a corroborative, not as a primary, argument in favor of its *iʿjâz*.[85] His younger contemporary, the famous Abû ʾl-ʿAlâʾ al-Maʿarrî (d. 1058), seems to have been the last poet of note to try to rival the Koran, or rather one or the other passage of it.[86]

It would seem that, quite aside from theological considerations, the Holy Book as a literary monument deeply impressed even the sophisticated reader of the ʿAbbâsid age.

ʿAlî aṭ-Ṭabarî is at a loss to find the proper words to do justice to the beauties of the Koran. "Among the miracles of the Prophet is the Koran. It has, indeed, become a miracle of meanings which no writer on this subject has tried to explain without recognizing his incompetence and renouncing his discourse and his claim to such an explanation. When I was a Christian, I did

[82] Koran 17:90.

[83] Koran 10:39. For other passages cf. Abdul Aleem, *Islamic Culture*, VII (1933), 67–68.

[84] Aleem, *op. cit.*, p. 222.

[85] Cf. his *Iʿjâz al-Qurʾân* (Cairo, 1349), pp. 127–28; the Introduction to the author's forthcoming translation contains a detailed study of the growth of the *iʿjâz* concept with references.

[86] E.g., Koran 77:30–33; cf. Goldziher, *Muh. Stud.*, II, 403. Muhaḏḏib ad-Dîn al-Ḥillî (d. 1204/5) is accused of emulating the Koran (*ibid.*, p. 404).

not cease to say in accordance with an uncle of mine who was one of the learned and eloquent men among Christians that rhetoric was not a sign of prophetic office on account of its being common to all nations.[87] But when I waived traditions and customs, and broke with the promptings of habits and education, and examined the meanings of the Koran, then I found that the question was as its holders believed it to be. I have never met with a book written by an Arab, or a Persian, or an Indian, or a Greek, which contained, like the Koran, unity, praise, and glorification of the Most High God; belief in His Apostles and Prophets; incitement to good and permanent works; injunction for good things, and prohibition of evil things; exhortation to heaven and restraining from hell. Who has ever written, since the creation of the world, a book with such prerogatives and qualities, with such influence, sweetness and charm upon the heart, and with such attraction, felicity and success, while its producer, the man to whom it was revealed, was unlettered,[88] not even knowing how to write, and having no eloquence whatever? This is without doubt and hesitation a mark of prophetic office."

And aṭ-Ṭabarî adds thoughtfully: "Moreover, I found that all books worthy of everlasting fame do not fail to deal either with the world and its inhabitants, or with religion."[89]

His Spanish contemporary, Alvaro, implacable enemy of

[87] But Augustine, *De Doctrina Christiana*, Book iv, essayed to show the rhetorical virtues of the Scriptures in accordance with classical rhetorical theory. His object was to encourage the Christian preacher to improve his sermons along the lines of ancient rhetoric. For details cf. the author's *A Tenth-Century Document of Arabic Literary Theory and Criticism* (Chicago, 1950), p. xviii, n. 24.

[88] *Ummî;* his alleged illiteracy heightens the miracle of Mohammed's literary achievement. The same attitude is exhibited by the Greek biographer of Symeon the Young (d. 1041 or 1042), who considers it a special wonder that the unlearned Symeon was able to write about the mysteries of religion. Actually, however, Symeon was much better schooled than his biographer cares to admit (cf. K. Holl, *Enthusiasmus und Bussgewalt beim griechischen Mönchtum* [Leipzig, 1898], pp. 26–27). But *ummî*, used by Mohammed in the Koran, probably refers to the fact that he belongs to a nation without a literature, or else it corresponds to Greek *ethnikos*, *gentilis*. There is little doubt but that Mohammed knew how to read and write. For Jesus as *ummî* cf., e.g., Origen, *Contra Celsum* i. 29 and vi. 16.

[89] *Kitâb ad-daula waʾd-dîn*, pp. 44–45; trans., pp. 50–51; the greater part of the passage was also translated by Aleem, *op. cit.*, pp. 222–23.*

Islam that he was, cannot help admiring the style of the Koran. "The composition of its words and the prayers contained in all its parts, we today read in their volumes and much do we admire them for their elegant facility and their awesome (or: venerable) eloquence." Nevertheless, Alvaro is quick to assert, these accomplishments constituting but a sinful forgery will prove to the Muslims not a spiritual remedy but rather a cause of eternal punishment. For "any word or work not rooted in the faith of the Christ will be found vain, and harmful at the time of the Judgment."[90]

Less favorably impressed was the Christian al-Kindî (writing after 912).[91] He first points out that "every nation regardeth its own language the most beautiful, while the Arabs hold every other tongue but their own as barbarous; and similarly the Arabic, held by them as the most beautiful, is regarded by other nations to be barbarous."[92] He then deduces from the foreign words Mohammed used his lack of skill in handling the Arabic language. Finally, al-Kindî assails the Koran's claim to poetical beauty. "If, again, the claim put forth be, that there is in the Koran a supernatural harmony and cadence of language, and beauty of conception, that will be determined by the accuracy of the measures, the purity and fitness of the composition, and the point and charm of thought and imagery. But thy book throughout is broken in its rhythm, confused in its composition, and in its flights of fancy unmeaning."[93]

Five centuries later Ricoldus de Santa Cruce turns the beautiful style of the Koran into an argument against its genuineness. "We must realize that the Koran is not the law of God because its style (*phrasis*) does not resemble that of the divine law. For its language is rhythmical, or metrical, it is full of adulation in its sermons,[94] and like fables (*mythikon*) in its reasoning. That

[90] *Indiculus luminosus*, chap. 29; *MPL*, CXXI, 546. The first part of the passage is referred to by Th. W. Arnold, *The Preaching of Islam* (2d ed.; London, 1913), p. 138, n. 4.

[91] For the date cf. L. Massignon, *EI*, II, 1021.

[92] *Apology*, trans. by Sir Wm. Muir (London, 1882), p. 29.

[93] *Ibid.*, pp. 30–31.

[94] With this taunt the author probably refers to the glorifying epithets which God uses when talking of himself.

its style is rhythmical throughout is patent to its readers. I cannot here insert an example because neither rhythm nor wording can be truly and in every respect preserved when translated into Latin. The Saracens and the Arabs in this do glory to excess that the style of their law is both elevated and rhythmical, and they hold this to indicate that God composed the Book which then was revealed to Mohammed (*Môámeth*) verbatim. Mohammed, being unlettered, would never of himself have known such thought and such style. It is evident that the opposite (of this theory) is correct. For we see in the Holy Scriptures how God conversed with Moses, Job and the other prophets, never once using rhythm or verse in addressing them. Mohammed avers the law of Moses and the Gospel to be from God and God to have given their books to Moses and the Christ. These, however, are neither metrical nor rhythmical. And no other of the prophets who heard the voice of the Lord indicated that God had spoken in meter, which (manner of speech) is also spurned by human philosophers and wise men."[95]

VI

Interest in theology grew continuously after the low of the first twenty-five years following Mohammed's death had been overcome. Religion was well on its way to enwrapping the totality of man's life when the accession of the ᶜAbbâsids both speeded and intensified the process. While the heart strove ever more desperately to establish a personal relationship with the Lord, the mind was at work to clarify and systematize the data of revelation in order to wring from them the answers to questions the Prophet had never envisaged.

The group of thinkers known as Muᶜtazilites, Abstainers,[96]

[95] *MPG*, CLIV, 1057–58, chap. 4 (beginning). Ricoldus' argument is rather curious in view of the metrical character of much of the Old Testament, which, in many instances, had been recognized by the Fathers of the Church; cf., e.g., Jerome's *Preface to the Book of Job*, with its analysis of the meters occurring in it, and his subsequent remarks on Hebrew prosody, *Vulgate* (Frankfort/M, 1826), pp. xxv–xxvi.

[96] Originally, from declaring for any of the contenders for the caliphate; cf. C. Nallino, *RSO*, VII (1916–18), 429–54, on the interpretation of the name.

championed ᶜ*aql*, reason, as judge in matters of belief. The remodeling of its basic doctrines that Greek philosophy once had forced upon nascent Christianity, Christianity now forced upon Islam. The problems of man's freedom, God's qualities, and, as a special case of this question, the metaphysical position of the Logos, the Word of God, now held the attention of Muslim thinkers as they had commanded that of the Fathers of the Church; and their discussion roused the same passion among the believers of both faiths.

The Muslims appropriated and handled with increasing skill the scholastic method perfected by the church. To refute the dissenters, orthodoxy had reluctantly to use their weapons. By 900, perhaps even earlier, both sides employ the same techniques in arguing, although their results continue to differ widely. The compromise theology propounded by al-Ashᶜarî (d. 935), a seceder from the Muᶜtazila, which leans heavily to the conservative side, ultimately came to be accepted as embodying the tenets of orthodox belief.

In its treatment of the idea of God, the Muᶜtazila was primarily concerned with vindicating God's justice and his unity. To safeguard his justice, God had to be absolved from causing man to go wrong, he had to be conceived of as necessarily just, as compelled by his justice to reveal himself to man so as to acquaint him with conditions and means of salvation. To safeguard God's unity, the idea of him had to be cleansed of anthropomorphism and his attributes defined in such a way as not to suggest a plurality of divine entities.

In the main, Ashᶜarite theology ruled the Muᶜtazilite positions out of court. Al-Ashᶜarî's creed upholds God's direct responsibility for both good and evil;[97]* it maintains God's possession of hands and eyes in accordance with the koranic text, although with the qualification that we have no means of specifying their modality (*bi-lâ kaifa*);[98] and, while making some verbal concessions on the subject of his attributes, it canonizes with regard to the most important application of this doctrine, viz.,

[97] Al-Ashᶜarî, *Maqâlât al-Islâmiyyîn*, ed. H. Ritter (Istanbul, 1929–30), I, 291.

[98] *Ibid.*, pp. 290 and 291.**

the nature of the Word of God, a view diametrically opposed to that of the Muᶜtazilites.[99]

Some time before 738 the caliph Hishâm (724–43) had Jaᶜd b. Dirham put to death for advancing the doctrine that the Koran was created.[100] At about the same time John of Damascus suggests that it was dangerous to hold this view, for those who did were, in the eyes of the orthodox, "a contemptible abomination."[101]

Orthodoxy held that, even as his other attributes, God's speech was to be considered eternal, having no beginning and continuing without interruption. Consequently, his revelation did not originate in time, owing to a specific act of creation, but has been in existence from all eternity. Applied to the Muslim revelation, the inevitable conclusion is that the Koran is uncreated. The Muᶜtazilites, on the other hand, realized that the idea of an entity issuing from and inherent in, but still other than, Allah, posited as coeval and coexistent with him, meant in the last analysis the association with God of another divine being.

The ingenious tricks by which they thought to eliminate the danger of hypostatizing Divine Speech, or the Koran, are not especially conclusive; but there can be little doubt that their instinct was well directed and that, to protect the idea of the unity of God, the createdness of his Word had to be upheld. Nor can it be doubted that it was not the specious and devious reasoning of the orthodox divines which secured the victory for their viewpoint. The strength of the orthodox position actually derived from the fact that the believers at large in their boundless reverence for the Koran were demanding or at least backing any rationalization of their sentiment which would safeguard this veneration even to the peak of its unrestrained but devo-

[99] The teachings of the *falâsifa,* whose basic assumptions are Aristotelian rather than koranic, remained ineffective as far as the development of Islamic dogma is concerned.*

[100] He is said to have been the first to propound this view; cf. Ibn Ṭâhir al-Baghdâdî, *al-Farq bain al-firaq,* Vol. II, trans. A. S. Halkin (Tel-Aviv, 1935), p. 101, n. 5.

[101] *MPG,* XCVI, 1341–42; Becker (*op. cit.,* I, 433) quotes the passage but fails to connect it with Jaᶜd's fate.

tionally satisfying absurdity. The subtleties of the Muᶜtazilites stood in the way of their acceptance, but the arguments of the orthodox were no less hair-splitting, and their conclusions a hurtful challenge to intelligence. Their success, however, was not owed to any considerations of probability but solely to their agreement with the yearnings of the naïve believer.

Long after the battle had been decided, ash-Shahrastânî (d. 1153) summed up the Muᶜtazilite argument: "We agree that God is a speaker, but a real speaker is one who makes speech, so that God is a maker of speech in a substrate (*maḥall*) . . . . because if, as you say, a speaker is one in whom speech subsists it must either subsist eternally or temporally. If it were eternal (*qadîm*) there would be two eternals. . . . . What makes the eternity of speech impossible is that if the speech which is command and prohibition were eternal God would have had to lay commands on Himself. . . . . There can be no possible doubt that the words 'We sent Noah to his people'[102] when (*ex hypothesi*) there was no Noah and no people is a report of what did not exist, an impossibility, and a lie. The words 'Take off thy shoes,'[103] addressed to Moses when he did not exist . . . . is speech with the non-existent, and how can a non-entity be addressed? Therefore all commands and narrations in the Koran must be speech originated at the time the person addressed was spoken to. Therefore the speech is in time."[104]

From another vantage point the same conclusion is reached. "Speech consists of an ordered arrangement of words, whether in this world or the next; they are created and subsist in a temporal substrate (*qâʾima bi-maḥall ḥadîṯ*). When God gives them existence they are heard in the substrate, and as they come into being so they cease to exist."[105]

The extent to which public interest was aroused is hardly comprehensible today. Every stratum of society took up the theological discussion. A poet satirizes the circle of the Chief

[102] Koran 7:56.

[103] Koran 20:12.

[104] A. Guillaume, *The Summa Philosophiae of al-Shahrastânî* (London, 1934), pp. 279–80 of text; trans., p. 95.

[105] *Ibid.*, p. 288; trans., p. 97.

Judge Aḥmad b. abî Duʾâd (d. 854), one of the principal advocates of the "Created Koran," by saying: "While his friends drink till the small hours of the morning they searchingly investigate whether the Koran was created."[106]

In the beginning official opinion sided with orthodoxy. When Hârûn ar-Rashîd (786–809) heard that Bishr al-Marîsî maintained that the Koran was created, he threatened to "kill him in such a way as he had never yet killed anyone." Thereupon Bishr remained in hiding for about twenty years until Hârûn died.[107] But in 827 al-Maʾmûn publicly adopted the doctrine of the Koran's creation. In his last year, 833, the caliph went one step further. He instituted a test, *miḥna,* as to the creation of the Koran to which all *qâḍîs,* divines, and traditionists were to be subjected. Those whose answers were unsatisfactory were to be barred from public office and their testimony no longer accepted in court.

In language somewhat less subtle than that of the Muʿtazilite theologians the Commander of the Faithful professed himself greatly disturbed by the corruption and the harm threatening Islam through "the sayings which the Muslims are passing round among themselves as to the Koran," particularly the "confusedness of many of them about it until it has seemed good in their opinions and right in their minds that it has not been created; and, thus, they expose themselves to the risk of denying the creating by God of all things, by which (act) He is distinguished from His creation. He in His glory stands apart in the bringing into being of all things by His wisdom and the creation of them by His power, and in His priority in time over them by reason of His being Primitive Existence, whose beginnings cannot be attained and whose duration cannot be reached. Everything apart from Him is a creature from His creation—a new thing which He has brought into existence. (This perverted opinion they hold) though the Koran speaks clearly of God's creating all things, and proves it to the exclusion of all difference of opinion. They are, thus, like the Christians when they claim that ʿÎsà b. Maryam was not created be-

[106] Quoted by Goldziher, *Muh. Stud.*, II, 58.

[107] Cf. W. M. Patton, *Aḥmed b. Ḥanbal and the Miḥna* (Leiden, 1897), p. 48.

cause he was the word of God."[108] Those who fail to see the truth of this position do not, in the opinion of the caliph, have "any share in the real religion, or any part in the real faith and in well-grounded persuasion."[109]

The more prominent divines were summoned to the governor of Iraq and asked to declare themselves concerning the Koran's creation. Most of them declared their agreement with the prescribed view; some evaded the issue by shrewd verbiage; a few stood by their convictions. In the next reign torture and imprisonment were added to persuade recalcitrant theologians of their error. There were a few executions. Al-Maʾmûn's third successor, al-Mutawakkil (847–61), reversed the policy. He abolished the *miḥna* and aligned himself with orthodoxy. Whatever his immediate reasons, it must by then have been clear that the masses of the faithful could not be won over to the new dogma and that there was no point in creating a rift between ruler and ruled that was bound, sooner or later, to lead to political complications.

Orthodox thought now went to great lengths to fortify its theological position. The Word of God was understood to be everything between the two covers of the Holy Book. Thus the individual copy of the Koran with all its letters formed of ink was considered uncreated as well as the daily recitation of the Koran as it pours forth from the mouths of the faithful. "The Fathers (*as-salaf*) and the Ḥanbalites said: Agreement has established that what is between the two covers is the word of God, and what we read and write is the very speech of God. Therefore the words and letters are themselves the speech of God. Since the speech of God is uncreate the words must be eternal, uncreate."[110] Al-Buḫârî (d. 870), whose collection of traditions yields only to the Koran in holiness, was exposed to tribulations for not accepting the uncreatedness of the individual recitation of the Koran.[111]

[108] *Ibid.*, pp. 66–67, quoting Ṭabarî, *Annales*, III, 1118.

[109] *Ibid.*, p. 68, Ṭabarî, *Annales*, III, 1120.

[110] Shahrastânî, p. 313; trans., p. 104. Cf. the quotation from Aḥmad b. Ḥanbal (d. 855), *Kitâb as-sunna* (MS), in J. Schacht, *Der Islâm mit Ausschluss des Qorʾâns* (Tübingen, 1931), pp. 36–38.

[111] Cf. Goldziher, *Vorlesungen*, p. 116, and Patton, *op. cit.*, pp. 34–35.

This very radicalism of orthodox theology gave rise to compromise formulas. Al-Ashʿarî at first took up the position that one could not go beyond declaring that the Koran was the uncreated Word of God. It should neither be maintained that the utterance of the Koran is created nor that it is uncreated.[112] Later, however, he receded toward the extremist position.

"If anybody says, 'Tell us, do you believe that God's Word is on the Preserved Table?' the answer is: That is what we believe, because God has said, 'Yet it is a glorious Koran, written on the Preserved Table,'[113] (and therefore the Koran is on the Preserved Table); and it is in the breasts of those whom the knowledge has reached (God has said, 'but it is a clear sign in the breasts of those whom the knowledge has reached');[114] and it is read by the tongue (God has said, 'Move not the tongue in haste').[115] The Koran is in reality (*fîʾl-ḥaqîqa;* i.e., not figuratively speaking or as copy or quotation of the heavenly original) written in our books, in reality preserved in our breasts, in reality read by our tongues, and in reality heard by us (as He has said, 'Grant him an asylum, that he may hear the word of God')."[116]

Al-Ashʿarî's contemporary, al-Mâturîdî (d. 944), took a more conciliatory view. God's eternal Word cannot be heard.[117] The text contained in our copies of the Koran is the Word of God, and so is the recitation of the Koran in the mosque; but the actual letters and sound are things created.[118] Aṭ-Ṭaḥâwî, an Egyptian lawyer (d. 933), shows a similar tendency to let the controversy rest. "We believe," he says in his *Creed,* "that the Koran is the speech of Allah. From Him it began as an utterance without any modality. He sent it down to His Prophet as a

[112] *Maqâlât,* I, 292.

[113] Koran 85:21–22.

[114] Koran 29:48.

[115] Koran 75:16.

[116] Koran 9:6. *Al-Ibâna ʿan uṣûl ad-diyâna,* trans. from the edition, Cairo, 1348, p. 32, by W. C. Klein (New Haven, Conn., 1940), p. 81; cf. also Goldziher, *Vorlesungen,* pp. 116–117. O. Pretzl, *Sitzungsberichte d. Bayr. Akad., phil.-hist. Kl.,* 1940, Heft 4, pp. 26–35, restates various theories on the nature of the Koran from al-Ashʿarî's *Maqâlât.*

[117] Cf. Klein, *op. cit.,* Introduction, p. 37.

[118] Cf. Goldziher, *Vorlesungen,* p. 115.

revelation. The believers assented to the Koran in this way as a reality.

"They assured themselves that it was in reality the speech of Allah and not something created like the speech of mankind. Whoever on hearing it asserts that it is the speech of mankind is thereby an unbeliever. Allah has reprehended him, rebuked him and threatened him with hell-fire, since Allah has said, 'I will broil him in hell-fire.'[119] When Allah threatened with hell-fire whosoever said, 'This is only the speech of mankind,'[120] we know and are assured that it is the saying of the Creator of mankind, and the saying of mankind does not resemble Him."[121]

The solution decreed by orthodox Islam to the question of the Koran's creation is another testimony to the tremendous influence exerted by the believers' mood on the development of doctrine. The abstract form of the discussion and the tortuous argumentation should not be allowed to conceal the simple fact that the Muslim community was animated by the ardent desire to exalt the Book, their guide and distinction, beyond anything human imagination could conceive. In this sense the doctrine of the Koran is emotional theology. It attempts to put into rational terms that feeling of the Revelation's sublimity which had made Mohammed exclaim:

> Verily, it is a Koran noble,
> In a book treasured,
> Touched only by the purified;
> A down-send from the Lord of the Worlds.[122]

[119] Koran 74:26.

[120] Koran 74:25.

[121] E. E. Elder, *The Macdonald Presentation Volume* (Princeton, 1933), pp. 134–35, from two Cairo manuscripts of aṭ-Ṭaḥâwî's *Bayân as-sunna waʾl-jamâʿa.* J. Hell (*Von Mohammed bis Ghazâlî* [2d ed.; Jena, 1923], p. 40) translates a shorter version of the passage from a Berlin manuscript and a print, Kazan, 1893.

[122] Koran 56:76–79. The Ashʿarites integrate the anthropomorphic concept of God in respectable theology, which is one more instance of the success, in Islam, of "emotional theology." Cf. in this context R. Otto's statement about the preponderantly numinous character of Allah and its theological consequences (*The Idea of the Holy* [London and New York, 1936], p. 94).

CHAPTER FOUR

THE RELIGIOUS FOUNDATION: PIETY

I

ISLAM aims at comprehending life in its totality. It posits the ideal of a life in which, from the cradle to the grave, not a single moment is spent out of tune with or merely unprovided for by religious ruling. The distinction between important actions and unimportant detail of daily routine loses much of its meaning when every step is thought of as prescribed by divine ordinance. Profane and sacred no longer denote the area withdrawn from, and the area subject to, religious supervision. No sphere is left in which our doings are inconsequential for our fate in the hereafter. The relevancy of our failings will vary according to their moral and social significance, but nowhere shall we find a no-man's land to which religion does not lay claim. The Prophet had been charged with revealing not merely the great metaphysical truths but the rules of daily conduct as well. The Lord wanted the faithful to organize their commonwealth in a certain manner, he enjoined them to follow a certain code of law, and he selected for them a certain way of life. Thus, by accepting Islam, the believer accepted a ready-made set of mandatory answers to any question of conduct that could possibly arise. As long as he obeyed sacred custom, the Muslim's life was hallowed down to its irksome and repulsive episodes, and he would be fortified by the assurance of his righteousness.

The model to follow is the Prophet. Where the Koran fails to supply the necessary information, his *sunna*, his personal custom or the custom practiced by his community in the earliest times of Islam, fills the lacuna. Mohammed's *sunna* is usually recorded in a *ḥadîṯ*, a saying of his or about him which directly or by implication describes his usage or else contains a statement touching the present or future condition of his community.

The pagan Arab had endeavored, though to a much smaller extent, to follow the *sunna* of his ancestors; now pre-Islamic custom was replaced by the precedent set or the tradition approved by the Prophet. What could be proved to have been practiced by Mohammed was thereby admitted as normative. At the time of ᶜUmar II (717–20) doubt prevailed as to when a youth would come of age. The question was solved when somebody found a *ḥadîṯ* telling of a boy being rejected for military service by the Prophet at fourteen but accepted at fifteen.[1]

To convince, an opinion had to issue from the Prophet. Innovation, even change in small matters, when based on personal reasoning was to be rejected. Every thesis that cannot be traced in the age of the Prophet, every custom not authorized by the example of his times, is abomination. It is maintained by some that those mentioned in the first sura of the Koran "upon whom anger falls" have incurred God's wrath by *bidᶜa*, innovation, and those "that go astray"[2] are straying off the beaten tracks of the *sunna*.[3]

The tendency to canonize the usage, supposed or actual, of the Prophet's day—a tendency which, thanks to the lack of historical perspective, in many ways aimed at the canonization of the status quo of the recorder's time—led as early as the eighth century to preference being accorded the *sunna* in case it conflicted with the Koran. "The *sunna* is judge over the Koran, not the Koran over the *sunna*."[4] It is true that this verdict was not generally agreed upon. Al-Ashᶜarî records four different opinions, but only one of these maintains the supremacy of the Book over the *sunna*, while another denies any possible opposition of the two authorities.[5] The Ḥanbalite, Aḥmad Ghulâm Ḫalîl (d. 888), well expresses pious sentiment when he declares: "The *sunna* . . . . is the foundation on which the community is built. They (the models) are the companions of Mohammed, the people of the (authoritative) *sunna* and the community (*ahl as-sunna waʾl-jamâᶜa*). Whoso fails to follow them, errs and commits innovation. Whoso deviates from the companions of Mo-

[1] Cf. Margoliouth, *Early Development*, p. 98, and Goldziher, *Muh. Stud.*, II, 17.

[2] Koran 1:7.

[3] Goldziher, *Muh. Stud.*, II, 24–25.

[4] Yaḥyâ b. Kaṯîr (d. 738), quoted *ibid.*, II, 19.*

[5] *Maqâlât*, II, 608–9.

hammed in any religious matter is an unbeliever. Whoso alleges that there is any matter in Islam for which the companions of Mohammed do not suffice us has lied about them[6] and launched slanderous attacks against them. He is an innovator, he goes and leads astray, and introduces into Islam what does not pertain thereto. Know that there is no *qiyâs* (inference from analogy) in the *sunna*, nor can any rules (*amṯâl*) be formulated for it or any fleeting emotions[7] followed with regard to it. It is the recognition of the Prophet's model (*âṯâr*) without qualification (*bi-lâ kaif*) and explanation, without a Why? or a How? To discourse, polemize, dispute, argue is an innovation that rouses doubt in the heart even if one hits the truth and the *sunna* (in this fashion)."[8]

The extreme rigidity of the *sunna* concept was mitigated by a variety of factors. Obviously, absolute faithfulness to the mores of the past was an ideal for which the theologians might fight but which was by no means acceptable to everyone. One could perhaps say that a number of *sunnas* strove for supremacy. Pagan ethos, on the one hand, and Persian manners, on the other, offered precedents that would differ from those set by the early believers and prove more attractive to some circles. Neither tradition was, however, sufficiently complete to displace the *sunna* of the Prophet even had there been general readiness to yield it. But the Prophet's *usus* did not cover every contingency either, or, if it did, much evidence had slipped the memories of his companions or their heirs.

The very urge to have every detail covered by prophetic precedent forced a certain amount of forgery. Modern practices had to be justified or combated, and a *ḥadîṯ* was the only weapon to achieve either. Moreover, the *ḥadîṯ* was a convenient means of Islamizing such Christian or Jewish matter as was felt to be attractive and spiritually akin to the Muslim faith. It was not too difficult for the experienced traditionist to construct a con-

[6] The text has *kaḏḏaba-hum*, "declared them liars," which does not seem to fit.

[7] *Ahl al-ahwâʾ*; cf. at-Tahânawî, *Dictionary of Technical Terms* (Calcutta, 1862), p. 1543.

[8] Arabic text in L. Massignon, *Recueil de textes inédits* ... (Paris, 1929), p. 213; German trans., Schacht, *op. cit.*, p. 40.

vincing chain of authorities who were supposed to have transmitted any particular saying of the Prophet to the theologian's own day. It is freely admitted that the pious are only too ready to lie when it comes to *ḥadîṯ*.

Mohammed's prophetic powers made it possible for him to have enounced the most detailed predictions as to events and problems, mostly aberrations from the true *sunna* or the true doctrine, that were to trouble his community many centuries after his death. There was nothing improbable in his describing the setting and the virtues of towns to be founded long after he had departed this life. The growing strength of the popular belief in Mohammed's miraculous gifts made it difficult for internal criticism of his reputed sayings to be generally admitted. Instead, criticism of the enormous mass of traditions had to concentrate on the formal correctness of the *isnâd*, the chain of witnesses. Once it was established that all the links in this chain had been God-fearing and upright men who at least could have been in personal contact so as to hear the tradition in question one from another, nothing was to be done to invalidate it except perhaps to launch an equally well-authenticated *ḥadîṯ* of different impact.

Despite the huge quantities of *ḥadîṯ* weeded out by the most respected collections, such as the two *Ṣaḥîḥ* (Correct Ones), of al-Buḫârî (d. 870), arranged by subjects, and of Muslim (d. 875), arranged by the names of the authorities immediately following the Prophet, tradition remained an almost uncontrollable body consisting of an ever increasing number of individual items. When it had been widely realized that not all *ḥadîṯ* could truly be attributed to the Messenger of God, a saying of his was circulated wherein he predicted that after his demise more and more apothegms would be ascribed to him even as the earlier prophets had been credited with many a word not really theirs. Any such apothegm should be compared with the Book. If it is in harmony with revelation, it is his whether he actually pronounced it or not. Thus "the Prophet said" comes to mean little more than "it is correct, the Prophet would approve."[9]

[9] Cf. Goldziher, *Vorlesungen*, p. 47, and *Muh. Stud.*, II, 48–49. For the attitude cf. Seneca *Ad Lucilium* xvi. 7: "quicquid bene dictum est ab ullo, meum est."*

Other critics had the consensus of the believers decide about the "genuineness" of a *ḥadîṯ*. If it found favor, it was true—the collective judgment of the Muslims would not be erring. In this fashion the *bidʿa* concept comes to be modified to include both good and bad *bidʿa*. Ash-Shâfiʿî (d. 819) declared: "An innovation that contradicts the Koran, a *sunna*, an *aṯar*,[10] or the consensus, is the heretical *bidʿa;* an innovation, on the other hand, that is neither bad in itself nor stands in contradiction to any of the religious authorities mentioned, is a laudable and unobjectionable *bidʿa*."[11]

To reduce the flood of forgeries the Prophet was—in invented *ḥadîṯ*—quoted as inveighing against such invention. "Whoso deliberately lies about me, let him enter unto his place in hell-fire." Mohammed predicts: "At the end of the times there will arise forgers and liars who will bring you traditions neither you nor your forebears ever heard. Beware of them lest they lead you into error and temptation."[12]

Such warnings were as appropriate as they were ineffective. Since in theory no legal opinion, no religious reform, no political cause could be promoted except on the strength of a decision of the Prophet, manufacture of *ḥadîṯ* simply could not be helped. It is a quaint spectacle to watch the Muslims fight their spiritual battles through an exchange of predated authoritative verdicts in favor of each contestant. The present is made to appear as the materialization of a situation envisaged and predicted by the Prophet long ago. Contemporary conflicts had been outlined and prejudged by Mohammed. What happened today was, in a sense, the re-enactment of a drama first staged in the anxious heart of the Apostle of God.

Each political party cites the Prophet in support of its cause. When the rebels make ready to dethrone the caliph al-Walîd II (in 744), a saying of the Prophet made the rounds in which he rebuked a man for calling his son "al-Walîd." "You call your children by the names of your Pharaohs. Verily, there will arise a

[10] A tradition going back to a companion or successor of Mohammed, not to the Prophet himself.

[11] Goldziher, *Muh. Stud.*, II, 26.*

[12] *Ibid.*, pp. 132–33.

man by the name of al-Walîd, who will do more damage to my people than Pharaoh did to his." The recorder adds maliciously that people had related this saying to al-Walîd I (705–15) until they experienced the rule of al-Walîd II.[13]

When the Prophet left for his Tabûk campaign, he put ᶜAlî in charge of Medina. ᶜAlî made difficulties, not wishing to be excluded from the fight. Thereupon Mohammed said: "Are you not satisfied to occupy with me the position Hârûn (Aaron) occupied with Moses?"[14] Could any partisan of ᶜAlî hope for better support of his champion's claim to Mohammed's succession? When in the ninth century popular hatred of the Turks had reached fever pitch, it must have been comforting to hear quoted the Prophet's prediction that "the Hour (of Judgment) would not arrive before the small-eyed, red-faced, and flat-nosed Turks with faces like shields clad with sinew one above another (i.e., having rough, or broad and coarse faces) would be (victoriously) fought."[15]

The traditionist, thus, held the keys to the correct arrangement of all human activities; his knowledge of the *sunna* guarded the integrity of the faith, and his authority made him an indispensable instrument of organized power, legitimate or usurped. He administered the treasures bequeathed by the Prophet to his community, and he saw to it that those treasures, which had a way of increasing under his hands, were properly used. Hard was his task but great his glory.

When Sufyân b. ᶜUyaina died (in 814), al-Aṣmaᶜî (d. 831), in eulogizing him in an elegy, drew up a complete picture of the traditionist's function and importance.

Let him weep for Sufyân who seeks a *sunna* that has become effaced, and him who asks as his food morsels of extinct knowledge (*aṯârât*) and sayings of the Companions (*âṯâr*);

And him who desires a short chain of witnesses (i.e., traditions that quickly lead up to the Prophet) and an admonition (on good authority), and those that roam the four corners of the earth (in their quest for knowledge), coming from afar.

[13] *Ibid.*, pp. 109–10.

[14] Al-Buḫârî, *Ṣaḥîḥ*, ed. L. Krehl (Leiden, 1862–1908), III, 177; a shorter version, *ibid.*, II, 436.

[15] *Ibid.*, p. 401.

(The place of) his sessions has become desolate, emptied of its (regular) inhabitants (i.e., his permanent students) and the pilgrims (lit., those that come for the *ḥajj* and those that come for the *ᶜumra*).

Who will now that he has settled (in his grave) take care of a *ḥadîṯ* handed on from (i.e., on the authority of) az-Zuhrî (d. 742) and ᶜAmr b. Dînâr (d. 743 or 744)?

No Bedouin and no town-dweller will after his demise ever again hear anyone say: az-Zuhrî related to us.

May his decease bring no happiness to the spiteful ones who are overjoyed (by his death)—heretics they are, or deniers of predestination,

Or else miscreants (*zanâdiqa*), led by Jahm (b. Ṣafwân, d. 745–46) straight into the wrath of the Merciful and the Fire,

Or atheists and skeptics who have mixed with Allah's *sunna* absurdities upon absurdities.[16]

II

The spirit that moved the traditionists whatever their sentiments as individuals doubtless operated in favor of a formalistic or ritualistic concept of religion. The Lord exacts a certain amount of ritualistic devotion and is pleased with its precise execution down to the last detail.

The prayer, *ṣalât*, which it is obligatory for every believer to perform five times a day, is not so much an effort to achieve personal communication with Allah as a set of ceremonies expressing the Muslim's obedience, worship, and devotion. These prayers are preferably said in common with other faithful, lined up in well-ordered rows behind a prayer-leader, *imâm*. Nothing in the service is left to the initiative of the individual. From the ablution preceding the beginning of the ceremony to its very conclusion every act and every utterance are minutely regulated. Inadequate performance voids the validity of the *ṣalât*. The services are of different length, the morning service consisting of two, sunset, of three, noon, midafternoon, and evening, of four *rakᶜa* each, where *rakᶜa* means the main part of the *ṣalât*,[17] a sequence of mostly koranic formulas pronounced in various positions of the body (standing, bowing, prostrate).

[16] Ibn Qutaiba, *ᶜUyûn al-aḫbâr* (Cairo, 1343–48/1925–30), II, 135–36.

[17] In the Introduction of his translation of Book IV of al-Ghazâlî's *Iḥyâᵓ ᶜulûm ad-dîn*, published as *Worship in Islam* (Madras, 1925), pp. 6–18, E. E. Calverley describes in detail the Muslim prayer service. In his diagram of the service that dissects it in forty phases, this "main part" covers Phases 3–30.

Al-Ghazâlî (d. 1111), when describing the *ṣalât*, has this to say of the prostration.[18] "Next he (the believer) goes down for the Prostration, saying the *takbîr* (the formula: *Allâhu akbar*, God is greatest), and then places his knees on the ground and places his forehead, nose and palms (on the ground), uncovered. He says the *takbîr* while lowering himself, but he does not raise his hands in anything but the Bowing.[19] It is fitting that his knees should be the first to be placed on the ground, and after them his hands, and after them his face; and that he should place his forehead and his nose on the ground; and that he should turn his elbows away from his sides (but a woman should not do that); and that he should keep his feet apart (but a woman should not do that); and that in his Prostration he should leave an open space on the ground (but a woman should not leave a space); —'leaving a space' means raising the stomach from the thighs and separating the knees;—and that he should place his hands on the ground opposite the shoulders, without separating the fingers but rather joining them and joining the thumb to them (but, if he were not to join his thumb, it would not matter); and without extending his arms on the ground, as a dog does, since that is forbidden, and that he should say, 'O the praise of my Most High Lord!' three times (but if he increases the number, it is well, unless he is acting as *imâm*)."[20]

There have been acrimonious disputes about detail. Early authorities oppose the raising of the hands in the *ṣalât*. The exact height to which their raising might be permitted was under discussion. Popular custom retained the age-old gesture against weakening protests on the part of many a traditionist. This, as other disagreements on seemingly minor points of ritual that have exercised the minds of the Muslim divines, is seen in its true light when it is realized that the raising of the hands perpetuates a pagan gesture used to coerce the deity in curse, vow, and prayer.[21]

18 Phases 21–23 in Calverley's diagram. 19 Phase 16.

20 Calverley, *op. cit.*, pp. 70–71. Schacht (*op. cit.*, pp. 27–35) translates al-Ghazâlî's chapter on the *ṣalât* from his *Kitâb al-wajîz* (Cairo, 1317). Pictorial representation and description of the *ṣalât* in T. P. Hughes, *Dictionary of Islam* (New York and London, 1885), *s.v.* "Prayer."

21 Cf. Goldziher, *Nöldeke-Festschrift* (Giessen, 1906), pp. 320–28.

The spiritual significance of this elaborate procedure is suggested by ᶜIkrima (d. 724) when he proposes "the tying (of man to God)" as etymology of *ṣalât*.[22] A *ḥadîṯ* depicts its cleansing power. "The *ṣalât* is like a stream of sweet water which flows past the door of each one of ye; into it he plunges five times a day; do ye think that anything remains of his uncleanness after that?"[23] Al-Ghazâlî discusses the six "inner realities" which "bring the life of the *ṣalât* to perfection"[24] as the presence of the heart, understanding, respect, reverence, hope, and humility. The heart is to the Muslim not the seat of emotions but the seat of the mind, the receptacle of the "inmost, most secret and genuine thoughts, the very basis of man's intellectual nature."[25] The obstacle to achieving the presence of the heart is distraction, *ghafla*, that *ameleia* which for St. Afrêm is the typical state of the impious.[26] External causes of distraction can be removed with comparative ease; the internal causes are more stubborn. They are anchored in earthly cares, preoccupations, desires. Meditation on the future world will counteract them most effectively. The "inner realities" give their true meaning to each phase of the prayer. The physical prostration acquires significance as "the highest degree of submission, for the dearest of your members, which is your face, gets hold of the humblest thing, which is the dust. . . . . Whenever you place yourself in the place of lowliness, know that you have placed it in its proper place, and have returned the branch to the trunk, for of the dust were you formed and to it you return.

"So at this, renew to your heart the remembrance of the greatness of Allah, and say, 'O the praise of my Lord Most High!' and confirm it by many repetitions, for one repetition is of weak effect. Then, when your heart is moved, and that is evident, let your hope find assurance in the mercy of Allah, for

[22] L. Massignon, *Essai sur les origines du lexique technique de la mystique musulmane* (Paris, 1922), p. 259. He apparently connected the word with *ṣila*, from √*wṣl*. Actually, *ṣalât* is an Aramaic loan-word.

[23] A. J. Wensinck, *EI*, IV, 103.

[24] *Ibid.*, p. 105.

[25] D. B. Macdonald, *The Religious Attitude and Life in Islam* (Chicago, 1909), p. 221.

[26] Cf. Andrae, *Kyrkohistorisk årsskrift*, XXIII, 289–90, XXIV, 51 and 59.

His mercy makes haste towards weakness and lowliness, and not towards pride and conceit."[27]

And Abû Huraira (d. 677) said: "The nearest a creature is to Allah is when he prostrates: so, do much supplication."[28]

Full spiritualization of the *ṣalât* was reached by Ḥâtim the Deaf (*al-Aṣamm;* d. 851–52), who said: "When the time for the *ṣalât* arrives, I perform a copious ablution and go to the place where I want to perform the *ṣalât*. There I sit till my limbs are rested, then I stand up, the Kaᶜba straight in front of me, the *ṣirâṭ* under my feet, Paradise on my right, Hell on my left, and the Angel of Death behind me; and I think that this *ṣalât* is my last. I then stand wavering between hope and fear. . . . (and after finishing the prescribed prayer) I do not know whether my *ṣalât* has been graciously accepted by Allah or not."[29]

III

The *ṣalât,* however, did not suffice as either vantage point or culmination of devotion. The ritual allows for personal conversation (*munâjât*) of the believer with his God at the end of the service, and pious prayer or pious request (*duᶜâᵓ*) is recognized and recommended when the believer feels the need to supplement the *ṣalât*.

It seems that such people as were not, so to speak, professionally concerned with religion or in whose life religion was not the dominant interest were rather slow in making their devotional attitude articulate. More often than not early poetical utterances that sound a religious note are actually expressions of a political program whose slogans happen to be of a more or less doctrinal character. Sayings of the Prophet, scraps from the Koran, are versified. Sometimes the believer declares his allegiance not without naïveté.

[27] Calverley, *op. cit.*, p. 118.

[28] *Ibid.*, p. 54.

[29] Wensinck, *EI*, IV, 105 = Calverley, *op. cit.*, p. 59. Cf. also P. Klappstein, *Vier turkestanische Heilige* (Berlin, 1919), p. 26, who translates the slightly different version of the saying recorded by Farîd ad-Dîn ᶜAṭṭâr (d. 1230), *Taḏkira al-awliyâᵓ*, ed. R. A. Nicholson (Leiden, 1905–7), I, 248–49. *Ṣirâṭ* is the narrow bridge across the infernal fire which conducts to Paradise and from which the wicked will fall into the flames of Hell.

"We are satisfied with Allah's religion in every respect," says Jârûd b. ᶜAmr, perhaps in 630, "we are satisfied to have Allah and (!) ar-Raḥmân as Lord."[30] Ḥassân b. Ṯâbit strikes a more moving note in an elegy on a victim of the Battle of Uḥud (625). "I said to her: Martyrdom, O Umaima, is a going to rest, and (the gaining of) satisfaction of a Lord, prone to forgiveness."[31]

Occasionally, the basic tenets are summarized in poetical guise.

He (the Lord) coined for him (the Prophet) a name after (or: from) His own in order to exalt him: the Lord of the Throne is worthy of praise (*maḥmûd*) and he is highly lauded (*muḥammad*).
A prophet who came to us after despondency and after there had been a break (in the advent of) messengers while the idols were worshipped on earth.
He became a lamp, shining and guiding, radiating like the well-polished Indian sword.
He warned us of a Fire and brought the cheering message of a Garden, he taught us Islam; so we are (now) praising Allah.
You are God forsooth, my Lord and my Creator. To this I shall testify amongst the people as long as I live.
O Lord of men, you are too exalted to be touched by the word of those that claim a god beside you; you are most high and most glorious.
Yours are Creation, Grace, and Command; to you we come for guidance, and it is you we worship.[32]
For Allah rewards every confessor of His unity with (a place in) a Garden of Paradise in which he will be allowed to live for ever.[33]

ᶜAbdallâh b. Rawâḥa (d. 629) finds a drastic phrase for a conflict that must have been frequent in those early days.

O my soul,
I notice that you show no taste for Paradise.
But I swear by God you will get there,
Obediently, or else be forced![34]

The life of the pious is threatened by hostile demons. When Saᶜd b. ᶜUbâda dies (in 636), the *jinn* are heard to sing:

[30] Ibn Saᶜd, *Ṭabaqât*, V, 408; cf. O. A. Farrukh, *Das Bild des Frühislam in der arabischen Poesie* (Leipzig, 1937), p. 21.

[31] *Dîwân*, No. 38.3. Cf. Farrukh, *op. cit.*, p. 29.

[32] The second half of the verse reflects Koran 1:4.

[33] Hassân, *Dîwân*, No. 154.1–8; Poem 91 is somewhat alike, but shorter.

[34] Ibn Saᶜd, *op. cit.*, III, ii, 82.

> We killed the lord (*sayyid*) of the Ḫazraj, Saᶜd b. ᶜUbâda;
> We shot him with two arrows and did not miss his heart.[35]

The Bedouins' relation to Allah remained indifferent to theological considerations. Sulaimân b. ᶜAbdalmalik (715–17) was amused by a Bedouin's prayer in a year of drought.

> O Lord of the devotees (*ᶜibâd*), what is the matter with us and you?
> You used to give us water—what has possessed you (to withhold it)?
> Do send rain down on us, exert yourself![36]

People became interested in, and were moved by, the destinies of the past heroes of the faith. Fed by a stream of legends, their imagination appropriated every detail of the lives of the former prophets. Religious truth was impressively brought home to the simple-minded believer when he heard it reiterated by the elect of yore.

Masᶜûdî records these verses composed by Adam himself when he was informed that Abel had been slain by his brother.

> A change has come over the lands and those (that live) in them. The face of the earth has turned dusty and ugly.
> An enemy has settled close to us; he never forgets (his enmity), he is accursed; he does not die so we could find rest.
> Cain has killed Abel in an unprovoked misdeed. Alas for his handsome face!
> Length of life is but grief to me, and never can I get rest from my life.

Satan replied:

> Forsake this land and its inhabitants. This wide earth has become too strait for you.
> You and Eve, your wife, thought yourselves safe here from the hurts of this world.
> But my ruses and my guiles never ceased ere this precious prize escaped you.
> But for the mercy of the Most Powerful (*jabbâr*) a gust of wind would have driven you from the Garden of Eternity.[37]

Despite official discouragement, popular piety at all times favored legendary themes that offered their somewhat trite edification through a captivating display of saintly personages.

[35] *Ibid.*, p. 145.

[36] Al-Mubarrad, *Kâmil*, ed. W. Wright (Leipzig, 1864–92), p. 562; for similar passages cf. Goldziher, *Muh. Stud.*, I, 88. The Bedouin's prayer reminds one of the popular Athenian prayer to Zeus to grant rain, quoted by Marcus Aurelius *Commentationes* v. 7.

[37] Al-Masᶜûdî, *Murûj aḏ-ḏahab* (Paris, 1861–77), I, 65–66; of Adam's poem only vss. 1, 4, 5, and 7 have been translated here.

Toward the end of the seventh century, religious phraseology and perhaps a certain amount of religious feeling penetrated into love poetry. The poets appropriated the notions of sin and eternal damnation to discourage the cruelty of their beloved. The fair lady is warned that she will become guilty of murder if she continues her resistance and that the Lord will visit condign punishment on her. "Fear God with regard to us, O Ruqayya, and dread a punishment for our case—do not slay us!"[38]

It is God himself who has decreed the lover's passion.[39] The girl is asked to free the poet or be generous—for God, too, is generous and prone to forgiveness.[40] God is implored to grant the lover perseverance.[41]

> I bring complaint of unrequited love to God, and not to men.
> A lover frightened by his love must bring complaint.
> Do you not stand in awe of God for whom you slew
> Albeit he approached you meek and full of humbleness?
> O Lord, endear me to her, make her feel for me—
> For it is you Who gives and Who withholds.[42]

Not many poems are as serious in their appeal to the Almighty. More often than not a touch, and more than a touch, of frivolousness can be sensed in the employment of hallowed words and concepts. ᶜUmar b. abî Rabîᶜa (d. 719) uses the form of a prayer in addressing his beloved.

> O you whom I love with all my soul
> And who stands me in stead of all mankind,
> And who wrongs me that am always ready to forgive,
> And who does not care whether her sins are forgiven.[43]

The poet's impertinent play with things sacred is obvious when Kuṯayyir ᶜAzza exclaims: "Do not despair that Allah will wipe off your sins when you pray at the place where she has prayed!"[44]

[38] Ibn Qais ar-Ruqayyât, ed. N. Rhodokanakis, *SBWA*, Vol. CXLIV (1902), Abh. 10, Poem 52.4.

[39] E.g., ᶜUmar b. abî Rabîᶜa, ed. P. Schwarz (Leipzig, 1901–9), Poem 106.9.

[40] ᶜUmar, No. 40.5.

[41] ᶜUmar, No. 38.12.

[42] Jamîl, ed. F. Gabrieli, *RSO*, XVII (1938), 146–47, Poem 73.4, 5, 11.

[43] Poem 343.1–2; the genuineness of these lines is not above suspicion.

[44] Ed. H. Pérès (Algiers, 1928–30), Poem 4.3.

The lady's sight is Paradise to the poet.[45]

She is Paradise in this world to him who obtains her favor,
She is Paradise as long as she stays near your folk—
But does anything remain for long in this world?[46]

O ornament of those whom Eve bore,
But for you the world would be neither beautiful nor sweet.
To whom Allah shows your appearance (*ṣûra*)
Obtains Paradise (or: eternal life), never aging nor greying.[47]

The sentiment of the age encouraged both frivolousness and piety. It allowed both attitudes to mingle, and sudden switches from one to the other are frequent and do not necessarily reveal any bitter conflicts in the poet's heart. The style of Islam tinges his every effusion, but the worldly spirit continues in light disguise.

Waḍḍâḥ al-Yaman (*fl.* 700) records in a love poem:

I told her one day: yield! She smiled and said: Heaven forfend that I should do the forbidden.
And she would not yield before I humbled myself before her and instructed her how leniently the Lord treated venial sins![48]

But in another poem Waḍḍâḥ's mood is completely changed.

What is the matter with you, Waḍḍâḥ, who always dally with love-songs—are you not afraid of the approaching end?
Pray to the Master of the Throne and take such steps as will save you on the Day of Stumbling and Slipping.
O Death, you never cease to interfere with a hope long before that hope will have come to fruition.
Could anyone save himself by fleeing from you I should hasten the journey of my camel.
But your long arms reach beyond where the camels of noble breed will give up for fatigue.
Were I not on my guard against my doom and stood I not trembling from fear of it,
I should yield to the passion of my heart; verily its passion goes out to the ladies of the bridal chambers.[49]

45 ᶜUmar, No. 121.5.

46 The play on the words *ḫuld*, "eternity, Paradise," and *ḫulûd*, "eternity," cannot be rendered (Kuṯayyir, No. 8.7*b*–8).

47 Anonymous; quoted ᶜ*Uyûn*, IV, 29.

48 *Aghânî* (3d ed.), VI, 228.

49 *Ibid.*, pp. 229–30 (vss. 1–5, 7, 8).

By that time the sectarians, and primarily the Ḫârijites, had succeeded in purifying and deepening religious sentiment. The Ḫârijites who liked to call themselves *shurât*, "vendors," i.e., those who have sold their souls for the cause of God, while outlawed and hunted down as enemies of society, were driven by the passionate and somewhat gloomy piety of earliest Islam both to atrocious crimes against anyone who did not share their views and to a fervent desire for a martyr's death. They lived under the shadow of the end which they did not fear but welcomed.

Qaṭarî b. al-Fujâ᾽a, one of their leaders and a great poet (d. 698 or 699), thus glorified the Ḫârijite murderer of the caliph ᶜAlî (656–61).

O blow delivered by a God-fearing man who desired with it nothing but the satisfaction of the Master of the Throne!
On the Day I shall invoke his name and I am certain that of all creation he will weigh most heavily in the scales of the Lord.[50]

Muᶜâḏ b. Juwain b. Ḥuṣain thus exhorts his comrades before a battle:

O you vendors of your souls! The time to depart has arrived for him who wishes to sell his soul!
Would you want to remain in the house of the sinners out of ignorant carelessness, when every one of you is hunted to be killed?
Attack the host of the foes, for prompted by reasoning led astray they have singled you out for slaughter.
Onward, O men, to a goal which whenever it is mentioned stands out as the most pious and the most just.
Would I was with you on the back of a fleet horse of strong ribs, clad in a coat of mail, not without arms!
Would I was with you battling your foes so as to drink the first the cup of death.
Apprehension weighs on me that you might be gripped by fear and driven off the field before I could draw the sword against those whom it is meet to slay.[51]

The piety of the Shiites seems somewhat more concerned with the dogma and thus strikes a less obviously emotional key.

[50] Masᶜûdî, *Murûj*, IV, 435.

[51] Lit., the sacrilegious heretics, *al-muḥillûn;* Ṭabarî, *Annales*, II, 36 (anno 663), vss. 1–7.

Statements against the caliphs who deprived the Alids of their right to the throne[52] and highly speculative discussions take up a sizable proportion of their religious utterances.[53] But the doctrinal attachment to the House of the Prophet engenders sometimes a warm feeling of personal devotion to its members, past and present, which introduces a new note into Arabic verse.

When as-Sayyid al-Ḥimyarî (d. 789) was told that the Prophet had allowed his grandchildren, al-Ḥasan and al-Ḥusain, to ride on his back, he composed these lines in the simple style of the popular legend.

The Prophet came to Ḥasan and al-Ḥusain while they sat in their quarter and played.
He greeted them "May I be your ransom!" and "May the Lord keep you alive!" Such was the rank they held with him.
Then they marched around sitting on his shoulders (lit., and under them his shoulders). How excellent mount and riders!
Two children, whose mother was a pious and a modest woman who kept herself pure for a chaste (husband; i.e., ᶜAlî).
And their father (lit., elder, *shaiḫ*) was the son of Abû Ṭâlib. How excellent the children and the parents!
My two friends, do not refrain from taking a stand (on the question of who is entitled to the throne; *lâ turjiʾâ*), and know that right guidance is not what you claim,
And that the blindness of doubt after certainty, and the weakness of sight after keen perception
Is an error. So do not persevere in them (i.e., blindness and weak-sightedness). How bad, by your life, are those qualities![54]

The upsurge of religious feeling that characterizes the period after the accession of the ᶜAbbâsids finally installed religion as a regular subject of poetic endeavor. A modicum of piety had by then become part and parcel of every man's spiritual provisions, and even those that were inclined to skepticism were deeply concerned with religious issues as such. It is not too surprising, then, that we find Abû ʾl-ᶜAtâhiya (d. 828), to whom Arabic religious poetry owes the first great collection of "Ascetic Songs,"

[52] E.g., Kuṯayyir, Poems 76–79.

[53] E.g., Kuṯayyir, Poem 150, and much of Kumait's (d. 743) *Hâshimiyyât*, ed. and trans. J. Horovitz (Leiden, 1904).

[54] *Aghânî* (3d. ed.), VII, 259, vss. 1–8.

zuhdiyyât, accused of unorthodox views.[55] His simply worded lines spoke the mind of the many inarticulate believers.

Fear of God alone gives standing (or: rank; ᶜ*izz*) and nobility—to love the world makes you poor and destitute.
As long as he keeps his fear of God unimpaired it is no shortcoming of the pious slave (of Allah) to be a weaver or a cupper.[56]

This type of poetry is fond of moralizing.

No profit comes to man from his reason;
his good deeds are man's best store.
Youth, leisure and passion
are apt to corrupt you, O how apt!
Each and every one has two natures,
one good, one bad, that are each other's opposites.
Poverty is felt only with regard to what exceeds bare sustenance.
He who fears God is torn between hope and fright.[57]

IV

Driven by his feeling of helpless dependence on God's mercy and by the disquieting consciousness of his sins, the believer turned to God. The Almighty had revealed a few rules of faith, he had prescribed a rather exacting ritual, and he had indicated that the obedient servant could count on his grace on the Day of Distinction. But the sensitive conscience realized the uncertainties of the promise.

In the last resort it was the Lord's unfathomable pleasure that would decide the crucial issue of salvation. There was nothing whereby the believer could compel God's forgiveness, and, what was worse, the heedlessness of a moment might nullify the merit of a lifetime spent in the fear of God. In his waking hours as well as in his sleep the faithful had to be on his guard. Never once was he to lose sight of the Hour and the punishment await-

[55] Cf. G. Vajda, *RSO*, XVII (1938), 215–20. Abû ᵓl-ᶜAtâhiya took great pains to refute the accusation.

[56] *Aghânî* (3d ed.), IV, 5.

[57] From the *urjûza*, *ibid.*, pp. 36–37. The *moralia* of the *zindîq* Ṣâliḥ b. ᶜAbdalquddûs, executed in 783, are on a slightly higher level; they have been edited with an introduction by Goldziher, *Transactions of the Ninth International Congress of Orientalists*, II (London, 1893), 104–29. In *JAOS*, LX (1940), 23–29, the writer attempts a study of the development of Arabic religious poetry from a different vantage point.

ing him should he slip. Life was a fearful test; somber submissiveness the mood in which it had to be faced.

By asking for prayer, the Lord had shown what kind of service he favored. Evidently, supererogatory prayer would be to his liking. In his Book he deprecated the joys and values of this world—the less one partook of them the more he would approve of one's devotion. Thus, a numerically small but in the long run highly influential group of the truly pious, not organized but led to similar conclusions by similar impulses, threw overboard the level-headedness of the Prophet's rules. Where he had wished to strike a healthy balance between the duties to this and to the other world, they would have nothing of the contaminating rewards of the Here and withdrew from its obligations out of fear of temptation.

The ascetic mood of the Christian and the pre-Christian Near East had gripped the pious who forced their undernourished bodies into vigils of prayer and Koran readings, into orgies of contrition and fear, and into feats of abstinence which seemed quaint and forbidding to the average follower of the Prophet. The Prophet's injunctions against celibacy, in part, perhaps, provoked by the influence of Nestorian Christianity, removed virginity from the ascetic ideals, and the community was not prepared to countenance the development of organized monasticism on Christian lines. The God-fearing fought their battles alone or in small and informal groups, and even when, from the twelfth century on, those groups of a master and his personal followers crystallized into regular fraternities, the vows of the members were never as stringent or as final as those of the Christian friar.

The type of piety that animated the Muslim devotee directly continues the emotion so well described by St. Basil: "The ascetic life has one object, the salvation of the soul, and so it is necessary to keep with fear as a divine commandment everything that can contribute to this very purpose. For even God's commandments have no other purpose than that he who obeys them may be saved."[58]

Ḥasan of Baṣra (d. 728) declares that "fear and hope are the

[58] W. K. L. Clarke, *The Ascetic Works of Saint Basil* (London, 1925), p. 141.

two mounts of the believer," but "fear must be stronger than hope, for when hope is stronger than fear, the heart will rot."[59] And likewise St. Basil had held that "to those who are just being introduced to piety, instruction through fear is more profitable, according to the advice of Solomon, wisest of men, who said: 'The fear of the Lord is the beginning of wisdom' (Prov. 1:7)."[60]

Some feel that the struggle for salvation should be conducted in retirement, but others see in good works their best hope and thus keep within the community. In any event, laughter and mirth are to be avoided. Ḥasan of Baṣra is reported not to have laughed once in thirty years.[61] Tearfulness is commended. The "weeper," *abîlâ*, of the Syrian church is paralleled by the Muslim *bakkâ*ʾ. ʿAbdalwâḥid b. Zaid (d. 793) exhorts his fellow-ascetics: "O brethren, will ye not weep in desire for God? Shall he who weeps in longing for his Lord be denied the Vision of Him? O brethren, will ye not weep in fear of the Fire? Him who weeps in fear of the Fire the Lord will rescue therefrom. O brethren, will ye not weep in fear of the thirst on the Day of Resurrection? O brethren, will ye not weep?"[62] Shaʿwâna, one of the earliest woman ascetics, when warned by her friends that she might lose her sight through much weeping, replied: "Verily to be blind in this world through much weeping is better, to my mind, than to be blind in the next through the fires of Hell." And she also used to say: "Let the one who is not able to weep pity those who weep, for the one who weeps, weeps only because he knows himself and his sins and that towards which he is going."[63] St. Afrêm had been much admired for his gift of tears. "As with all men to breathe is a natural function unceasing in exercise, so with Afrêm it was natural to weep. There was no day, no night, no hour, no moment, however brief, in which his eyes were not

[59] Quoted by H. Ritter, *Islam*, XXI (1933), 14.

[60] Clarke, *op. cit.*, p. 158.

[61] Chapter xvii of St. Basil's *Longer Rules*, in Clarke, *op. cit.*, pp. 180–81, enjoins that "it is necessary also to refrain from laughter."

[62] Massignon, *Recueil*, p. 5; the beginning is translated by M. Smith, *Studies in Early Mysticism* (London, 1931), p. 157. Cf. also Schacht, *op. cit.*, p. 89.

[63] M. Smith, *Râbiʿa the Mystic and Her Fellow-Saints in Islam* (Cambridge, 1928), pp. 145–46.

wakeful and filled with tears, while he bewailed the faults and follies now of his own life, now of mankind."[64]

Silence is recommended. "Silence produces beauty of adornment and the manifestation of awe and the cessation of evil utterances and the graces of gratitude and praise to God—if it be right, the servant speaks, and if it be wrong, he betakes himself to something else, and therefore his speech is listened to and his comment followed. Silence is a safe refuge, and in quietness is peace."[65] However, while "silence is safer, speech is more excellent if directed towards the praise of God and the furtherance of His purposes."[66] In this qualification al-Muḥâsibî (d. 857) is in agreement with the Prophet, who is supposed to have forbidden Anas b. Mâlik to practice continuous silence, arguing that it was better to exhort people to the virtuous life and the abandonment of sin than to refrain from talking to them.[67] It hardly needs mention that silence as a devotional exercise goes back to pre-Christian antiquity.

Together with silence, humility, and the remembrance of God, poverty is of great help toward the attainment of salvation. Worldly possessions are dangerous. "Two bad companions, the Dînâr and the Dirham! They profit you only when they leave you!"[68] It is not so much poverty that is desirable but freedom from greed, avoidance of the temptations incident to wealth. The rich man is tied to this world with stronger cords than the poor. To be given a share in this world is likely to entail a threat to one's share in the next. The Prophet is represented as saying: "The rich will be admitted to Paradise five hundred years later than the poor."[69] Nothing, it is stated, "of all the works that follow us is more effective in obtaining for us a place

[64] Smith, *Early Mysticism*, pp. 156–57, quoting from *Ephraim the Syrian, Life and Writings*, trans. H. Burgess and J. B. Morris (Oxford, 1898), p. 126.

[65] Al-Muḥâsibî (d. 857), *Kitâb az-Zuhd*, fol. 3*a*, quoted by M. Smith, *An Early Mystic of Baghdad* (London, 1935), p. 165.

[66] *Ibid.*, pp. 55.

[67] Goldziher, *Revue de l'histoire des religions*, XXXVII (1898), 320.

[68] Ḥasan of Baṣra, quoted by Ritter, *loc. cit.*, p. 24.

[69] Quoted by Goldziher, *Muh. Stud.*, II, 385.

in the other world than renunciation of this world (*zuhd*)."[70] Likewise, St. Afrêm had said:

> Alas for thee, O world, how much art thou loved,
> Thy beauties are many, but they are not permanent,
> For thou are but a dream, without real existence;
> I renounce thee henceforth, O wicked world!
>
> Woe be to whoever shall love thee, O world!
> For he will be caught in thy snares, and in the nets thou
> layest for him,
> He shall lose his soul and yet not possess thee;
> I renounce thee henceforth, O wicked world![71]

Abû Bakr, the first caliph (632–34), is quoted as saying: "Our abode is transitory, our life therein is but a loan, our breaths are numbered, and our indolence is manifest." By this, al-Hujwîrî (d. probably after 1072)[72] explains, he "signified that the world is too worthless to engage our thoughts; for whenever you occupy yourself with what is perishable, you are made blind to that which is eternal: the friends of God turn their backs on the world and the flesh which veil them from Him, and they decline to act as if they were owners of a thing that is really the property of another. And he (Abû Bakr) said: 'O God, give me plenty of the world and make me desirous of renouncing it.' "[73] But being in the world does not necessarily disqualify from attaining spiritual perfection. Al-Muḥâsibî sees more profit accruing to one's soul from contact with a God-fearing rich man than with a poor man of not quite the same moral standing.[74]

Poverty, especially if voluntarily preferred to security, perfects man's confidence in God. It is not for man to fret about his sustenance. He who created him also will provide for him. The ever present vision of death makes hoarding of provisions appear futile. Complete trust, *tawakkul*, in the Lord will arise in consequence of complete renunciation of the world.

[70] Abû Ṭâlib al-Makkî, *Qût al-qulûb* (Cairo, 1310), I, 243.

[71] S. Ephraim, *Renunciation of the World*, trans. M. Smith, *Early Mysticism*, p. 140.

[72] *Kashf al-maḥjûb*, trans. R. A. Nicholson (Leiden and London, 1911), Preface, p. xviii.

[73] Hujwîrî, pp. 70–71.

[74] *Kitâb ar-riᶜâyâ li-ḥuqûq Allâh*, ed. M. Smith (London, 1940), pp. 185–86.

An-Niffarî (d. probably 965) professes to have been told by the Lord:

Satisfy Me as to thine eye, and I will satisfy thee as to thy heart.
Satisfy Me as to thy feet, and I will satisfy thee as to thy hands.
Satisfy Me as to thy sleeping, and I will satisfy thee as to thy waking.
Satisfy Me as to thy desire, and I will satisfy thee as to thy need.[75]

"Fear of God and firm faith are the two scales of the balance and *tawakkul* the tongue by which you can tell the more and the less."[76] "Entrust your affairs to God and take your rest."[77] You are to lie "as little children in the bosom of God."[78] Al-Ghazâlî explains that *tawakkul* results from belief in the Unity of God. "Since God is the sole cause of all that exists or can exist, and all His acts are the result of His perfect goodness and wisdom, and all things depend on His power, then the servant can in perfect trust give up his will to the Divine Will and abandon himself to God, trusting in Him to provide for all needs."[79]

Here again Islam continues the mood of Syrian Christianity. In the second half of the seventh century, Isaac of Nineveh had written: "The man whose soul is night and day given to the works of God, and who therefore neglects to prepare dress and food, and to fix and prepare a place for his shelter and the like, that such a man trusts in God that He will prepare in due season all he needs, and that He will care for him . . . . this is really true trust and a trust of wisdom."[80]

But the social consciousness of Islam tries to counteract the exhortation to begging and idling which seemed to be, and frequently was, implied in this attitude of complete passivity. The Prophet is shown as rebuking a man who devoted all his time to prayer, leaving the preparation of his food and the care of his beast to others.[81] Al-Muḥâsibî points out that God expects his

[75] Muḥammad an-Niffarî, *The mawâqif and muḫâṭabât*, ed. and trans. A. J. Arberry (London, 1935), *muḫâṭaba* 34.6–9 (trans., p. 162).

[76] Sahl at-Tustarî (d. 896), quoted *Qût al-qulûb*, II, 3.

[77] ᶜÂmir b. ᶜAbdallâh (d. 721/2), quoted Smith, *Early Mystic of Baghdad*, p. 185.

[78] Ash-Shiblî (d. 773), quoted Smith, *Early Mysticism*, p. 172.

[79] Cf. Smith, *Râbiᶜa*, pp. 81–82.

[80] Quoted by Smith, *Early Mysticism*, p. 172, from Isaac's *Mystical Treatises* trans. Wensinck (Amsterdam, 1923).

[81] Cf. Goldziher, *Vorlesungen*, pp. 144–45.

children to work for what he provides. Every prophet has had to work as a shepherd.[82] *Tawakkul* means acquiescence in earning what one needs—and it is for God to decide of what exactly those needs consist. Abû Ṭâlib al-Makkî (d. 996) devotes a separate chapter to showing the compatibility of laying up stores with *tawakkul*.[83]

Was the devout to appeal to medical skill when stricken? Opinion is divided, but it is remarkable how here again the common-sense element so characteristic of Islam comes to the fore. While D̲û'n-Nûn (d. 857) reprimanded a friend who complained of his illness to the extent of asking for his prayers,[84] the Prophet is cited: "There is a remedy for every disease, some know it, some don't—only death is beyond cure."[85] Once Moses lay ill and the Jews told him to use such-and-such a preparation, but he refused twice, desirous of being cured by God, who cures without preparations. Finally, God ordered him to take the customary remedy, and he was cured. Then God told him: You wanted to nullify my wisdom by not trusting completely him who conferred their usefulness on medical drugs.[86] The same argument is used by St. Basil to reconcile reliance on medical art with complete reliance on God. "The medical art . . . . has been given us by God who directs all our life to advise the removal of what is in excess or the addition of what is wanting. . . . . The herbs which are appropriate to each disease did not grow out of the ground automatically, but, to be sure, were produced by the will of the Creator with the object of benefiting us."[87]

Palladius (wrote 419–20) realizes that the pious disposition of the mind "is naturally exposed to waves of evil, both visible and invisible, and can enjoy calm only with the help of continuous prayer and spiritual self-culture."[88] Centuries earlier the sentiment had been expressed that prayer was not to be the request for something the devotee lacked but thanksgiving for what he

[82] Cf. Smith, *Early Mysticism*, p. 184.

[83] *Qût al-qulûb*, II, 19–21.

[84] As-Sarrâj (d. 988), *Kitâb al-luma' fî 't-taṣawwuf*, ed. R. A. Nicholson (Leiden and London, 1914), p. 235.

[85] *Qût al-qulûb*, II, 21.

[86] *Ibid.*, bottom.

[87] Clarke, *op. cit.*, pp. 224–25.

[88] *Historia Lausiaca*, Prologue, 7; trans. W. K. L. Clarke (London, 1918), p. 42.

had been given.[89] These ideas, together with the experience of being drawn nearer and nearer to God through the effusion in worshiping prayer of the innermost self, determine the character of the Muslim pious' converse with his Lord.

When asked how to enter upon prayer, Abû Saᶜîd al-Ḫarrâz (d. 899) said: "You approach the Lord Most High as you will approach Him on the Day of Resurrection. When you stand before Him there is no interpreter between you and Him. He draws near you and you commune with Him, fully conscious of Who it is before Whom you are standing, for He is the great King."[90]

Therefore, in the words of as-Sarrâj: "Before the time of prayer comes, the servant must be in a state of preparation, and his attitude must be that which is essential for prayer, namely, a state of meditation and recollection, free from wandering thoughts, and consideration or remembrance of aught save God alone. Those who enter thus upon prayer, with heart intent only upon God, will proceed from prayer to prayer, in that same state of recollection, and will remain therein after they have ceased to pray."[91] To the Prophet "every time of prayer was an Ascension and a new nearness to God."[92] While it is permissible to ask the Lord for a lawful favor,[93] some tender consciences refrained

[89] E.g., Maximus Tyrius, *Dissertationes*, ed. H. Hobein (Leipzig, 1910), v. 8 (p. 63). It may be mentioned here that Maximus seems to be the oldest source for Arab stone worship. In *Diss.* ii. 8 (pp. 25–36) he says: "I do not know whom the Arabs worship, but I have seen (the deity's) *agalma*, a quadrangular stone, *lithos tetragonos*."

Agatharchides of Knidos (2d cent. B.C.), *On the Red Sea*, 85 (*Geographi Graeci Minores*, ed. K. Müller [Paris, 1882], I, 176), quoted by Diodor iii. 42, only mentions "an altar of hard stone and great age inscribed with archaic and unknown, *ἀγνώστοις*, letters," near Poseidion (which D. H. Müller, Pauly-Wissowa, *Real-Encyclopädie der class. Altertumswissenschaft*, new ed., III, 348, tentatively identifies with ᶜAqaba). Agatharchides does not, however, suggest that the stone as such was an object of worship.

Clement of Alexandria (d. after A.D. 211) *Protreptikos iv.* 1 (Stählin, I, 40), and Arnobius (d. after A.D. 325) *Adv. gentiles vi.* 11, include the stones adored by the Arabs in their lists of oddities of pagan worship.

[90] Sarrâj, p. 152.

[91] *Ibid.*, p. 154; trans. Smith, *Early Mysticism*, p. 163.

[92] Hujwîrî, p. 302.

[93] E.g., al-Qushairî (d. 1074), *ar-Risâla fî ᶜilm at-taṣawwuf* (Cairo, 1330/1912), p. 120. The *Risâla* was composed in 1045.

from prayer altogether lest the Lord should tell them: "If you ask for something We think fit for you, you (falsely) suspected us (that We would withhold it from you), but if you ask something We do not think fit for you, you have given Us bad praise. If you acquiesce We shall bestow on you what We have destined for you from all eternity."[94]

Al-Qushairî begins his chapter on *tauba*, repentance, with the koranic admonition: "Turn penitently to Allah as a body, O ye believers, mayhap ye will find happiness."[95] If God wants man to be freed from his desires, he first throws open to him "the gate of repentance."[96] Here repentance corresponds to "conversion" in Christian theology.[97] It involves three elements, "remorse for disobedience and immediate abandonment of sin, and determination not to sin again." Contrition leading to repentance "may be due to three causes: (1) fear of Divine chastisement and sorrow for evil actions, (2) desire of Divine favor and certainty that it cannot be gained by evil conduct and disobedience, (3) shame before God."[98] Repentance has a different meaning depending on the spiritual standing of him who repents. D̲û ᵓn-Nûn said: "The repentance of the common is from sin; the repentance of the elect is from forgetfulness; the repentance of the prophets is from seeing that they are unable to reach what others have attained."[99]

In describing the perfect ascetic, al-Muḥâsibî lists the characteristic features of this type of piety. "The believer who is seeking for godliness renounces all that is destructive to him in this world and the next, and leanness is manifest in him, and mortification and solitude and separation from the companionship of the pious, and the appearance of grief and absence of joy, and he chooses all that, hating to indulge in pleasure which

[94] Al-Wâsiṭî (d. after 932), quoted by Qushairî, *op. cit.*, p. 121.

[95] Koran 24:31 (Bell translates: "ye will prosper"); Qushairî, *op. cit.*, p. 45.

[96] Abû Saᶜîd b. abî ᵓl-H̲air (d. 1049), quoted by R. A. Nicholson, *Studies in Islamic Mysticism* (Cambridge, 1921), p. 51.

[97] Cf. Smith, *Early Mysticism*, p. 170.

[98] Hujwîrî, pp. 294 and 295.

[99] Al-Kalâbâd̲î (d. 990 or 995), *Kitâb at-taᶜarruf li-mad̲hab ahl at-taṣawwuf*, trans. A. J. Arberry (Cambridge, 1935), p. 83. Sarrâj, p. 44, quotes a different version of this saying.

may incur the wrath of the Lord and make him worthy of His chastisement, and he hopes that his Lord will be well pleased with what he does, and that he will be saved from chastisement, and will be permitted to come into His presence and to taste of the joys of Paradise, unalloyed and unabated, and to abide therein to eternity, enjoying the good pleasure of his Lord, the All-Gracious and All-Glorious."[100]

V

At the same time that theologians and philosophers strove to define and rationalize the absolute unity of the divine being, groups of devout strove after an emotional understanding of the essence of the One. On the basis of Neo-Platonic ideas the Ṣûfîs, so called for the wool, *ṣûf*, of which their coarse frock was made,* attributed reality to God alone. Man participates in reality only inasmuch as he has attained to identification with the divinity. An elaborate path, *ṭarîqa*, of spiritual perfection leads to the gnosis, *maᶜrifa*, of the divine Unity and to the bridging of the gap between the creature and its Creator when the soul transcends the confines of personality by losing itself in the intuition of the One. The mere attribution of reality to any entity besides the One is polytheism, *shirk*.[101] The finite soul views the Infinite with love. Love implies longing. And longing makes man renounce the world for the beatific vision in which no distinction is felt any more between himself and the Most High, in whom the individual mind has become completely absorbed.

Love is the mood of the Ṣûfî, gnosis his aim, ecstasy his supreme experience. "Man's love toward God is a quality which manifests itself in the heart of the pious believer, in the form of veneration and magnification, so that he seeks to satisfy his Beloved and becomes impatient and restless in his desire for vision of Him. . . . . He is cut off from all habits and associations, and renounces sensual passion and turns towards the court of love and submits to the law of love and knows God by His attributes of perfection. And believers who love God are of two kinds—(1) those who regard the favor and beneficence of God towards

[100] *Riᶜâya*, p. 199; trans. M. Smith, *Early Mystic of Baghdad*, pp. 169–70.

[101] Lit., association, i.e., of other gods to God.

them, and are led by that regard to love the Benefactor; (2) those who are so enraptured by love that they reckon all favors as a veil (between themselves and God) and by regarding the Benefactor are led to (consciousness of) His favors. The latter way is the more exalted of the two."[102]

Love, al-Qushairî states, is a "noble state" in which God reveals himself to the servant. God loves the servant and the servant loves him.[103] Love of God on the part of man is a state of his heart too subtle to bear description. This state will move man to glorify God, to prefer his satisfaction (to anything else), to be impatient of separation from him, to yearn for him, to be restless without him, and to feel close to him in his heart through remembering him unceasingly. But the servant's love of God does not mean that God should show him affection nor that he should join (or: comprehend?) God. How could this be, seeing that true infinity is too holy to be reached, attained, or joined. It comes closer to the truth to say that the lover perishes in the Beloved than to say that the lover joins the Beloved.[104] Qushairî seems to feel that there is no better word than "love" to explain the servant's state, however much this may leave unexplained.

Found weeping and asked the reason, Sulaimân ad-Dârânî (d. 830) said: "Why should I not weep? For, when night falls, and eyes are closed in slumber, and every lover is alone with his beloved, and the people of love keep vigil, and tears stream over their cheeks and bedew their oratories, then God Almighty looks from on high and cries aloud—'O Gabriel, dear in my sight are they who take pleasure in My Word and find peace in praising My name. Verily, I am regarding them in their loneliness, I hear their lamentation and I see their weeping. Wherefore, O Gabriel, dost thou not cry out aloud amongst them—"What is this weeping?" Did ye ever see a beloved that chastised his lovers? Or how could it beseem Me to punish folk who, when night covers them, manifest fond affection towards Me? By Myself I swear that when they shall come down to the Resurrection I

[102] Hujwîrî, pp. 307–8.

[103] *Op. cit.*, p. $144^{3, 4}$.

[104] *Op. cit.*, p. $144^{16–19}$; cf. R. Hartmann, *Al-Ḳuschairîs Darstellung des Ṣûfîtums* (Berlin, 1914), pp. 62–63.

will surely unveil to them My glorious face, in order that they may behold Me and I may behold them.' "[105]

For at the end of his path, at the end of what the Muslims called "the science of Ṣûfîdom" or "the esoteric science,"[106] the mystic will receive the gnostic experience of the Divine. He will see God face to face, and, in seeing him, will become one with him. Love leads to gnosis.[107] Gnosis is "the meeting of the Friend," the first step in establishing fellowship with him. Such fellowship leads to tranquillity and satisfaction, which "is the quiescence of the heart under the events which follow from the Divine Decree."[108]

Beyond this experience lies *fanâ*ʾ, extinction of personal consciousness, *Entwerden* in the language of the German mystics. In three stages man cleanses himself of his self. The passing-away of his evil qualities is followed by exclusive concentration on the thought of God. Thus freed from the world of perception, he may advance to the cessation of all conscious thought. When wholly immersed in the contemplation of the Divine, the mystic loses consciousness even of his loss of consciousness and attains to the highest beatitude of the soul.[109]

One feels reminded of the word of Plotinus (d. 270): "The Soul thus cleansed is all Idea and Reason, wholly free of body, intellective, entirely of that divine order from which the well-spring of Beauty rises and all the race of Beauty."[110] And this is how Plotinus tells the unspeakable experience. "Many times it has happened: Lifted out of the body into myself; becoming external to all other things and self-centered; beholding a marvellous beauty, then, more than ever, assured of community with the loftiest order; enacting the noblest life, acquiring identity with the divine."[111]

105 Qushairî, *op. cit.*, p. 15; trans. R. A. Nicholson, *JRAS*, 1906, pp. 308–9.

106 E.g., Sarrâj, pp. 23–24; Ibn Ḫaldûn, *Prolegomena*, III, 59 (trans., III, 85).

107 M. Smith (*Early Mysticism*, p. 209, n. 1) observes: "Euagrius Ponticus had already connected love and knowledge, 'For the end of love is the knowledge of God.' "

108 Hujwîrî, p. 180, quoted by Smith, *Early Mystic of Baghdad*, p. 231.*

109 Cf. R. A. Nicholson, *JRAS*, 1913, p. 61.

110 *Ennead* i. vi. 6; trans. S. MacKenna (London, 1917), p. 85.

111 *Ennead* iv. viii. 1; trans. S. MacKenna (London, 1924), p. 143.**

Obviously, the doctrine of the *fanâ*ʾ goes far to bridge the infinite abyss between God and man on which, one might say, Islamic doctrine is predicated. Fusion of the individual soul with the Divine Essence is hardly compatible with the absolute transcendence and remoteness of the koranic Allah. Orthodoxy struck back when al-Ḥallâj (d. 922) proclaimed the merging of the divine and the human spirit, identifying himself in his ecstasy with the Creative Truth.

> I am He whom I love, and He whom I love is I,
> We are two spirits dwelling in one body.
> If thou seest me, thou seest Him,
> And if thou seest Him, thou seest us both.[112]

The core of Islam seemed threatened by the idea of *ḥulûl*, incarnation, and the execution of the overbold visionary caused the mystics to explain carefully that *fanâ*ʾ did not mean loss of essence or destruction of personality.[113] What passes away in the mystic's ecstasy are the attributes, not the essence, of humanity. And, correspondingly, the mystic enters into God's qualities but not into his essence.[114]

Even as orthodoxy had to resist the pantheistic proclivities of the pious, it had to counteract those antinomian tendencies which everywhere and at all times accompany the process of interiorization of the religious experience. It would be wrong to assume that the many Ṣûfî brotherhoods, which were organized independent of one another in all parts of Islam, maintained the same attitude toward the religious law. Some groups insisted on the necessity of keeping the formal rules of the *sharî*ʿ*a* but added that these would become truly meaningful only when joined with the "works of the heart."[115] Others profess to discover a certain symbolical value in the ritualistic injunctions of the

[112] *Kitâb aṭ-Ṭawâsîn*, ed. L. Massignon (Paris, 1913), p. 134; trans. R. A. Nicholson, *The Idea of Personality in Ṣûfism* (Cambridge, 1923), p. 30.

[113] Cf. Hujwîrî, p. 243.

[114] Cf. Nicholson, *JRAS*, 1913, pp. 58–60. The Greek (but not the Roman) Church went somewhat further in allowing for "deification," θέωσις. Maximus Confessor (d. 662) explains deification as "sharing in the essence of God, through grace." Euagrius Ponticus (d. *ca.* 400) preceded, Symeon the Young followed, him in this doctrine. Cf., e.g., J. M. Hussey, *Church and Learning in the Byzantine Empire, 867–1185* (London, 1937), p. 223.

[115] Cf. Goldziher, *Vorlesungen*, p. 167.

canon law. A third section places the gnostic above the formalistic requirements of conventional religion. They would, in some cases, go so far as to consider him free not only of ritual but of moral precepts. The unreality of this world entails the nothingness of all its attributes. What, then, could the statutes and demands of society, what the tenets of this or that specific faith, mean to him who had seen through the meaningless mirage?

Law and dogma claimed a basis in reason. Dialectics was the means to ascend from truth to truth. The Ṣûfî spurned the logical process. Knowledge gained by demonstration was a very different thing from gnosis vouchsafed the intuitive soul. Not from outside with the aid of sagacious combinations of abstract concepts, but from within, under the dictation of the Friend who illuminates the self-searching heart, does the mystic arrive at his insights. Not ratiocination, but union with the One is the source of their cognition as it is the goal of their way.

By accepting the law but with important reservations and by deprecating the religious value of reason and rational proof, the Ṣûfîs, who, by the tenth century, had become the strongest spiritual force among the people, provoked a vehement opposition on the part of the official theologians and legists of all schools. In 1045 al-Qushairî, himself a Ṣûfî leader, wrote his famous *Risâla* with a view to bringing about reconciliation. The path and the truth presuppose the law. This, one might say, is the basis of his attempt at bridging the gap between official and mystical piety, between the rational and the intuitive life.*

Toward the end of the same century theology took the decisive step to guarantee emotional religion its proper place within the structure of orthodoxy. Al-Ghazâlî (d. 1111), deprecating the religious significance of legal hair-splitting and of scholastic oversubtlety, called for a renewal of religious fervor from the experience of the heart. He does not relinquish the principles of Islamic law, but he reinterprets this law as a means and a guide for the soul to work its salvation by winning its share of the divine secret that is accessible only when approached in fearful longing for the love of the Lord.

When al-Ghazâlî's ideas had been adopted by the consensus, the great movement of mysticism, which in spite of Greek (and

Indian) origin of much of its philosophical skeleton and terminology is the most significant genuinely Islamic contribution to the religious experience of mankind, had been secured for orthodox Islam. It is perhaps only a slight overstatement that almost all personal devotion of the individual Muslim down to this very day is somewhat tinged with Ṣûfism and thus inclined, be it ever so lightly, toward pantheism.

Ṣûfism has added the saint to the human typology of Islam. The Koran speaks of the "friends, *auliyâ*ʾ, of God,"[116] on whom no fear shall come and who shall not grieve. In another passage God himself is said to be the "friend, *walî*, of those who believe."[117] Popular sentiment identified those friends of the Lord with the perfect mystics in whom it recognized the supernatural powers of saintship. Here as often the consensus of the believers defeated the unambiguous doctrine of the Prophet that ruled out the existence of saintship even as it had defeated his assertion of his own fleshly nature. Popular piety canonized its saints during their lifetime. After their death their tombs became centers of worship to which people would pilgrimage for aid and blessing.

What makes the perfect mystic a saint is his intimacy with God which is documented by his ability to work miracles. "God has saints (*auliyâ*ʾ) whom He has specially distinguished by His friendship and whom He has chosen to be the governors of His Kingdom and has marked out to manifest His actions and has peculiarly favored with diverse kinds of miracles (*karâmât*) and has purged of natural corruptions and has delivered from subjection to their lower soul and passion, so that all their thoughts are of Him and their intimacy is with Him alone. . . . . He has made the Saints the governors of the universe; they have become entirely devoted to His business and have ceased to follow their sensual affections. Through the blessing of their advent the

[116] Koran 10:63. The concept of the "friend of God" is an heirloom of the Hellenistic world; cf., e.g., Epiktet *Diss.* iv. 3. 9 and the long list of Christian references, both Greek and Latin, in Holl, *Enthusiasmus*, p. 129, n. 1. In *ibid.* (p. 214) "Friend of God" appears as a frequent honorary epithet of the monk. Cf. also Augustine *Confessions* viii. 6, where an official upon relinquishing this world for the monastic life explains: "amicus autem dei, si voluero, ecce nunc fio."

[117] Koran 2:258.

rain falls from heaven, and through the purity of their lives the plants spring up from the earth, and through their spiritual influence the Muslims gain victories over the unbelievers."[118]

The doctrine did not, however, go unchallenged. "The Muᶜtazilites . . . . deny special privileges and miracles, which constitute the essence of saintship. They affirm that all Muslims are friends (*auliyâ*ᵓ) of God when they are obedient to Him, and that anyone who fulfils the ordinances of the faith and denies the attributes and vision of God . . . . and acknowledges only such obligations as are imposed by Reason, without regard to Revelation, is a 'friend' (*walî*)." Al-Ḥujwîrî adds maliciously that "all Muslims agree that such a person is a 'friend,' but a friend of the Devil."[119] But theology overruled the Muᶜtazilite protest. Ash-Shahrastânî asserts that "the miracles of the saints are intellectually possible and traditionally guaranteed." And he observes: "Individually these miracles might not be credible but their cumulative testimony is proof that the miracles happened at the hands of the saints."[120]

Opposition against basing saintship on *charismata, karâmât*, came from the saints themselves. Abû Saᶜîd b. abî ᵓl-Ḫair, himself a recognized saint, was told: "So-and-so walks on the water."

"It is easy enough: frogs and waterfowl do it," he replied.

"So-and-so flies in the air," they said.

"So do birds and insects," he replied.

"So-and-so goes from one town to another in a moment of time," they said.

"Satan," he rejoined, "goes in one moment from the East to the West. Things like this have no great value. The true saint goes in and out among the people and eats and sleeps with them and buys and sells in the market and marries and takes part in social intercourse, and never forgets God for a single moment."[121]

No protest, however, was of any avail. The people got the saints they wanted. With admiration did the populace accept

[118] Hujwîrî, pp. 212–13.

[119] Hujwîrî, p. 215.

[120] Shahrastânî, *Nihâya*, p. 497; trans., p. 157.

[121] Nicholson, *Studies*, p. 67.*

the unmeasured self-glorification of some of their *auliyâ'*. To describe his rank with the Lord, ʿAbdalqâdir al-Jîlânî (d. 1166) said of himself: "Before the sun rises, he greets me; before the year begins, it greets me and reveals to me everything that will happen during its course. I swear by the majesty of the Lord that the saved and the damned are brought before me and that my eye rests on the well-guarded tablet (of destiny). I dive into the oceans of God's sciences and I have seen Him with my eyes. I am the living proof of His existence, I am the deputy of the Prophet and his heir on earth."[122]

While recognizing the *karâmât* of the saints, theology was careful to set them apart from the *muʿjizât* of the Prophets. Both kinds of miracles are alike in that it is God who displays the miraculous power in the prophet or the saint, as neither prophet nor saint possesses any control of his own over nature. But "the miracle of the saint consists in an answer to prayer, or the completion of a spiritual state, or the granting of power to perform an act, or the supplying of the means of subsistence requisite and due to them, in a manner extraordinary: whereas the marvels accorded to prophets consist either of producing something from nothing, or of changing the essential nature of an object."[123]

This definition needs supplementation: "*Muʿjizât* involve publicity and *karâmât* secrecy, because the result of the former is to affect others, while the latter are peculiar to the person by whom they are performed. Again, the doer of *muʿjizât* is quite sure that he has wrought an extraordinary miracle, whereas the doer of *karâmât* cannot be sure whether he has really wrought a miracle or whether he is insensibly deceived. He who performs *muʿjizât* has authority over the law . . . . ; on the other hand, he who performs *karâmât* has no choice but to resign himself (to God's will) and to accept the ordinances that are laid down upon him."[124]

[122] Goldziher, *Muh. Stud.*, II, 289–90. It may be noted here that the Greek Church did not contest the right of the faithful to honor persons of outstanding piety as saints, even during their lifetime.

[123] Kalâbâḏî, p. 60.

[124] Hujwîrî, pp. 220–21. Schacht (*op. cit.*, pp. 65–66) quotes al-Baghdâdî's (d. 1037) more systematic exposition of the subject.

The saint is the member of a hierarchy, headed by the *quṭb*, or axis, who wanders through the world, always unknown and frequently invisible. It is this hierarchy "by which the invisible government of the world is carried out."[125] The mystic speculation of the thirteenth and fourteenth centuries identifies prophets and saints as "Perfect Men." The Perfect Man, the *anthropos teleios* of the Gnostics, is a cosmic power. "He unites the One and the Many, so that the universe depends on him for its continued existence."[126] "As a microcosmos of a high order he reflects not only the powers of nature but also the divine powers as in a mirror."[127]

In every age the Perfect Men are an outward manifestation of the essence of Mohammed, who thus is shown as an Islamic Logos. Mohammed appears as the ideal type of humanity, the Perfect Man; and the Perfect Man is "a copy of God."[128] It is in Mohammed as his mirror that the Lord's names and attributes should be seen. The beauty of this world is borrowed from him and subsists through his Light. This pre-existent Light that had been revealed in all the prophets from Adam to Jesus continues to affect the world through the saints who commune with Mohammed in the oneness won by love.

In this fashion the circle is closed. The Messenger of God is vindicated in his supernatural uniqueness when the power of the mystic saint who upholds the world is comprehended as issuing from his participation in the prophetic essence of the Perfect Man whose "heart stands over against the Throne of God."[129]

125 Macdonald, *Attitude*, p. 163.

126 Nicholson, *Studies*, p. 78.

127 *Ibid.*, p. 82, reproducing an idea of Goldziher's. On the Perfect Man cf. also D. B. Macdonald, *Moslem World*, XXII (1932), 163–65.

128 ʿAbdalkarîm al-Jîlî (d. between 1406 and 1417), quoted by Nicholson, *Studies*, p. 106, and *Personality*, p. 60.

129 Al-Jîlî, quoted by Nicholson, *Studies*, p. 106.

CHAPTER FIVE

THE BODY POLITIC: LAW AND THE STATE

I

ISLAM is the community of Allah. He is the living truth to which it owes its life. He is the center and the goal of its spiritual experience. But he is also the mundane head of his community which he not only rules but governs. He is the reason for the state's existence, he is the principle of unity, the *Staatsgedanke,* which both upholds and justifies the continuance of the commonwealth. This makes the Muslim army the "Army of Allah," the Muslim treasury, "the Treasury of Allah." What is more, it places the life of the community in its entirety as well as the private lives of the individual members under his direct legislative and supervisory power.

The burden of lawmaking rests on Allah's shoulders. His ordinances may vary in scope but not in stringency. Every order issuing from him carries the same compulsion. It is not for man to grade his rulings as more or less important. Nor is there any differential to separate the sphere of his direct interference from a neutral or purely human zone. The only indifferent areas are those where lack of information bars man from the knowledge of Allah's detailed regulations, and by various methods the community labors to supply the missing instructions.

By its very nature Allah's word must be considered final. He is known to have changed his mind a certain number of times abrogating specific injunctions given his Prophet and replacing them by "equally good or better ones."[1] The death of the Prophet ended this means of organic, or opportunistic, change.

Conflicts between the inspired precedent of the Prophet's *sunna* and the inspired stipulation of the Koran were but apparent and could be resolved through well-directed ingenuity.

[1] Koran 2:100.

It fell thus to the lot of the legist to arrange the relatively restricted number of explicit regulations and the much more numerous records of the usage in the earliest times of the faith in such a fashion as would clearly describe the precedent of the golden prime of the Muslim community.

The ten years of the Prophet's rule in Medina and perhaps the thirty years following his death constituted the age in which human society had come as near perfection as could be hoped for. So the institutional, legal, financial, and, of course, religious precedent of that period was to yield the terms, concepts, and prescriptions of that perfect order which was Allah's.

The political situation of the subsequent times discouraged the majority of the legists from active participation in the government. But even the most harmonious co-operation of jurisprudents and executive officialdom could not have prevented the gap between the ideal and the actual, the normative and the practical, the precedent of sacred law and the makeshift decision of the executive order, from widening until it became unbridgeable. The pious condemned the ruler's deviations from the established norm of the Prophet's days, and in fear for their souls they evaded his call when he summoned them to take office. However ready the state might be to accept the legist's pronouncements, too many emergencies of change would call for arbitrary rulings, and the faithful would risk his salvation by lending his authority to the ephemeral iniquities of power.

Thus the government of Allah and the government of the sultan grew apart. Social and political life was lived on two planes, on one of which happenings would be spiritually valid but actually unreal, while on the other no validity could ever be aspired to. The law of God failed because it neglected the factor of change to which Allah had subjected his creatures. When legal theory stooped to take this element into account, it succeeded in reaching a workable compromise. But it had, unwittingly perhaps, relinquished that grandiose dream of a social body operating perpetually under the immutable law which God had revealed in the fulness of time.

To be sure, God's will was manifest in the transformation of his community. Still there was deterioration and failure in falling away from the standards set in the Prophet's age. To this very day that failure continues, and the Muslim lives under two laws: one, eternal, applicable to him because of his membership in his faith; the other, revocable and subject to modification, a device to cope with the complications and to bridle the sinfulness of this our irremediably backsliding existence.

II

Law, constituting the will of God and in no way depending for its authority on human reason or human values, purposes to limit the original liberty of man with a view to his own benefit and that of society.

The original state of man is liberty. It is the exigencies of social life that compel the abridgment of this liberty. Mohammed voiced God's desire to attune the law to man's frailty. "Allah wishes to make it easy for you, and does not wish to make it difficult for you."[2] The Prophet's common sense discouraged exaggeration of any kind. Law is intended as the complement of faith regulating man's actions even as faith regulates his beliefs. Happiness and its transcendental counterpart, salvation, reward the believer.

From these starting-points, "Islamic jurists have reached a twofold conclusion: (1) Liberty finds its limit in its very nature, because liberty unlimited would mean self-destruction—and that limit or boundary is the legal norm, or Law. (2) No limit is arbitrary, because it is determined by its utility or the greatest good of the individual or of society. Utility, which is the foundation of law, traces also its boundary and extent."[3]

Accordingly, Muslims have defined jurisprudence as "knowledge of the practical rules of religion." The Muslim legists scrutinize human actions and classify them in agreement with Allah's rulings. This procedure makes jurisprudence, in Ibn Ḫaldûn's words, "the knowledge of the rules of God which concern the actions of persons who own themselves bound to obey

[2] Koran 2:181.

[3] D. de Santillana, in *The Legacy of Islam*, ed. Sir. Th. W. Arnold and A. Guillaume (Oxford, 1931), p. 292.

the Law respecting what is required, forbidden, recommended, disapproved, or merely permitted."[4]

The body of these rules is called *fiqh,* which originally and even as late as the Koran means merely "knowledge" of any kind. Together with *kalâm,* scholastic theology, *fiqh* builds the *sharîca,* the "straight path," the Sacred Law, where "sacred" relates to the source rather than the subject matter of the regulations.

In its purposing, then, *fiqh* is "like the *jurisprudentia* of the Romans, *rerum divinarum atque humanarum notitia* and in its widest sense it covers all aspects of religious, political and civil life. In addition to the laws regulating ritual and religious observances, as far as concerns performance and abstinence, it includes the whole field of family law, the law of inheritance, of property and of contract, in a word, provisions for all the legal questions that arise in social life, it also includes criminal law and procedure and finally constitutional law and laws regulating the administration of the state and the conduct of war."[5]

Before the word *fiqh* attained to this comprehensive meaning it had been used together with, or in opposition to, *ᶜilm,* which denoted the accurate knowledge of Koran, tradition and legal precedent, whereas *fiqh* carried the connotation of independent finding of judgment. Thus it could be said, Wisdom consisted of Koran, *ᶜilm* and *fiqh.*[6]

The encyclopedic system of jurisprudence, worked out, to use this old terminology, through *ᶜilm* and *fiqh,* arranges the individual subjects in a manner strikingly different from that suggested by Western legal thinking—even if we overlook the absence in *fiqh* of the fundamental Western division of private and public law and if we acquiesce in having the criminal law distributed over a number of sections.

The Shâfiᶜite *faqîh,* Abû Shujâᶜ al-Iṣfahânî (eleventh century), divides the material into sixteen books which treat of cere-

[4] That is, legally and religiously indifferent. *Prolegomena,* III, 1; trans., III, 1. The above rendering is that of R. Levy, *An Introduction to the Sociology of Islam* (London, 1931–33), I, 213.

[5] Goldziher, *EI,* II, 101.*

[6] *Ibid.*

monial purity, prayer, the poor rate, fasting, pilgrimage,[7] barter and other business transactions, inheritance and wills, marriage and related subjects, crimes of violence to the person, restrictive ordinances (e.g., concerning fornication, drinking, apostasy; a chapter of miscellanies), holy war, hunting and the slaughter of animals, racing and shooting with the bow, oaths and vows, judgment and evidence (i.e., legal procedure), and manumission of slaves.[8]

The actual codification of the good life as proposed by *fiqh* would, of course, depend on the source material which the legislator would recognize as authoritative. The assumption seemed obvious that the statute of Allah's commonwealth ought to be promulgated by the Lord himself. But equally obvious was the observation that he had not done so. Only by a dangerous extension of the interpretative abilities could it be maintained that the Koran supplemented by the Prophet's *sunna* contained or implied the answers to every question brought up by the change of events, the change of conditions. But to admit any other source of law was to acknowledge the impossibility of building the life of the individual and the life of society exclusively on the command of Allah, it meant the renunciation of the ideal for whose realization the Muslim community had been called into being. Not to admit any other source was, on the other hand, a dishonest evasion of the facts; at best, a pious fiction bound to result in disastrous inadequacy in meeting the exigencies of everyday life.

Viewed in this light, the acrimonious fight among the law schools concerning additional sources of legislation entirely loses the character of a squabble over words. In the last analysis no legist could escape the necessity of using "opinion" or "analogy" besides Koran and *sunna*, whether he openly acknowledged them as "bases," *uṣûl*, or whether he admitted them cov-

[7] These four books are devoted to the so-called "pillars," *arkân*, of Islam, the basic minimum obligations that rest upon each and every believer. These *arkân* include the pronouncing of the creed, *shahâda*, at least once during maturity of age.

[8] Cf. D. B. Macdonald, *Development of Muslim Theology, Jurisprudence and Constitutional Theory* (New York, 1903), pp. 351–57. Already ash-Shâfiʿî's (d. 819) *Kitâb al-umm* shows essentially the same structure.

ertly through subtle and elaborate interpretation of the Holy Book. The identity of their plight and the essential identity of their solutions lend the disputations of the schools a flavor of futility. However, while a sizable proportion of their debates and of their differences amply warrants this condemnation, the great cause at stake actually resolved itself into the burning question whether or not the Lord had revealed the full statute of a *civitas Dei*, whether or not the concept of divine rulership of man and society could be carried through to its logical conclusion, whether or not through a compromise a human element had to be admitted into the structure.

The Prophet apparently was unaware of the dilemma. He does not seem to have considered the completeness of revelation or custom. We are told that once he was sending a judge to the Yemen and asked him on what he would base his legal decisions.

"On the Koran," he replied.

"But if that contains nothing to the purpose?"

"Then upon your usage."

"But if that also fails you?"

"Then I will follow my own opinion." And the Prophet approved his purpose.[9]

And even under ᶜUmar II (717–20) the problem was still faced without much theoretical reflection. When the *qâḍî* of Egypt referred to this prince "a case dealing with an assault of a particular kind by a youth on a girl, the caliph replied that he could find no precedent for such a case and that the *qâḍî* must use his own judgment."[10] But the next generation awakened to the importance of admitting or banning "opinion," *ra*ᵓ*y*, as a source of law.

The great orthodox schools differ in the early phases of their development according as they allow or disallow the validity of the *ra*ᵓ*y*.[11] And it is worth noting that the later the date of a school the more intolerant it proves itself of *ra*ᵓ*y*—each of the great teachers, Abû Ḥanîfa (d. 767), Mâlik b. Anas (d. 795), ash-Shâfiᶜî (d. 819), Aḥmad b. Ḥanbal (d. 855), and Dâ'ûd aẓ-

[9] Macdonald, *op. cit.*, p. 86; also Goldziher, *Die Ẓâhiriten* (Leipzig, 1884), p. 8.

[10] Levy, *op. cit.*, I, 235.

[11] Goldziher, *Ẓâhiriten*, p. 3.

Ẓâhirî (d. 883), is less inclined to admit *ra'y* than his predecessor.

Qiyâs (analogy, analogical deduction), which came to be admitted as a source of law by all but one of the four great law schools—only Ibn Ḥanbal rejected it—represents an attempt at restricting or at least disciplining the use of the *ra'y*. There are two ways in which *qiyâs* can be practiced. The analogy may be deduced from a material similarity in the configuration of the two cases, or problems, one of them already decided by Koran or *sunna* indicating the appropriate decision of the other. Or a more liberal attempt could be made to co-ordinate cases by investigating the *ʿilla* (ratio, motive) of the koranic provision. In judging the present problem, the same *ʿilla* must be found as prompted the Prophet's verdict.

The Koran forbids wine because it causes intoxication. In passing on the permissibility of another beverage, its intoxicating potential will have to be made the basis of legal opinion. In the same fashion the penal provisions of the Koran touching theft can be extended to cover burglary as well. The *ʿilla* of the koranic provision,[12] viz., the punishment of "taking secretly the possessions of another," can easily be shown to apply to burglary, too.[13]

It will be admitted that the gain in prophetic authority obtained by such restriction of the *ra'y* was bought at the price of a certain crudity of classification, since, to limit consideration to the present example, burglary and theft are not identical offenses nor were they so considered by the Muslim legists, who, on the strength of *qiyâs*, found themselves compelled to establish identical penalties for both types of lawbreaking.

The advocates of *qiyâs* looked to the Koran for support, but they met with slight success, and their opponents could with even greater ease adduce counterarguments culled from the Book.[14] The authorities who refused to admit the *qiyâs* were advised that they, too, applied analogical deduction in their legal reasonings: that, in fact, no legal finding could be arrived at

[12] Koran 5:42.

[13] Cf. Levy, *op. cit.*, I, 237–38.

[14] Koran 4:62, 4:85, and 59:2 (a.o.) were adduced in support of *qiyâs;* Koran 6:38, in combating its lawfulness.

from the sacred text and the *sunna* unless the arguments or reasons prompting the divine decisions or the Prophet's actions were established. And it is pathetic to hear the deniers of the *qiyâs* defend their position with the allegation that they did not subject the passages in question to the processes of analogy, but only stated explicitly what those passages stated implicitly—that, in other words, they were dedicated to exegesis, not to deduction.[15]

The demands of life necessitated further concessions. In connection with the *qiyâs* the Ḥanafites developed the principle of *istiḥsân*, or "regarding as better." Carried to its logical conclusion, this principle would have allowed the complete setting-aside of the revelatory basis of the law in favor of local custom, popular prejudice, or simple expediency. It provided for the relinquishing of the *qiyâs* for what would be more convenient for the people in the particular case.[16] The Mâlikites replace *istiḥsân* with *istiṣlâḥ*, or "regarding in the general interest," allowing considerations of the commonweal to enter into the motivation of a legal opinion. It is in no way surprising that bitter opposition stunted the growth of these trends which might have led to a system of equity.[17]

The means by which Muslim law succeeded at once in preserving its foundations of Koran and *sunna* and in attuning its provisions to the ever changing needs of different places and times was the recognition of the *ijmâ*ᶜ, the consensus, as another source of law. It is the consensus which can accept an innovation, at first considered heretical, and, by accepting it, make it part and parcel of the *sunna*, overriding traditional views in its way. Independent of "written, traditional or inferred law" *ijmâ*ᶜ constitutes the application of the Roman principle "consuetudinem aut rerum perpetuo similiter judicatarum auctoritatem vim legis obtinere deberi."[18] The *ijmâ*ᶜ of the doctors functions like the Roman *consensus prudentum*.

[15] Cf. Snouck Hurgronje, *Revue de l'histoire des religions*, XXXVII (1898), 187; Th. W. Juynboll, *Handbuch des islamischen Gesetzes* (Leiden and Leipzig, 1910), p. 51, n. 2.

[16] Goldziher, *Ẓâhiriten*, p. 12.

[17] Cf. Macdonald, *op. cit.*, p. 87.

[18] I.e., usage and precedent are to obtain force of law. Quoted by Goldziher, *EI*, II, 101–2.

Being empowered to set a new *sunna*, the *ijmâ*ᶜ outranks the *sunna*. The Koran says: "We have made you a people in the middle."[19] This, al-Baiḍâwî (d. 1282) explains, is to say that the Muslims are fair-minded and purified in thought and action. They will strike the golden means between avarice and profligacy, temerity and cowardice, etc. Their character being as it is, the koranic line implies that their *ijmâ*ᶜ is authoritative, for, were they to agree on something vain, it would reflect upon their sense of balance.[20] More conclusive is the second part of the koranic verse where it is stated that this was done to make them witnesses in regard to the people. Elsewhere the Book assails the separatist. "But him who splits from the messenger after the Guidance has become clear to him, and follows any other way than that of the believers, We shall consign to what he has turned to, and roast in Gehenna—a bad place to go to!"[21]

By asserting that "never will my community be united in an error," the Prophet eliminated the uneasiness that the consensus might, on occasion, be misguided and thence misguiding. In the beginning the consensus of the Companions was considered authoritative. Mâlik thought the consensus of the holy places, Mecca and Medina, decisive. Gradually *ijmâ*ᶜ came to be interpreted as the agreement of those competent to judge in religious matters; it became the agreement of the learned. There being no organization of the learned, it is not possible to poll them and to obtain a decision on a moot question.

The *ijmâ*ᶜ, then, cannot be determined by resolutions of any kind regarding future settlement of this or the other problem. It rather is to be determined by retrospection. At any given moment one is in a position to realize that such and such opinions, such and such institutions, have become accepted through *ijmâ*ᶜ. Deviation from the *ijmâ*ᶜ is unbelief, *kufr*.

The doctrinal area covered by decision of *ijmâ*ᶜ—these decisions may be expressed in statements, actions, or silence—constantly widens as the scope of what is left to its decision as steadily narrows. The questions to be settled by future *ijmâ*ᶜ

[19] Koran 2:137.

[20] Al-Baiḍâwî, *Tafsîr*, ed. H. O. Fleischer (Leipzig, 1846–48), I, 88–89.

[21] Koran 4:115.

will tend to become ever more minute and insignificant. This natural development diminishes considerably the potentialities of *ijmâ*ᶜ in reforming Islam. It may, of course, develop that, at some future time, the agreement will lend the *ijmâ*ᶜ wider scope so as to allow it to sanction far-reaching changes concerning validity and content of the *fiqh*.

The consensus has, in former times, compelled the admission of the cult of the saints as well as that of the infallibility, *ᶜiṣma*, of the Prophet, in both cases disregarding koranic statements and the early *sunna*.* Thus, the *ijmâ*ᶜ could, for instance, by shifting its stand on *ijtihâd*, remove one of the main obstacles to the modernization of the Islamic structure.[22] A tradition of the Prophet has it that he who applies himself to form his own opinion through his personal exertion (*mujtahid*) will receive a reward even though he reach the wrong conclusion. The fallible *ijtihâd* of the individual would always be corrected by the inerrant *ijmâ*ᶜ of the community. However, the view has been held, and sanctioned by *ijmâ*ᶜ, that with the passing of the founders of the great law schools the *ijtihâd muṭlaq*, the absolute, i.e., unrestricted *ijtihâd*, had disappeared. Their successors were entitled to *ijtihâd* only within the framework of their respective schools, and the subsequent generations of jurisconsults possess an even more reduced authority in that they may answer specific legal questions on the basis of their knowledge of precedent. This commonly accepted theory was, from time to time, contested by theologians who claimed farther-reaching rights of *ijtihâd* for themselves. The *ijmâ*ᶜ has, so far, sided against their claim. But a reversal of popular sentiment could and would reopen the "door of personal exertion" and thereby possibly pave the way for a thorough overhauling of the *sharîᶜa*.

Ash-Shâfiᶜî, to whom Islam owes the first theoretical exposition of *ijmâ*ᶜ, quotes the Prophet as saying that in three matters the heart of a Muslim will never fall into error: sincerity toward Allah, sound advice to the fellow-Muslim, and clinging to the Muslim community. And ash-Shâfiᶜî explains such clinging to mean just one thing: Since actually the Muslim community is widely dispersed and most places are inhabited by both be-

[22] On *ijtihâd* cf. D. B. Macdonald, *EI*, II, 448–49.

lievers and unbelievers, both pious and impious, attachment to the physical community is irrelevant if not impossible. Therefore, the Prophet's injunction can have no other meaning than to require the faithful to consider lawful or unlawful whatever the community so considers, to hold what the community holds in point of doctrine. Error springs from segregation. No error is conceivable within the community with regard to the implications of Koran, *sunna*, and *qiyâs*—if God willeth.[23]

This view, and with it the whole theory of *ijmâᶜ*, became tenable only through a significant addition, to wit, the doctrine that, on secondary points, divergence of opinion, *iḫtilâf*, was admissible. "The variety of opinion is a blessing to my community." With these words the Prophet is made to forsake the absolutist claim of divine law, the idea of the exclusivity of the one inspired truth down to the last detail of belief and conduct. The playing-down of the differences between the four great *maḏâhib*[24] which, for all practical purposes, divide the Sunnite world among themselves is justified by the minor nature of their disagreements. Without the recognition of their equal standing before God the fanatical struggle between them as it threatened to develop in the fifth and sixth centuries A.H. would have rent asunder the unity of Islam. So once more the exigencies of real life forced the abandonment or at least the curtailment of the expectation to organize life in submission to direct and unequivocal regulation from the Almighty.

The distribution of the leading schools was influenced by political events as well as by the location of the schools' original seat. Teachers who lived too far from the beaten paths of travel would find it difficult to find students.

At present the Ḥanafite rite—the only one to permit recita-

[23] Abridged from ash-Shâfiᶜî, *Risâla* (Cairo, 1321), p. 65; a full German translation in Schacht, *op. cit.*, pp. 25–26. It hardly needs to be said that the Shîᶜa rejects the *ijmâᶜ* of the Sunnites. Nor do they accept *raʾy*. But they maintain the continuance of the *ijtihâd muṭlaq* exercised by authorities who wield powers that properly belong to the Hidden Imâm; see later, chap. vi, Part III. The kinship of the *ijmâᶜ* concept with, and most likely its descent from, the Stoic-Epicurean idea of the demonstrative force of the κοιναὶ ἔννοιαι, is fairly obvious. Cf., among many passages, Cicero *De natura deorum* i. 16 and Seneca *Ad Lucilium* cxvii. 6.

[24] Sg. *maḏhab*, rite, school.

tion of the Koran in a language other than Arabic—dominates India and most of the countries formerly subjected to the Ottoman Turks; the Shâfiᶜites, southern Arabia, the Dutch Indies, Lower Egypt, and Syria; the Mâlikites hold Upper Egypt and North Africa; while the Ḥanbalites are practically confined to the Wahhâbî territory in central Arabia.

Despite the triviality of their distinctions, transfer from one rite to another is generally frowned upon. It is approved of only if suggested by migration to a country dominated by a different rite or else if undertaken to evade legal inconvenience, such as might result from the absence, in some territory, of a judge of one's original school. Political developments have, of course, frequently entailed wholesale changes in the distribution of the rites. Thus the Ottoman Turks forced the transfer of Iraq from the Shâfiᶜite rite to the Ḥanafite in the sixteenth century.

Within the limitations incident to the realities of history the Muslim has tried to build up a life under God rather than in God. In spite of extensive borrowings from the law of the countries he conquered, the *fiqh* as a system is profoundly original. Fortified behind his law, the Muslim braved successfully the vicissitudes of time. But the observation is saddening that much of his earthly success and of the solidity of his establishment in this world is due to his readiness to compromise by admitting the changing verities of this life into the unchanging verity of revelation.

III

Nowhere was the discrepancy between the normative dreams of the lawyers and the actual conditions of life so loud and so hurtful to the community as in the sphere of political organization.* No aspect of Muslim civilization lends itself more convincingly to the demonstration of that grandiose and sublime failure to strike a balance between aspiration and achievement, that incapacity to institutionalize with reasonable adequacy the divinely revealed principles of the body politic so keenly grasped and so unrealistically pursued by the legists. But in the end the cleavage between the real and the ideal, becoming intolerable and ludicrous, forces the renunciation of the ideal without allowing more than the thinnest disguise of such abdication to protect the conscience of the community which continues to think of itself as the community of Allah.

Mohammed had set up his followers as a theocracy, a commonwealth in which the political power was held by the Lord, who had it administered by his apostle and deputy, the prophet Mohammed. His divine mission conveyed to him political power. The community knew no distinction between the temporal and the spiritual when it came to defining this power. The split in Christendom between church and state was unthinkable in Islam. The temporal power was at one with the spiritual; the state was the church in that it safeguarded and expanded the area of the faith and took care of the business of the believers.* But it was restricted to administration; it was reduced to an executive function as soon as the Prophet died and Allah ceased to manifest the faith through his messenger and friend.

Thus, religion and politics, or administration, became inextricably joined in the task of the functionary of the early state. The caliph ᶜUmar is supposed to have addressed his governor at Baṣra in these terms:

"People have an aversion from their rulers, and I trust to Allah that you and I are not overtaken by it, stealthily and unexpectedly, or by hatreds conceived against us. See to the execution of the laws even if it be for only one hour of the day, and if two matters present themselves to you, the one godly and the other worldly, then choose as your portion the way of God. For the present world will perish and the other world remain. Strike terror into wrongdoers and make heaps of mutilated limbs out of them. Visit the sick among Muslims, attend their funerals, open your gate to them and give heed in person to their affairs, for you are but a man amongst them except that God has allowed you the heaviest burden."[25]

When the newly converted chief of an Arab tribe said to the Prophet, "Thou art our prince," the Prophet answered quickly: "The prince is God, not I."[26]

The only type of ruler the Arab had known in his own country

[25] Ibn Qutaiba, *ᶜUyûn al-aḫbâr*, ed. C. Brockelmann (Berlin and Strassburg, 1900–1908), p. 28; trans. Levy, *op. cit.*, I, 283–84.

[26] Santillana, *loc. cit.*, p. 286.

had been the *sayyid,* the chieftain of a tribe (or possibly leader of an agglomeration of tribes). The *sayyid* held this office thanks to his personal prestige, which in part was due to his noble lineage, but which mostly sprang from his qualities as a leader, his generosity, and his ability to deal with people. The *sayyid* had no power to enforce his bidding. Sometimes he became guilty of arrogancy, but as a rule his prerogatives did not infringe on the essential equality of all members of the tribe. He was freely accessible. No ceremonial protected him and his position. His heir would succeed him only if his capabilities recommended him, but socially the descendant of a reverenced leader had a considerable advantage.

ᶜÂmir b. aṭ-Ṭufail, a famous *sayyid,* contemporary of the Prophet, said:

As for me, though I be the son of the Chief of ᶜÂmir, and the Knight of the tribe, called on for help in every adventure,
It was not for my kinsmen's sake that ᶜÂmir made me their chief: God forbid that I should exalt myself on mother's or father's fame!
But it was because I guard their peculiar land, and shield them from annoy, and hurl myself against him that strikes at their peace.[27]

The princes of the Umayyad dynasty (661–750) tried to maintain the mores and mannerisms of the *sayyid,* although intrinsically their position as rulers of an enormous empire, as successors, caliphs, of the Prophet, and as "Princes of the Believers" (*amîr al-muʾminîn*) had completely outgrown frame and scope of the ancient ideal.

The accession of the ᶜAbbâsids, made possible largely through the support of Persian Muslims, brought to the fore the humanly less attractive but politically more adequate concept of kingship to which the Iranians had been accustomed from their native rulers. The prince, isolated from the uniform herd of his subjects, consecrated by divine designation for his office, legitimized by his descent from a long line of kings, guarded by an elaborate etiquette devised to guard his person from defiling contact with the lowly crowd and to overawe the slaves over whom he had been set by the Lord of the Worlds[28]—this type of

[27] *Dîwân,* ed. and trans. C. J. Lyall (Leiden and London, 1913), I, 1–3.

[28] On the influence of Persian on Byzantine ceremonial cf. the interesting paper by E. Stein, *Byzantinisch-Neugriechische Jahrbücher,* I (1920), 50–89.

despot now merged successfully with the theocratic representative of Allah and, much less successfully, with the Arab chieftain of olden days. It would seem that the ᶜAbbâsids attempted upon occasion to exhibit different aspects of their kingship to the several sections of their subjects. But, on the whole, the mores of the desert receded. Legitimistic and pietistic absolutism, attractive to the rulers and supported by the cultural superiority of its Persian proponents, steadily gained ground, mitigated only by the time-honored administrative weakness of the Eastern state.

Each of the three concepts of rulership carried its own principle of succession. The *sayyid*'s office was perpetuated by the consensus of the tribesmen; the Persian kings held sway on the strength of their legitimate descent from their predecessor; the theocratic state, however, allowed of two principles to fill the vacancy on the throne. Since the Lord was not pleased to continue the prophetic office by raising a spiritual successor to Mohammed, either kinship to the deceased Apostle of God might entitle to succession on the ground that a spark of his inspiration, or of the divine substance distinguishing him as Allah's elect, would continue in his lineage, or else more crudely that Mohammed had designated his cousin and son-in-law, ᶜAlî b. abî Ṭâlib, as his executor, *waṣî;* or, the consensus of the community might intrust one of the Muslims with taking care of the business of the state as a procurator and manager.

The latter view won out in the beginning. But, while the function of the ruler remained defined in this manner, the principle of heredity soon was admitted *de facto;* and, after it had been strengthened by the Persian tradition, no attempt was made over more than five centuries to displace the ᶜAbbâsids, relatives of the Prophet, from the caliphal throne.

On these somewhat slender premises theory developed its idea of the caliphate, harmonizing the divergent forces of history, aiming at glorification of the Muslim state, and laboring to make actual conditions measure up to the demands of the ideal.

Al-Mâwardî (d. 1058) begins his *Statutes of Rulership* (*al-aḥkâm as-sulṭâniyya*) with the statement that the imamate (or caliphate) was divinely appointed to supplant the office of prophethood that had expired with the death of Mohammed.[29] It purposes the defense of the faith and the administration of this world. It is a necessary institution. Some base it on reason, because man would live in lawlessness without a leader; some on law, because the caliph is primarily concerned with its maintenance. To appoint an *imâm* is a compulsory duty of the Muslim community. The Koran enjoins obedience to the ruler.[30] The *imâm*'s authority is therefore of divine origin. The Koran says that, were there any gods except Allah in the heaven or on the earth, both heaven and earth would go to ruin.[31] Correspondingly there can be only one *imâm* on earth. Should different sections of the Muslim world each elect an *imâm*, such election would be invalid. This view is proffered, although, by the time al-Mâwardî wrote, Islam had acquiesced for more than a hundred years in a multiplicity of caliphates (the caliphate of the ᶜAbbâsids in Baghdad, that of the Fâṭimids in Egypt and Syria, and that of the Umayyads in Spain). Ibn Ḫaldûn is more realistic when he acknowledges the legality of two *imâms* holding office at the same time provided only there was sufficient distance between them to prevent friction and confusion.[32]

The imamate is an elective office. Every Muslim man of good moral character and possessing the knowledge and the judgment requisite to discern the qualities required in an *imâm* is qualified as an elector. Nearness to the seat of the caliphate will influence, but should not decide, who actually participates in the election. The number of electors necessary for a valid election is controversial. Precedent deriving from the accession of ᶜUṯmân points to a minimum of five. Others carry this attempt to reconcile the theory of election with the actual procedure even further by allowing for a quorum of no more than three, or even for one single elector whose verdict is able to confer the caliphate on a qualified candidate, thus obligating the communi-

[29] The following presentation is mostly based on al-Mâwardî (ed. M. Enger [Bonn 1853], trans. E. Fagnan [Algiers, 1915]) and Ibn Ḫaldûn, *Prolegomena,* I, 278 ff. (trans., I, 318 ff.); cf. also Levy, *op. cit.,* I, 295–317.

[30] Cf., e.g., Koran 4:62.

[31] Koran 21:22.

[32] *Prolegomena,* I, 347–48 (trans., I, 391–92).

ty to obedience. The reduction of the body of electors to a membership of one is tantamount to the acknowledgment of accession through appointment by the predecessor, for which method history provided many an example.

To be eligible as *imâm*, a person must meet these requirements: (1) he must be morally beyond cavil; (2) he must be possessed of such knowledge as will enable him to pass personally on questions of government that will present themselves to him; (3) his hearing, speech, and sight must be unimpaired; (4) he must enjoy soundness of limbs; (5) he must possess the judgment and the experience necessary for the conduct of affairs; (6) he must show the courage and energy required to protect the *dâr al-Islâm* and to fight the enemy; and (7) he must be descended of the Quraish, the clan of the Prophet.[33]

This last condition was not universally accepted. The Ḫârijite sectarians held that any pious Muslim could be invested with the imamate—even an Abyssinian slave. And Ibn Ḫaldûn feels that the requirement of Qurashî descent is due to erroneous interpretation of various *ḥadîṯ*.

Disability to carry out his duties disqualifies the incumbent. The caliph cannot continue in office when taken prisoner by a foreign power. Since from the tenth century the caliphs in Baghdad had been little more than figureheads under the thumb of generals, the legists ruled that, as long as the actual potentate governs in the best interest of the Muslims, the *imâm*, although personally deprived of executive power, may stay in office. Should this proviso, however, not be fulfilled, then the Muslims are to look out for someone powerful enough to restore the caliph to his rightful position. One may perhaps detect in this stipulation the recognition of a limited right (or, duty) of revolution.

The prerogatives of having his name mentioned in the *ḫuṭba*, the address of the preacher in the Friday service, of having his

[33] It may be noted that al-Fârâbî (d. 950) in his *Model City*, which is inspired by Platonic and Neo-Platonic ideas but which has remained inconsequential in the development of Arabic political theory, lays down about the same requirements for the ruler whom he considers Man become active Intellect through control of the Intelligibilia. Cf. F. Dieterici, *Der Musterstaat des Alfârâbî* (Leiden, 1900), pp. 92–96.

name on the coins, of attending service in the *maqṣûra,* the "confined part" of the mosque, and of wearing the Prophet's mantle, *burda,* remained with the caliph even in the worst debasement of his position.

Theory, however, circumscribed his functions as rather vaster than they had been at the peak of his influence. Al-Mâwardî enumerates his duties under ten heads. (1) He is to maintain Islam in accord with tradition. The caliph is to disabuse innovators of their errors and in every way to safeguard religion from deterioration. (2) He is to make justice rule throughout the land and to see to it that judgments are carried out properly. (3) It is for him to protect the borders of the *dâr al-Islâm* so as to safeguard life and property of the individual believer. (4) He must apply the penalties provided by the *sharîᶜa* against transgressors. (5) He must garrison the borders so as to prevent enemy incursions. (6) He is under obligation to combat those unbelievers who reject an invitation to Islam until they either become converted or agree to become tributaries of the Muslims. (7) He is to levy taxes in accordance with the koranic prescriptions; (8) to regulate public expenditure; (9) to appoint the right people to public office; and (10) to keep administration and all other state affairs under close personal surveillance.[34]

IV

In dealing with the lower ranks of the administrative hierarchy, al-Mâwardî shows himself much more inclined to describe realistically the situation as he found it.

Just as Moses had Aaron appointed as his minister or helper, *wazîr,*[35] the caliph appointed an assistant whose concern was primarily with the affairs of the pen, that is, with civil government. The vizierate was developed by the Arab Muslims, Sassanian tradition shaping no more than some of its paraphernalia.[36] Al-Mâwardî distinguishes between a vizierate with restricted powers, *wizâra tanfîḏ,* and a vizierate with unrestricted

[34] Mâwardî, *op. cit.,* pp. 23–24; trans. pp. 30–31.*

[35] Koran 20:30–33.

[36] This has been proved conclusively by S. D. Goitein, "The Origin of the Vizierate and its True Character," *Islamic Culture,* XVI (1942), 255–63, 380–92.

powers, *wizâra tafwîḍ*, whose holder parallels in many respects a modern prime minister with the added power of levying taxes and spending public moneys according to his judgment. His tenure of office depended on the good graces of the caliph. The crises of the tenth century were accompanied by frequent exchange of viziers.

Aṣ-Ṣûlî (d. 946) quotes one Ibn Isrâʾîl as saying: "Formerly this office (i.e., the vizierate) lasted for quite a while (*muzâmana*), then it became limited to a year (*muʿâwama*), then to a month (*mushâhara*), then to a day (*muyâwama*), and finally"—but here Ibn Isrâʾîl had difficulties in expressing himself correctly—"to an hour."[37]

The vizier supervised the heads of the various bureaus (*dîwân*), the most important of which was the *bait al-mâl*, the treasury. Anticipating modern usage, the vizier not infrequently took personal charge of one or more of those bureaus or ministries. Each of the provinces which "formed more or less a loose confederation"[38] within the caliphate was administered through its own *dîwân* in the capital. Around 900 these *dîwâns* were incorporated in one central bureau (*dîwân ad-dâr*), with three branches for east, west, and the Sawâd (i.e., central and lower Iraq). The war office, the bureau of expenditure, the general post office (whose head was in charge of the secret police), two *dîwâns* dealing with official correspondence, and the caliph's cabinet, concerned with petitions to the ruler, constituted the main organs through which the central authority asserted itself.[39]

Theory assigned the treasury income from three sources: *faiʾ*, tribute from lands conquered by the Muslims; *ghanîma*, the loot of the battle; and *ṣadaqa*, alms tax. *Ṣadaqa* includes tithe, *ʿushr*, paid on agricultural lands and orchards; and *ṣadaqa*, in a more narrow sense, also called *zakât*, paid on cattle. With regard to *zakât* the Koran determines rates of payment and the charitable use to which the money is to be put.[40]

[37] Ibn Isrâʾîl wrongly forms *musâʿât* instead of *musâwaʿa*. Aṣ-Ṣûlî, *Adab al-kuttâb* (Cairo, 1341), pp. 185–86.

[38] Mez, *op. cit.*, p. 76.

[39] Cf. *ibid.*, pp. 76–81, for detail.

[40] Koran 9:60. Cf. Levy, *op. cit.*, I, 331.

The tribute from conquered lands was the so-called *ḫarâj* to be levied from territory whose inhabitants have concluded a treaty with the Muslims which placed them under Muslim sovereignty. Such land may not be sold, and conversion to Islam of the owner does not affect his obligation to pay *ḫarâj*. The enforcement of this tax from Muslim taxpayers was one of the great controversial issues of the Umayyad age, but finally the consensus acquiesced in the necessary but un-koranic arrangement.

Actually, the treasury enjoyed income from other sources as well: taxes levied on non-Muslims, local and municipal imposts, tolls, sales taxes, and—an irregular but lucrative source—sums extorted from fallen officials and confiscations of one sort or another, especially profitable being the appropriation of the fortune left by the rich.

Ibn al-Muᶜtazz (d. 908) says: "Woe to him whose father dies rich! Long does he remain incarcerated in misfortune's home, the unrighteous officer saying unto him: How do I know that you are the rich man's son? And when he rejoins: 'My neighbors and many others know me,' they pluck his moustache one by one, assault him, knock him about until strength ebbs away from him and he faints. And in the dungeon he languishes until he flings his purse to them."[41]

Tax farming and collective liability of community or province for the amount assessed did their usual damage to the national economy. But it was only in the tenth century, when the diminution of the territories under direct caliphal sway aggravated the lessening of the income to be derived from the several sections of the empire, that the decline became disquieting In 306/918–19, the total receipts of the treasury amounted to about fourteen and a half million *dînâr*—but expenditure exceeded the receipts by over two million. The maladministration prevailing becomes patent when it is learned that, of the total expenditure, only about one million went toward what might be called empire expenses, such as maintenance of frontier posts, the imperial mail, the pilgrim roads, and the salaries of empire officials, whereas some fourteen million were appropriated for

[41] *Dîwân* (Cairo, 1891), I, 131; trans. Mez, *op. cit.*, p. 113.

the caliphal household, the policing of the capital, and the salaries of minor officials working in the central government offices.[42]

Al-Mâwardî intrusts the provincial governor with civil and military power in his area and, contrary to the usage of the better period, with the levying of taxes as well. In this he only portrayed the conditions of the later times when the possession of this prerogative in addition to his other functions had made the governor practically independent. As he also possessed the right to nominate the judges, his influence reached every compartment of public life.

The cleavage between norm and usage again becomes painfully apparent in theory and practice of the judgeship. Al-Mâwardî stipulates as requisites of a valid appointment that the appointee be (1) an adult and a male; (2) intelligent; (3) free; (4) a Muslim; (5) possessed of the high moral qualifications necessary for admission to the number of approved witnesses; (6) of sound sight and hearing; and (7) well instructed in the law. This last requirement is understood to include the correct attitude toward the various roots of the *fiqh*.[43]

Unless specifically restricted, the *qâḍî*'s function will include, among other things, the decision of disputes, enforcing liabilities, enforcing the rights of the incapacitated, the management of pious foundations (*auqâf*, sg. *waqf*) or the supervision of the appointed manager, giving effect to testamentary dispositions, the infliction of fixed penalties, the protection of his district against violations of safety and building regulations, and the meting-out of equal justice to the weak and the strong, the high and the low.[44]

What seems the ideal dispensation and process of law is contained in a letter allegedly written by ᶜUmar I to one of his judges. Whatever its date, the missive was familiar to Muslim writers no later than the middle of the ninth century.

[42] Cf. A. von Kremer, "Ueber das Einnahmebudget des Abbasiden-Reiches vom Jahre 306 H. (918–919)," in *Denkschriften der Kais. Akad. d. Wiss.*, XXXVI (1886), 283–362; see also Kremer's paper, "Ueber das Budget der Einnahmen unter der Regierung des Hârûn alrašîd," *Verhandlungen des VII. Internationalen Orientalisten-Congresses, Semitische Section* (Wien, 1888), pp. 1–18.

[43] Mâwardî, *op. cit.*, pp. 107–11; cf. H. F. Amedroz, *JRAS*, 1910, 762–65.

[44] Mâwardî, *op. cit.*, pp. 117–19; Amedroz, *op. cit.*, pp. 768–69.

"The judge's office is (the application of) either an unequivocal ordinance of the Koran (*farîḍa muḥkama*) or a practice that may be followed (*sunna muttabaᶜa*). Understand this when considerations are put before you, for it is useless to utter a plea when it is not valid. Equalize all Muslims in your court and your attention, so neither the man of high station will expect you to be partial, nor will the humble despair of justice from you. The claimant must produce evidence, from the defendant an oath may be exacted. Compromise is permissible between Muslims, provided no law be violated thereby. If you have given judgment, and upon consideration come to a different opinion, do not let the judgment which you have given stand in the way of retraction; for justice may not be annulled, and you are to know that it is better to retract than to persist in injustice." In the following, ᶜUmar enjoins *qiyâs* in a manner to suggest origin of this passage perhaps toward the middle of the eighth century. After regulating the fixing of a term for the absent defendant and the admission of testimony, the letter concludes: "God concerns Himself with your secret character, and leaves you to follow appearances. Avoid fatigue and the display of weariness or annoyance at the litigants in the courts of justice, wherein God enables you to earn reward and make a handsome store. For when a man's conscience towards God is clear, God makes His relations with man satisfactory; whereas if a man simulate before the world what God knows that he has not, God will put him to shame."[45]

The dispensation of justice is a duty on the Muslim community. A *qâḍî* must be appointed. In places like Baghdad a chief judge constituted the highest judicial authority. Frequently, a judge was named for each *maḏhab* represented in a big municipality.

Actual practice severely curtailed the *qâḍî*'s function. Not only did the early caliphs frequently sit in person, as did even much later governors in the several provinces, but the local authorities, especially the police, arrogated the administration of justice to a considerable extent. In other words, a goodly por-

[45] Ibn Qutaiba, *ᶜUyûn*, p. 87 (=Mâwardî, *op. cit.*, pp. 119–21); trans. D. S. Margoliouth, *JRAS*, 1910, 311–12.

tion of the *qâḍî*'s jurisdiction was handed over to the executive arm of the government to be decided by the vizier, or the governor, who presided over the so-called *maẓâlim* (lit., "wrongs") court.

This tribunal was supposed to take charge of the following matters: (1) "acts of injustice and tyranny committed against people by governors"; (2) injustice in the assessment or the levying of taxes; (3) supervision of the financial acts of the public officials in the various government bureaus; (4) "claims by regular troops in respect to reduction in, or withholding of, their pay"; (5) "restoring property taken by force"; (6) surveillance of *auqâf;* (7) "enforcing decisions given by the *qâḍî* which have remained unenforced"; (8) "open evildoing which the *muḥtasib* (censor, trade inspector) is not strong enough to repress"; (9) care of public worship; and (10) hearing of litigation in general; here no clear line is drawn as against the competence of the *qâḍî*'s tribunal.[46]

The greater enforcement power of these "worldly" courts due to their closer relationship with the highest executive officer relegates the ordinary judge to a secondary position. It is characteristic that the four "orthodox" caliphs are never presented as sitting in *maẓâlim* court—it is the practical emergencies of the later period that compelled this innovation which fatally wounds the ideal of uniform administration of divinely ordained justice among the Muslims. The full extent to which the regular judge's authority had been weakened by the eleventh century becomes clear from what al-Mâwardî, himself for a time a chief judge in Baghdad, has to say on the difference of the jurisdiction of the *maẓâlim* court from that of the *qâḍî*. Of the ten points he lists, these five are the most significant: (1) The *maẓâlim* court is superior in dignity and power; (2) its jurisdiction is "wider and more unfettered, both in scope of action and in sentence"; (3) it possesses "greater power of intimidation"; (4) it also possesses "power of checking open wrongdoing and visiting open transgression with correction and discipline"; and (5) it exercises full power of subpoena.[47]

[46] Mâwardî, *op. cit.*, pp. 135–41; cf. Amedroz, *JRAS*, 1911, pp. 637–41.

[47] Mâwardî, *op. cit.*, pp. 141–42; Amedroz, *op. cit.*, pp. 641–42.

In part, it is the peculiar shortcomings of the *sharîᶜa* which caused the rise of the *maẓâlim* courts. The *qâḍî* is bound to adjudicate a case at once—the *maẓâlim* judge may delay the verdict if such delay appears to further the finding of the truth. The *qâḍî* cannot summon witnesses directly; he has to wait until the complainant brings forward witnesses and examines them. The *maẓâlim* judge is free to act as he sees fit in the best interests of justice. The koranic law contained penalties repellent to the more delicate sentiment of later times. Already one of the Companions is presented as advising a woman arraigned before him for theft to deny the accusation so as to spare him the necessity of having her right hand cut off.[48] The *maẓâlim* judge, on his part, could more easily decide in accord with contemporary feeling.

The *ḥisba* jurisdiction represents another attempt to supplement the function of the *qâḍî*. It is an institutionalization of the koranic admonition to all believers, "And let there be (formed) of you a community inviting to good, urging what is reputable and restraining from what is disreputable."[49]

The official in charge of it, the *muḥtasib*, usually a jurist, is "at liberty to deduce principles of decision from custom, *ᶜurf*, as distinct from revealed law, *sharᶜ*."[50] His duties are intermediate between those of the *qâḍî* and the *maẓâlim* judge. He hears and decides complaints in cases of short measure and weight, sales fraud, and withholding of debits that have fallen due. But his jurisdiction is restricted to obvious rights and wrongs and to incontested liabilities. He cannot hear evidence or administer an oath. On the other hand, he can examine into matters without a complaint being brought, and his powers of execution exceed those of the regular judge. To al-Mâwardî, the *maẓâlim* tribunal ranks highest, the *ḥisba* lowest.[51]

The *muḥtasib* is primarily a supervisor of the morals of the community. The trespasses he is supposed to prevent or to punish are, in a general way, infringements on proper behavior.

[48] Cf. Amedroz, *JRAS*, 1910, p. 793.

[49] Koran 3:100.

[50] Mâwardî, *op. cit.*, p. 404; cf. Amedroz, *JRAS*, 1916, p. 77.

[51] Mâwardî, *op. cit.*, pp. 405–8; cf. Amedroz, *loc. cit.*, pp. 78–80.

Thus he is to see to it that prayer is performed at the correct hours and in the manner sanctioned by usage. He is responsible for protecting the faithful from being exposed to the temptation of the bad example, for instance, with regard to the drinking of wine and the playing of musical instruments. It is for him to safeguard the community against fraudulent commercial practices, to keep the roads open, and to enforce building regulations (a task which the *sharîʿa* reserves for the *qâḍî*). He may be called upon to act as inspector of industries[52] and to correct unfair treatment and payment of laborers. He is not entitled to deliver judicial opinions, but he upholds what may be called the common law. His activities partake of those of the police officer and of those of the judge; his authority is both executive and judicial, but it is restricted to application and enforcement of prior rulings of the "higher" courts or of the popular feeling of equity.

Unfortunately, the *ḥisba,* so admirably devised in the flexibility of its tasks to suit the contingencies of everyday life, had, in al-Mâwardî's time, "declined in people's estimation when rulers neglected it and conferred it on men of no repute whose object was to profit and get bribes."[53] At no time has the Muslim municipality proved capable of developing institutions which, over a protracted period of time, would have resisted the shortsighted encroachments of an irresponsible government.

The awkward position of a judge vis-à-vis a recalcitrant executive, also, generally speaking, the near-impossibility of preserving a clean conscience when pressured by the caliph on the grounds of *raison d'état,* and, finally, the unwillingness of sitting in judgment over fellow-Muslims whose moral standing might be vastly superior to that of the judge made the office one to be shunned by the pious. Only compulsion could justify its acceptance in the eyes of the devout. Too often did the legist have to use his knowledge to justify the inexcusable, or at least, the

[52] Cf. Mez, *op. cit.*, p. 269.

[53] Mâwardî, *op. cit.*, p. 431; cf. Amedroz, *loc. cit.*, p. 101. In the *Arabian Nights* the *muḥtasib* shares the *qâḍî's* ill repute; cf. O. Rescher, *Islam*, IX (1919), 72–73.

unlawful, by ingenious twists of interpretation, or even falsification of textual tradition.[54] The pious were afraid of courting eternal damnation when the office of *qâḍî* was thrust upon them. Abû Ḥanîfa had to be flogged into taking the judgeship of Baghdad.

The reputation of the judges went down. Too often did they have to collude with those in power to suppress the innocent; too often did they allow themselves to be bribed into condoning injustice.[55] Unprotected against executive transgression, the administration of the law not infrequently broke down altogether. Once more, the sublime Muslim dream of the divinely regulated life eluded the faithful under the impact of ruthless realities. Theocratic authoritarianism failed to stimulate that sense of civic responsibility which is, in the long run, the sole guardian of the law, human or divine. The Muslims in the great cultural centers not only were aware of being misgoverned (as were their fellow-subjects in the countryside) but they had no illusions as to the vicious circle of oppression in which they found themselves caught. But no analytical acumen could force the government to rid itself of the foreign mercenaries on which it relied for its stability, nor could a government harassed by the rapacity of shortsighted armed hordes be expected to forego the disastrous profits of corruption.[56]

With all this it still would seem that nowhere did the Muslims cling more desperately to their axioms and illusions than in their concept of the highest office. And nowhere were the faithful to experience more bitter disappointment; nowhere did they have to acknowledge defeat more openly and with less saving grace.

The steady decay that, beginning as early as the ninth cen-

[54] Cf. the instances cited by Goldziher, "Muhammedanisches Recht in Theorie und Wirklichkeit," *Zs. f. vgl. Rechtswiss.*, VIII (1889), 406–23.

[55] Cf. E. Tyan, *Histoire de l'organisation judiciaire en pays d'Islam*, Vol. I (Paris, 1938), chap. v, "Les Moeurs judiciaires," pp. 423–500, and Rescher, *loc. cit.*, p. 73, for the verdict on the judge of the *Arabian Nights*.

[56] Cf., e.g., Ibn Miskawaih (d. 1030), *The Eclipse of the Abbasid Caliphate*, ed. and trans. D. S. Margoliouth and H. F. Amedroz (Oxford, 1920–21), II, 279 (trans., V, 298–99).

tury, ate away the strength of Islam and had, by the middle of the tenth, ruined the central authority of Baghdad beyond repair compelled acquiescence in conditions only too far removed from those postulated by political theory. It may be doubted whether the caliphate as designed by the legists ever had any real existence, but in the eleventh century the discrepancy between reality and ideal had become so flagrant it could no longer be overlooked by the body of the believers.

So the requirements of legitimate power had to be redefined with ever greater leniency, until the low had been reached and the theoretical dream abandoned. The believer was thought under obligation to obey whosoever held sway, be his power *de jure* or merely *de facto*. No matter how evil a tyrant the actual ruler, no matter how offensive his conduct, the subject was bound to loyal obedience.

That disillusionment bordering on cynicism with which the Oriental still is inclined to view the political life begins to speak through the mouth of al-Ghazâlî. "There are those who hold that the imamate is dead, lacking as it does the required qualifications. But no substitute can be found for it. What then? Are we to give up obeying the law? Shall we dismiss the *qâḍîs*, declare all authority to be valueless, cease marrying and pronounce the acts of those in high places to be invalid at all points, leaving the populace to live in sinfulness? Or shall we continue as we are, recognizing that the imamate really exists and that all acts of the administration are valid, given the circumstances of the case and the necessities of the moment?"[57]

Al-Ghazâlî continues: "The concessions made by us are not spontaneous, but necessity makes lawful what is forbidden. We know it is not allowed to feed on a dead animal: still, it would be worse to die of hunger. Of those that contend that the caliphate is dead for ever and irreplaceable, we should like to ask: which is to be preferred, anarchy and the stoppage of social life for lack of a properly constituted authority, or acknowledgment of the existing power, whatever it be? Of these two alternatives, the jurist cannot but choose the latter."[58]

[57] Quoted by Levy, *op. cit.*, I, 306.

[58] Santillana, *loc. cit.*, p. 302.*

That utter hopelessness and resignation which marks the political life of the later period is well expressed by the *qâḍî* Ibn Jamâ^ca of Damascus (d. 1333). "The sovereign has a right to govern until another and stronger one shall oust him from power and rule in his stead. The latter will rule by the same title and will have to be acknowledged on the same grounds; for a government, however objectionable, is better than none at all; and between two evils we must choose the lesser."[59]

The *civitas Dei* had failed, and the Muslim community had accepted its failure.

[59] *Ibid.*, pp. 302–3. In Byzantium, too, success legitimized usurpation, on the ground that the victor had won his crown by a vote, *ψῆφος*, of the Lord; cf. Buckler, *op. cit.*, p. 243, n. 4, and K. Holl, *Gesammelte Aufsätze zur Kirchengeschichte*, III (Tübingen, 1928), 194. R. Guilland (*EOS: Commentarii societatis philologae Polonorum*, XLII [1947], 142–68) analyzes the resulting ideas of loyalty; his conclusions illuminate certain Islamic patterns of political behavior.

CHAPTER SIX

THE BODY POLITIC: THE SOCIAL ORDER

I

ISLAM is concerned with salvation or damnation of the individual believer. The believers are equal before God, except for such distinction as is established by their greater or lesser piety.[1] It is explained that "through piety are souls brought to perfection and persons may compete for excellence in it; and let him who desires honor seek it in piety."[2] But the Muslim's personal equality with his fellows in the faith which is guaranteed, so to speak, by his right to a direct relationship with his Lord does in no way preclude elaborate social stratification within the community of Islam.

The Muslim shares, to a very high degree, in the sensitivity about rank which is so characteristic of the Middle Ages. Not only is he rank-conscious but he is keenly concerned with expressing social distinctions through a delicate system of etiquette. Questions of precedence are of considerable importance. Politeness is carefully graded to manifest the relative position of the interlocutors. Conversation as well as correspondence begins with public recognition of the social relationship of the participants. Rank is stressed, not glossed over for the sake of tact or politeness. But this emphasis on social inequality, however offensive it may appear to the modern Occidental, does not touch the core of the personalities involved. The ceremonial registers the accident of their relative position at any given moment. It implies recognition of a social fact that may be short-lived, but it does in no way suggest inequality of substance. Nevertheless, Islam itself has given rise to a new set of criteria to grade and stratify society.

Abû Bakr had divided the spoils of war evenly among the Muslims, no matter whether the recipient was "young or old,

[1] Cf. Koran 49:13.

[2] Baiḍâwî, II, 276, to Koran 49:13; trans. Levy, *op. cit.*, I, 78.

slave or free, male or female."[3] ʿUmar, although preserving the fundamental assumption of Islam leveling all distinctions of birth, insisted that the Muslims were not equal in the matter of faith. As it would hardly have been practicable to rank the faithful for the depth of their devotion, the caliph adopted two principles of a very different character to determine the share of the individual in the distribution of the booty. Kinship with the Prophet and the date of conversion decided the standing of the believer, inasmuch as this standing expressed itself in the yearly emoluments paid out to him from the public treasury.[4]

Alongside of the idea of a religious aristocracy, other concepts of the structure of society compelled acceptance. The Barmakid vizier al-Faḍl b. Yaḥyà (disgraced in 803) is reported to have divided mankind into four classes.

"(1) The ruler, whom merit has placed in the foremost rank; (2) the vizier, distinguished by wisdom and discrimination; (3) the high-placed ones, whom wealth has placed aloft; (4) the middle class who were attached to the other three classes by their culture (*taʾaddub*). The rest of mankind is mere scum who know but food and sleep."[5]

And long before al-Faḍl, al-Aḥnaf b. Qais (d. after 687) is supposed to have expressed a similar opinion. The value of culture for social advancement is stressed and the advice is voiced to study history, literature, and astronomy, as the kings are interested in these kinds of information. A littérateur tells how he maintained himself in favor with successive monarchs by achieving proficiency in their respective fields of interest: as-Saffâḥ's (750–54) predilection for sermons was followed by al-Manṣûr's (754–75) for history; al-Hâdî (785–86) preferred poetry—but when Hârûn was taken with asceticism, our courtier forgot all the information he had amassed in previous reigns.[6]

[3] Abû Yûsuf, *Kitâb al-ḫarâj* (Bûlâq, 1302), p. 24; trans. Levy, *op. cit.*, I, 81.

[4] For details, cf., e.g., Mâwardî, *op. cit.*, pp. 347–48; see also P. K. Hitti, *History of the Arabs* (3d ed.; London, 1943), p. 172.

[5] Ibn al-Faqîh (*fl.* 902), *Muḫtaṣar kitâb al-buldân*, ed. M. J. de Goeje (Leiden, 1885), p. 1; translations by Mez, *op. cit.*, pp. 147–48, and Levy, *op. cit.*, I, 96.*

[6] Ibn al-Faqîh, pp. 1–2.

Ibn al-Mudabbir (d. 892) enjoins the secretary to be careful to address people according to their "grandeur, exalted position, and elevation." He groups them in eight classes, the higher four comprising caliphs, their viziers and highest secretarial or civil officials, their generals and governors of the frontier districts, and their judges; the lower four include kings (either foreign potentates or such as are under the caliph's suzerainty), their viziers and other high officials, then the jurisconsults or theologians, *ᶜulamâʾ*, and, finally, educated people of influence.[7]

Isḥâq al-Mauṣilî (d. 850), the greatest musician of his time and a man of encyclopedic erudition, asked al-Maʾmûn as a special favor to allow him to present himself before him not among the singers but among the littérateurs. His request was granted, and later he was given permission to appear together with the jurisconsults and judges.[8] But the common prejudice against musicians prevented al-Maʾmûn from appointing him to a judgeship, although he thought highly of Isḥâq's legal knowledge.[9]

It is not always easy to ascertain the proprieties of the Muslim hierarchy. When in hiding between two terms of office, Ibn al-Furât (d. 924) took refuge in the house of a haberdasher at Baṣra. "While enjoying this refuge, he said to his host: 'If I should be made vizier, what would you like me to do for you?' The man said that he would like to have some government appointment. Ibn al-Furât replied: 'Unfortunately you cannot be made into a minister, or a governor, or a chief of police, or a secretary of state, or a general: so what post can I offer you?' 'I leave it to you,' said the host. Ibn al-Furât then suggested a judgeship and he consented."[10]

Each Muslim, then, had his fixed position in three intersecting hierarchies. Before his God he was saint or sinner, a prospective dweller of Paradise or timber for Hell; in the aristocracy of Islam he might be a kinsman of the Prophet or the descendant of humble non-Arabic clients with no claim to the glamour of

[7] Ibn Mudabbir, pp. 10–11.

[8] *Irshâd*, II, 199.

[9] *Ibid.*, p. 198, and *Aghânî* (3d ed.), V, 272–73.

[10] At-Tanûḫî (d. 994), quoted by Levy, *Baghdad Chronicle*, p. 139.

early conversion; and in official society he might hold an appointment as vizier or lead, as poet or singer, a precarious existence on the outer fringes of the courtly set. There was no supplementing hierarchy of political rights. What could be achieved under an absolutist government was a personal share in executive power whose exact amount would determine one's exact position in the official world—a position, therefore, which the slightest change of the political constellation would raise or lower.

The social order of the Islamic world accommodated non-Muslims as well as Muslims. Both groups lived under the same basic conditions, and the eagerness to assert rank and power affected the Jew and the Christian as it did the Muslim. It would seem that outside of the capital the religious groups lived fairly apart, except for their co-operation in official business. But the yardsticks of social success, the mechanisms of social advancement or decline, appear to have been the same everywhere within the *dâr al-Islâm*. Naturally, the dice were loaded in favor of the Muslims. Muslim appreciation of a Christian would raise his prestige in his community; Christian praise of a Muslim, on the other hand, need not be as beneficial to the recipient among his coreligionists. The mores and even the personal law of the religious communities differed to a considerable extent, but the fundamental social values were held in common. The three great religious groups evinced the same attitude toward power and the government. And Christians and Jews stood with Islam on the side of urban as against rural, or desert, life.

Islam, from its very outset unfolding in an urban milieu, favored city development. The legislation of the Koran envisages city life. The nomad is viewed with distrust. The Book speaks of the Bedouin as very strong "in unbelief and in hypocrisy and more apt not to know the limits of what Allah hath sent down to His messenger."[11] Wherever the Muslim conquerors came, they founded cities. Only in a city, that is, a settlement harboring a central mosque, *jâmi*ᶜ, fit for the Friday service and a market (and preferably a public bath), can all the requirements of the faith be properly fulfilled. Migration into town, *hijra*, is recommended and almost equalized in merit to

[11] Koran 9:98.

that more famous migration, again called *hijra*, of the Prophet from Mecca to Medina. To forsake town for country life is severely condemned.[12]

While he duly respects their military virtues, Ibn Ḫaldûn has no doubts concerning the anticultural proclivities of the Bedouin. Where they rule, civilization will perish. Stable political forces must center on cities. No state can achieve continuity on desert ground. It is true, nomadism and a settled existence are equally natural ways of life; nevertheless, the latter represents a more satisfactory condition. The lack of restraint and discipline that go with nomadism are hostile to progress of any sort. The Bedouin will oppress the settled population to such a degree as to ruin them economically, break up their social order, and thus bring about the downfall of civilization.[13]

It is again the custom of the city that prevailed in enforcing the veil and the seclusion of the free Muslim woman. It seems that the Meccan woman of standing wore the veil. Mohammed's wish to have women share in the devotional practices and, to a certain extent, in the spiritual life of the community ran counter to established habit, especially in the eastern provinces, and the learned, adopting when in doubt the more severe interpretation of the law, made the *sharᶜ* press home rigorously woman's aloofness from any activity likely to attract public attention to her. Woman saints, woman preachers, and woman scholars are met with and are accorded generous recognition, but it is obvious that the average Muslim preferred his womenfolk to stay home rather than to gain fame by unusual achievement.

Mohammed allowed women free disposal of their property, and he improved their position with regard to inheritance. But he did not do away with the general attitude which relegated women to a secondary place in the esteem of society. "The men are overseers over the women by reason of what Allah hath bestowed in bounty upon one more than another, and of the

[12] On this subject cf. W. Marçais, *Académie des Inscriptions et Belles-Lettres: Comptes rendus, 1928*, pp. 86–100. Max Weber, *Wirtschaft und Gesellschaft* (Tübingen, 1925), p. 358, errs when he assigns the town in Islam "only political importance" contrasting Islam in this respect with Judaism and Christianity as the bearers of a specifically "*bürgerlich-städtische*" religious attitude.

[13] Cf. *Prolegomena*, I, 220 ff., esp. pp. 270–72 (trans., I, 254 ff., esp. pp. 310–11).

property which they have contributed (i.e., the marriage-price); upright women are therefore submissive, guarding what is hidden in return for Allah's guarding (them); those on whose part ye fear refractoriness, admonish, avoid in bed, and beat; if they then obey you, seek no (further) way against them; verily Allah hath become lofty, great."[14]

The axiom of the natural superiority of the male sex which is made to justify its legal and social prerogatives is still maintained in Muslim lands, where "excessive" liberty for the woman continues to be eyed with apprehension and where the *ijmâᶜ* only slowly sanctions outward assimilation to European custom without imposing too much change in the basic attitudes that regulate the relation of the sexes in general and the public position of women in particular.[15]

The Koran allows polygamy but restricts it to simultaneous marriage with four lawful wives. To these, however, an unlimited number of slave concubines may be added. Divorce is easy for the man. No reasons need be specified.

The elimination of woman from public and social life—a free woman may be seen only by her husband and next of kin within the prohibited degrees—was completed by the time of Hârûn ar-Rashîd. While it probably made for easier contact across class lines, it impoverished social life to a remarkable degree. It also became responsible for the emergence of conditions strongly resembling antiquity in that the educated man shared his intellectual interests and enjoyments with a set of women entirely divorced from those with whom he shared his family life.

In imitation of the custom of the ancient Orient and of the Byzantine Empire, eunuchs came to be employed to guard the women of distinguished households. The caliph al-Amîn (809–13) did much to invalidate in practice the prohibition placed upon the institution by Koran and *ḥadîṯ*. Christians and, to a less extent, Jews were active in the procurement of, and the trade in, eunuchs. The people despised and loathed the eunuchs,

[14] Koran 4:38.

[15] Cf., e.g., Muḥammad Kurd ᶜAlî, *Al-Islâm waʾl-ḥaḍâra al-ᶜarabiyya* (Cairo, 1934–36), I, 85–93; also H. A. R. Gibb's opinion in *The Near East: Problems and Prospects* (Chicago, 1942), pp. 39–40.

but high society was fond of them and paid exorbitant prices for them.[16] In fact, together with well-trained singers they were among the most expensive slaves.

In anecdotes such as those collected in the *Kitâb al-aghânî* ("Book of Songs") the more glamorous aspects of the life of skilled slaves and slave girls are represented. But even in those records of the successes of singers and musicians it cannot be overlooked how, at the barrier between bond and free, interest in the feelings of the fellow-human and awareness of his dignity are silenced only too frequently. Muslim society harbored a considerable number of slaves, but it was not wholly dependent on slave labor. In most places free, or freed, labor served its needs equally well. Therefore, the humane tendencies toward amelioration of the slave's lot which are embodied in both Koran and Tradition were never actively opposed. The law imposes certain disabilities on a slave: his testimony in court is, as a rule, not acceptable; his trespasses are more lightly punished, as he cannot be held responsible for his doings in the same way as the free; his blood would not atone for a free man's blood, etc. On the whole, the trend was toward kindliness and liberality in emancipating them. The illimited right of concubinage with slave girls made, in many instances, for shocking degradation whose only alleviation may have sprung from reduced sensibility of the victim due to prolonged social pressure and the commonness of the experience.

To this day, slavery continues in one form or another in certain parts of the Muslim world. Travelers, almost unanimously, report favorably on the lot of the unfree. Be this as it may, the only redeeming feature—and this of not too much saving force—is the absence of that self-righteous rationalization of slavery with all the cheap flattery it affords the masters and the equally cheap contempt it piles on the slaves that was developed in Christian lands in order to justify what conscience knew could not be justified. As the Koran took the institution for granted, its continuance did not warp too badly the souls of those who upheld it. The disregard for lowly human life, which is still to be felt throughout the Arab world, may in part be due to the

[16] On eunuchs cf., e.g., Mez. *op. cit.*, pp. 353–57.

age-old custom of slavery. But the attitude is shared by the descendants of those slave aristocracies, Turkish and Circassian, who for many a generation ruled *de facto* in Baghdad, *de jure* in Egypt. The institute of the slave army that gains control of the state and whose members, theoretically at least, combine supreme political power with extreme social and legal disabilities is perhaps the strangest paradox with which medieval Islam confronts us.

II

Society in the medieval Muslim world was intersected by four principal lines of division: the first separating the Muslim from the non-Muslim, the next setting apart the several religious groups within Islam, the third marking off the different nationalities united under Islam, and the last delimiting the more narrowly social distinctions that assigned people to a more or less definite hierarchy of professions.

Of these dividing lines, the most incisive was the barrier that kept apart believer and unbeliever. The relationship between these two kinds of people is determined by this fundamental fact: there is not and there cannot be equality of the Muslim and the non-Muslim. "Islam is the final religion, the right way, the ultimate truth. Those who follow it are therefore the elect of Allah and are necessarily in a position of superiority to other groups who still follow something which is less than the final truth, which belongs to what is outmoded, inferior, and, in a word, passé. Muslims thus are conscious that in virtue of this superiority they have sovereign rights to rule."[17]

The world belongs as of right to the true believer, who has certain obligations to those communities who possess some part of the divine revelation but none whatever to the pagan. Muslim law leaves the idolaters only the choice between conversion and death. Thus theory does not admit the possibility of a pagan minority. It is only the Christians, the Jews, and the Zoroastrians who may be legally recognized as an organized minority. But the assignment of a clearly circumscribed position within the Muslim world does not bridge the gap in social distinction.

[17] A. Jeffery, *Journal of Near Eastern Studies*, I (1942), 392.

By virtue of his being a Muslim, the believer is superior in substance, and there is nothing the unbeliever could do to ameliorate his position but to accept Islam and to become himself a member of the ruling group. The fact that, in contrast to the faithful of most great religions, never in their early history were the Muslims subject to prolonged and large-scale persecution doubtless strengthened this conviction of being the elect of the Lord.

Aloofness is enjoined by the Prophet. "O Believers! take not the Jews or Christians as friends! . . . . If any one taketh them for his friends, he surely is one of them. God will not guide the evildoers."[18] The official attitude toward Christians and Jews is mirrored in a *fatwà*, legal opinion, of the fourteenth century.[19]

"It is known that the Jews and the Christians are branded with the marks of the wrath and malediction of the Lord because they give Him associates and stubbornly deny His signs. God has taught His servants the prayers which they are to use in addressing Him. He has commanded them to march in the direction of those on whom He has showered His grace, in the path of His prophets, the righteous, the martyrs, and the virtuous among men; He also has commanded them to keep away from the path of the profligate from whom He has withdrawn His mercy and whom He has barred from Paradise. Those that have roused His wrath and those that have gone astray[20] are fraught with His vengeance and His curse. Now, according to the text of the Koran, the people of the wrath are the Jewish people, and the people led astray by error are the trinitarian Christians who adore the Cross."

This attitude to the People of the Book, as Jews and Christians are called, does not entail any obligation on the part of the Muslim either to convert or to exterminate them. And it is here that Islam's reputation as a religion of toleration arises. This reputation is undoubtedly justified, inasmuch as both Christians and Jews are permitted to profess their own religion; but

[18] Koran 5:56 (Rodwell's translation).

[19] Trans. from *Journal asiatique*, XVIII (sér. 4, 1851), 468.

[20] Allusion to Koran 1:7: "(Guide thou us on the straight path, the path of those . . . .) with whom Thou are not angry, and who go not astray."

it is entirely unjustified, inasmuch as for the West toleration implies an equal footing before the law and participation in civil and political life on terms of equality.

The People of the Book are considered as *ḏimmî*, that is, as persons in possession of a protective treaty, *ḏimma*,* in which they renounce certain rights and in return enjoy the practice of their religion and their customs. Much has been made of the so-called Covenant of ᶜUmar as a document of liberalism. That this document is rather an abstract from many individual covenants or, better still, an approximate description of the actual state of affairs around A.D. 800 is not too important in this context. It demonstrates beyond doubt the isolation of non-Muslims within their own religious groups. Their personal safety and their personal property are guaranteed them at the price of permanent inequality. The briefest version of the Covenant is the following; it is given in the form of a letter from ᶜUmar in which he quotes a letter from some Christians.

"When you (i.e., ᶜUmar) came to us we asked of you safety for our lives, our families, our property, and the people of our religion on these conditions: to pay tribute out of hand and be humiliated;** not to hinder any Muslim from stopping in our churches by night or day, to entertain him there three days and give him food there and open to him their doors; to beat the *nâqûs* (the wooden board which serves as 'bell' amongst the Eastern Christians) only gently in them and not to raise our voices in them in chanting; . . . . not to build a church, convent, hermitage, or cell, nor repair those that are dilapidated; nor assemble in any that is in a Muslim quarter, nor in their presence; not to display idolatry, nor invite to it, nor show a cross on our churches, nor in any of the roads or markets of the Muslims; not to learn the Koran nor teach it to our children; not to prevent any of our relatives from turning Muslim if he wish it; . . . . not to resemble the Muslims in dress, appearance, saddles . . . . ; to honor and respect them, to stand up for them when we meet together; . . . . not to make our houses higher (than theirs); not to keep weapons or swords, nor wear them in a town or on a journey in Muslim lands; . . . . not to strike a Muslim; not to keep slaves who have been the property of Muslims. We impose these terms on ourselves and on our coreligionists; he who rejects them has no protection."[21]

It is true that, with all those restrictions, non-Muslims frequently became influential in the government. But it is equally true that appointments to executive posts of non-Muslims were, strictly speaking, illegal, that the appointees held their places on sufferance, and that pious circles always fought such laxity of practice on the part of certain rulers. The decisive point is not that in certain periods Jews and Christians trespassed without punishment the several restrictions imposed on them but that both communities, the Muslim as well as the non-Muslim, were constantly aware of the fact that there were irrevocable restrictions incorporated in the canon law and that there obtained in everyday life conditions of laissez faire not compatible with the sterner ordinances of this law.

This is not, of course, to deny that there was in the East during the Middle Ages less physical persecution of nonconformists than in the West, where by the way, with the exception of the Jews, sizable religious minorities were as good as nonexistent. The minority situation within the world of Islam is, however, portrayed most clearly by saying that the minorities bought their safety at the price of *Geschichtslosigkeit*, at the price of having more or less the status of crown colonies in our day: no influence on taxation and no influence on the foreign policy of the sovereign body to which they belonged. Within this framework their economic life suffered comparatively little interference. Individual rulers might harm the communities or some prominent members—this happened regularly after a period of conspicuous prosperity and political ascendency—but the Muslims themselves were equally exposed to the arbitrary and unrestrained power of the monarch.

The Covenant did not always protect the Christians of Arab blood. It was sometimes felt a disgrace that Arabs should not be Muslims,[22] and measures of repression were taken against them with the barbarity customary at the time. Throughout Muslim

[21] A. S. Tritton, *The Caliphs and Their Non-Muslim Subjects* (London, 1930), pp. 4–5. For the stipulations of the Covenant cf. also D. C. Dennett, Jr., *Conversion and the Poll Tax* (Cambridge, Mass., 1950), p. 63.

[22] Tritton, *op. cit.*, p. 89.

history, it should be noted, the tension, virtual or actual, between Christians and Muslims was much more marked than that between Jews and Muslims, probably on account of the backing the Christians were likely to receive from the West. The *Arabian Nights* eloquently describes the deep hatred caused by the Crusades, which led to a deterioration of the status of the Eastern Christians. It was during this time that a legist laid down the principle: "When the infidel attempts to rise above the Muslim in whatever respect and when he revolts against him, the *imâm* has the right to put him to death."[23]

The inclusion in its framework of a number of semiautonomous bodies of potential enemies obviously constituted a dangerous weakness of the Muslim state. The Byzantine Empire did not tolerate a Muslim organization on its soil. It is surprising that there were comparatively few attempts at forcible conversion of Christians.[24] Religious law permitted the use of *ḏimmî* soldiers, provided they could be trusted. But it was exactly this condition which could hardly ever be considered reliably fulfilled. Thus, excepting the event of foreign invasion, the burden of warfare, internal and external, fell entirely on the Muslims, an inequality which was in part remedied by the considerably more oppressive taxation to which the non-Muslims were subjected.

The law safeguarded the stability of the ratio between the religious groups—not only was apostasy from Islam liable to be punished with death but conversion of a Christian to Judaism or of a Jew to Christianity was prohibited as well. In course of time the non-Muslim communities appear to have somewhat shrunk, but it is astounding that they survived in considerable size, seeing the reward incident upon joining the majority group.

Muslim law and, even more so, Muslim mentality insisted upon emphasizing without letup the disabilities to which the

[23] *Journal asiatique*, XIX (sér. 4, 1852), 115–16.

[24] Cydones lists a few instances from the late period; cf. Eichner, *Islam*, XXIII (1936), 243–44. Th. W. Arnold, *The Preaching of Islam* (2d ed.; London, 1913), has no instance from Arabic Islam where the government practiced compulsion in making converts.

dimmî was subjected. However much influence he and his community might actually wield, ways were found to prevent him from forgetting, and be it only for a moment, that he was, in modern terms, a second-class citizen. Time and again the texts assert the intention of humiliating the *dimmî*. Never was he to be left in doubt about his inferior status. This anxiousness on the part of the ruling group to cajole their own susceptibilities by hurting those of the non-Muslims increased as time went by. And it must be said that, on the whole, relations between the communities steadily deteriorated. The decline of their power made the Muslims more and more nervous; and, on the part of the Christians, the continued policy of alternating pin pricks and blows had its effect, too.

In the early days relations between Muslims and Christians had been fairly satisfactory and decidedly better than those between Muslims and Jews. This situation was gradually reversed. Under al-Mutawakkil (847–61) a wave of anti-*dimmî* feeling swept the capital. This caliph, Barhebraeus (d. 1286) reports, "was a hater of the Christians, and afflicted them by ordering them to bind bandlets of wool round their heads; and none of them was to appear outside his house without a belt and girdle. And if any man among them had a slave, he was to sew two strips of cloth of different colors on his tunic from the front and from behind. And the new churches were to be pulled down. And if they should happen to have a spacious church, even though it was ancient, one part of it was to be made into a mosque.[25] And they were not to lift up crosses during their feasts of Hosanna. In a similar manner he laid these same commands, and many others which were like unto them upon the Jews also."[26]

[25] It may be mentioned in this connection that there is some evidence to suggest that in the twelfth and thirteenth centuries the Great Mosque in Damascus was, to a certain extent, shared with the Christians. Ibn Jubair (*Travels*, ed. M. J. de Goeje [Leiden and London, 1907], p. 266 [referred to by K. A. C. Creswell, *Early Muslim Architecture* (Oxford, 1932–40), I, 121]) in 1184 saw "foreign" anchorites living in the western minaret. (Reference owed to Mr. M. B. Smith.) For the thirteenth century cf. Bartholomew of Edessa, *MPG*, CIV, 1444, and Eichner, *loc. cit.*, pp. 144–45.

[26] *Chronography*, trans. E. A. Wallis Budge (London, 1932), I, 141.*

To promote hatred of the Christians, al-Jâḥiẓ wrote a *risâla* in which he pointed out the reasons of their comparative popularity and then went on to explain why they should be detested and abhorred. The *Epistle* makes it clear that their social position had not been unfavorable up to the writer's time. "Another cause for the admiration accorded by the masses to the Christians is the fact that they are secretaries and servants to kings, physicians to notables, perfumers, and money-changers, whereas the Jews are found to be but dyers, tanners, cuppers, butchers and cobblers.[27] Our people observing thus the occupations of the Jews and the Christians concluded that the religion of the Jews must compare as unfavorably as do their professions."[28]

Al-Jâḥiẓ admits the Christians' wealth and their assimilation to Muslim manners. He even grants their superior education. But each of these assets he turns into one more reason for their suppression. "Our nation has not been afflicted by the Jews, Magians, or Sabians as much as by the Christians; for (in the polemics with us) they choose contradictory statements in Muslim traditions (as the targets of their attacks). (They select for disputations) the equivocal verses of the Koran, and (hold us responsible for) *ḥadîṯs*, the chains of guarantors of which are defective. Then they enter into private conversation with our weak-minded, and question them concerning the texts which they have chosen to assail. They finally insert into the debate the arguments that they have learned from the atheists and accursed Manichaeans. And notwithstanding such malicious discourse they often appear innocent before our men of influence and people of learning; and thus they succeed in throwing dust in the eyes of the staunch believers and in bewildering the minds of those who are weak in faith. And how unfortunate that every Muslim looks upon himself as a theologian, and thinks that everyone is fit to lead a discussion with an atheist!"[29]

[27] It need hardly be said that this represents no adequate statement on the economic position of the Jews, although some crafts such as the dyer's trade were almost exclusively plied by them.

[28] *Radd* ᶜ*alà 'n-naṣârà*, trans. J. Finkel, *JAOS*, XLVII (1927), 327–28.

[29] *Ibid.*, p. 331. Throughout his *Descriptio*, al-Muqaddasî considers the presence of many Jews or Christians a blemish, ᶜ*aib*, of a particular town or area.

Despite their participation in public life, in which they were, however, severely handicapped by their inability to depose in court, the better part of their activities was spent within their communities. The tendency of their leaders was to stimulate aloofness rather than co-operation. The appeal to the Muslim courts in cases where the *shar*ᶜ did not require it was discouraged. The *d̲immî* communities developed their own law and had power to enforce it within their confines. The communities designated their chief, whom the government had the right to reject. The positions of Jacobite Patriarch and Nestorian Catholicus were highly esteemed and apparently lucrative, too, for huge sums were paid upon occasion to secure confirmation.[30]

In reading works of Christian authors of the kind of Thomas of Marga's (d. 840) *Book of Governors*,[31] or in following up the fate of a non-Muslim community in a provincial town,[32] one feels very strongly how much their interests are divorced from those of the Muslim state. It is as though the author was barely touched by the events of the Islamic world despite the repercussions these must have had even on his personal fate. Muslims might scoff at, or assail the influence exercised by, the *d̲immî* in administration, finance, or the cultural life of the Muslim community—actually, a good deal, if not most, of the energy of a member of any subject group was spent apart from the main stream of development, devoted primarily to assuring the survival of the church or the synagogue that were source and goal of his social and spiritual existence. It is remarkable how tenaciously these non-Muslim communities maintained themselves throughout and beyond the Middle Ages, and it is equally remarkable to observe how little the Muslim state was really hampered in its operation by the dead weight of those semiforeign organizations within its structure.

The system of harboring autonomous religious communities

[30] A letter of appointment from the *Tad̲kira* of Ibn Hamdûn is printed, *JRAS*, 1908, pp. 467–70, and in part translated by Mez, *op. cit.*, p. 35.

[31] Ed. and trans. E. A. Wallis Budge (London, 1893).

[32] Cf., e.g., E. von Dobschütz, "Edessa unter der Araberherrschaft," *Zs. f. wiss. Theologie*, XLI (1898), 364–91.

inside the Muslim state recommended itself to every nationality group that captured power in the Islamic world. It was carried to perfection by the Ottoman Turks, a state of affairs which persisted until the Young Turk Revolution in 1908. The personal status before the law of an Ottoman subject depended entirely on the privileges enjoyed by the religious community, or *millet*, to which he belonged.[33] The Turks never tried to assimilate the subject peoples, although they placed no obstacles in the way of voluntary assimilation. The *millet* was self-governing in its internal affairs and elected its head, who received the confirmation of the sultan and in whom just enough executive power was vested to enable him to collect the taxes imposed on his community by the state.[34]

It was highly convenient from an administrative point of view to deal with the religious minorities through this machinery. The state never contemplated using their military strength, which, in time, became negligible. The modernization of the Ottoman state, after 1839, resulted in a diminution of the legal autonomy of the minorities, some topics being withdrawn from the religious community law to be settled uniformly for all Ottoman subjects. The contempt for the non-Muslim groups, the *raya*—Turkish pronunciation of the Arabic *ra*ᶜ*âyâ* (lit.: "herd animals")—remained along with their exclusion from the Empire's policy-making bodies. With all this it must be admitted that, the over-all conditions of the East being what they were, this situation was the most advantageous that could be hoped for and definitely preferable to the change brought about by the impact of the West.[35]

[33] Cf. Cte F. van den Steen de Jehay, *De la situation légale des sujets ottomans non-musulmans* (Brussels, 1906), p. 7. W. Cahnmann, *American Journal of Sociology,* XLIX (1943–44), 524–29, describes the *millet* system and discusses its recession before the "territorial society of the West."

[34] Van den Steen, *op. cit.,* pp. 347 ff.

[35] As late as 1899 did the so-called "Mad Mullah" build up a state in Somaliland in which his dervishes, in virtue of their religious superiority, constituted the ruling "tribe," with the political organizations of the old tribes left more or less intact (cf. E. Cerulli in *Aspetti e problemi attuali del mondo musulmano* [Rome, 1941], pp. 91–92).

III

The consensus of Muslims has always condoned theological disputation, but it has been slow in recognizing that a group of dissenting believers had put itself outside the pale. As a rule, exclusion from the body of the faithful was the consequence of political disagreement fought out on religious ground. Exclusion never meant a formal excommunication of the sectarian—there would have been no authority to pronounce it. It only meant that majority sentiment held his teachings incompatible with received beliefs. Such majority sentiment may relent—as it seems to be relenting at present toward Wahhâbîs and Ibâḍites—and the survival of the sects is owed mainly to the individualistic zeal of the socioreligious minority groups themselves.

The Prophet's death caused dissension touching the succession. One section of the believers insisted that ᶜAlî, Mohammed's cousin and son-in-law, was the sole rightful heir to leadership of the Muslims. The majority rejected this view. After the assassination of the third caliph, ᶜUṯmân, during whose last days ᶜAlî had been rather lukewarm in his support, the highest dignity fell to him. Civil war ensued between him and the Umayyads, ᶜUṯmân's kin, who fought to avenge his murder. The dispute in which Iraq backed ᶜAlî against the Syrian governor, Muᶜâwiya, ended with a Ḫârijite stabbing ᶜAlî to death. ᶜAlî's son, Ḥasan, sold his rights to the throne to Muᶜâwiya, and here the matter would have rested but for a curious development that had commenced well during ᶜUṯman's reign but had been consistently disowned by ᶜAlî himself.

The entire community of the faithful reverenced the House of the Prophet and highly respected ᶜAlî for his close relationship with Mohammed, his early conversion, his learning, eloquence, and other qualities of which it is difficult to ascertain whether he actually displayed them or whether they were his as the result of pious attribution. His political record, at any rate, is not too impressive. The community did not, however, accept the allegation proffered by a small conventicle of ardent partisans that the Prophet himself had selected ᶜAlî as his successor and had confided to him secret knowledge of a metaphysical character. For reasons that will probably never be satisfactorily accounted for, this group saw in ᶜAlî and his offspring the embodiment of their concept of the ruler, *imâm*. Whoever else was in possession of the highest dignity was no better than a usurper and a tyrant. It is the *imâm*, and only the *imâm*, who is entitled to direct the faithful.

He is infallible and thus competent to teach and to guide. The existence of the *imâm* cannot be dispensed with. The imamate is a necessary institution—necessary in the sense that it constitutes the organ through which divine guidance manifests itself on earth at any given moment. No reconciliation is conceivable between the idea of the caliph as it was evolved by the majority of the so-called Sunnîs—an executive charged with the defense of the faith and the faithful—and the idea of the *imâm* as it was promulgated by the *shîᶜat ᶜAlî*, the party of ᶜAlî, the Shiites. This *imâm* is not only a ruler; he is a teacher and heir to the prophetic office. He is more than a mere mortal man. His function as a ruler is not acquired; it is innate. He differs in substance from the rest of mankind. The spark of divine light that, from Creation, has passed from prophet to prophet until it was held by the common grandfather of Mohammed and ᶜAlî is now part of the spiritual substance of ᶜAlî and his descendants. This spark marks out its bearer as the *imâm* of his age. It cleanses him of sinfulness.[36] It endows him with superior powers of the mind and of the heart.[37]

In the Koran we are told how after the creation of man God said to the angels: " 'Do obeisance to Adam,' and they did obeisance, except Iblîs who was not one of the doers of obeisance. (11) He (Allah) said: 'What prevented thee from doing obeisance when I commanded thee?' He replied: 'I am better than he; Thou hast created me from fire, but him Thou has created from clay.' (12) He said: 'Get thee down from it (i.e., probably, Paradise)! It is not for thee to show pride in it; so get out!' "[38] The Lord's request whose refusal led to Satan's downfall was, according to the Shîᶜî, based on his wish to have

[36] When, much later, the impeccability of Mohammed was accepted by the Sunnîs, this *ᶜiṣma* was considered not inherent in the Prophet's substance, but a favor, *luṭf*, from Allah.

[37] For this characterization of the *imâm* cf. Goldziher, *Vorlesungen*, pp. 217–18.

[38] Koran 7:10–12.

the spark of divine light that rested within Adam adored by all creation.

The specific impulses which made the Shiite conventicles recognize the Light in this or that scion of the House cannot now be ascertained. As a matter of fact, the early Shîᶜa split over the personality of each subsequent *imâm* and broke apart into a considerable number of sects of varying importance. All of them, however, unquestioningly upheld the concept of the necessary *imâm* of the House of ᶜAlî, distinguished from ordinary man by his share in the divine substance.

Political discontent found a dignified rallying-point in these legitimist speculations. Philosophical notions of Persian or late Greek origin secured survival by attachment to Shiite theology. The Sunnite government was forced to repress the movement which not only was politically dangerous—the number of Alid pretenders is legion—but which through its idea of the *imâm*'s infallible authority in doctrine and morals might lead, and in the case of some ultra-Shiite groups did lead, to the destruction of the core of Islam, the belief, that is, in the finality of Mohammed's message. Did not certain extremist circles go so far as to condemn Mohammed for usurping what would rightfully have been ᶜAlî's place? Was it not suggested by others that Gabriel made a mistake in intrusting the Lord's message to Mohammed instead of to ᶜAlî?[39] To be sure, the moderates disclaimed responsibility for those excesses, even as they repudiated any doctrine smacking of incarnation of the godhead in the *imâm*, but the fundamental rift in political and theological reasoning was not to be healed.

Persecution, blunted by the jerky inconsistencies of oriental administration and, even more, by the general veneration of the Prophet's family, did nothing to prevent the growth of the Shîᶜa. The movement spread right in the center of the Empire, even in the capital itself. Shiite scholars were busy fortifying the foundations of their claim. Toward the end of the ninth century the Shiite historian, Ibn Wâḍiḥ al-Yaᶜqûbî (d. after 891), thus describes the selection by Mohammed of ᶜAlî as his successor. It happened on his return from his farewell pilgrimage to Mecca.

[39] Cf. Goldziher, *Vorlesungen*, p. 219.

"Mohammed set out at night, straight for Medina. When he came to a place in the vicinity of al-Jaḥfa, which was called Ghadîr Ḫumm (the Pond of Ḫumm) . . . . , he stood up to deliver an inspired utterance. Taking the hand of ᶜAlî b. abî Ṭâlib, he said: 'Am I not dearer to the believers than their own lives?' They replied: 'Yes, O Apostle of God.' He then declared: 'Whoever recognizes me as his master, will know ᶜAlî as his master.' He went on to say: 'O ye people, I will now go ahead of you, and you will meet me at the drinking-fountain in Paradise. . . . . And I will ask you when you arrive concerning two treasures, so be careful how you look after them.' They inquired: 'What treasures, O Apostle of God?' He answered: 'The greatest treasure is the Book of God, because it is from Him, given as it were by the hand of God, and entrusted to your hands. Hold fast to it and do not lose it and do not change it. The other treasure is the line of my descendants, the People of the Household.' "[40]

In 962 the Bûyid, Muᶜizz ad-Daula, a Shîᶜî from Dailam in northwestern Persia, introduced the celebration of this day of the Pond of Ḫumm in Baghdad.[41]

With the rise of the Shîᶜa from the tenth century onward quarrels between them and the Sunnîs multiplied. In Baghdad as elsewhere the Shîᶜîs lived together. Their slow expansion beyond the quarter of Karḫ testifies to their gradual but irrepressible growth in numbers and influence. The most insignificant incident might stir up a riot. The mutual dislike of the two groups was easily fanned into hatred. It would seem that, on the whole, the Shîᶜa displayed greater intransigence. It was a Shîᶜî vizier (of the Sunnî caliph) who suggested to the Mongol prince Hûlâgû the conquest of Baghdad, and it was another Shîᶜî dignitary who persuaded him to kill the captured caliph after Baghdad had fallen (1258). The Shîᶜîs in general looked upon the pagan Mongols as liberators from the Sunnî yoke.

The law of the Shîᶜa differed from that of the Sunnites only in a few points of major importance. Thus, the Shîᶜa permits marriage to be contracted for a specified time, an arrangement

[40] Yaᶜqûbî, *Historiae*, ed. M. Th. Houtsma (Leiden, 1883), II, 125; trans. D. M. Donaldson, *The Shîᶜite Religion* (London, 1933), pp. 1–2.

[41] Mez, *op. cit.*, p. 69.

which the Sunna, not unjustly, equalizes with prostitution. The similarity of their *fiqh* entails a profound similarity in their everyday lives. Aside from minor changes in the *ṣalât* ritual, there would not have been much to emphasize the cleavage of the groups in their daily relations.

What did keep them apart and provoked ceaseless friction was their different attitude to the Muslim community and to their fellow-men. To an unusual degree the Shîᶜa had developed the traits so often met with in small and suppressed religious groups. Their attachment to their own creed was coupled with an inclination to accept speculative extravagancies that must have been deeply repugnant to the far more sober judgment of the Sunnîs. A most unpleasant aggressiveness made them develop the cursing of their opponents, especially the three usurping caliphs, into a religious duty. To the Sunnî those caliphs were little short of heroes of the faith. This petulant aggressiveness manifests itself again in an almost morbid urge to oppose the Sunnî at all cost on any controversial detail. The Shiite legist, Kulînî (d. 939), declares: "What runs counter to the consensus of the Sunna is correct."[42]

Sunnite Islam in the good periods exhibits an unmistakable trend toward humanization of interdenominational relations. The Koran declares the polytheists to be "simply filth,"[43] that is, ceremonially unclean. Sunnite Islam practically limits the application of this statement to excluding the non-Muslim from the Kaᶜba, which, incidentally, the context shows it was meant to justify. The Shîᶜa, on the other hand, reads into Mohammed's observation a prohibition so much as to touch the unbeliever. If he drinks from a vessel, the vessel can no longer be used by a believer, that is, by a Shîᶜî, etc. The Koran permits Muslim men to marry Jewish or Christian women of good repute.[44] The Shîᶜa, impelled by its intense separatism, explains this permission away. Wherever possible the non-Shiite Muslim is included in this sectarian intolerance. It is even suggested to bar all adversaries of the Alid cause from receiving charity.

Intransigence and intolerance are made particularly unpleas-

[42] Goldziher, *Vorlesungen*, p. 247, and n. 17.26 on p. 277.

[43] Koran 9:28.

[44] Koran 5:7.

ant by the doctrine of *taqiyya* (lit., precaution). The Koran states: "Whether ye conceal what is in your hearts or reveal it, Allah knows it."[45] This verse has been taken to condone concealment of one's convictions in the event their open profession would endanger the believer's safety. The Shîᶜa, however, built upon this slender foundation a doctrine, considered fundamental, of the believer's duty to hide his true allegiance when under the sway of the unbeliever. The Shîᶜî is bidden to act like a Sunnî when dominated by a Sunnî government. The injunction met with sufficient response to imbue medieval Shiism with a most unattractive flavor of moral ambiguity. The Shîᶜî in non-Shîᶜî territory lives the life of a conspirator. He curses in private whom he joins in public. The laws of morality are valid only within the conventicle. Oppression engendered a tearful mood. The marks of suffering were declared the marks of the true Shîᶜî. A blend of self-pity and self-righteousness, unmeasured hatred and unmeasured devotion, made up the atmosphere surrounding the Friends of the Household.

The attraction of Shiism was heightened by the accommodation it provided for age-old concepts and manners of reasoning debarred from the system of Muslim orthodoxy. But its appeal gained even more strength by supplying a justification for emotionalism toward which Sunnite Islam had always shown a certain reserve. The Shîᶜa distrusted Ṣûfism. It was not for the individual believer to establish contact with the divinity—the *imâm* mediated, logos-like, between the godhead and the God-seeking soul. But while the highest experience of the Ṣûfî was, by its very nature, confined to the few, everybody might share in the intoxication of grief that swept the faithful in the commemoration of Ḥusain's death.

This son of ᶜAlî and grandson of the Prophet had been slain, in 680, at Kerbela in the course of an abortive revolt. The pathetic figure of this incompetent but courageous nobleman deserted in his hour of need by those who had prompted his rebellion impressed itself upon the imagination of Islam, and especially of Shiite Islam, as no other Muslim personality except the Prophet himself and possibly ᶜAlî. With pride does the

[45] Koran 3:27.*

Shîʿa refer to its sanguinary defeats. "Our dooms are the swords while you die on your thrones like the full-breasted (women)."[46] But pride yields to despair when it comes to the slaughter of Ḥusain. Moaning for Ḥusain has become the paramount mood of the Shîʿa. The true believer will never cease to weep for the martyred prince, not even in Paradise. In 962 "solemn wailings and lamentations"[47] for Ḥusain were instituted in Baghdad to mark the tenth of Muḥarram, the chief festival of the Shîʿî. As time went on, regular passion plays were performed on this day. The plays we possess, all of them of unknown authorship and in part of no mean artistic value, are hardly older than 1800, but there is every reason to believe that they give vent to emotions that were as vehemently experienced many centuries earlier.

When the government troops have closed in on Ḥusain, after endless conversations in his camp and after he has declined the assistance of the king of the *jinn*, the Umayyad general asks for a volunteer to kill the Prophet's grandson. Shimar responds and says:

> I am he whose dagger is famous for bloodshed. My mother has borne me for this work alone. I care not about the conflict of the Day of Judgment; I am a worshipper of Yazîd (the Umayyad caliph), and have no fear of God. I can make the great throne of the Lord to shake and tremble. I alone can sever from the body the head of Ḥusain the son of ʿAlî. I am he who has no share in Islam. I will strike the chest of Ḥusain, the ark of God's knowledge, with my boots, without any fear of punishment.
>
> Ḥusain: Oh, how wounds caused by arrows and daggers do smart! O God, have mercy in the Day of Judgment on my people for my sake. The time of death has arrived, but I have not my Akbar[48] with me. Would to God my grandfather the Prophet were now here to see me!
>
> The Prophet (*appearing*): Dear Ḥusain, thy grandfather the Prophet of God has come to see thee. I am here to behold the mortal wounds of thy delicate body. Dear child, thou hast at length suffered martyrdom by the cruel hand of my own people! This was the reward I expected from them; thanks be to God! Open thine eyes, dear son, and behold thy grandfather with dishevelled hair. If thou hast any desire in thy heart, speak it out to me.
>
> Ḥusain: Dear grandfather, I abhor life; I would rather go and visit my dear ones in the next world. I earnestly desire to see my companions and friends—above all, my dearly beloved son ʿAlî Akbar.

[46] ʿAlî at-Tanûḫî (d. 953–54), *Irshâd*, V, 342[8]; the poem by Ibn al-Muʿtazz to which at-Tanûḫî replies is *Dîwân*, I, 16.

[47] Mez, *op. cit.*, p. 68.

[48] His son, killed previously.

THE PROPHET: Be not grieved that ᶜAlî Akbar thy son was killed, since it tends to the good of my sinful people on the day of universal gathering.

ḤUSAIN: Seeing ᶜAlî Akbar's martyrdom contributes to the happiness of thy people, seeing my own sufferings give validity to thy office of mediation, and seeing thy rest consists in my being troubled in this way, I would offer my soul, not once or twice, but a thousand times, for the salvation of thy people!

THE PROPHET: Sorrow not, dear grandchild; thou shalt be a mediator, too, in that day. At present thou art thirsty, but tomorrow thou shalt be the distributor of the water of al-Kausar (in Paradise).[49]

In this manner the incident of Kerbela is reinterpreted as an action of cosmic significance and as a drama strongly reminiscent of the death of the Christ.

At present Shiite strength is greatest in India, Iraq, and especially Persia, where Shiism has been the state religion since 1502. At the height of the Middle Ages it was, in its several ramifications, a powerful force in Egypt, Mesopotamia, and southern and eastern Arabia. The Persian East was won, but Egypt lost, only during and after the eleventh century. For a long time Baghdad was the center as of all theology so of the polemics between Sunna and Shîᶜa—polemics which extended from insults exchanged by the populace through the discussions of the learned to the rhymed invectives of the poets.

Not those controversies but political events determined the development of Shiite doctrine. In 873 there died in Samarra Abû Muḥammad al-ᶜAskarî, whom the most numerous branch of the Shîᶜa, the "Twelvers," count as their eleventh *imâm*. His son, Muḥammad Abû ʾl-Qâsim, the twelfth *imâm*, disappeared in his own home in 880 at the age of perhaps nine years. He did not die but went into concealment whence he will return at the end of time.

The idea that a personality of metaphysical significance is temporarily removed from this world, or at least from the sight of mankind, to introduce the millennium by his reappearance is anchored in the Judeo-Christian milieu and corroborated by Zoroastrian eschatology. Sunnite Islam, too, has been receptive to messianic hopes. The Muslim masses beset by injustice

[49] Sir L. Pelly, *The Miracle Play of Hasan and Husain* (London, 1879), II, 101–2.*

and political uncertainty cherished the belief in the Mahdî, the absolutely guided (by Allah), who would when the end of the world was at hand bring about a short period of perfection.

Ibn Ḫaldûn states, though with little sympathy for this popular expectation, that "it has been commonly accepted among the masses of the people of Islam, as the ages have passed, that there must needs appear in the End of Time a man of the family of Mohammed who will aid the Faith and make justice triumph; that the Muslims will follow him and that he will reign over the Muslim kingdoms and will be called al-Mahdî. The appearance of ad-Dajjâl[50] and of the other signs of the Last Day which are established in sound tradition will come after him. ᶜÎsà (Jesus) will descend after his appearance and will kill ad-Dajjâl or will descend along with him and aid him in that killing; and in worship ᶜÎsà will follow the Mahdî as his *imâm*."[51]

Popular imagination was backed by numerous traditions elaborating on the Mahdî's personality as on every other eschatological detail. The worse the lot of the Muslims, the more fervent their belief in this savior, the greater their readiness to adhere to pretenders masquerading as such. For at least four hundred years after their fall did the people of Syria hope for the advent of the Sufyânî who would bring back the glories of the Umayyads. The dynasties in power retaliated by spreading traditions deprecating the role of the Sufyânî and having him killed by the Mahdî. Not to this day has the appeal of the Mahdî concept died out in the less Westernized parts of the Muslim world.

But, despite the Mahdî's intrenchment in the hearts of the multitude, Sunnite theology never made him a part of the official creed. The Shîᶜa, on the other hand, includes the belief in the "hidden *imâm*," the Lord of the Age (*qâᵓim az-zamân*), among its fundamental doctrines. His absence, *ghaiba*, does not prevent his being the true ruler of the world. His sinless existence is necessary, and even in concealment he aids and comforts the faithful.

"When the *imâm* Zain al-ᶜÂbidîn (d. *ca.* 714) was asked: 'How

[50] An eschatological personage of the antichrist type.

[51] *Prolegomena,* II, 142 (trans., II, 158); trans. D. B. Macdonald, *EI*, III, 113.

could men profit from a Proof of God that was concealed and hidden from them?' he replied, 'They would profit in the same way they do from the Sun when it is concealed by a cloud.' "[52]

There are four answers "to the statement that a concealed *imâm* can be of no profit to mankind. The first is that all the time there is the expectation that the *imâm* will appear, and this expectation in itself makes for abstinence from numerous sins. . . . . The second answer is that the Most High has by His grace given the *imâm*, and the reason he is concealed is on account of his enemies among men. The situation is similar to that of the Prophet in Mecca, when the unbelieving Quraish prevented men from coming to him. . . . . During the time he was in exile, and up until the time when he appeared as a Prophet in Medina, there can be no doubt that his status was that of a Prophet and was always advantageous to men. The third answer is that it is perfectly possible that God knows that there are friends of the *imâm* during his concealment who would deny him if he appeared, so that his appearance would thus become a reason for their loss of faith. The fourth answer is that it is not at all necessary that all should profit equally. It might be that a select number would see him and be thus advantaged, just as they say that there is a city where the descendants of the *imâm* live and that the *imâm* will go to that city. Although the people of the city may not see him, yet they will utter their requests to him, as it were behind a curtain."[53]

Its obvious remoteness from Mohammed's teaching notwithstanding, Shiite dogma is in the faithful's mind based on Koran and tradition. The Shîᶜî is as *sunna*-conscious as the so-called Sunnî. The custom of the Prophet makes law for him as well as for the main body of believers. It is only in the selection of *ḥadîṯ* where the distinction shows. The Shîᶜa receives exclusively such *ḥadîṯ* as are related by Shîᶜî—or at least pro-Shîᶜa Sunnî—authorities, and innumerable forgeries have been circulated to support Shîᶜa teaching and Shîᶜa attitude toward the Alids.

Adoption of allegoresis as the principle of interpretation pro-

[52] Majlisî (d. 1699), quoted by Donaldson, *op. cit.*, p. 310.

[53] Sayyid Murtaḍà (d. 1044), quoted by Majlisî, *Ḥayât al-qulûb*, trans. Donaldson, *op. cit.*, pp. 311–12.

cured the necessary backing of revelation. While the Shîᶜa contends that their early antagonists suppressed pro-Alid passages in the Book, it recognizes the genuineness of the material extant and has never pressed too hard the claims to genuineness of certain verses or suras allegedly rediscovered at various times. But the Shîᶜa did tamper with the standard text to vindicate its tenets through minor changes in the Koran's wording. Appropriate interpretation of the received context remained, however, its most powerful proof.

The Koran says: "To whom Allah giveth not light, for him there is no light."[54] Al-Qummî (*fl.* in the tenth century) explains this to mean that he to whom Allah does not give an *imâm* of Fâṭimid birth will, on the Day of Resurrection, have no *imâm* in whose light he could appear.[55] In another verse the Lord addresses the bee[56]—here the bee is taken to stand for the family of the Prophet. The "drink varied in color" which comes forth from the bees' bellies[57] is the Koran intrusted by God to the *ahl al-bait*, the Household of the Prophet.[58] In another passage man is asked: "Does he think that no one has seen him? (8) Have We not given him two eyes, (9) A tongue and two lips, (10) And have guided him the two paths?"[59] Here the two eyes represent the Prophet, the tongue, ᶜAlî, the two lips, Ḥasan and Ḥusain, and the two paths are understood as leading to loyal attachment to the last-named.[60]

Infiltration of non-Islamic matter is even stronger in the systems of the "Sevener" Shîᶜa, so called because of their belief that it was the seventh *imâm*, variously identified as Mûsà al-Kâẓim (d. 799) or Ismâᶜîl b. Jaᶜfar (d. 762) or rather his son Muḥammad, who went into concealment. The Ismâᶜîlîs, supporters of Ismâᶜîl's claims to the imamate, were organized in a semisecret society whose members were classed according to the degree of their initiation into the esoteric doctrines of the sect.

[54] Koran 24:40.

[55] Goldziher, *Die Richtungen der islamischen Koranauslegung* (Leiden, 1920), p. 298.

[56] Koran 16:70.

[57] Koran 16:71.

[58] Goldziher, *Richtungen*, pp. 299–300.

[59] Koran 90:7–10.

[60] Goldziher, *Richtungen*, p. 300.

The Qarmaṭians, with their center in Baḥrain, whose strength in Syria and Mesopotamia between *ca.* 870 and 1000 derived as much from the social discontent of the times as from their religious message, stood in close but not yet completely explained connection with the Fâṭimids.

ᶜUbaidallâh who seized power in the Maghrib in 909 and whose descendants conquered Egypt in 969 to maintain themselves for two centuries as a small Shiite caste ruling a huge majority of Sunnî subjects, this ᶜUbaidallâh was the first "hidden *imâm*" who emerged from concealment. While it can hardly be said that the Fâṭimids brought the millennium to Egypt, the flourishing state of this country at the middle of the eleventh century when its conditions were far happier than those prevailing in any Eastern Muslim land so impressed the Persian Sunnite Nâṣir-i H̱usraw (d. 1088) that he let himself be converted to the Ismâᶜîlian doctrine as the truth directly responsible for Egypt's prosperity.

Starting from the Neo-Platonic philosophy of emanation, the Ismâᶜîlîs, who have been called *taᶜlîmîs*, "devotees of teaching," because of their insistence on the necessity of an *imâm* for the authoritative instruction, postulate a sequence of "speakers," periodic manifestations of the universal intellect. The first of these speakers was Adam, who was followed by Noah, Abraham, Moses, Jesus, Mohammed, and, finally, the seventh *imâm*. During his life the speaker, *nâṭiq* or prophetic *imâm*, is assisted by his "base," *asâs*, who interprets the esoteric significance of the speaker's message. Thus Aaron assisted Moses and ᶜAlî assisted Mohammed. Between two speakers there arises a "silent *imâm*," *ṣâmit*, who maintains the tradition of the preceding and prepares the way for the next *nâṭiq*. Each manifestation is more perfect than the previous one. The seventh *nâṭiq* will be followed by the Mahdî who will represent a still higher manifestation of the universal intellect and thus outdo the work of all prior manifestations including, of course, the prophet Mohammed.

This doctrine evidently destroys the basis of traditional Islam, of the Sunnî as well as the Shîᶜî persuasion. Allegorical interpretation of the Koran, which unearths the inner, *bâṭin*, meaning of the text, justifies the Ismâᶜîlî system which in its higher grades disparages all positive religion and stresses the relative truth of all theological systems. The Iẖwân aṣ-ṣafâ, whose views parallel in many respects those of the Ismâᶜîlî, declare: "It befits our brothers that they should not show hostility to any kind of knowledge or reject any book. Nor should they be fanatical in any doctrine, for our opinion and our doctrine embrace all doctrines, and resume all knowledge."[61]

Serious social grievances, the support given to the established order by Sunnite Islam, and the steadily worsening political situation made the Ismâᶜîlî and related movements very influential until deep into the thirteenth century.[62] The progressive impoverishment of the country was the mainspring of "revolutionary Shiism." The social crisis brought about by the rise of industry and trade in the ᶜAbbâsid Empire had filled wide strata of the population with enmity against organized religion. Around 1000, Aḥmad b. Muḥammad al-Ifrîqî, known as al-Mutayyam, sang:

> No, certainly, I shall not pray to God, as long as I shall be poor. Let us leave prayers to the Shaiẖ al-Jalîl, to Fâᵓiq . . . .
> To the chief of armies, whose cellars bulge with measures. But why should I pray? Am I mighty? Have I a palace, horses, rich clothes and golden belts?
> To pray, when I do not possess a single inch of earth, would be pure hypocrisy.[63]

The populace would follow any leader who would bring them hope couched in the authoritative terms of religious expectation. Political vicissitudes favored or uprooted the individual sects. But the movement outlasted the disappointment of centuries.[64]

[61] Quoted by B. Lewis, *The Origins of Ismâᶜîlism* (Cambridge, 1940), p. 94.

[62] The full significance of those "Sevener" heresies for philosophy, on the one hand, and for the history of the Muslim world, on the other, is only beginning to be realized. A great deal remains to be done. Further investigation will result in a better understanding of the social stratification of the day, the relations of the political powers, and the Greek and Gnostic heritage in Islamic thought.

[63] *Irshâd*, II, 81; trans. Lewis, *op. cit.*, p. 92.

[64] The ruthlessness of the Neo-Ismâᶜîlites of Ḥasan Ṣabbâḥ (d. 1124), who freely used terrorist methods to spread their influence, brought them into disrepute with Crusaders as well as orthodox Muslims as *Assassins*. Hûlâgû broke their power, but they survive to this day in an insignificant group in Syria and in a

IV

Islam was not a social movement in the sense that it aimed at reforming the existing order. But, while Mohammed did not attack the distribution of property as he found it, he attacked the traditional foundation of the Arab hierarchy by deprecating noble ancestry as of no avail in the eyes of the Lord and by stressing the equality of all believers within the fold of the new faith. Political considerations did not permit him to adhere too strictly to this principle. Powerful adversaries were reconciled, potential disloyalty forestalled by economic concessions of considerable magnitude as well as by tacit recognition of social prerogatives. While, on the one hand, Islam promoted egalitarianism, on the other, it strengthened the traditional aristocratic proclivities of the Arabs by providing a new and, to the Muslim, unimpeachable basis for social distinction, the closeness to the Prophet in blood and in faith. Thus there was added to the pagan nobility of descent the *ashrâf*, nobles, of the Prophet's line, of his clan, of his tribe, the offspring of the Meccan companions of his migration, *muhâjirûn*, and of his Medinese helpers, *anṣâr*. Throughout the ᶜAbbâsid Empire the Hâshimids, the members of the Prophet's family, enjoyed financial privileges.

The conquests made the Arabs the leading group throughout the Empire. Whatever their internal distinctions, their political power ennobled them as a nation. They began to consider themselves as the true aristocracy of the Muslim world. The facts of the situation together with this presumptious attitude engendered a number of disquieting problems. There was, first of all, the question where to place the non-Arab Muslim. The foreigner who stuck to his religion—Christian, Jewish, or Zoroastrian—lived in a social setting of his own the structure of which did not have to be attuned to Arab prejudice. But for those Persians, Copts, Greeks, Nabataeans, Negroes, and Turks who accepted Islam, room had to be made in Muslim society.

These recent converts, then, had to supplement their change

---

much more influential body in India, where the well-known Aga Khan is at present heading their main subsect, the Khojas (*ca.* 150,000 adherents) in his capacity as their forty-seventh *imâm.*

of religion by obtaining affiliation with an Arab tribe who would extend its protection to them[65] but in return consider them its clients, *mawâlî*. The word *maulà* as a technical term covers three very different relationships. The manumitted slave becomes a client, *maulà*, of his former master. An Arab of one tribe, and in exceptional cases even a non-Arab, could, according to age-old custom, become the affiliate of another tribe, enjoying the same standing as the natural-born members of his new community. Such equality was not enjoyed by the non-Arab *mawâlî* converts. In fact, their social disabilities, mainly enforced by convention, which, however, under the Umayyads found ready support from the authorities, proved much more irksome to the *mawâlî* than the special taxation to which they were liable.

Their situation was not only unsatisfactory but in many ways paradoxical and thus extremely provoking. A sizable proportion of the *mawâlî* lived in easy circumstances, or were actually rich, through control of certain trades or as landowners and merchants. Their proportionate contribution to religious and mundane studies easily outranked that of the Arabs. Although *mawâlî* of Persian background quickly became Arabicized as far as language went and although they were among the most pious of Muslims, the consciousness that their ancestors had been bearers of a civilization much higher than that of their Arab masters never left them. But neither wealth nor learning, or even political influence, could free them from Arab contempt. This contempt directed against non-Arab nationalities as if they were nothing but an inferior social class lost little of its acrimony but much of its effectiveness when the ᶜAbbâsids came into power. There was actually nothing to maintain it except the intense and, with their fall from the leading position in the state, increasingly vindictive race-feeling of the Arabs aided, in some degree, by the glory accruing to them from having given the world its last and greatest prophet.

Every other factor operated against the supremacy of the pure-blooded Arab. The rise of city civilization favored the

[65] On the practical aspect of this protection in desert travel see G. Jacob, *Altarabisches Beduinenleben* (2d ed.; Berlin, 1897), p. 211, n. 1.

maulà and the *ʿajam*, the non-Arab (especially the Persian), over the Bedouin tribesman. However tenaciously clung to, in the long run tribal feeling was bound to wane in the great urban centers. The Empire was maintained primarily from taxation of the non-Arab elements. It had long since become impossible to govern it as the private domain of the Arab aristocracy. The growing strength of Muslim orthodoxy, too, worked toward equality.

Around 750, Abû Ḥanîfa had ruled that "all Quraishites were of equal standing in a class by themselves, and that all other Arabs were equal irrespective of their tribes. Amongst non-Arab Muslims, a man was by birth the equal of an Arab if both his father and grandfather had been Muslims before him, but only then if he were sufficiently wealthy to provide an adequate marriage endowment."[66] This combination of *ancienneté* in the faith, wealth, and descent as yardsticks of social standing marks a decided advance over the *mawâlî*'s position, say, two generations earlier. It should be noted, too, that the Mâlikites acknowledged their full equality with the Arabs.

By that time the Arabization of the *mawâlî* had made big strides. They had even invaded, though not without opposition, the field of Arabic poetry. An ever growing number of the great masters of the Arabic language was recruited from people of non-Arab ancestry. Imperceptibly, Arabic civilization becomes Muslim civilization, and it is the spontaneous collaboration of the best minds of all the Empire's nationalities that accounts for the stupendous rise of this civilization in those two hundred years, from 750 to 950, so breathlessly crowded with cultural exploits in the most disparate areas of human accomplishment. It might be suggested, although with a grain of salt, that Arab leadership declined just when the Muslim, and to a certain extent also the non-Muslim, population had successfully assimilated the two great gifts the Arabs had to bestow—their language and their faith. And it is obvious that under the hands of the Arabicized Muslim both this language and this faith gained such literary and spiritual richness as could never have been evolved in the isolation of the peninsula.

[66] *Al-Jâmiʿ aṣ-ṣaghîr* (Bûlâq, 1302), p. 32, quoted in Levy, *op. cit.*, I, 91.

Arab race pride survives to this day. But in the cosmopolitan world of the Muslim empire racial separation could not be maintained. The Koran's permission of unlimited concubinage with slave girls, coupled with the provision that the offspring of such unions was to be considered legitimate, made for speedy intrusion of foreign blood in the greatest houses of the Arab aristocracy. Only three ᶜAbbâsid caliphs were born of free mothers, and all these belong to the eighth century. The ancient Arab concept of nobility had been based on descent from a noble father and a noble mother; now the idea gained acceptance that, as a poet put it, "the mothers of men are but vessels . . . . ; the fathers account for nobility."[67]

Greek culture permeated the Roman Empire. But the Greeks remained barred from political power. Persian influence on the development of the Islamic world, comparable in many ways to that exercized by the Greeks on the Latin West, was promoted by the leading positions in the government which Persian Muslims attained under the ᶜAbbâsid dynasty. It was not only the etiquette of the court which became Persianized or the style of the administration—Iranian thinking habits, Iranian prejudices, Iranian social and economic traditions, even outright Iranian nationalism were introduced in the capital albeit under the cloak of the Arabic language and under careful, if upon occasion somewhat specious, preservation of Islamic orthodoxy.

In contrast to the ordinary run of converted Persians who had sought and found identification with Arab society, however superficial and disadvantageous, wide strata of the Persian nobility had succeeded, upon adopting Islam, in maintaining their landed property, their social standing, their political influence—all this while keeping within their own traditional class hierarchy. With their inclusion in the leading stratum of the ᶜAbbâsid capital two social systems came to coexist at court: the Arab-Muslim, which relegated the non-Arab to the bottom of the ladder, and the Iranian, which classed people according to profession rather than descent.

The Avesta originally recognized three classes—priests, warriors, and agriculturists—to which later the artisans were add-

[67] Cf. Goldziher, *Muh. Stud.*, I, 124.

ed.[68] Accordingly, Ardashîr, the first Sassanian king, divided his subjects into (1) knights and princes, (2) religious officials, (3) physicians, scribes, and astrologers, and (4) farmers and other people of low standing.[69] The classifications recorded by Ibn al-Faqîh[70] follow the same basic principle, which is again reflected in the vizier Niẓâm al-mulk's (d. 1094) *Treatise on Government* (*ca.* 1092), in which the population is graded in this order: "(1) the king, (2) the provincial governors or tax-gatherers, (3) the vizier, (4) feudal landowners, (5) the peasants subject to them, and (6) *qâḍîs*, preachers, police officers, etc."[71] A compromise can be discovered when in 1532–33 ᶜAlî b. Ḥusain al-Kâshifî proposes a similar list but has it headed by the Prophet, his Companions, and the *imâms*.[72]

Pride in Iranian descent rooted in pride in the glories of their history lent emotional strength to those social concepts. Prestige and charm of the Persian manner proved equally winsome. ᶜAbdalmalik (685–705) rebuked Ibn Qais ar-Ruqayyât for representing him as an *ᶜajam* in a panegyrical poem.[73] But Abû Tammâm (d. 846) incurs criticism when he compares the caliph to Ḥâtim Ṭayy and other Arab models of generosity. How dare he compare the Prince of the Faithful to those barbarians![74]

When Ismâᶜîl b. Yasâr, a *maulà* of Persian ancestry, had sung before Hishâm (724–43):

Princes were my ancestors, noble satraps of high breeding, generous, hospitable . . . .
They humbled the kings of the Turks and Greeks, they stalked in heavy coats of mail
As ravenous lions stalk forth.
There, if thou askest, wilt thou learn that we are descended from a race which excels all others;[75]

[68] Cf. E. Benveniste, *Journal asiatique*, CCXXI (1932), 117.

[69] Al-Jâḥiẓ (?), *Kitâb at-tâj*, ed. Aḥmad Zekî Pasha (Cairo, 1914), p. 25.

[70] Cf. above, p. 171.

[71] Levy, *op. cit.*, I, 99.

[72] *Ibid.*, p. 100; for detail see H. Ethé in W. Geiger and E. Kuhn, *Grundriss der iranischen Philologie* (Strassburg, 1896–1904), II, 332.

[73] *Aghânî* (3d ed.), V, 79; the objectionable verse, *Dîwân*, I, 18.

[74] Goldziher, *Muh. Stud.*, I, 148.

[75] Trans. from A. von Kremer's German version in S. Khuda Bukhsh, *Contributions to the History of Islamic Civilization* (Calcutta, 1905), p. 90.

the caliph had him thrown into a pond, and he narrowly escaped with his life. But, in the tenth century, Abû Saᶜîd ar-Rustamî may ask with impunity:

The Arabs boast of being the masters of the world and the lords of the peoples.
Why don't they rather boast of being shepherds and camel drivers?[76]

And another poet calls on them to vacate the throne of the Persians, to withdraw to Ḥijâz, and to eat lizards and herd camels.[77]

Mastering as they did the techniques of Arabic literary presentation, it was not long before the non-Arab Muslims, and especially those of Persian ancestry, lifted their fight for equality to the plane of scientific discussion. This intellectual nationalism took its name, *shuᶜûbiyya*, from a koranic passage in which the Lord tells the faithful, "We have created you of male and female and made you races, *shuᶜûb*, and tribes, *qabâᵓil*, that ye may show mutual recognition; verily the most noble of you in Allah's eyes is the most pious."[78] This verse was, and it would seem correctly, interpreted as enjoining equal standing of all Arab tribes, *qabâᵓil*, and all non-Arab peoples, *shuᶜûb*. As happens frequently in similar situations, the spokesmen who had started by vindicating the equality with the ruling Arabs of their national group ended by proclaiming its superiority. And again in accordance with the fate of other literary movements, the *shuᶜûbî* controversy outlived the period of its significance, being carried on deep into the twelfth century, when history had long since decided the issue against the Arabs.

On the whole, the dispute was conducted in a manner not worthy of the excellent scholarship of a goodly portion of the contestants. It is strange to observe what type of arguments seemed then conclusive evidence as to the greater or lesser value of a nation before God. We can sympathize with the Arab insistence on Mohammed's compatriots being ennobled by the very fact of their relationship with the greatest of messengers. And we will be ready to admit that this argument had to be countered with the reminder that all the other prophets that

[76] Goldziher, *Muh. Stud.*, I, 162.

[77] At-Taᶜâlibî, *Der vertraute Gefährte des Einsamen*, ed. G. Flügel (Vienna, 1829), No. 314 on p. 272; cf. Goldziher, *Muh. Stud.*, I, 164.

[78] Koran 49:13.

preceded him were of non-Arab stock. To have given the world those many apostles naturally increased the dignity of the non-Arabs. Moreover, if the Arabs were descended from Abraham through Ismâ^cîl, the Persian genealogists showed their people descended from him through Isaac.

The present political supremacy of the Arabs lost some of its splendor when the allegedly much greater splendor of the ancient Persian kings was recalled. And even should the Arab power exceed that wielded by the Iranian monarchs it could be urged that they had attained and promoted civilization at a time when the Arabs had not so much as emerged into the light of history. All well considered, what did the Arabs have to their credit? Their language, yes, although weaknesses could be found even in this instrument of revelation.[79] Their endless genealogies? Perhaps. But what did it signify if you could trace your descent from a long line of robbers, camel-drivers, and lizard-eaters? And, what is more, their own tradition cast weighty suspicions on the genuineness of many a family tree, on the modesty of many a woman who appeared as a key figure in tribal genealogy. On the strength of their own records most of those proud Bedouin aristocrats were of mixed blood, bastards, and the sons of bastards. Their nomadism, their foods, their customs—every conceivable item was taken to lower the standing of the Arabs. Did not the *shu^cûbiyya* go so far as to turn the Arab orator's habit of carrying a staff in his hand into evidence of his nation's inferiority?

The *shu^cûbî* movement was not confined to Persians. But with them it was one aspect of a national renascence which seems to have begun late in the eighth and won a somewhat limited victory in the tenth century. The partly religious and partly political rebellions of Bihâfrîd (d. *ca.* 750), Sinbâḏ the Magian (d. 756), Ustâḏsîs (d. 768), al-Muqanna^c (d. 780), and Bâbak (d. 838) were followed by the purely political sedition of the Ṣaffârids (868–903) in Sijistân, North and East Persia, and the Sâmânids (874–999) with the center of their power in Ḫurâsân. The Sâmânids had their scholars link up their genealogy with

[79] Cf. the Persian who, *ca.* 800, taunts the Arabs for having borrowed so many foreign terms (Ṣûlî, *op. cit.*, p. 193).*

the Sassanians so as to prove the legitimacy of their claim to power over Persian territory, and they patronized literary activity in Persian which after timid beginnings was growing into full bloom during the tenth century.

Balᶜamî, who prepared the Persian version of Ṭabarî's *Annales,* was a Sâmânid vizier. Rûdagî (d. 940–41), the first great Persian poet, lived at the Sâmânid court. Daqîqî (d. 952) began the monumental versification of Iranian history and legend which was to be completed by Firdausî (d. *ca.* 1020) as the *Shâh-Nâma* (Book of Kings), one of the great masterpieces of all times, under Sâmânid auspices. Thus *shuᶜûbî* anti-Arabism, the struggle for Persian independence, and the revival of learning and poetry in the Persian language must be considered three fronts of the same fight.*

It is doubtful, however, whether complete severance from the Arab sphere was ever envisaged. The Ṣaffârids and the Sâmânids, just as many a dynasty of later times, were anxious to receive the formal confirmation of the caliph in Baghdad. The Persian littérateurs of the tenth century were almost all bilingual, composing Arab and Persian verse with equal facility. And scholarship, especially in the religious sciences, continued to use Arabic as its vehicle. Persian literature rose to unrivaled heights of expressiveness during the subsequent four or five centuries, but Arab ways of thought as embodied in Muslim tradition were never really discarded and the interaction of Arab and Persian writing never ceased. Persian scholarship continued to contribute to research and speculation carried on in Arabic, but it outlasted for some time the decline of learning which the political developments forced upon the centers of the Arab world. It is extremely important for the understanding of the Persian resurgence in the tenth century that it was during this period that the last strong nuclei of Zoroastrianism yielded to the religion of the Arab Prophet.

Of all the non-Arab nationalities, the Persians ranked highest. Therefore, the poet Ibn Mayyâda (d. *ca.* 766) claimed Persian descent for his mother, who actually was either Berber or Slav.[80] The Nabataeans—not to be confused with those whose

[80] *Aghânî* (3d ed.), II. 261.

kingdom with the capital of Petra was destroyed by Trajan in A.D. 106—badly suffered from Arab arrogancy. Those "eaters of lentils"[81] were not too successful in vindicating their claim to equality by means of various literary forgeries destined to demonstrate the venerable age of their civilization[82] and the favor shown them by the early heroes of Islam.[83] The Aramaic-speaking peasantry of Mesopotamia, to which the Arabs extended the name of Nabataeans from its original application to the non-military settlers of Syria and Iraq,[84] never quite made the grade. Nor did the Turks.

They came to the capital as the caliph's bodyguard and at once incurred the dislike of the population. Al-Muᶜtaṣim's removal to Samarra, in 836, did not improve matters. By the middle of the ninth century the Turkish praetorians were all-powerful, appointing and deposing caliphs, and enjoying great liberty in the handling of public moneys. Their influence declined temporarily during the next generations, but ultimately it was their kin who came to control the Near East.

Ibn Lankak of Baṣra (d. 912–13) sings:

The free have passed away, they are gone and destroyed: Time has left me amongst barbarians.
They tell me: You are staying at home too much. But I say: Because it does not give pleasure to go out.
Whom would I meet looking around me: just apes riding in saddles.
(This is) a time in which nobility has risen so high it is all by itself in the highest mansions of the stars.[85]

The Turks could not be denied a measure of recognition because of their warlike qualities. Their horsemanship, their courage, and their hardiness caused admiration. But they were credited with the vices of their virtues. "The Turk would rather ob-

[81] *Aghânî* (1st ed.), XVIII, 144⁷; cf. Goldziher, *Muh. Stud.*, I, 156, n. 2.

[82] Ibn al-Waḥshiyya, or perhaps Aḥmad b. Zayyât, in his *Nabataean Agriculture, ca.* 930, attempts to glorify the Nabataeans by showing the superiority of Babylonian over Arab civilization. The Nabataeans are introduced as heirs of Babylonian culture. Having nothing to go by, he invented all the evidence (cf. *GAL*, I, 242, and Suppl., I, 430–31).

[83] For the Nabataeans in tradition cf. Goldziher, *Muh. Stud.*, I, 156–58.

[84] Cf. E. Honigmann, *EI*, III, 802.

[85] Aṯ-Ṯaᶜâlibî, *Yatîmat ad-dahr* (Damascus, n.d.), II, 118; quoted in part, Goldziher, *Muh. Stud.*, I, 152.

tain a maintenance by violent means than a kingdom freely: he cannot enjoy his food at all unless he has got it by hunting or by plunder."[86]

Poetry, and later art, accepted Turkish (and Mongol) features as beautiful. Many are the verses where slanted eyes, sleek dark hair, and a round face are praised without restraint. Only too often did the Turkish slave become the favorite of his master. But when the Turks first attracted the interest of the Arabs it was for their military virtues. They occupy in war the position of the Greeks in science and the Chinese in art.[87] Al-Jâḥiẓ, who appears to have been particularly interested in "national psychology,"[88] credits them with simple virtues. "The Turks know not how to flatter or coax, they know not how to practice hypocrisy or backbiting, pretence or slander, dishonesty or haughtiness on their acquaintance, or mischief on those that associate with them. They are strangers to heresy[89] and not spoiled by caprice, and they do not make property lawful by quibbles."[90]

They are a proud people. They do not acquiesce in playing a subordinate role. "They are more offended when anyone is ignorant of their claims than they are when anyone refuses to give them what they ask." But when they meet with a fair-minded king, they cast in their lot with him "and submit to parting from their country and accept the imamate rather than tyrannical lordship and justice to custom."[91] But what impresses al-Jâḥiẓ most about them is the tenacity with which they resist assimila-

[86] Al-Jâḥiẓ, *Tria opuscula*, ed. G. Van Vloten (Leiden, 1903), p. 37; trans. C. T. Harley Walker, *JRAS*, 1915, p. 675.

[87] *Opuscula*, p. 46; Walker, *loc. cit.*, p. 685.

[88] Cf. *Opuscula*, p. 44 (trans. Walker, *loc. cit.*, p. 683): "The Greeks know the theory, but do not concern themselves with the practice. The Chinese do concern themselves with the practice, but do no know the theory." Not all his observations are as happy, though. Ibn Ḥazm, *Fiṣal*, IV, 181, well characterizes al-Jâḥiẓ as "one of those frivolous men who are mastered by the desire for a joke, and one of those who lead into error, yet one, as we found, who in his books never sets forth a lie deliberately and assertively, though he often enough sets forth the lies of others." The passage is quoted by I. Friedlaender, *JAOS*, XXVIII (1907), 1st half, p. 50.*

[89] *Al-bidaᶜ*. The aversion to independent theological speculation remained with the Turks throughout the period.

[90] *Opuscula*, pp. 39–40 (trans. Walker, *loc. cit.*, p. 678).

[91] *Ibid.*, pp. 42–43 (trans. Walker, *loc. cit.*, pp. 681–82).

tion. While the Arabs who settled in the East become indistinguishable from the natives of those provinces, the Turks retain their national characteristics. Love of one's country is common to all nations, "but it is peculiarly strong amongst the Turks, and counts for more among them owing to their mutual similarity and homogeneity of idiosyncrasy."[92]

With this opinion there should be compared what the physician Ibn Buṭlân (d. after 1063) says of the Turkish slave girls. "Fair-skinned, the Turkish women are full of grace and animation. Their eyes are small but enticing. They are thick-set and are inclined to be of short stature. There are very few tall women among them. They are prolific in breeding, and their offspring are but rarely ugly. They are never bad riders. They are generous; they are clean in their habits; they cook well; but they are unreliable."[93]

History brought equality of Persian and Arab and of Turk and Arab, but it did not help the Muslim Negro to vindicate his birthright. When al-Jâḥiẓ in one of his paradoxical moods sets out to prove the superiority of the blacks over the whites,[94] he includes Indians, Abyssinians, Nubians, Copts, and Negroes in the designation "blacks." He points out that their color is due to the climate of their homeland and in no way constitutes a punishment of God.[95] He also defends them against the opinion that their intelligence is inferior and ranks with that of white women and children.[96] The H̱ârijites declared that even "an Abyssinian slave" was eligible for the caliphate, thus showing that such a person was considered at the very bottom of the social order. A Medinese woman rebuked Kuṯayyir for praising the scent of her sleeves that had been touched by the smoke of aloe-wood,[97] instead of suggesting that it is her fragrance which permeates her clothes with sweetness, by remarking: Even a

[92] *Ibid.*, p. 41 (trans. Walker, *loc. cit.*, p. 679).

[93] Mez, *op. cit.*, p. 162. Cf. the ethnological remarks made apropos the purchase of slaves by Kaikâ'ûs b. Iskandar, prince of Gurgân, in his *Qâbûs Nâmah* (written in 1082/3), ed. R. Levy (London, 1951), pp. 64–66 (trans. Levy, *A Mirror for Princes: The Qābūs Nāma* [London, 1951], pp. 102–5).

[94] *Opuscula*, pp. 57–85; a brief summary of his *Risâla fî faḫr as-sûdân ʿalà ʾl-bîḍân* in O. Rescher, *Excerpte und Uebersetzungen aus den Schriften des .... Ǧâḥiẓ* (Stuttgart, 1931), pp. 210–12.

[95] *Opuscula*, pp. 81–82.

[96] *Ibid.*, pp. 76–77.

[97] *Dîwân*, ed. H. Pérès, No. 12.9.

Negro woman's sleeve would smell pleasant if scented with aloe.[98] Nuṣaib, celebrated as the best Negro poet (*fl.* 700), is painfully conscious of his color and declines invitations for dinner as he is afraid his table companions might not really like to have a meal with him.[99] The famous Negro singer, Ibn Musajjiḥ, is equally apprehensive of giving offense when traveling incognito.[100]

The Negro *shuᶜûbiyya* emphasized the hospitality enjoyed by the first Muslim *émigrés* in Abyssinia. The Prophet is visited by an Abyssinian who addresses him with this question: "You Arabs excel us in every respect; you are more shapely, and of more gainly color; also the Prophet has arisen amongst you. Now, if I believe in your mission shall I be awarded a seat in Paradise alongside of the believing Arabs?" "Yes," the Prophet assures him, "and the black skin of the Abyssinian will spread splendor at a distance of a thousand years."[101]

The Negroes, *zanj*, formed an important part of the slave army, which, in an attempt at breaking social oppression, fought the government under an Alid leader for fifteen years (868–83). The workers employed in making the Shaṭṭ al-ᶜArab arable[102] from whom the insurgents were largely recruited desired betterment of their position, not a reorganization of society. Although a considerable proportion of them were themselves slaves, they showed no desire to abolish slavery but instead took to keeping slaves of their own. It cannot be said that the final suppression of this movement affected the position of the Negro in Muslim society. The offspring of a Negro mother and a white father was admitted to full equality; the full-blooded Negro generally remained an outsider. The barrier was not, however, sufficiently strong to exclude Negroes from high office. From 946 to 968, Egypt was governed by Kâfûr, a Negro born in slavery.

The Christian physician, Ibn Buṭlân, discusses the relative

[98] *Kâmil*, p. 498.

[99] *Aghânî* (3d ed.), I, 352; Nuṣaib refuses to answer when attacked for his color.

[100] *Ibid.*, III, 282–84; the story is retold at length by Levy, *op. cit.*, I, 88–90.*

[101] Slightly abridged from Goldziher, *Muh. Stud.*, I, 74.

[102] On their activities cf. the details given by L. Massignon, *EI*, IV, 1213.

merits of colored slave girls. Of the Negress he has this to say: "At the markets Negresses were much in evidence; the darker the uglier and the more pointed their teeth. They are not up to much. They are fickle and careless. Dancing and beating time are engrained in their nature. They say: were the Negro to fall from heaven to the earth he would beat time in falling. They have the whitest teeth. . . . . The Abyssinian woman, on the other hand, is weak and flabby and frequently suffers from consumption. She is ill-suited for song and dance and languishes in a foreign country. She is reliable and has a strong character in a feeble body." Of all the "black" women, Ibn Buṭlân prefers the Nubian as "the most adaptable and cheerful."[103]

V

The viceroy of Iraq and half-brother of the caliph Muᶜâwiya, Ziyâd b. Abîhi (d. 676–77), asked his chamberlain in what order he admitted people to his presence. The chamberlain replied: First those who belong to a great house, then the aged, then the well-mannered and educated.[104] If the chamberlain really had been bent on giving everyone his social due, this simple rule-of-thumb would hardly have sufficed him to grade his master's visitors.

Muslim society of the great age was stratified according to a number of incompatible criteria. Position might be owed to membership in an aristocratic family of Arabic, or perhaps of Persian or even Jewish or Turkish, background. Among the Arabs nobility would derive from relationship to great tribal leaders of past or present or else to the household of the Prophet in any of its ramifications. Alids and Hâshimids were singled out from the population by being organized under a *naqîb* (*Adelsmarschall*). Money, though deprecated by the moralist, played

[103] Mez, *op. cit.*, pp. 161–62, trans. from a Berlin manuscript. The Negro's fondness of the dance is referred to by the poet Abû ᵓsh-Shamaqmaq (*fl.* end of eighth century), quoted by aṯ-Ṯaᶜâlibî, *Ṯimâr al-qulûb* (Cairo, 1908), p. 435 (Frag. xxxiv 2 of the writer's forthcoming edition). *BGA*, V, 330, quotes Plato(!) as declaring that the Negro knows no sorrow.

It would seem that in Byzantium there was even less of a color prejudice than among the Muslims (cf. Runciman, *op. cit.*, p. 182).

[104] Lit., those with *adab;* Ibn ᶜAbdrabbihi, *al-ᶜIqd al-farîd* (Cairo, 1353/1935), I, 37, and III, 238.

its customary part. Education opened the doors of the great to the ambitious poor, and it was a prerequisite for public office, although princely whim did not always stoop to scrutinize a favorite's qualifications. Political influence, military power, administrative rank, wealth, birth, and schooling, in every possible combination, strengthened or counteracted one another in assigning a given individual his place in society.

Position and influence were closely related. The Alids during the early reign of the ᶜAbbâsids provide the closest parallel to the familiar European phenomenon of a class like the ancient aristocracy in the Third French Republic maintaining its social prerogatives while withdrawing from the leading positions in the state. The will of the prince could transfer a subject from one class to another with the greatest ease and speed. Thus society remained flexible and fluid, but all the more intent upon bestowing on prevailing conditions an appearance of solidity through the enforcement of a rigid ceremonial of rank and station. Titles sought after and granted in steadily increasing numbers to civil and military officials as well as to judges and scholars constituted one device of holding fast to success attained. The office would be lost, but the former holder would continue to be addressed as "Pillar of the Faith," "Sword of the Empire," or "Adornment of Islam." The less reliance could be placed on actual conditions, the more those tokens of dignity and standing were craved.

Al-Bêrûnî (d. 1048) observes: "When the ᶜAbbâsids had decorated their assistants, friends and enemies indiscriminately, with vain titles, compounded with the word *daula* (that is, 'empire,' such as Helper of the Empire, Sword of the Empire, etc.) the empire perished; for in this they went beyond all reasonable limits. This went on so long that those who were especially attached to their court claimed something like a distinction between themselves and the others. Thereupon the Caliphs bestowed double titles. But then also the others wanted the same titles and knew how to carry their point by bribery. Now it became necessary a second time to create a distinction between this class and those who were directly attached to their court, so the Caliphs bestowed triple titles, adding besides the title of

Shâhinshâh. In this way the matter became utterly opposed to common sense, and clumsy to the highest degree, so that he who mentions them gets tired before he has scarcely commenced, he who writes them loses his time writing and he who addresses them runs the risk of missing the time for prayer."[105]

Offices were not hereditary. But administrative appointments were likely to be made from candidates belonging to a rather narrow circle of families. These families were in possession of the secrets of governmental technique, they were familiar with empire conditions, and they had the necessary connections. Slaves and freedmen, who were numerous among the military, were, therefore, fairly rare among the clerks. All the professions that presupposed special training tended to develop a certain exclusivity. Judgeships as well as the place of the court physician, the higher, but not necessarily the highest grades of the civil service, not infrequently remained within the same family or group of families for generations on end.

The judge and the theologian were expected to be experts in the sciences of tradition, canon law, and scholastic theology. The civil servant, among whose duties might be the conduct of state correspondence and the phrasing of edicts, represented a different type of education. His training was based on grammar, belles-lettres, and history, aiming at amassing universal if somewhat superficial information. Facility and elegance of written expression, mastery of etiquette and style, and a pleasant handwriting were the chief skills he could hope to display. "He who would be a savant," Ibn Qutaiba says, "should cultivate a particular branch of learning, but he who would be a littérateur let him range over the entire domain of learning."[106] The civil servant wore the *durrâ^ca*, an unlined woolen garment with a slit in front. The distinctive feature of the theologian's dress was the *ṭailasân*, a sort of pointed hood resting on the shoulders but sometimes worn over the turban.[107]

[105] *Chronology of Ancient Nations*, trans. E. Sachau (London, 1879), p. 129; quoted by Donaldson, *op. cit.*, pp. 275–76.*

[106] Mez, *op. cit.*, p. 170.

[107] Cf., e.g., *Irshâd*, I, 234, where al-Battî (d. 1012/3) first dons the dress of the legist, then that of the scribe. See also Ibn al-Mudabbir's description of the appearance of the *kâtib* (*Risâla*, pp. 8–9).

In addition to this entourage of court officials, the rulers surrounded themselves frequently with a group of "friends," *nudamâ*ʾ (lit., table companions), selected from the most personable and educated people of the capital. These *nudamâ*ʾ, who drew a salary, might but need not include prominent members of the prince's official family. The institution which dates back to the Parthian kings from whom the Roman emperors had borrowed it gave great influence without saddling with the responsibilities of office. Literary education, social graces, and the gift of improvisation would admit into, boorishness and pomposity exclude from, this circle. Successful poets, independent men of literary attainments, even singers and musicians would be invited to keep the sovereign company, and the educational movement which focused attention on *polymathia* and on style tied in only too well with the needs of the *nadîm*.

The poet, who again wore a peculiar dress when presenting himself at court—al-Jâḥiẓ prescribes for him embroidered silk fabric, a black cloak, or any other striking garment[108]—would upon occasion receive fabulous gifts from the ruler in reward for a happily formulated flattery or else in recognition of his services as a semiofficial spokesman for the government. How lucrative he, and the singer, might at times find his employ, for the most part he maintained himself not without difficulty on the fringes of high life. His position varied depending on his personal success. The power of the word counted for much, and his abilities would be sought for purposes of blackmail[109] or government publicity. The poet al-Ḫalîʿ as-Sâmî (d. 864) proclaimed the principle: It is one of the duties of princes to give presents to the poets.[110] And this viewpoint was generally accepted. While a court poet might rise to great wealth and even greater

[108] *Bayân*, III, 78.

[109] Cf. *Aghânî* (3d ed), IV, 162–63, the story of the rich man who seeks to buy a poet's support against another poet. *Kâmil*, p. 259, stresses the fact that Yaḥyà b. Naufal al-Ḥimyarî never praised to obtain gifts.

[110] At-Taʿâlibî, *Ḫâṣṣ al-ḫâṣṣ* (Cairo, 1326), p. 60. For the classical attitude, cf., e.g., Dio of Prusa *Or*. ii. 13: "Philip (of Macedonia) laughed and said, 'You observe, Alexander, that one must not offend good poets or clever writers, since they have the power to say anything they wish about us' " (trans. J. W. Cohoon, "Loeb Classical Library," I, 59).

Story-tellers, astrologers, and letter-writers connect respectable society with those marginal groups, part outsider and part outcast, whose place at the bottom is not regularized like that of the slaves but who are entirely at the mercy of chance. Such are the jugglers, of whose art the Iḫwân observe that "it is not anything real but just quickness of movement and concealment of the means (whereby the tricks are executed). . . . . The fools laugh, but the reasoning marvel at the skill of the performer."[127] Such are the beggars, who, however, not infrequently take up this pursuit to satisfy the rigorous unworldliness prescribed by some Ṣûfî conventicles. It is urged in those circles that the giver would get his return through Ṣûfî intercession in the next world. The authorities were likely to take a different view, though. Al-Mâwardî makes it clear that "a beggar who is sturdy and able to work should be reproved and told to earn his living by his craft, and if he persists he should be kept from begging by punishment."[128]

Abû Dulaf al-Ḫazrajî, a famous traveler (*fl.* 930–50), composed a long poem, full of the slang of vagrants and criminals, in which he describes the various types of the Banû Sâsân, the swindlers and *fahrende Leute* of his time.

When a country becomes too narrow for us we remove from it into another country.
The whole world is ours, (both) the (territory of) Islam and (that of) Unbelief.
We despise laws and regulations and are by no means devoid of pride (?).
To us belong man and woman playing insane, iron charms (*shîshaq?*) around their neck,
(And so does) he who inflicts wounds upon himself or anoints himself (so as to appear) badly beaten up.
And (to us belong) such as wander about in monkish garb or beg as pilgrims and share the dough.
And such as pretend to lead a thoroughly ascetic life, or keep the law most strictly or act saintly in hair garments.
And to us belongs the mourning weeper (over Ḥusain) and also the reciter of lavish praise (on Ḥusain).
And those who preach (inspired) by love for ᶜAlî and Abû Bakr (and so collect alms from Shîᶜî and Sunnî).[129]

[127] *Rasâᵓil,* Tract 8, p. 33.

[128] Al-Mâwardî, *op. cit.*, p. 416; trans. Amedroz, *JRAS*, 1916, pp. 87–88.

[129] Cf. Mez, *op. cit.*, p. 348; also Ibn al-Jauzî, *Kitâb al-aḏkiyâᵓ*, trans. O. Rescher (Galata, 1925), p. 143, where this practice is described in detail.

(And he) who sees the snake and goes up to him without fear nor fright
And pulls out what terrifies of the teeth of the small-eyed (snake).
And to us belongs every leader of wild animals, the master of lion and rat.[130]

It is a bitter reflection on the times when Abû Dulaf continues:

And to us belongs the Guardian of the Faith, al-Muṭîᶜ (caliph, 946–74), whose reputation is widespread.
He begs from Muᶜizz ad-Daula (945–67, his *amîr al-umarâ*ᵓ) the bread as much as he can get.[131]

Not infrequently people begged under the pretense of collecting the funds necessary to ransom relatives who had fallen into the hands of the Christians. Abû Dulaf knows the trick,[132] and it was the witnessing of an incident of this kind that prompted al-Ḥarîrî (d. 1122) to undertake his *maqâmât*. He saw a stranger in a mosque at Baṣra who persuaded the *qâḍî* to donate a substantial sum toward rescuing his daughter from the Greeks. Later, al-Ḥarîrî discovered that the man had been lying. But, when called to account, Abû Zaid of Sarûj retorted in verse:

Live by deceit, for we live in times whose sons resemble the forest lions.
Try to cull the fruit, if the fruit escapes thee, be satisfied with the leaves remaining;
And ease thy heart from distracting thoughts at the frowns of fickle and adverse fortune,
For the ceaseless change of vicissitudes proclaims the doom of our life's unstableness.[133]

130 *Yatîma*, III, 177–87; vss. 20–22, 30, 36, 42–43, 63–64, 93–94, 103.

131 *Ibid.*, p. 187, vss. 110–11.

132 *Ibid.*, p. 178, vs. 37.

133 Ed. F. Steingass (London, 1897), p. 395; trans. by the same, *Assemblies of al-Ḥarîrî*, II (London, 1898), 169.

CHAPTER SEVEN

THE HUMAN IDEAL

I

MUSLIM theology, Muslim philosophy, and, above all, the Muslim literatures document the evolution of a human ideal, but slightly affected by changes in time and place, under the impact of three main trends.

The individual is depersonalized. This depersonalization operates in two ways. It induces the spectator to reduce the people he views and studies to types, blunts his interest in the distinctive traits, and stimulates emphasis on trueness to pattern. On the other hand, it induces the individual to cultivate as the highest aim of life the mystical experience of complete unity with the divine essence when the consciousness of any separate personality is blotted out. In this state not only do the limits —and this means also the characteristics—of the individual dissolve but the experience is necessarily identical for everyone who achieves it, and thus it nullifies whatever differences there are at the outset between the individuals striving after ecstasy.

Moral education, therefore, does not purpose either the unfolding of the self and its fullest possible realization or its progressive sanctification through what may be called selective realization; it purposes nothing but assimilation to established type of the individual self. One definition of the mystic life describes it as "to form one's self on the character of God."[1] But the outstanding trait of Allah is his superb impersonality. Even the popular anthropomorphism never succeeded in rescuing his character from dazzling indistinction except for the whimsicality with which he was supposed to exercise his power.

Ashᶜarite theology had to eliminate as much as the semblance of insight in his personality by listing his features and qualities with the express confession of inability to specify their modes.

[1] Nicholson, *Personality*, p. 52.

Thus to mold the self after God implied that it was to be emptied of its individuality whose transitoriness, in any event, rendered it metaphysically valueless. Salvation and the experience of unity, interrelated to a point, seemed to necessitate the stripping of the human being of all the accidents that defined him in this world as the particular man or the particular woman in whose guise he was compelled to travel the road of life.

From its inception Islam had professed slight esteem for man. With a view to impressing him with the lowliness of his physical origin, the Koran describes the individual's genesis in detail.

> We have created man of an extract of clay;
> Then We made him a drop in a receptacle sure;
> Then We created the drop a clot,
> Then We created the clot a morsel,
> Then We created the morsel bones,
> And We clothed the bones with flesh,
> Then We produced him, another creature. . . . .[2]

No glory accrues to man from his beginnings. Not only is he formed of mean matter; he is weak and insensitive when he enters upon life and is maintained in his precarious existence only by the will of God. He is beset by disease and pain. Whether he likes it or not, he suffers from hunger and thirst. He desires knowledge, but ignorance is his lot; he wishes to remember but forgets. He plans his own undoing and never reaches safety of life or station. And what is his end, al-Ghazâlî reflects,[3] but death reducing him to the nameless insensibility of his beginnings and subjecting him to repelling decay.

The only experience in which this creaturely frailty may be overcome, at least for one beatific moment of repose in God, is the soaring of the soul past its bodily confinement, away from its prison of corporeal individuality into the light of the One where it reaches infinity by losing its identity.

The mystical teacher, the prophet, the king and the poet, and even the beggar—they are important not for what they are as individuals but for what they signify in the great order of being.

[2] Koran 23:12–14.

[3] When discussing pride, *Iḥyâʾ*, Book 29; cf. Carra de Vaux, *Gazali* (Paris, 1902), pp. 164–65.

They are known by certain marks. When their lives are studied, they have to be identified as casts from well-known molds. Their importance derives from their being representative of a type, and the type is but the materialization of a function. The particular accomplishments of this or that saint, of this or that ruler, are of interest only inasmuch as they will decide his rank among the several representatives of the type.

Arabic literature never had been at its best when individualizing its figures. The satirist had shown a keen eye in discerning human inadequacies, but only rarely did the writer round off his acute observations to achieve the portrayal of a character who would act out the qualities ascribed to him by his inventor. Accuracy of description, such as is met with in the *ayyâm* tales and throughout poetry, mostly regards the physical appearance and, even in this respect, is far from unconventional. Persian tradition was more versatile. The epic—historic, romantic, and mystic-didactic—does present characters who are sufficiently individualized to seem alive. In other words, it is not lack of technical skill when, more and more, the individual is presented in his typical rather than his personal aspect. As is so frequently the case with the "Lives" of the Christian saints, the "Lives" of the great mystics are told in such a manner as to obliterate the distinctive peculiarities both of character and of fate. They are individualized just enough to establish their typological genuineness and their position within the hierarchy of the type.

The biography of the saintly man begins with a laudatory statement exalting him as model of the great, apex of perfection, an upright devotee, unequaled ascete and thaumaturge, close friend of the Lord, teacher of other accomplished initiates. But for his name and that of his home town there is nothing about him that could not and would not be repeated with regard to any number of fellow-saints. This éloge which places him in the right category is followed by a description of the most significant incident in his life—his conversion. The experience of conversion explains and proves his holiness. The remainder of his *Vita* is made up of sayings and possibly the events that provoked them. Dates are practically never given. They do not matter. The year in which he received his call has no bearing on the saint's transcendental significance. As a person he would not be worth remembering. But as a saint he must be commemorated by the very deeds and words that identify him as such. Everything besides these is merely personal and, therefore, incidental and meaningless.[4]

In the same spirit the poet is spoken of. ᶜAufî (*fl.* early thirteenth century) and Daulatshâh (*fl.* 1487), to mention two representative Persian historians of literature, begin their biographies with a panegyric that establishes their heroes firmly as poets, describing their virtues with elaborate vagueness. They may then place them at the court of this or that king or otherwise hint at their circumstances, but they will shift quickly to quoting some of their outstanding verses. This is, of course, not to say that biographical facts are always avoided; it does, however, mean that the poet's individuality is likely to be forgotten for his typical features as a specimen of the pattern "poet." And it may be added that political figures, kings and viziers, do not escape the same fate. Persian authors may exhibit this trend more patently than Arabic, but the gradual strengthening of this depersonalizing outlook on people is unmistakable throughout the Muslim literatures. The same spirit is at work when "the ten best poets,"[5] or, in imitation of the Canon of the Attic Orators, ten *bulaghâ*ᵓ, "eloquent speakers," are grouped together.[6] In glaring contrast to classicism that wishes to evidence the universal significance of the individual in its very uniqueness, the individual is considered here only for his typical traits.

The deindividualizing tendency engulfs the presentation of happenings and actions as well. The early Arab historian concentrates on detail. The particular incident is what interests him. He may lose sight of the larger aspects and connections, but he will record accurately what he has seen or what he has been told. This attitude changes radically. When, to select an instance at random, Aḥmad b. ᶜArabshâh (d. 1450) describes the bellicose life of Timur (d. 1404), he makes no attempt to depict

[4] The biographies in Farîd ad-Dîn ᶜAṭṭâr's (d. 1230) *Taḏkirat al-Auliyâ*ᵓ (Leiden and London, 1905–7) will illustrate this point.

[5] Cf. the *muzdawij* poem, *Irshâd*, VI, 158.

[6] *Irshâd*, VI, 3.

a battle as it actually occurred. What he does is to identify the incident as a battle and then give rein to his imagination, which can be counted on to draw a glowing but entirely unspecific picture of the exploit.

"Then both armies, when they came in sight one of the other, were kindled and mingling with each other became hot with the fire of war and they joined battle and necks were extended for sword blows and throats outstretched for spear thrusts and faces were drawn with sternness and fouled with dust, the wolves of war set their teeth and fierce leopards mingled and charged and the lions of the armies rushed upon each other and men's skins bristled, clad with the feathers of arrows, and the brows of the leaders drooped and the heads of the heads (i.e., the captains) bent in the devotion of war and fell forward and the dust was thickened and stood black and the leaders and common soldiers alike plunged into seas of blood and arrows became in the darkness of black dust like stars placed to destroy the Princes of Satan, while swords glittering like fulminating stars in clouds of dust rushed on kings and sultans nor did the horses of death cease to pass through and revolve and race against the squadrons which charged straight ahead or the dust of hooves to be borne into the air or the blood of swords to flow over the plain, until the earth was rent and the heavens like the eight seas." It comes as an embarrassing anticlimax when Ibn ᶜArabshâh concludes: "And this struggle and conflict lasted about three days."[7]

Depersonalization was favored by the moralist's habit of decomposing the human character into individual qualities, such as pride and humility, liberality and miserliness, truthfulness and dishonesty, which were discussed one after another, preferably in pairs of opposites. Here again individual man was interesting merely as an illustration of a general observation which was owed to the sagacity of one of the wise. In well-ordered and well-written chapters al-Mâwardî discusses, for example, the avoidance of arrogance and self-conceit, modesty, urbanity and

[7] Book I, chap. 47; trans. J. H. Sanders (London, 1936), pp. 81–82.

irascibility, envy and emulation, silence and speech, etc.[8] The number of similar works testifies to the public response.

Ideal types of behavior were evolved and identified with certain personages. These identifications sometimes go back to pre-Islamic times, such as the selection of Ḥâtim Ṭayy as the paragon of generosity. So the reader was taught to think in types, to appraise people for individual traits, to disregard the fulness of their humanity. This outlook fosters the idea of the human character as a compound of unintegrated traits—traits which are found typified here or there, for the most part arbitrarily, and which, it was felt, could be put together so as to produce a perfect individual.

Ibn Buṭlân records the opinion of an experienced slave broker. "The ideal slave is a Berber girl who is exported out of her country at the age of nine, who spends three years at Medina and three at Mecca and at sixteen comes to Mesopotamia to be trained in elegant accomplishments. And, thus, when sold at twenty-five, she unites, with her fine racial excellences, the coquetry of the Medinese, the delicacy of the Meccan, and the culture of the Mesopotamian woman."[9]

According to the Iḫwân, "the ideal, and morally perfect man, should be of East Persian derivation, Arabic in faith, of ᶜIrâqî, i.e., Babylonian, education, a Hebrew in astuteness, a disciple of Christ in conduct, as pious as a Syrian monk, a Greek in the individual sciences, an Indian in the interpretation of all mysteries, but lastly and especially, a Ṣûfî in his whole spiritual life."[10]

Depersonalization was accelerated by what may be called the progressive literarization of the Muslim outlook on, and, even more, of the Muslim response to, life. Literature has always been the art of the Muslim world, masterpieces of painting and architecture notwithstanding. The one great contribu-

[8] *Kitâb ad-dunyâ waᵓd-dîn* (Cairo, 1343/1925).

[9] Mez, *op. cit.*, p. 161. Cf. also Ibn Ḥauqal's description of a perfect man in the person of Abû ᵓs-Sarî al-Ḥasan b. al-Faḍl b. abî ᵓs-Sarî al-Iṣfahânî, characterized as the pure type of scholar and *adîb* (*op. cit.*, p. 2).

[10] T. J. de Boer, *The History of Philosophy in Islam* (London, 1903), p. 95.

tion of the Arabs to Muslim civilization was their literary tradition, which includes the Koran.

The range of intellectual activity considered subject to the laws of literary style constantly widened. The upsurge of the educational ideal of the *kâtib*, the civil official or the clerk, drew first history, then ethics, and, finally, philosophy into the orbit of belles-lettres. Elegance of presentation became obligatory. Illustrations culled from poems, anecdotes, and parables were discovered as effective means to please the public; frequent switches from one subject to another would keep fatigue from the reader. Effortless instruction, amusing edification, and informative witticism were eagerly applauded. The result was the philosophical causerie, a gossipy and clever historiography, the encyclopedia, or simply a collection of miscellaneous and unintegrated information interspersed with rhymes and stories—all these presented in a glamorous garb of verbal splendor. Style came to be cultivated for its own sake, wit degenerated into punning, and the substance of what the author had set out to convey almost evaporated in a fireworks of rhetoric.

On a lower plane, and rather crudely, Arab and Persian literature of the *bas empire* reproduce the decay of classical literature in the last centuries of antiquity. The rhetorical tradition of this era had largely survived. The craving for the anecdote, the delight taken in a point nicely made, the concentration on the isolated detail in hand, and the heedlessness of leading ideas from which to justify the sparkling detail bespeak and promote the same spirit that is responsible for the declining comprehension of the human personality as a whole. The writer no longer cares for the incident he describes; he cares only for his description. The facts are degraded to occasions for display—display, that is, of his literary skill, his wit, his erudition. The author outweighs the work, and effect relegates truth to the background.

The same disrespect for his subject matter and the same conceit reveling in his facile virtuosity disfigure Philostratus' introductory paragraph to his life of the rhetorician Scopelian (written *ca.* A.D. 235), which was applauded in the *Letters* of Abû ʾl-ʿAlâʾ al-Maʿarrî (d. 1058).

"I will now speak of the sophist Scopelian but first I will deal with those who try to calumniate him. For they say that he is unworthy of the sophistic circle and call him dithyrambic, intemperate in his style, and thick-witted. Those who say this about him are quibblers and sluggish and are not inspired with extempore eloquence; for man is by nature prone to envy. At any rate the short disparage the tall, the ill-favored the good-looking, those who are slow and lame disparage the light-footed swift runner, cowards the brave, the unmusical the musical, those who are unathletic disparage athletics; etc."[11]

Obviously, Philostratus is interested only in his beautiful phrasing, in the exhibition of his abilities. Scopelian is just a pretext. The same must be said of Abû ʾl-ʿAlâ's display of affection for the recipient of the following lines.

"Love (*mawadda*) is of two sorts, the sound and the faded. That which is sound is from God Almighty, and that which gets obliterated is from the accursed devil. Now He that knows secrets is aware that my affection for you . . . . if left to itself suffices, and if compared with any other surpasses and outtops it.

"I shall not syncopate my affection for you as the first order of (the meter) *munsariḥ* is syncopated, nor contract it as the fourth foot of (the meter) *ṭawîl* is contracted, nor elide it like a trochee, nor make it like a shifting syllable, affected by aphaeresis and chronic complaints. On the contrary, I shall preserve it from alteration as the rhyming syllable is preserved from alteration of the vowel or consonant; and I shall maintain its purity and truth. The relations between us shall not require to be kept fresh by interchange of presents, for our love is in a well-guarded place, secure against time's ravages."[12]

It was in the same vein that six hundred years earlier Augustine assured Pope Celestine (422–32) of his affection. "I always owe you love, the only debt which, after being repaid, still keeps one a debtor. For it is repaid when it is expended, but is still

[11] *Lives of the Sophists* i. 21 (beginning); trans. W. C. Wright ("Loeb Classical Library," 1932), pp. 71–73.

[12] *Letters*, ed. and trans. D. S. Margoliouth (Oxford, 1898), No. 35 (text, p. 118; trans., p. 137).

owing even if it has been repaid, since there is no time when it does not require to be expended. Nor is it lost when it is repaid, but rather by repayment it is multiplied, for it is repaid by retaining it, not by getting quit of it. And since it cannot be repaid unless it be retained, so it cannot be retained unless it be repaid—nay rather, when a man repays it, it increases in him, and the more lavishly he expends it, the more of it he gains. . . . .

"Love, then, is not expended like money, for in addition to the fact that money is diminished by expenditure and love is increased, they differ in this too, that we give greater evidence of good-will toward anyone if we do not seek the return of money we have given him; whereas no one can sincerely expend love unless he tenderly insist on being repaid; for when money is received, it is so much gain to the recipient but so much loss to the donor; love, on the other hand, is not only augmented in the man who demands it back from the person he loves, even when he does not receive it, but the person who returns it actually begins to possess it only when he pays it back.

"Wherefore, my lord and brother, I willingly repay to you, and gladly receive back from you, the love we owe each other, and that which I receive back, I still claim; that which I repay, I still owe."[13]

Abû ᵓl-ᶜAlâᵓ's letter is an extreme but by no means isolated example of that dissolution of thought and sentiment into musical phrase, that sacrifice of sense to sound, which so deeply affected the literatures of the Muslim peoples. The trend begins in the eighth century, to win an uncontested victory during and after the eleventh century. Literarization of ideas and rhetorization of style—there is no Arabic or Persian author after A.D. 1000 who does not, in some measure, exhibit their trace. Presentation and content interact. The supremacy in prose and poetry of the writer-virtuoso goes far to inject into any concept

[13] Augustine, *Select Letters*, ed. and trans. J. H. Baxter, ("Loeb Classical Library" [London and New York, 1930]), No. 44, pp. 341–43; the letter, No. 192 of the complete collection, was written in 418. Basil (d. 379), at the end of Letter 208 (*Letters*, ed. and trans. R. J. Deferrari, III, 192–93), expresses himself in the same vein but with much greater simplicity. "Surely, it is just for those who began an affection to be repaid in like manner." Incidentally, the idea propounded by Basil and Augustine is frequently used by Arabic poetry.

of human perfection an element of the versatile, widely read, quick-witted, and entertaining littérateur.

There is an element of sober reasonableness in Islam which works toward a humane application of its precepts. The Prophet was sent not to make life more difficult but to facilitate it. Religion or civilization is meant to supply information likely to smooth the believer's rough road through this and into the next world. Usefulness is, therefore, the criterion by which the selection of knowledge is to be guided. What is useful is not necessarily practical. Usefulness in or for the hereafter overrides usefulness for the here. Islam is eminently human in that it takes man for what he is, but it is not humanist in that it is not interested in the richest possible unfolding and evolving of man's potentialities, in that it never conceived of the forming of men as civilization's principal and most noble task. Man is to be directed and guided toward salvation rather than educated to develop his self in developing this world as the deed most deserving of everlasting reward. Humanism does not have to be godless. For the sake of the Lord and in grateful service to him, man may be required to exploit his innate possibilities to the full. But while the great Muslim scholars allowed themselves to be driven to their most significant achievements by sheer intellectual curiosity and while detached interest in the mysterious world around and in us inspired thinkers to undertake laborious tasks, the consensus never advanced beyond justifying scientific activity by pointing out its usefulness.

When al-Ḫafâjî weighs the relative merits of poetry and prose, he adduces as one of his arguments in favor of prose the fact that the need for prose and the art of the scribe, *kitâba,* are evident, whereas poetry could be dispensed with. Besides, the *kâtib* may reach a higher position with the king through his art than the poet through his verse. Thus *kitâba* is shown to be more noble, *ashraf,* than poetry.[14] Ibn Ḫaldûn designates as the highest rated "arts" or crafts those that are indispensable for society—farming, masonry, weaving, and the like—and those

[14] *Sirr al-faṣâḥa,* p. 272. It should not go unmentioned that Tacitus, *De Oratore,* chap. ix, proffers a similar argument in favor of oratory over against poetry.

that are "noble," thanks to their object. Here his examples include obstetrics, medicine in general, music, librarianship, and *kitâba*. The last three bring their masters into contact with the greatest princes and thus possess a degree of nobility which the others are lacking.[15]

In another passage Ibn Ḫaldûn echoes the theologians' division of the sciences in praiseworthy and blameworthy sciences. Although his own studies clearly were stimulated by a desire of knowledge for knowledge's sake, in his theoretical statement on the subject he proclaims that matters that do not profit us either "religiously, that is for our final salvation, or temporally, for our living in this world," are none of our concern. It is "part of the beauty of a man's *islâm*, resignation to God," to leave alone what does not concern him.[16]

The absence of a humanist concept of man's nature and task and the baneful submission to usefulness as a yardstick of values are largely responsible for the comparative ineffectiveness of the Greek heritage. Taken over without the idea of man that gave it unity, the many details proved stimulating but remained disparate and disturbing. The cultural development of the later part of the Middle Ages could with some justification be characterized as a concerted effort to eliminate the alien touch.[17] When today the Muslim youth is warned not to imitate the

[15] *Prolegomena*, II, 316–17 (trans., II, 367–68). Similarly, statistics, geography, and economics gain distinction as needed by kings (Ibn Ḥauqal, *op. cit.*, p. 3). The honor accorded to poets by princes, the so-called defense by testimonial, still appears in sixteenth-century apologies of poetry; cf., e.g., B. Willey, *Tendencies in Renaissance Literary Theory* (Cambridge, 1922), pp. 16–17.

[16] *Ibid.*, III, 136 (trans., III, 186); al-Ghazâlî, *Iḥyâ'*, Book I, chap. 2, voices the same sentiment. See D. B. Macdonald, *Religious Attitude*, pp. 119–20; cf. also his *Aspects of Islam* (New York, 1911), pp. 308–9, and Ṭaha Ḥusain's observation, *La Philosophie sociale d'Ibn-Khaldoun* (Paris, 1918), p. 207, that for Ibn Ḫaldûn the goal of education is not the citizen capable of forming the best government but the man who understands the business of living.

[17] On this subject see this writer's "Attempts at Self-interpretation in Contemporary Islam," in *Proceedings of the 6th and of the 10th Conf. on Science, Philosophy and Religion* (New York, 1946), pp. 785–820, and (New York, 1950), pp. 135–84. Cf. F. Rosenthal's remarks on the attitude of the ninth-century translators from which the "esthetic enjoyment" and the "unselfish pleasure merely in possessing what the Ancients had possessed" was conspicuously absent. "What they sought was . . . . but the practically and theologically realizable knowledge they offered" (*Islamic Culture*, XIV [1940], 392).

West except in matters of material usefulness,[18] the fear is justified that this most narrow of selective principles will stunt once more the potential contribution of the Islamic world. The fascination of the useful blinded the medieval Muslim to the realization that the real gift of the ancients was not Greek science but the spirit that made it possible; and today the pressure of politics reinforces the appeal of the immediately practical and makes the impatient Easterner forget that the power of the West does not spring from its technical accomplishments but from the spirit that brought them about.

Those principal tendencies of depersonalization in viewing and purposing of human experience, literarization of its comprehension and reproduction, and usefulness as the criterion of its selection and evaluation, are, in turn, directly responsible for three attitudes of slightly lesser bearing which again permeate almost all the Muslim ideas about man.

Depersonalization naturally entailed a restriction of the interest in reform to an interest in reforming one's self. The ego has to be changed to fit the pattern, to become responsive to, and worthy of, the supreme vision. The illuminatus is kind and charitable; he may wish to open the high road to God to as many as he can reach, but social conditions as such, the fate of the multitude as such, are none of his concern. The social reformer, unless disguised as prophet or heretic, is not provided for in the scheme of patterns; and the best minds are not interested in his task nor do they feel too keenly the sting of the evils that rouse the sociopolitical innovator.

Literarization provokes, well-nigh implies, eclecticism. Selection reveals the scope and the hue of the littérateur's mind. Epitomes and anthologies have been popular ever since the ninth century A.D. "There is more information than can be counted. So take the nicest of everything."[19] Saws of wisdom, anecdotes, and didactic material are collected from everywhere. Greek and Persian, Jewish and Christian, sources are ransacked. Ideas,

[18] Muḥammad Kurd ᶜAlî, *Al-Islâm waᵓl-ḥaḍâra al-ᶜarabiyya* (Cairo, 1934–36), II, 538–39.

[19] Al-Washshâᵓ, *Kitâb al-Muwashshà*, ed. R. E. Brünnow (Leiden, 1886), p. 4.

imagery, mores, anything and everything is acceptable as long as it lends itself to presentation in Muslim garb, and the cloak may be of the thinnest. The littérateur and the scholar under his impact develop into avid collectors of miscellaneous matter. They supply (or borrow) the categories of arrangement—the matter is gathered in from everywhere. The catholicity of educated taste is restrained only by religious and, to some slight extent, national prejudice.

Usefulness must be vindicated by success. And success is taken to mean happiness for the successful. The Koran desires happiness for the believer. Popular ethics develop the same theme. For once, Aristotelian philosophy, declaring happiness the supreme end of human effort, pulls in the same direction. On the highest level happiness derives from the mystic approach to God; the average faithful reaches it through a certain moderation—the Aristotelian concept of virtue as the mean between two vices has been absorbed by much of Muslim ethical theory—an equilibrium in conduct and human relations. Philosophy and belles-lettres teem with suggestions and injunctions how to attain that happiness which is the rarely questioned objective of man's endeavors. Equilibrium, in familiar fashion, is dissected into a number of component qualities that are then traced through history and all over the world, civilized and uncivilized.

Islam never followed the West in changing the purpose of conduct from the static ideal of happiness to the dynamics of the "pursuit of happiness." In fact, Islam as the perfect vehicle of happiness continues as one of the most forceful claims of the modern apologist. Spokesmen as far apart as Jamâl ad-Dîn al-Afghânî (d. 1897)[20] and Muḥammad Ḥusain Haikal (1888——)[21] have stressed Islam's unique capacity to produce happiness. The realization that this happiness is, in large measure, dependent on satisfactory contacts with one's fellows counteracts somewhat the asocial bliss to which the elect aspire in egotistical isolation.

[20] Cf. C. C. Adams, *Islam and Modernism in Egypt* (London, 1933), pp. 15–16.

[21] *Ḥayât Muḥammad* (2d ed.; Cairo, 1935), pp. 501–28.

II

Another set of basic attitudes can be shown to have gone into the conceptions of the human ideal, although perhaps on a slightly less significant plane.

The most influential of these attitudes is doubtless the immense appreciation and reverence of knowledge as such. Usefulness and the varying limitations of the day may restrict the range of knowledge actually mastered, but, irrespective of its actual contents, knowledge is an indispensable mark of true humanity and ignorance among its most disfiguring scars.

The messenger of God said: "The quest for knowledge is incumbent upon every Muslim man and every Muslim woman."[22] He also said: "Acquire knowledge, because he who acquires it in the way of the Lord performs an act of piety; who speaks of it, praises the Lord; who seeks it, adores God; who dispenses instruction in it, bestows alms; and who imparts it to its fitting objects, performs an act of devotion to God. Knowledge enables its possessor to distinguish what is forbidden from what is not; it lights the way to Heaven; it is our friend in the desert, our society in solitude, our companion when bereft of friends; it guides us to happiness, it sustains us in misery; it is our ornament in the company of friends; it serves as an armor against the enemies. With knowledge, the servant of God rises to the heights of goodness and to a noble position, associates with sovereigns in this world, and attains to the perfection of happiness in the next."[23]

Knowledge has an important bearing "on all the other qualities (of the human character) such as generosity and avarice, cowardice and courage, arrogance and humility, chastity and debauchery, prodigality and parsimony, and so on. For arrogance, avarice, cowardice, debauchery and prodigality are illicit. Protection against them is not possible except through

[22] Az-Zarnûjî (*fl.* 1203), *Taᶜlîm al-mutaᶜallim* (Cairo, n.d.), p. 3; trans. T. M. Abel and the writer.

[23] Quoted by Syed Ameer Ali, *The Spirit of Islam* (rev. ed.; London, 1922), pp. 360–61; this passage, by the way, exhibits to perfection the quest for usefulness and happiness. Cf. also *Mustaṭraf*, I, 52.

knowledge of them and their opposites. So knowledge thereof is prescribed for all of us."[24]

Since deeds are judged by intentions, the spirit in which knowledge is acquired counts for much.

Whoso strives for knowledge for the life to come saves himself because of an increase in righteousness.
But woe to those that strive for it to obtain an advantage over their fellow-servants![25]

Proficiency is attainable only when knowledge is duly esteemed and profound respect is felt toward the learned and, above all, one's teacher. ᶜAlî is quoted as saying: "I am the slave of him who taught me one letter of the alphabet. If he wishes he may sell me, and if he so desires he may set me free, and if he so desires he may make use of me as a slave." And he added these verses:

It seems to me the greatest duty is that which is due the teacher, and that which it is the most necessary thing for each Muslim to observe.
Indeed it is a duty to offer him a thousand drachmas as a token of honor for his instruction in one single letter of the alphabet.[26]

In what is considered his very first revelation to Mohammed, God emphasizes that he taught man by the pen what man did not know.[27] Az-Zamaḫsharî (d. 1144) has this to say on the meaning of that statement: "God taught human beings that which they did not know, and this testifies to the greatness of His beneficence, for He has given to His servants knowledge of that which they did not know. And He has brought them out of the darkness of ignorance into the light of knowledge, and made them aware of the inestimable blessings of the knowledge of writing, for great benefits accrue therefrom which God alone encompasses; and without the knowledge of writing no other knowledge could be comprehended, nor the sciences placed within bounds, nor the history of the ancients be acquired and their sayings be recorded, nor the revealed books be written;

[24] Zarnûjî, p. 4.

[25] Abû Ḥanîfa (?), quoted by Zarnûjî, p. 5.

[26] Zarnûjî, p. 9.

[27] Koran 96:4–5.

and if that knowledge did not exist, the affairs of religion and the world could not be regulated."[28]

Al-Ghazâlî sets forth that the true knowledge consists in knowing one's self and in knowing the Lord. Such knowledge is gained through humility only. Those who are led to pride by their learning are occupied with crafts rather than knowledge; they are merely dealing in philology, or mathematics, or poetry, and brag of amassing information.[29] Such experts might get involved in bitter rivalries and their knowledge be tested rather rudely.

Ṣâᶜid al-Baghdâdî (d. 1026) was received at the court of al-Manṣûr b. abî ᶜÂmir (d. 1002) in Spain, but his exorbitant claims to scholarship antagonized the local lights. One day al-Manṣûr had them examine the newcomer in his presence. He did not do too well in grammar but felt insulted when asked easy questions about accidence. He then shifted his ground by emphasizing his specialty was poetry, history, the solving of riddles, and music. In these fields his showing was excellent: whichever rare expression was proposed to him for explanation he elucidated by quoting verse as evidence or by telling a story hinging on the particular word. And all present were duly impressed.[30]

Theory excels practice but should not be divorced from it.

> Knowledge is for the practitioner what the string is for the builder;
> And practice for the learned what the cord is for him who hauls water.
> Without string building will not be exact;
> Without cord the thirst will not be slaked.
> Who aspires to perfection,
> Let him both be learned and practise.[31]

From this viewpoint the Greeks fall down. "Do you not see that the Greeks, who have studied causes and effects, have not been good as merchants and in manual industry? . . . . The best of their genius being theoretical, not practical."[32] Thus, "knowl-

[28] Ameer Ali, *op. cit.*, p. 361; Baiḍâwî, II, 410, may also be compared.

[29] Cf. Carra de Vaux, *Gazali*, pp. 160–61.*

[30] *Irshâd*, IV, 104. Cf. the similar situation, Lucian *De mercede conductis* 11–12.

[31] Az-Zamaḫsharî, *Aṭwâq aḏ-ḏahab*, ed. and trans. Barbier de Meynard (Paris, 1876), Maqâla 77, p. 172.

[32] Al-Jâḥiẓ, *Opuscula*, pp. 43–44 (trans. Walker, *JRAS*, 1915, pp. 682–83).

edge should not be separated from action."[33] Neither is superior to the other. Neither is deserving of recompense without the other.

The ultimate aim of knowledge is the knowledge of God. Although reason can prove his existence and establish the structure of his being,[34] it is not discursive but intuitive knowledge, gnosis, that leads to the realization by the believer of God's essence and of the deepest secrets of the faith. Mind and heart,[35] knowledge and gnosis, *ᶜilm* and *maᶜrifa* of the Arab thinkers, are engaged, as it were, in a rivalry of cognition, with the heart and *maᶜrifa* holding the edge. It is al-Ghazâlî's depreciation of the religious merits of logical and legal finesse which secured official acknowledgment for the superior potentialities of *maᶜrifa*, of which Ṣûfism already had convinced the body of the nonprofessional pious.

Gnosis transcends the limits imposed on rational knowledge. Only gnosis reaches to the true core of the universe through immediate experience and vision. Only gnosis opens the door to the understanding of the self and of God's grace. Al-Muḥâsibî classifies "knowledge, *ᶜilm*, as being of three types: first, knowledge of what is lawful and unlawful, which is knowledge of what concerns this world and is outward knowledge; second, knowledge of what concerns the next world, which is inward knowledge; third, knowledge of God and His laws concerning His creatures in the two worlds, and this is a fathomless sea, and only the most learned of the faithful attain to it."[36]

Scholasticism divides *ᶜilm* into "eternal and originated according as it exists in God or in a creature." Between these two kinds of knowledge there is no resemblance. Originated knowledge comprises "intuitional, necessary (i.e., warranted by the evidence of the senses and by unanimous assertion), and de-

[33] Hujwîrî, p. 11.

[34] The Spaniard Abû Bakr Ibn Ṭufail's (d. 1185) *Ḥayy b. Yaqẓân* ("Alive son of Wakeful") is written to evidence this tenet.

[35] On their respective provinces cf. J. Obermann, *Der philosophische und religiöse Subjektivismus Ghazâlîs* (Vienna and Leipzig, 1921), pp. 31–41.

[36] M. Smith, *Early Mystic of Baghdad,* p. 57, summarizing al-Muḥâsibî's *Kitâb al-ᶜilm* from a Milan manuscript.

ductive."[37] This analysis of our cognitive faculties acknowledges the inadequacy of pure reason and its processes.

The theoreticians of mysticism tried again and again to describe the ineffable experience of the gnosis. When al-Qushairî discusses it, no doubt is left but that *maᶜrifa* has come to include a standard of behavior and purification of the heart which are at once a means of obtaining the "knower's" state and owed to the insight vouchsafed through this state.[38] In this vein, Hujwîrî gives "the name *maᶜrifa* to every knowledge that is allied with (religious) practice and feeling."[39]

The Syrian physician and mystic Simon of Ṭaibûtheh (d. *ca.* 680), a Christian, had explained that "a part of knowledge is apprehended not by words, but through the inward silence of the mind . . . . it lifts itself up towards the sublime ray of the hidden Godhead . . . . it becomes a knowledge that is higher than all knowledge, for it has reached the Divine Knowledge of the hidden Godhead, which is higher than all understanding."[40] As though in elaboration of this view Ḏû ᵓn-Nûn defines: "Gnosis is in reality God's providential communication of the spiritual light to our inmost hearts."[41] Illumination isolates the recipient. "He who belongs to God and to whom God belongs is not connected with anything in the universe."[42]

The primate of *maᶜrifa* supplements and thus strengthens the asocial strain in the concept of man's nature and man's task. But, correspondingly, it is the concentration on individual salvation, on individual fulfilment by submergence in the Universal Soul, which is the most powerful promoter of a theory of knowledge which culminates in the discarding of the rational processes for the raptures of vision. The enthusiast carried away by the beatitude of losing his consciousness in God may even lay the ax to the whole structure of human cognition and proclaim:

[37] D. B. Macdonald, *EI*, II, 470.

[38] Cf. the quotations in Hartmann, *Qushairî*, pp. 57–58.

[39] Hujwîrî, p. 382. For the genesis of the gnosis concept cf. H.-C. Puech, *Le Manichéisme* (Paris, 1949), pp. 70–72 (and the notes).

[40] Quoted by M. Smith, *Early Mystic*, p. 101, n. 2, from A. Mingana, *Early Christian Mystics*, p. 11.

[41] Hujwîrî, p. 275.

[42] Hujwîrî, p. 274.

"Real gnosis is the inability to attain gnosis."[43] One glimpse of the ineffable effaces the wisdom of the wise. Such emphasis on the mind's limitations—not alleviated by their exact definition in the manner of a Kantian critique of pure reason—bears its share of responsibility for the ultimate stunting of the philosophical spirit in Islam.

Every believer is a fighter for the faith. Every Muslim is liable to military service. Not infrequently compulsion was used to fill the ranks. Many an army contained a contingent of volunteers who enlisted for religious reasons. Immediate danger or a sudden wave of enthusiasm would gather sizable numbers of volunteers. When the Byzantines attacked the border regions, it was mostly contingents of local inhabitants who rallied to the colors. Upon occasion, these home guards were reinforced by Muslims from far-off districts who joined in little bands, leaving a trail of fanaticism along their route to the front. The caliph was the supreme commander; the local potentate or governor, or else any appointee of the court, the actual leader.

The Muslim community was a warlike community, prowess an indispensable quality of the noble. Arab and Persian tradition combined in emphasizing courage and soldierly ability as essential traits of the good man. A considerable part of every able-bodied Muslim's life was spent under arms, particularly in the early period before professional mercenaries took over most of the warring. The crown of the martyr rewarded the supreme sacrifice of the fighter for the faith.

Nevertheless, Muslim civilization is a civilian civilization. Civilian patterns of human development such as the scholar, the saint, or the littérateur have attracted most of Islam's creative energy. In the social stratification the civilian outranks the soldier. The vizier, a civil servant, is supposed to have precedence over the general. Governmental theory discusses the vizierate before the generalship. The soldier as a caste has frequently ruled Muslim states, but such *de facto* supremacy in no way changed the consensus that assigned the state civilian leadership. The Muslims of the seventh century lived, as it were, in an

[43] Ash-Shiblî, quoted by Hujwîrî, p. 276.

armed camp. But more and more did their leader, the caliph, change into their chief administrator. By 800 the transformation was complete. However often the caliph might command his troops in person, however much the poets would vaunt his bravery, he was to be an official first and a soldier only in an emergency. The concepts of representative humanity characteristic of Muslim civilization are nonmilitary, even though the soldierly virtues would continue to be acclaimed.*

The Muslim is painfully conscious of the instability of all things human. He bears up under the cruel vicissitudes of fate and resigns himself to the awesome uncertainties destiny is fond of inflicting upon him. He overcomes the precariousness of his existence by deprecating the significance of his outward circumstances; he integrates insecurity and the anguish it entails into his view of the world by accepting its moral of the worthlessness of this transitory abode. He is inured to sudden turns of the wheel of fortune and is equipped with the philosophical apparatus to master life's every whim.

Still, the Muslim hates change. The ideal life and the ideal community are static. The West expects change to be for the better; the Muslim knows it to be for the worse. The best Islam was in the beginning. And now it deteriorates with every generation. There is nothing man can do to reverse the decline preordained to continue until the Mahdî appears only a short time before this world meets its end. Did not man begin his days in Paradise? And what state has change brought him to! While man cannot arrest the decay, he may slow it. By clinging to the ways of the forebears, by upholding and reliving the tradition of the ancients, by eschewing innovation, the standing of his betters who preceded him would be preserved one instant longer.

The decomposition of societies, the downfall of empires, draw sighs and saws. Condemned to live in futility, man grows despondent and holds fast to what is tested and proved. This atmosphere discourages reformers. Society is prepared to applaud only such change as will restore the simpler, better conditions of earlier times when contact with the Lord was more immediate and more intimate. Stagnation is cultivated, but the ensuing sterility deplored as another piece of evidence of the increasing weakness of man.

The rebel is condemned. Experience has shown too often that his victory means but a change in personnel. Shaken by ceaseless convulsions, Islam appreciates order. The established tradition is binding, in politics and religion as well as in poetry and thought. Few communities underwent so many changes, and were molded by so swift and so startling developments, as Islam. But it was never more than a sprinkling of the intellectual élite that recognized their values, that braved prejudice by extolling the modern over the ancient.[44] For about three centuries the believers in progress kept up their losing fight. Around 1100 the spectacle of political decline became too appalling, the consolidation of conservative orthodoxy too final, for the cultural optimists to carry on. Only toward the very end of the period did Ibn Ḫaldûn take up development in history as a subject of theoretical consideration.

In terms of achievement this leaning toward the past, this craving for the static, are expressed in depreciation of originality. Invention became less important than formulation; wording outranked meaning. The delight in form as self-protection against upsetting innovation lent powerful support to that literarization of sentiment and thought to which Islam was to succumb in graceful complacency.

III

The dominant attitudes of Muslim society favored the scholar as a normative pattern of human character and activity. In the beginning, it would seem, the learned man was supposed to be practically omniscient and something of a wizard to boot. The

[44] When al-Muqaddasî (*op. cit.*, p. 127) enumerates his reasons for joining the Ḥanafites, he lays great stress on their reverence for the oldest authorities. He quotes the well-known tradition which has the Prophet say: The best of you are those of my generation, then those of that immediately following; then again those of the next following. Thereafter falsehood will spread, etc. The same Muqaddasî (*ibid.*, p. 310) praises the inhabitants of Balîkân in Ḫurâsân as "sound, upright people, of the first clay, *min aṭ-ṭîna al-ûlà*." For the history of this conflict in the field of literature cf. the author, *JNES*, III (1944), 246–51.

absence of accepted standards of credibility made it difficult to separate scholarly from inspirational insight.

Wahb b. al-Munabbih (d. 728) when confronted with a slab covered with strange lettering read the inscription without a moment's hesitation, recognizing it as a Greek text from the days of Solomon, son of David. The text began with the formula, "In the name of Allah, the Merciful, the Compassionate," and consisted of a series of moral expostulations of the familiar kind.[45] When ᶜAlî al-Karḫî in 955 read the cuneiform inscriptions of Persepolis to his master, the Bûyid ᶜAdud ad-Daula (949–83),[46] such unblushing pretense was no longer necessary to maintain a scholarly reputation in respectable circles.

Al-Jumaḥî (d. 845) had denied the authenticity of ᶜÂdite and Ṯamûdite poems quoted by Ibn Isḥâq (d. 767).[47] Two centuries later al-Ḫaṭîb al-Baghdâdî (d. 1071) showed up the spuriousness of a letter allegedly written by Mohammed to the Jews of Ḫaibar. He pointed out that one of the witnesses recorded on the missive had died before the fall of Ḫaibar, while another accepted Islam only some time after the event.[48] Even some of Wahb's contemporaries had the strength of character to confess their ignorance. Traditionists in the van and philologists close behind appear to have been the first to lay down the conditions of honest research.

As-Suyûṭî (d. 1505), looking over the completed development, lists those early scholars who braved public expectation by avowing their lack of information. He follows up a chapter on "Those who answered a question with 'I don't know,' " with another listing those who referred a problem they found themselves unable to solve to another authority, and he finally discusses a number of authorities who had dared to change their opinion after prolonged investigation.[49] These steps seem to

[45] Masᶜûdî, *Murûj*, V, 361–62; the incident happened in 706.

[46] G. Wiet, *Répertoire chronologique d'épigraphie Arabe* (Cairo, 1931 ff.), Vol. IV, Nos. 1475–76.

[47] *Ṭabaqât ash-shuᶜarâʾ*, ed. J. Hell (Leiden, 1916), p. 4.

[48] *Irshâd*, I, 247–48.

[49] *Muzhir*, II, 163–66. The difficulty of professing ignorance when the scholar is not supposed to have any gap in his information is shown by Jerome's experi-

have been accepted practice around 800. A little later, al-Mubarrad (d. 898) formulates a principle on which to justify self-correction: it erases the sin incident in making and spreading mistakes.[50]

The great age of Muslim civilization achieved a truly lofty ideal of the savant. "Learning only unveils herself to him who wholeheartedly gives himself up to her; who approaches her with an unclouded mind and clear insight; who seeks God's help and focusses an undivided attention upon her; who girds up his robe and who, albeit weary, out of sheer ardour, passes sleepless nights in pursuit of his goal rising, by steady ascent, to its topmost height; and not to him who seeks learning by aimless flights and thoughtless efforts or who, like a blind camel, gropes about in the dark. He should not yield to bad habits or permit himself to be led astray by vicious tendencies. Nor must he turn his eyes from truth's depth. He should discriminate between the doubtful and the certain, between genuine and spurious, and should always stand firm by the clear light of reason."[51] Muṭahhar aspires to presenting his subject purified of all embroidery, the errors of the washing-women, old wives' tales, and the apocryphal assertions of unreliable traditionists.[52]

In this spirit al-Muqaddasî, in the Introduction to his *Description of the Muslim Empire* (written in 987), proposes to be guided by personal observation first and by bookish authorities last. Research, not speculation, will yield an exact account of the world. Many are the ways in which he managed to travel

---

ence. In *Letter* lxxvii. 7 he relates how Fabiola asked him "the meaning and origin" of each place-name mentioned in the list of halting-places of the Israelites on their way from Egypt to the river Jordan. "In very many cases I had frankly to confess ignorance. Thereupon she began to press me harder, expostulating with me as though it were not allowed me to be in ignorance of what I do not know." In the end Jerome promises her to write a treatise on the subject (trans. F. A. Wright, *Select Letters of Saint Jerome* ["Loeb Classical Library"], pp. 327–29).

[50] *Ibid.*, p. 265. For a more detailed study of the development of the idea of scholarly fallibility cf. the author's paper in *Corona: Studies in Celebration of . . . . S. Singer* (Durham, N.C., 1941), pp. 142–47, and F. Rosenthal, *The Technique and Approach of Muslim Scholarship* (Rome, 1947), pp. 62–63.*

[51] Muṭahhar b. Ṭâhir al-Maqdisî (*fl.* 966), *Livre de la création et de l'histoire*, ed. and trans. C. Huart (Paris, 1899–1919), I, 4–5; trans. Mez., *op. cit.*, p. 171.

[52] *Ibid.*, I, 5–6.

and to gather information. "I have given instruction in the common subjects of education and morals; I have come forward as a preacher, and I have made the minaret and the mosque resound with the call to prayer. I have been present at the meetings of the learned and the devotions of the pious. I have partaken of broth with the Ṣûfîs, gruel with monks, and ship's-fare with sailors. Many a time I have been seclusion itself, and then again I have eaten forbidden fruit against my better judgment. I associated with the hermits of Lebanon, and in turn I lived at the court of the Prince. In wars I have participated: I have been detained as a captive and thrown into prison as a spy. Powerful princes and ministers have lent me their ear, and anon I have joined a band of robbers, or sat as a retail-dealer in the bazaar. I have enjoyed much honor and consideration, but I have likewise been fated to listen to many curses and to be reduced to the ordeal of the oath, when I was suspected of heresy or evil deeds."[53]

Before him, al-Yaᶜqûbî had felt the same irrepressible impulse to accumulate firsthand information. From earliest youth he had wanted to explore the geography and history of foreign lands. He systematically interrogated foreigners on the nature of their countries, their food, dress, religion, and government. If the informant seemed trustworthy, he put down his answers. The information thus accumulated he supplemented by traveling.[54]

In 887/88 Ibn al-Muᶜtazz wrote his *Kitâb al-badîᶜ*, the "Book of the New Style." He was fully conscious of being the first to undertake in this work a systematic study of poetics. After listing the five principal figures of this New Style, he expresses the hope that others will discover additional figures and thus improve on his contribution.[55] Ibn al-Muᶜtazz would thus be the first Muslim to conceive of knowledge as a task to be mastered

[53] Ed. M. J. de Goeje (Leiden, 1906), pp. 1–3; trans. of selected passage, De Boer, *op. cit.*, pp. 70–71. Cf. also the further illustration of his exertions, *Descriptio*, pp. 43–45.

[54] *Kitâb al-buldân*, ed. M. J. de Goeje (Leiden, 1892), pp. 232–33; Carra de Vaux, *Penseurs de l'Islam*, II (Paris, 1921), 4–7, discusses al-Yaᶜqûbî's method and accomplishment.

[55] Ed. I. Kratchkovsky (London, 1935), pp. 2–3; for the date cf. Kratchkovsky's Introduction, p. 16.

progressively and through co-operation over successive generations of scholars. As-Sakkâkî (d. 1229), who originally embraced learning because of the honors he saw bestowed on great savants,[56] speaks in upholding a noble tradition when, after stating his own view on a rhetorical problem, he clarifies the standpoint of his opponents and leaves the reader the choice.[57]

In the Preface to his *Chronology of Ancient Nations* (written in A.D. 1000) al-Bêrûnî, one of the greatest scholars of all times, accounts for the method he proposes to use in his researches. His objective "cannot be obtained by way of ratiocination with philosophical notions, or of inductions based upon the observations of our senses, but solely by adopting the information of those who have a written tradition . . . . and by making their opinions a basis, on which to build up a system; besides, we must compare their traditions and opinions among themselves, when we try to establish our system. But ere that we must clear our mind from all those accidental circumstances which deprave most men, from all causes which are liable to make people blind against the truth, e.g. inveterate custom, party-spirit, rivalry, being addicted to one's passions, the desire to gain influence, etc." It is, however, exceedingly difficult to use this method "on account of the numerous lies which are mixed up with all historical records and traditions. . . . . However, that which is within the limits of possibility, has been treated as true, as long as other evidence did not prove it to be false. For we witness sometimes, and others have witnessed before us, physical appearances, which we should simply declare to be impossible, if something similar were related from a far remote time. . . . . The matter standing thus, it is our duty to proceed from what is near to the more distant, from what is known to that

[56] Cf. F. Krenkow, *EI*, IV, 80. The same respectful attitude toward the scholar was entertained in the contemporary Greek world. In 1238, Irene, wife of the Nicean emperor John III Vatatzes (1222–54), called George Acropolita (d. 1282) a fool for advancing the opinion that eclipses were caused by the moon coming between the sun and the earth. But she apologized to the young scholar, who had barely reached the age of twenty-one, condemning her behavior as unbecoming, ἀπρεπῶς, and explaining that it was not right to apostrophize in such a manner anyone advancing scientific theories, φιλοσόφους λόγους (George Acropolita, *Opera*, ed. A. Heisenberg [Leipzig, 1903], I, 63; cf. Runciman, *op. cit.*, p. 229).

[57] *Miftâḥ al-ᶜulûm* (Cairo, n.d., *ca.* 1898), pp. 212–13.

which is less known, to gather the traditions from those who have reported them, to correct them as much as possible, and to leave the rest as it is, in order to make our work help him, who seeks truth and loves wisdom, in making independent researches on other subjects, and guide him to find out that which was denied to us, whilst we were working at this subject, by the will of God, and with His help."[58]

This critical consciousness of function and procedure of the scholar remained unparalleled for centuries to be almost but not quite reconquered by Ibn Ḫaldûn when he set forth in the Preface of his *History of the World* (first sketched in 1377) the principles by the aid of which he hoped to ascertain truth and separate it from falsehood.[59]

The savant who had an independent contribution to make rated higher than the mere *muqallid*, who confined himself to exposition and comment of earlier achievement.[60] But, as time wore on, public opinion became increasingly reluctant to admit or to recognize the pioneer. Tradition presaged the advent of a rejuvenator of the sciences each century.* A majority had accepted al-Ghazâlî as the *mujaddid* expected for the end of the fifth Muslim century. Four hundred years later, when Muslim science had been gripped by *rigor mortis*, the polyhistor, as-Suyûṭî, tried hard to convince the contemporaries that he was the only man alive whose all-inclusive erudition would fulfil the prerequisites of a *mujaddid* in his age. To corroborate his claim, as-Suyûṭî not only enumerates the fields of learning he has mastered, pointing to his five hundred published tractates, but he emphasizes that he is in the habit of not writing about any subject in which he has had a predecessor and of not relinquishing any matter before he has completely exhausted it.[61] By this time, however, independence of research had come to mean little more than independent arrangement of the traditional material.

[58] Trans. E. Sachau (London, 1879), pp. 3–4.

[59] *Prolegomena*, I, 8–50 (trans., I, 13–65).

[60] Cf., e.g., Zamaḫsharî, *op. cit.*, Maqâla 37, pp. 76–77.

[61] Cf. texts and the comments printed by I. Goldziher, *SBWA*, LXIX (1871), 15–16 and 21–22.

The scholar was supposed to stand his ground in disputation. These verbal combats were conducted in a sharp and what appears to us rather tactless fashion. As is inevitable on such occasions, the better man, even the better cause, might easily be worsted. In 932 the vizier Ibn Ḥinzâba Ibn al-Furât (d. 939) had gathered around him a splendid assembly of diplomats and intellectual leaders whom he addressed as follows.

"I desire someone to come forward and debate with Mattà[62] on the subject of Logic. He declares that it is impossible to know what is correct from what is incorrect, truth from falsehood, right from wrong, proof from sophism, doubt from certainty, except by our command of logic, our control of the system established and defined by its author, and our acquaintance through him with its doctrines.

"A general silence ensued. Presently Ibn al-Furât said: 'Surely there must be someone here who can meet him, and arguing with him refute his view, I regard you as seas of knowledge, champions of our religion and its followers, lamps to guide the seeker after truth. Why, then, this hesitation and alarm?'

"Abû Saʿîd as-Sîrâfî (d. 979) raised his head and said: 'Vizier, excuse us. The knowledge that is stored in the breast is different from that which is to be displayed before such an assembly, where there are listening ears, and gazing eyes, and stubborn minds, and critical spirits. Their presence occasions anxiety, and anxiety numbs the energy: it produces shame and shame presages defeat.' "

This is exactly what happens to Mattà when as-Sîrâfî, at the bidding of the vizier, takes up the cudgels against him. Mattà's Arabic eloquence seems to have been defective, and as-Sîrâfî swept his arguments aside with grandiloquent precision. The discussion reaches grammar. As-Sîrâfî asks:

"Here is a question more closely connected with the intelligible sense than with the verbal form. What would you say of the phrase 'Zaid is the best of the brothers'?"

Mattà: "It is correct."

[62] Mattà b. Yûnus al-Qunnâʾî (d. 940), the Christian translator into Arabic of Aristotle's *Poetics*.*

As-Sîrâfî: "Then what would you say of the phrase 'Zaid is the best of his brothers'?"

Mattà: "It is correct."

As-Sîrâfî: "If, then, both are correct, what is the difference between them?"

"Mattà was troubled and hung his head, and was choked by his saliva."[63]

Jealousies between scholars were the order of the day. When the great savant Naṣîr ad-Dîn aṭ-Ṭûsî (d. 1274) was vizier of the Mongol Hûlâgû, the conqueror of Baghdad, he came to Ḥilla, the seat of an important school of Shiite learning. Upon his arrival the scholars gathered around him. He asked the jurisprudent Najm ad-Dîn al-Ḥillî (d. 1277): "Who is the greatest scholar of this circle?" Najm ad-Dîn replied: "They are all outstanding in their field." Aṭ-Ṭûsî went on: "Who is the best expert in the principles of law and in speculative theology?" Najm ad-Dîn pointed out two of the professors present. A third *shaiḫ* resented Najm ad-Dîn's omission of himself and wrote him a letter in verse full of bitter reproach. Najm ad-Dîn wrote back to apologize. "If His Excellency had asked you a question on those 'principles' how would you have come out? And all of us would have had to feel ashamed!"[64]

The social function of the scholar is limited to his role as guardian of religious law and lore. There is no expectation that the results of his investigations will bring about human betterment. He may be supposed to criticize the existing government for its failure to live up to religious standards. This criticism, however, will be general, for the idea of social progress through increase in knowledge is foreign to the Muslim Middle Ages.

The ascete or the saint is the authorized spokesman for the

[63] *Irshâd*, III, 106 and 115 (from *Imtâᶜ*, I, 107–29); trans. D. S. Margoliouth, *JRAS*, 1905, pp. 111–12 and 120. On pp. 85–91 Margoliouth lists other similar debates.* The institute of public disputations among scholars continues a classical tradition. The Hippocratics appear to have held discussions before crowds (cf. B. Farrington, *Science and Politics in the Ancient World* [London, 1939], p. 34), and from Alexandrian times scholars, especially grammarians, disputed with one another at banquets, before the ruler, not without detriment to their achievements; cf. R. Hirzel, *Der Dialog* (Leipzig, 1895), II, 350.

[64] Cf. R. Strothmann, *Die Zwölfer-Schîᶜa* (Leipzig, 1926), pp. 48–49.

oppressed, the warner of the great, the conscience of the kings. The "wise fool"[65] brings home to those in power their lack in human understanding, the Ṣûfî beggar reminds them of the futility of their transitory splendor. The influence of religious heroes has been considerable, but on the whole the effectiveness of Muslim reformers has been impeded by their concentration on removing specific abuses and on curing the evils of the day by resorting to the generalities of the past. The saint as a wandering penitent and preacher, a living program rather than a personality, revered and feared, sometimes inviting contempt,[66] sometimes demanding submissive recognition, and the beggar without ties to this world—they provide patterns for escape to those who cannot bear what they see. The saint in all his disguises is more or less immune. He not only may but is expected to criticize, to castigate, to voice the ideals he lives, and to threaten the powerful transgressors with the vengeance of the Lord. And to the common folk every powerful one is a transgressor. The saint thus sides with the wronged, the disinherited, those whom life has cheated of their chance. But while he flays the wickedness of the rulers and asks them to reform, he does not attach too much weight to the grievances that pain his wards. Only a short while, and this shadowy life is behind us; only a short while, and death enforces the equality of the dust.

The king is shaken by the holy man's diatribe. He weeps and repents. He replaces a corrupt official. But fundamentally nothing changes. The perfect ruler works perfect justice. He protects his people against enemies without and oppression within. He sees to it that the law is kept. He is generous, devout, brave, and lends his ear to the pious. His punishment is swift, his reward lavish. He promotes happiness throughout the land.

But where is the perfect ruler to be found? The very exaltation of the ideal forces a discouraging cleavage between the actual sultan and the true king. A certain inability, or perhaps

[65] For this type cf., e.g., *Irshâd*, I, 150; II, 58; VI, 501; *Bayân*, II, 178 ff.; also Ibn al-Jauzî, *Kitâb al-adkiyâ*ʾ, trans. O. Rescher (Galata, 1925), pp. 301–5; and P. Loosen, *Die weisen Narren des Naisâbûrî*, d. 1015 (Strassburg, 1912).

[66] The best presentation of the *malâmâtî* is by R. Hartmann, *Islam*, VIII (1918), 157–203. For similar attitudes in the Greek Church, cf. E. Benz, *Kyrios*, III (1938), 1–55.

only a strong escapist reluctance, to see historical realities in their proper light, suggested a highly immoral equalization of any potentate with the ideal prince. Whoever accedes to power comes to be viewed as the embodiment of the canonical concept of the ruler which, in the popular mind, includes the almost divine stature of the mortal chosen to be absolute lord of life and property of his subjects.[67]

The literarized mind offers the same panegyrics to a worthless and to a model king. Power transforms its bearer. The vilest rulers promulgated the noblest proclamations and they may not always have been aware of the gruesome mockery in which they were indulging. The Muslim had become inured to living on two planes, the normative and the real, and it is no cause for wonder that he showed some inclination to mistake his vision for his experience and to slight the evidence of his experience for the higher truth which it was not worthy to displace.

IV

In supplementation of, and partial opposition to, the concept of scholarship purposing specialized knowledge, another educational concept developed that proposed to mold the individual as a whole and to regulate the form of his social relations as well as the style and ethics of his professional activities. The content of this polite education, *adab*, never was rigorously defined; it varied from age to age, although within rather narrow limits. The word *adab* itself, whose history remains to be written, originally connoting the discipline of the mind and its training, is perhaps somewhat arbitrarily chosen to designate a *Bildungsideal* which, whatever its components, is characterized by combining the demand for information of a certain kind with that for compliance with a code of behavior.*

[67] On the survival of the ancient concept of the god-king, cf. H. H. Schaeder's interesting sketch of the ideal ruler, *Biologie der Person*, ed. Th. Brugsch and F. H. Lewy (Berlin and Vienna, 1929), IV, 934–38, esp. pp. 937–38. G. Richter, *Studien zur Geschichte der älteren arabischen Fürstenspiegel* (Leipzig, 1932), has interesting illustrations of the concept of the ideal prince and the relationship between ruler and ruled. Ghuzûlî, *Maṭâliʿ al-budûr* (Cairo, 1299–1300), I, 12, quotes the caliph Maʾmûn as saying: "The best life has he who has an ample house, a beautiful wife, and sufficient means, who does not know us and whom we do not know."**

The information selected is arranged around belles-lettres (themselves frequently and confusingly referred to as *adab*), which are understood to include history. Further branches of knowledge are admitted as they prove necessary or serviceable to round off the mental range of the polite speaker or writer. The insistence on correctness and facility of expression accounts for the importance of grammar. There is a distinct high-society flavor about *adab*. Philosophy and its most recondite problems, arithmetic, law—nothing is excluded from enriching *adab*. But in the hands of the *adîb*, the representative of this type of education, the forbidding rigor of scientific debate gives way to pleasing converse, and depth is replaced by charm. European and particularly French society in the eighteenth century displays an attitude to learning not too dissimilar to that of the brilliant *udabâ*ᵓ of Baghdad. In both milieus wit and grace, and specifically literary wit and verbal grace, are sought after, and elegance, *ẓarf*, rates as the highest attainment.

Superficiality is hardly avoidable and easily condoned when cloaked by *esprit*. Ibn as-Sikkît (d. 857), a serious scholar and author of bulky tomes, advises to cull such *adab* as endears itself to the heart and as sounds desirable to the ear. Take from grammar what aids to rectify your discourse and leave aside the obscure and inaccessible. Of poetry choose the pleasing motives, get hold of as many historical tales and saws as possible, but avoid whatever is coarse.[68]

Adab, the general knowledge of everything, completes *ᶜilm*, the thorough possession of one area of information. But it leaves the basic structure of the Muslim's spiritual life untouched. It does not affect his religious standing. The *adîb* may be pious or impious, depending on his inclination. *Adab* as such is neutral. *Adab* does not require the taking of a stand on current questions or permanent problems. It is, in a sense, an outlook, a frame within which to integrate one's world. It is more only in so far as it will indicate what elements to select from the superabundance of experience, past and present, that threatens man with confusion. And it smoothes rough edges, conceals disquieting

[68] *Irshâd*, I, 19.

discrepancies, or harmonizes through clever formulation or recourse to age-old commonplace.

Elegance as the criterion of formal perfection is supported by taste, taking its place as supreme judge by the side of reason. And the reason, ᶜ*aql*, of the *adîb* is not the earnestly searching and argumentative tool of the philosopher; it is rather a compound of good sense and insight into the nature of people and the ways of the world. Therefore it could be said that there is no religious ethos, *dîn*, without discretion, *ḥayâ*ᵓ, and no discretion without prudence, ᶜ*aql*. Nor can there be discretion, prudence, and ethos without *adab*.[69]

To possess learning is not sufficient. The polish of *adab* must be added to perfect both the learning and the scholar who cultivates it. "The adornment of the learned is the beauty of his *adab*."[70] Al-Mubarrad contrasts *adab* with logic, condemning the excess of either.[71] ᶜ*Ilm* and *adab* are, in the words of Ibn ᶜAbdrabbihi (d. 940), the two poles on which religious and worldly behavior turn, the distinction between man and beast, between the angelic and the animal nature, the substance of rational thought, the lamp of the body, the light of the heart, and the pillar of the soul.[72] Neither ᶜ*ilm* nor *adab* do, however, make up for moral deficiencies. Al-Jâḥiẓ warns not to allow *adab* to be rated higher than character.[73]

Adab as a formal principle is all-inclusive and will fit everybody's needs. But it will suit best those to whom it owes the best part of its development and who were primarily responsible for its wide adoption—the littérateurs. It was the littérateur who found himself called upon to redact state correspondence. Official documents came to be judged by the elegance of their phrasing. Recondite allusions, ample quotations from Koran and poetry, rhymed prose, the conveying of the sovereign's ideas either by elaborate indirection or by poignant pun, gave dignity

[69] *Ibid.*, p. 15.

[70] *Ibid.*, p. 17^{14}.

[71] Quoted by al-ᶜAskarî (d. 1005), *Kitâb aṣ-ṣinâᶜatain* (Constantinople, 1320), p. 115.

[72] *Al-ᶜIqd al-farîd* (Cairo, 1353/1935), I, 264.

[73] *Bayân*, I, 86.

to the missive and evoked the recipient's admiration. A prince would be envied for having secured the services of an outstanding stylist.

In this manner literarization even affected the conduct of state affairs and the routine of the civil service. The *kâtib*, secretary, scribe, or civil servant, was to be erudite, and his erudition had to be exactly that mosaic of miscellaneous information kept in place by mastery of form and diplomatic grace that *adab* offered. Thereby *adab* came to be specialized so as to represent the education, both theoretical and practical, of the courtier-scribe or the courtier-poet, whose roles not infrequently would coincide. While there would be a special *adab*, code of behavior, for king, judge, or physician, the requirements of the *kâtib*, his *adab*, came to set the standard for the concept of *adab* par excellence.

The *kâtib* needed familiarity with every kind of literary document, Arab and Persian; he had to be able to compose any kind of state paper on the spur of the moment. But he had no chance of success in this art unless he was well versed not only in grammar and lexicology but in law as well. He had to be able to quote from the Koran and from an ample store of proverbs and verse.[74] In short, his knowledge had to be of an encyclopedic hue. Geography cannot be dispensed with, nor can mathematics or astronomy.[75] In fact, the *kâtib* should be so erudite that he could as well be known as a competent grammarian, legist, or scholastic theologian.[76] In addition to a natural gift of expression, which should not, as it usually is, be specialized to certain branches of poetry and prose, he stands in need of eight kinds of tools: (1) a thorough knowledge of Arabic, accidence and syntax, and (2) of lexicography and the distinctions between eloquent, obsolete, unusual, etc., expression; (3) an acquaintance with proverbs and *ayyâm* tales of the Arabs and with other incidents current among the people; (4) a wide reading in prose and poetry of earlier authors and a memorization of a great deal of their work; (5) a solid knowledge of political theory and the science of adminis-

[74] Ibn al-Mudabbir, p. 7.

[75] Ibn Qutaiba, *Adab al-kâtib* (Cairo, 1355), p. 12.

[76] Ibn al-Aṯîr, *al-Maṯal as-sâ'ir*, p. 3.

tration: (6) knowledge by heart of the Koran and (7) of the traditions issuing from the Prophet; and (8) command of prosody and poetics.[77] This list is not meant to exclude any other skill of which the *kâtib* may stand in need upon occasion. But it establishes clearly the predominantly literary character of his *adab* and of *adab* in general.

Erudition devoid of research interest and bent upon formal mastery rather than development of its subject matter is bound to become eclectic in addition to encyclopedic. At bottom it is irrelevant what sort of material is handled and formulated. Therefore, the *adab* collections abound with classical reminiscences and values, and mannerisms of the Greek rhetoricians' school are freely perpetuated. The *kâtib*'s *adab* largely continues, or at least builds on, Persian tradition. While much of the lore that is processed through *adab* is of Arabic origin, the trend toward literarization of all educational matter comes from Sassanian Persia and from Greece, especially the second sophistic tradition that had been so powerful in the East.

Some of the catalogues of the constituent elements of *adab* lean toward the Arabic, some toward the Persian usage. Both nations had been fond of physical exercise, but only the Persians had integrated such exercise into an ideal of chivalry. The Sassanian noble was expected to excel in riding and hunting, in games (including polo and chess), but also in *dipîrîh, kitâba*.[78] In *adab*'s propensity for miscellaneous learning and for treating knowledge of foods and drinks, clothing and etiquette, as full-fledged fields of study survives a like trend of the Sassanian age.[79] The occasional insistence in *adab* on courtly honor, *muruwwa* (not to be confused with the pagan ideal denoted by the same word), again in all likelihood goes back to *frahang*, the chivalrous education of the Persians. The vizier, al-Ḥasan b. Sahl (d. 850/51) explains: "The arts belonging to fine culture (*al-âdâb*) are ten: three Shahrajânic (playing lute, chess, and

[77] *Ibid.*, pp. 4–5; an-Nuwairî (d. 1332), *Nihâyat al-arab fî funûn al-adab* (Cairo, 1923 ff.), VII, 27–31, has a similar list, but puts knowledge by heart of the Koran first.

[78] Cf. Th. Nöldeke, *Bezzenbergers Beiträge*, IV (1878), 38, n. 1.

[79] Cf. *King Ḫusrav and His Page*, ed. J. M. Unvala (Paris, 1921); also A. Christensen, *L'Iran sous les Sassanides* (Paris, 1936), pp. 411–13.

with the javelin), three Nûshirwânic (medicine, mathematics, equestrian art), three Arabic (poetry, genealogy, and knowledge of history); but the tenth excels all: the knowledge of stories which people put forward in their literary gatherings."[80]

Whichever the details of its contents, *adab* is, above all, an approach; it is, so to speak, a principle of form, not an array of materials.

The Persian origin of much of attitude and substrate of *adab* accounts for the suspicions cast upon its main representatives. Al-Jâḥiẓ shows considerable irritation against the *kâtib* who prefers to base his decisions on the precedent of Sassanian kings and despises the wisdom of Muslim judges and teachers. He accuses the *kâtib* of neglecting the Muslim sciences, the Muslim *sunna*, and even the Koran for the outlandish wisdom of the Sassanian vizier, Buzurjmihr, and similar worthies.[81] Only too many of his ilk displayed heretical proclivities; they were not only active *shuᶜûbîs* but crypto-Zoroastrians.[82] The littérateur's Islam was believed to sit rather lightly. In the second half of the eighth century a wave of unorthodox feeling swept the intelligentsia. It petered out fairly soon, not so much because of official disapproval, even persecution, but because it was mostly a negative movement with leanings toward the obsolescent religious institutes of Manichaeanism and Zoroastrianism. It was during this short-lived epoch that the typology of the poet was enriched by the *mâjin*, the "lascivious," whose moral laxness made him *eo ipso* suspect of being a *zindîq*, a heretic of non-Islamic sympathies.[83] The promotion of *adab* by such figures could not but enhance popular distrust. But in the tenth century *adab* has become recognized and no longer is a subject for recrimination. The progress of narrow orthodoxy notwithstanding, Ibn al-Jawâlîqî (d. 1179/80) reads *adab*, probably belles-lettres, in a Baghdad mosque every Friday.[84]

[80] Goldziher, *EI*, I, 122, and *Muh. Stud.*, I, 168, n. 2, quoting from al-Ḥuṣrî, *Zahr al-âdâb*, I, 142.*

[81] Rescher, *Excerpte ...* , pp. 70–71.

[82] *Ibid.*, pp. 74–75.**

[83] Cf., e.g., *Irshâd*, VII, 303.

[84] *Irshâd*, II, 358. In the tenth century al-Muqaddasî, *BGA*, III, 205, finds in Egyptian mosques side by side study-groups of legists, Koran-readers, and people interested in *adab*, literature, and *ḥikma*, "wisdom."

Adab and *ẓarf* impose standards of decency, standards of manners, standards of emotional behavior. Loyalty to friends, liberality, and continence are expected of the *adîb*. Tact is greatly prized. Ḫâlid al-Barmakî (d. after 780) wins praise when he changes the term for "petitioners" from *as-suʾʾâl*, the insistent demanders, to *az-zuwwâr*, the visitors.[85] *Adab* takes up the idealistic concept of love which, promulgated by the Greek novel in antiquity, had begun to find favor in Arabic literature before 700 but was to be developed to ever greater subtlety and sophistication during the following centuries. The romantic love convention becomes so strong as to color even the most earthly relations.[86] Society philosophizes about love. Platonic love is glorified in the ᶜUḏrite lovers who die of their love. The psychology of love is studied. Resistance to passion is commended, as it is unbecoming to the *adîb* to lose control over his heart.[87] If he succumbs, the *adîb* is to realize that there is a definite tradition of conduct in love to which the enamored is to cling. If he deviates, he foregoes the name of *ẓarîf*. Such a *sunna* is established in the affairs of love even as in point of clothing, food, and the like, where the requirements of elegance again are minutely codified.[88]

Adab and literarization, largely identical in their effect on the Muslim mind, are primarily responsible for that merging of types (and professions) characteristic of the later Middle Ages. Not only does the scholar extend his scholarship over many fields to become more and more an encyclopedist or a polyhistor, but, while he attacks one field as a scholar, he attacks another as a littérateur. The poet Ḥâfiẓ (d. 1390)[89] taught theology and studied grammar; ᶜUmar Ḫayyâm (d. 1132) was a mathematician first; Ibn Ḥazm, the historian of religion, writes on love in the spirit of an *adîb*, following the precedent set by Ibn

[85] *Aghânî* (3d ed.), III, 173. Cf. also Salm al-Ḫâsir's (d. 803) verse in praise of the Barmakid vizier, Yaḥyà b. Ḫâlid (Frag. XL, 4, of this writer's edition, *Orientalia*, N.S., XIX [1950], 73, quoted in *Irshâd*, IV, 249): "He gives you before you ask him, sparing you the embarrassment of the request."*

[86] Cf., e.g., the stories, *Muwaššà*, pp. 95 ff.

[87] *Ibid.*, pp. 117–18.

[88] *Ibid.*, pp. 123–24.

[89] For the date cf. H. R. Roemer, *Abh. d. Akad. d. Wiss. u. d. Lit.* [*zu Mainz*], *Lit. Kl.*, 1951, p. 103.

Dâ᾽ûd (d. 909), the conservative legist and enthusiastic philosopher. Statesmen win acclaim as critics, kings as poets. Theologians tell stories; littérateurs write religious tracts. Whoever commands the established forms of expression has the means of rearranging the material conveniently prepared by the collector's zeal and the systematic scholarship of centuries. The skilled writer may treat of any subject. Everything that is to be known has been stored. It remains for scholarship to explain the results won by the great minds of the past and for literature to make them palatable and to popularize them for polite society. And more often than not the *ᶜâlim* is also the *adîb*.

Adab sharpened observation and insight into men. It set the style of social life in the great age of Islam and determined the form in which information was to reach the curious. It was not a concept productive in itself. In fact, it became the main tool of that literarization of all thought that marks the end of the contribution of medieval Islam to the progress of mankind. But, despite that potential sterility which it shares with all merely formal concepts, it beautified much that was trivial, ennobled much that was crude and coarse in the life of the period. It represented a humanistic rather than a vocational aspiration in raising scribe and littérateur to the level of ideal types. It is true that it soon lost the force to stimulate the creative effort. But to the end *adab* continued the perfect medium of expression for a society that had become tired and somewhat hopeless yet had remained eminently civilized.[90]

[90] The principal difference between *adab* and the Greek educational ideals would be the absence, in *adab*, of the political element, the *bürgerliche Tüchtigkeit,* to use H. von Arnim's expression (*Leben und Werke des Dio von Prusa* [Berlin, 1898], p. 8). The fate of the Muslim Empire brings to mind Plato *Laws* 697*C*, where the downfall of the Persian Empire is explained as due to the fact that the people were robbed of their freedom and annihilated through the suppression of the idea of community.

CHAPTER EIGHT

SELF-EXPRESSION: LITERATURE AND HISTORY

I

MAN stands revealed through any and all of his words and works. Depending on the medium in which his mind manifests itself, its bent is bared with greater or less immediacy. Despite their direct appeal to our emotions, confessions made through the filter of music or stone remain ambiguous, their verbal, even their psychological interpretation, conjecture.

Muslim civilization's greatest contributions to man's spiritual life were offered on the verbal level. Within limits, the retracing of which unveils the measure of interest and analysis this civilization allows the individual, literature bespeaks the concept Islamic civilization formed of man, and it does so both through explicit statement and through the selection of traits which it admits for disclosure.

Self-expression, then, in the medium of words, is of two kinds. You may simply describe what happens within you, and such description will have to include the discussion of objects or events that cause your experience. In fact, many times the element of explicit personal participation will seem subordinated to the copious background picture in which, however, the subjective element will always be traceable. This exteriorization of your experience inspires lyrics and autobiography.

On the other hand, experience could be rendered at one remove, so to speak, through the creation of characters other than yourself and of an action in which these characters are deployed. Depending on the technique chosen for the presentation of the action, this kind of self-expression takes the form of the epic, or prose narrative, or the drama.

In between those two basic types of self-expression and, in a sense, partaking of the peculiarities of both are history and its specialized twin, biography. The self-revelatory element in our apprehension of the historical process and in our interpretation of its protagonists is as obvious as is the fluidity of the boundaries between, for instance, historical and epical presentation of events.

The documents of self-expression, verse or prose, are conditioned by two sets of factors. One of these is the range of experience of which man not only has become conscious but has evolved the linguistic means of presenting. Progress means more than anything else the widening of this range of articulateness.

The other may be dubbed the literary tradition. No literary tradition has ever been all-inclusive. The most comprehensive tradition permitting, even encouraging, the treatment of a vast multitude of matters upholds a number of taboos, of untouchable subjects. More important, however, in curtailing the contents of literary self-expression is the continual existence of spheres of disinterest. The medieval mind expressed itself freely and subtly in dogmatics; modern man no longer finds in speculation of this type an appropriate medium of self-expression and self-representation.

The main factor, however, in shaping, and restricting, literary tradition is specific conventions that establish certain genres while ruling out others and enforce a certain manner of treatment—which frequently means limitations in treatment—with regard to subject matter assigned the individual genre. Thus not only number and kind of subjects are restricted but also the possibilities of dealing with the subjects admitted.

The strength of those conventions varies from civilization to civilization and, within a civilization, from age to age; but these variations tend to be rather slight. In the two principal literatures of Islam, the Arabic and the Persian, the rigidity and the tenacity of genre conventions were extreme even as they had been in classical antiquity. The critics, for the most part, made their influence felt on the conservative side. Theory desired the perpetuation of established tradition. The necessity of adapting expression to changes of impression was not generally recognized. Poetry, to those judges animated by an archaism, half-sentimental, half-philological, was primarily craftsmanship; its outstanding merit trueness to established form, not adequacy of self-expression.

The pre-Islamic ode, *qaṣîda*, in Ibn Qutaiba's much-quoted words, was to begin with the mention of "the deserted dwelling-places and the relics and traces of habitation. Then (the poet) wept and complained and addressed the desolate encampment, and begged his companion to make a halt, in order that he might have occasion to speak of those who had once lived there and afterward departed. . . . . Then to this he linked the erotic prelude, *nasîb*, and bewailed the violence of his love and the anguish of separation from his mistress and the extremity of his passion and desire, so as to win the hearts of his hearers and divert their eyes toward him and invite their ears to listen to him, since the song of love touches men's souls and takes hold of their hearts. . . . ." The poet goes on "to complain of fatigue and want of sleep and travelling by night and of the noonday heat, and how his camel had been reduced to leanness."[1] Finally, the poet reaches his destination, the home of a chief whose generosity he stimulates by praise or to whom he delivers a political request as the spokesman of his tribe.

Every detail in the setting of the *qaṣîda* is attuned to the desert and to pre-Islamic conditions. To the urban Muslim the *loci communes* of the *nasîb* sounded stale if not ridiculous. But Ibn Qutaiba insists: "The later poet is not permitted to leave the custom of the ancients with regard to those parts (of the ode), so as to halt at an inhabited place or to weep at a walled building, since the ancients halted at a desolate spot and an effaced vestige." Nor is the later poet allowed to ride a donkey or a mule and to describe them since the ancients rode "a male or female camel; nor is he to alight at sweet flowing waters, seeing that the ancients alighted at brackish and turbid waters. (Likewise) they are not supposed, on the journey to the man they praise, to traverse countries that grow narcissus, myrtle and roses, for the ancients traversed countries in which there grew only desert plants."[2]

[1] Ibn Qutaiba, *Kitâb ash-shiʿr waʾsh-shuʿarâʾ*, ed. M. J. de Goeje (Leiden, 1904), pp. 14–15; trans. R. A. Nicholson, *A Literary History of the Arabs* (London, 1914), pp. 77–78.

[2] Ibn Qutaiba, *Shiʿr*, p. 16. The plants named are *shîḥ*, *ḥanwa*, and *ʿarâra*.

Ḫalaf al-Aḥmar (d. 796) was asked: "Does it not surprise you that a poet was permitted to say: 'The land brought forth *qaiṣûm* and *jaṭjâṭ* (two desert plants),' while I was not permitted to say: '(The land) brought forth prune trees and apple trees'?"[3]

It may be assumed that Ḫalaf was in no way surprised. For in another context he made it clear that it was for the critics to pass on the quality of a verse as it was for the money-changer to pass on that of a coin. What does it avail you if you consider your coin genuine as long as the banker is not prepared to concur?[4] And the influence of the critics consistently indorsed the restrictive conventions of the ancient genre.[5]

The roots of Muslim self-expression—if such a generalization may be accepted for the sake of convenience—lie in three great literary traditions—the Arabic, the Persian, and the Greek. Of these, the Arabic has proved the most influential, especially with regard to the apparatus of poetry and to technique in general. The Persian tradition, unfortunately, is not always to be appraised exactly, since Sassanian literature, including its historiographical documents, is only incompletely preserved. To the Greeks are owed, aside from psychological and philosophical advances such as a deepening of the love concept and a sharpening of the logical abilities, patterns of narration, patterns of rhetorical presentation, and a goodly number of commonplaces and human paradigms that came to be of considerable assistance in the Arab writer's struggle to express ideas and experiences for the presentation of which his own literature would not yield a precedent.

Of the three strains, it is the Arabic we know best. But the unsatisfactory state of our insight into Sassanian literature and the details of the Greek contribution does in no way obscure the fact that the trend of self-expression responsible for the development of lyrics and autobiography derives its main strength from the Arabic tradition, whereas the trend leading to epic and dramatic representation is anchored in the Persian, and, on the whole, remains a Persian characteristic. The intermediate genres

[3] *Ibid.*

[4] Jumaḥî, p. 4.

[5] For countermovements and the *querelle des anciens et des modernes* in general, cf. the author, *JNES*, III (1944), 246–51.

of history and biography are nourished by both traditions, but it is probably fair to say that in the final forming of the historian's and the biographer's arts Arab ways and the Arab outlook on man asserted themselves somewhat more powerfully. The Greek spirit, on the wane after the tenth century, infiltrated everywhere. It did not, however, create new genres of self-expression but only affected those that existed by widening psychological experience and enriching the conceptual means of mastering it.

II

Ṯaᶜlab (d. 904) assigns to poetry a fourfold function: command, prohibition, and giving, and asking for, information.[6] These basic services of poetry branch out into "praise, polemical criticism (or satire, *hijâ*ᵓ), elegy, apology, love-making, comparison (*tashbîh*), and report of happenings."[7]

Arabic theory never quite outgrew this classification, operating rather confusingly with both formal and material differentials. Abû Hilâl al-ᶜAskarî (d. 1005) in one passage splits up poetry into four areas: panegyrics, *hijâ*ᵓ, self-praise, and love songs,[8] but elsewhere he declares for a division into five categories, replacing "self-praise" by "elegy" and adding "descriptive verse (*waṣf*)."[9]

It may be debatable whether those critics through their several classifications desired to lay bare the essential traits of classical, that is, pre-Islamic, poetry (documented *ca.* A.D. 450–620), but it is quite clear that they did not succeed. Leaving aside tribal and personal controversies, the poet's descriptive interest is paramount. This interest concentrates on objects rather than emotional experience. Perhaps it would be more accurate to say that the poet is freer in depicting the outside world than in giving an account of his sentiments. The richness and precision of his portrayal of the desert atmosphere—of his

[6] *Qawâᶜid ash-shiᶜr*, ed. C. Schiaparelli, *Actes du VIII*ᵉ *Congrès international des orientalistes*, Part II, Sec. I (Leiden, 1893), p. 183.

[7] *Ibid.*, p. 184.

[8] Abû Hilâl al-ᶜAskarî, *Dîwân al-maᶜânî* (Cairo, 1352), I, 31.

[9] *Ibid.*, p. 91. A very detailed division is given by Qudâma b. Jaᶜfar (?), *Naqd an-naṯr* (Cairo, 1933), p. 70.

mount, be it camel or horse, of the animals that enliven the steppe, of his weapons, and, in another sphere, of hunt and carousal—and of his beloved, the mixture of vividness and almost scholarly completeness, at first suggests considerable spontaneity and liberty of choice on the part of the artist. The alertness of his impressionistic response inspires striking comparisons but, at the same time, induces the poet to yield to fleeting associations and jeopardizes the unity of his work. But any cross-section of classical verse soon discloses the patterns to which the poet is supposed to cling.

A strict code selects the animals, even the landscape he is to describe—there is never a picture of the semiurban settlements in which many a poet spent a considerable part of his life. The amatory prelude, *nasîb*, so touching and colorful at first sight, is actually limited to less than half-a-dozen motive sequences, each with its own phraseology and imagery.[10] It is the same woman, one feels tempted to say, whose charms the poets set forth with varying skill. She is of high standing in tribal society and, by and large, conforms to the taste of Rubens' age, although, of course, her hair and her eyes are of a darker hue than that of the Flemish beauties whom Rubens immortalized as goddesses or nymphs.

When the poet speaks of love, it is of bygone days and lost hopes that he tells. It portends the end of classical song when Abû D̲uʾaib (d. *ca.* 650) in a *nasîb* voices hope for a passion still alive.[11] The actualization of love, the presentation of incident and feelings that either are valid here and now or point to future happiness or conflict, is one of the important advances owed to the so-called Medinese school of poets (*fl. ca.* 670–740). It testifies to the genius of the greatest classical poet, Imruʾulqais (d. *ca.* 540), that he discusses, without too much regard for the proprieties of the pattern, intimate personal experience. But even he never gets away from reminiscing, and, what is more, his amatory preludes remain fairly conventional, while his confessional verse is tucked away at some less prominent part of the *qaṣîda*.

[10] Cf. the writer, *Orientalia*, VIII (new ser., 1939), 333–36.

[11] *Dîwân*, ed. J. Hell (Hanover, 1926), No. 18.1.

Social custom supports impersonality. In Mohammedan times the family feels disgraced when one of their womenfolk is mentioned by a poet as the object of his affections. ᶜUmar I went so far as to forbid love poetry.[12] It may be doubted whether this sweeping condemnation was intended too seriously; but, in any event, it was bad manners to use other than fictitious names in erotic verse, however modest.[13] Slave girls might be named; ladies never. When Umm al-Banîn, the favorite wife of al-Walîd I, pilgrimaged to Mecca, the caliph warned the poets to refrain from addressing love songs to any member of his household.[14] Al-ᶜAbbâs b. al-Aḥnaf (d. 806) sings in detail and with great delicacy and finesse of his love, that turned from sweet to bitter, disguising and protecting his lady by calling her Fauz, "Success," a characteristic slave name. The rigor of convention relaxes as time wears on. But when the victory for genuineness in the portrayal of passion and affection is about to be won and the shackles of an obsolete pattern are almost removed, that fatal tendency of rhetorization sets in to stifle the warmth of personal feeling under the cover of verbal brilliancy.

The overpowering compulsion of poetical convention is impressively demonstrated in the experiences of two poets of the Umayyad age. Ibn Qais ar-Ruqayyât, after championing the loser in civil war, fled to Kufa, where a woman whom he had never met before hid him in her house. She never asked his name or circumstances. After he had stayed for one year, he heard the public crier make the announcement that whoever would shelter him would be held liable to severe penalties. Thereupon Ibn Qais told the woman he would leave immediately. But she told him not to worry, since this announcement had been made daily for the past year and she had been well aware of his identity. Nevertheless he departed. When he asked her about herself, she refused to answer. So the only thing he knew about her was her name, Kaṯîra, by which he had heard others address her. In due course the poet was pardoned by the caliph and, in token of

[12] *Irshâd*, IV, 154; see *Aghânî* (3d ed.), IV, 356, the comment of the poet Ḥumaid b. Ṯaur.

[13] Cf. ᶜUmar II's criticism of Nuṣaib, *Aghânî* (3d ed.), VI, 123–24.

[14] *Ibid.*, p. 218.

gratitude, wished to perpetuate in verse the memory of what the woman had done for him. At this point, however, Ibn Qais found himself the captive of convention. There being no precedent to follow, he could not do anything beyond introducing Kaṯîra into an ordinary *nasîb*. He tells of his grief for her and presents Kaṯîra as spurning his love on account of his gray hair—even as scores of poets had done before him. The peculiarity of their relationship is obliterated by the leveling weight of the age-old pattern.[15]

Aᶜshà Hamdân (d. 702) was liberated from captivity by the daughter of the Dailamite chief whose soldiers had taken him prisoner. Upon his promise to take her for his wife, she released him and some other Muslim captives. Aᶜshà celebrated the event in a long *qaṣîda*. He starts in the customary manner by deploring the departure of his love and describing the fair lady. Only after seventeen verses does he mention his fight in faraway lands. But for a few place-names the incident could have happened anywhere. No reference to the circumstances of his rescue is to be discovered. No sooner has Aᶜshà entered upon actual facts than he relinquishes the plane of actuality to rejoin convention in a passage of hearty self-praise.[16]

Self-praise, and even more so the eulogy of the dead, purposes to establish the speaker's or the deceased's conformity to the ideal. It is interesting because it clarifies our understanding of this ideal, but the specifically personal element of *iftiḫâr*, self-praise, or *faḫr*, praise, is rather slight (always disregarding, of course, references to events). It is only during the last three hundred years that the West has become sensitive to self-praise. The ancients, and the Greeks more than the Romans, and again the Middle Ages and the Renaissance tolerated it, and so did the Muslim world.[17] Plutarch,[18] and before him Quintilian,[19] dis-

[15] Ibn Qais ar-Ruqayyât, No. I, 1–4; the prose account, *Aghânî* (3d ed.), V, 84–85; cf. also Rhodokanakis, Introduction, pp. 33 and 46–47. For the whole problem cf. the writer's *Die Wirklichkeitweite der früharabischen Dichtung* (Vienna, 1937), pp. 106–9.

[16] Poem 32 (ed. Geyer).

[17] But the Old Testament discourages it. Cf. Prov. 27:2: "Let another man praise thee, and not thine own mouth."

[18] "De se ipso citra invidiam laudando."

[19] *Institutiones* xi. 1. 15–24.

cussed manner and extent to which it was to be permissible. Isocrates (d. B.C. 336) boasts unabashedly of his accomplishments.[20] As usual, the ancients behave less crudely than the Arabs, but on the whole the sentiment is the same.

When Plutarch[21] counsels to discourage praise of one's riches or power and to ask for a eulogy on moral grounds, viz., on account of one's goodness, urbanity, or usefulness, it is done in the same spirit that makes al-ᶜAskarî advise to confer praise or blame for the sake of (the presence or absence of) forbearance, knowledge, intelligence, and the like.[22] Physical handicaps should be overlooked by criticism. It is only character that counts. Convention backed by what might be called the atomizing outlook of the Arab on people and things[23] prevented for the most part the drawing of fully individualized portraits in poetical form. The Arab's attention was caught by the detail, which he would render with inimitable poignancy; but the totality of man, unless patternized, more often than not escaped while the poet skilfully vaunted bravery, generosity, decency, sportliness, and initiative of his hero.

In other words, poetry shows man poorer, or rather simpler, than he really was. The ideal is not infrequently engagingly painted with glaring colors, but the individual proved elusive. Malice would sometimes be successful where kindliness failed. But rhetorical hyperbole was likely to nullify the shrewdest vision.[24] As he is less well protected by social proprieties, the lowly receives the most accurate, if merciless, portrayal. The rough-handed, work-soiled, and ugly servant, who takes care of the camel turning the irrigation wheel,[25] the emaciated moun-

[20] *Antapodosis* 141 *et passim.*

[21] *Op. cit.*, chap. 12.

[22] *Dîwân al-maᶜânî*, I, 202.

[23] In point of form this tendency is operative, too, when the individual verse, not the poem in which it stands, is made the unit of critical study and when the demand is raised that it should constitute a complete and independent whole; cf., e.g., Shams-i Qais (thirteenth century), *Muᶜjam* (London and Leiden, 1909), p. 260, and al-ᶜAskarî, *Kitâb aṣ-ṣinâᶜatain*, pp. 26–27.

[24] Cf., e.g., Qudâma against exaggeration, quoted by al-Marzubânî (d. 994), *al-Muwashshaḥ* (Cairo, 1343), p. 354.

[25] Labîd, *Dîwân*, ed. Yûsuf al-Ḫâlidî (Vienna, 1880), No. 16.14 (p. 95).

taineer who looks for the honey of the wild bees,[26] and the caravan leader,

calm in his resolute way:
His loins well girt, and his shirt upon him ragged and torn, rough and ungentle of speech, crisp-haired, a masterful man[27]—

these figures represent beginnings that never quite came to fruition. It is perhaps of some significance that it was an outlaw who created one of the few outstanding character sketches of classical poetry. This is how Taʾabbaṭa Sharran speaks of his friend ash-Shanfarà.

Nay, I say not, when a Friend cuts short the bond and departs,
"Alas, my soul!" out of longing and soft self-pitying tears.
No! weeping, were I one to weep for him that has gone his way, should be for one keen of praise, a striver outstripping all—
Outstripping in all his tribe the racers for glory's goal, his voice resounds, strong and deep, mid his fellows bound on the raid:
Bare of flesh in the shins, his arms backed with sinews strong, he plunges into the blackest of night under torrents of rain;
The bearer of banners he, the chosen for council he, a sayer of words strong and sound, a pusher to furthest bounds.
For such a one do I care—to such goes my call for help when help is needed—shock-headed, hoarse as a raven's cry;
His hair like a rough sand-ridge, beaten oft by the feet of men,
I call him the Shepherd of the two small flocks, with the lambs and their ropes.[28]

The greatest advances in introspection were to be made in the analysis of love and in the unfolding of the stages through which the erring skeptic passes on his way to peace in God. Significantly enough, love experience never was admitted for discussion in the autobiography proper; neither the mores of the period nor the literary tradition which it developed were prepared to countenance its inclusion. The severity with which the incidental and the emotional (except for the specifically religious) are kept out of self-representation condemns the genre to

[26] Abû D̲uʾaib, No. 22.1–4.

[27] ʿAbîd b. al-Abraṣ, ed. and trans. C. J. Lyall (Leiden and London, 1913), No. 22.13*b*–14.

[28] *Mufaḍḍaliyyât*, No. 1. 9–15; trans., Vol. II, 3–4; vs. 9 voices conventional sentiment.

a certain dryness and one-sidedness in its understanding of personality.

In his *Dove's Neck-Ring*[29] Ibn Ḥazm follows in the footsteps of, but by far excels, Ibn Dâʾûd's erotic anthology, the *Book of the Flower*.[30] Ibn Dâʾûd endeavors to illustrate a number of psychological observations about love and the lover through verse. His analysis of passion does not go very far. It is romantic, or perhaps sentimental, love he is considering, and the reflection of Platonic philosophy is tangible in many a passage. His chapter headings reveal the scope of his work. "He whose patience is overcome, his weeping grows.—The emaciation of the body is the weakest proof of suffering.—The road of patience is long, the hiding of love is trying.—He whose patience is overcome, his secret shows up.—He whose love advances, his woes grow stronger.—The firmness of a pact is not known, except when a separation or an avoidance takes place.—Little fidelity after death is more sublime than much fidelity during life."[31]

Ibn Ḥazm's treatise preserves some traits of the anthology. Any statement he makes is corroborated by verse, frequently his own, and illustrative anecdote. However, the personal participation of the author is much more in evidence than in Ibn Dâʾûd's bulkier book, and his powers of penetration leave his playful predecessor far behind. Ibn Ḥazm treats his subject systematically. He begins with the origins of love, continues with the accidents of love and its praiseworthy and blameworthy qualities, then turns to calamities which occur in it and finishes with a condemnation of illicit practices and an éloge of continence, "so that," in his own words, "the conclusion of our wish and the last of our discussion be on inspiring the obedience of God and enjoining justice and forbidding evil: this is the duty of every believer."[32] There is an engaging lightness and elegance about the book which makes one forget its unevenness. Sometimes Ibn Ḥazm reaches the very limit of understanding; some-

[29] Ed. D. K. Pétrof (Leiden, 1914); trans. A. R. Nykl (Paris, 1931).

[30] Ed. A. R. Nykl and I. Ṭûqân (Chicago, 1932).

[31] Chaps. 41–44, 46, 49–50; trans. Nykl, *Neck-Ring*, Introduction, pp. cv–cvi.

[32] *Ibid.*, p. 5.

times he is satisfied with repeating, in graceful phrasing, what had been commonplace centuries before his day.[33] He is at his best when dissecting background and significance of the lover's behavior.

Among the calamities of love there is avoidance. These are its kinds: "(1) The first is the avoidance required by circumstances on account of a watcher who is present, and this indeed is sweeter than union itself; . . . . (2) Then comes the avoidance brought about by coquetry, and this is more delicious than many of the kinds of union, and on account of this it does not occur except when each one of the lovers has complete confidence in the other . . . . , and at that time the beloved feigns avoidance in order to see the lover's steadfastness. . . . . (3) Then comes avoidance occasioned by censure on account of some guilt committed by the lover. And in this there is some severity, but the joy of return, and the rejoicing of approval balances what has preceded. In the approval of the beloved after being angry there is a delight of heart which no other delight can equal. . . . . (4) There happens also both avoidance and reproach. And, by my life, if it lasts only a short time, there is a delight in it; but if it grows very serious it is not a good omen, and it is an indication of an evil consequence. . . . . (5) Then comes avoidance brought about by slanderers. . . . . (6) Then comes the avoidance (caused by) *ennui*. And *ennui* (getting soon tired of someone) is one of the natural innate characteristics of man; and what he who has been smitten by it deserves most is that no friend should be true to him, and no friendship toward him genuine; he is not firm in his promise, ... and no faith is to be attached to his swearing either love or hatred. . . . . (7) There is a case of avoidance where the initiative is taken by the lover: namely, when he sees his beloved treat him harshly and show inclination toward someone else . . . . ; so that he sees death and swallows bitter draughts of grief, ... and he breaks off, while his heart is cut to pieces. . . . . (8) Then comes the avoidance due to hatred: and here all writing becomes confused, and all cunning is exhausted, and troubles become great, this is

[33] Cf., e.g., the two discussions of the nature of love, *ibid.*, pp. 8–9 and 13.

the kind (of estrangement) which makes people lose their heads. . . . ."[34]

Much of Arabic autobiography is limited to the listing of significant dates: birth, study, public appointments. The personality behind the events remains shrouded. Another and smaller group of works perpetuates the tradition of Galen (d. *ca.* A.D. 200), the great Greek physician, who gave his *vita* in the form of an answer to a friend's request and in it listed his works in correct sequence. Only rarely does a scholar—and all the Muslim autobiographers are scholars or theologians of one sort or another—describe his personal character.

The Egyptian physician, ᶜAlî b. Riḍwân (d. 1061), asserts that he fulfils the stipulations of the Hippocratean oath[35] and gives an elaborate portrait of himself. "In my professional work, I endeavor to be humble, sociable, helpful to the dejected, to discover the distress of the unfortunate and to help the indigent. I make it my aim in all this to enjoy the satisfaction which comes from good deeds and sentiments, but at the same time this cannot but bring in money which I can spend. I am spending on my health and for the maintenance of my household, neither being a squanderer nor a niggard, as much as to practice the golden mean, as becomes a reasonable mind, at any time. . . . . I am wearing clothes which are adorned by the marks of distinguished people and by cleanliness. I make use of a delicate perfume, am silent and take care of my language where the failings of men are concerned. . . . . I avoid conceitedness and overweening, avoid eager desires and covetousness, and if an adversity befalls me, I rely on Allah the Most High and meet it reasonably without faintheartedness nor weakness. Whenever I transact business with anyone I pay in cash without giving nor raising credit, except if obliged to do so: . . . . In my leisure hours after having finished my practise, I devote myself to godliness, recreating myself by the thought about the 'Kingdom of Heavens and Earth'[36] and praising Him who laid their firm

[34] *Ibid.*, pp. 96–109 (selection).

[35] Cf. Ibn abî Uṣaibiᶜa (d. 1270), *ᶜUyûn al-anbâ*ᵓ (Cairo, 1299/1882), II, 102–3.

[36] Koran 7:185.

foundations. I read in Aristotle's treatise *On Economics* and endeavor to follow his prescriptions constantly from morning to evening. In the time of rest I review my actions and sentiments of the same day; what was good and nice and useful, I enjoy, and what was bad and ugly and nocive, I am grieved at and make up my mind not to repeat it."[37]

His contemporaries took a slightly different view of the great physician. Ibn abî Uṣaibiᶜa says: "Ibn Riḍwân was inclined to polemics against his contemporaries, physicians and others, and likewise against his predecessors. He was insolent in his utterings and abused those with whom he held argument."[38]

Ibn al-Muqaffaᶜ (d. 757) translated and edited the Sassanian physician, Burzôê's, autobiography composed on the occasion of his rendering into Pahlavî of the Sanskrit *Pancatantra*. Moved by idealism, he enters the medical profession. Despondency due to the impossibility of curing many a disease and the realization that religious knowledge frees from all infirmity makes Burzôê study the various faiths. Unable to decide which of them was the most excellent, he adopts ethical principles of universal applicability to direct his actions. He feels attracted by asceticism but too weak to cut his ties to this world. So he compromises, satisfied with such righteousness as he finds it possible to practice. In this resignation, this cessation of spiritual strife before the absolute goal is reached, Burzôê differs essentially from the later Muslim autobiographer who reviews his life only after having reached his spiritual objective.[39]

The Muslim autobiography of religious import is either the tale of a conversion—conversion, that is, from a bad to a good Muslim, from a worldly to a saintly person—or the description of the road from doubt to faith.

Conversion is usually due to some striking incident or else to a dream. The report not infrequently sounds like an anecdote,

[37] J. Schacht and M. Meyerhof, *The Medico-philosophical Controversy between Ibn Butlan of Baghdad and Ibn Ridwan of Cairo* (Cairo, 1937), pp. 36–37.

[38] *Ibid.*, p. 39.

[39] On Burzôê cf. the brilliant paragraph by F. Rosenthal, *Analecta orientalia*, XIV (1937), 10–11, where literature is listed.

but this impression is due to the omission of the preparatory developments that made the narrator's soul responsive to the decisive experience.

Some time toward the end of the year 1045, Nâṣir-i Ḫusrav (d. 1088), a minor official in Marv, fond of fast company and a poet of great promise, saw a personage addressing him in his dream and asking him: "How long will you drink of that beverage (i.e., wine) which takes away man's reason? It would be better for you to come to your senses." In his dream he answered: "But for wine the wise have never been able to find anything to alleviate this world's sorrow."

"Loss of self-possession and loss of reason do not procure rest of mind. No sage can have pointed to senselessness as guide. Something else will have to be sought to increase reason and sense."

"Where can I find this?" Nâṣir asked.

"He who seeks will find." Pointing in the direction of the *qibla*, the personage left without saying anything further. When he awoke, Nâṣir decided to reform. After imploring God for fortitude in his resolve, he asked to be relieved of his duties and set out on pilgrimage.[40]

The *Confessions* of Augustine (d. 430) are the earliest extant description of the psychological process leading a religious mind to a deepened reappropriation of the faith of his childhood. Tormented by doubts, Augustine turns to the study of any and all teachings within his reach. After going through disappointment and bottomless despair, he is shown the truth in the Catholic doctrine only then rightly understood by him. The life-story which, thanks to his artistic gifts, seems to transcend the mere framework of this transformation is actually told in careful selection so as to illustrate, justify, and above all organize in proper sequence the stages and the logic of the development. More normative than descriptive in intent, the *Confessions* present the stylized *vita* of a somewhat stylized personality trimmed of such authentic detail as appeared superfluous for the illustration of the author's ascent.

[40] *Safar Nâma*, ed. C. Schefer (Paris, 1881), pp. 2–3.

But for Augustine's literary mastership it would be obvious that he sacrificed the completeness of his self-vision to its didactic significance.

In spite of the limits Augustine imposed on his self-portrayal, the *Confessions* are full of incidents and reflections that bring his personality back to life. When lesser men, or just men of lesser literary ability, come to use their experience as an instructive paradigm of the path to truth, the integration of *vita* and development weakens, the biographical element loses the interest of the writer, and he tells his psychological recovery, merely providing the barest personal setting. To him, his life is noteworthy solely for its moral, or religious, lesson. Personality shrinks to be an instrument of truth-finding.

In an unassuming passage al-Muḥâsibî explains his way to God. Plunged into confusion by the disagreements of the theologians and unable to reconcile them even with the aid of the allegorical interpretation of the Holy Book, he sought the help of meditation, scrupulous observance of his ordinances and imitation of the Prophet. "My difficulties were increased by the lack of God-fearing guides, and I feared greatly lest death should cut short my life, through my anguish on account of the schisms among the faithful." But God gave him guidance "from those in whom I found indications of devoted piety, of abstinence, and of preference for the next world over this. . . . . They seek to make God loved by His servants, in reminding them of His favors and His loving-kindness and in calling upon the faithful to repent unto God." Following them, "I saw that no further proof was needed for one who had grasped the argument."[41]

It is not necessary that a religious solution beckon at the end of the path. The scholar Ibn al-Haiṯam (d. *ca.* 1039), pained by skepticism, scours the teachings of the sects for the truth. Disappointed in his searchings, he finds rest in Aristotelian philosophy. He recognizes study and research as his task in life. In accord with Galen he considers truth as attainable only

[41] *Waṣâyâ* (also called *Naṣâ'iḥ*), text in Massignon, *Recueil*, pp. 17–20; trans. Smith, *Early Mystic of Baghdad*, pp. 18–20.

through scientific effort.[42] Thus the result, but not the structure, of his experience differs from that of al-Muḥâsibî and his greater successor, al-Ghazâlî.

Al-Ghazâlî co-ordinates, to some extent, his actions and his psychological development. His *Savior from Error*,[43] while not measuring up in richness, or volume, to the *Confessions*, follows in its composition the pattern rendered famous by Augustine.* His longing for indubitable knowledge and the fallacies he has to discover in every teaching he reviews destroy his rest. He studies with the greatest thoroughness whatever opinions the learned hold in his day and finds them wanting. He had reached a respected position as expositor of the truth, while his uneasiness about the nature of this truth undermined his work and forced on his conscience a conflict of extreme bitterness. But it needed a collapse of his health before he could muster the strength to forsake his professorial chair and to retire from Baghdad to Jerusalem and Damascus, dedicated to self-purification and the apprehension of the Ṣûfî way and goal. Circumstances drew him back into the life of the world but not before he had found in the Ṣûfîs the competent guides toward rest in the Lord who imitated in their discipline the example of the Prophet.

It is disappointing but true to genre, and in accord with that discretion touching personal detail characteristic of so many Muslim authors, that, in accounting for his return to teaching, al-Ghazâlî refrains from setting forth his actual reasons and that, in general, the circumstantial narrative is of the slightest. And whereas in later European autobiographies—as well as in the *Confessions*—personages influencing the writer's outer or inner life are carefully recorded and described, al-Muḥâsibî, Ibn al-Haiṯam, and al-Ghazâlî are at one in concentrating on themselves and in excluding as far as possible men-

[42] It would seem that I find myself here slightly at variance with Rosenthal, who (*loc. cit.*, pp. 7–8) appears inclined to divorce Ibn al-Haiṯam more clearly from the literary pattern followed by al-Muḥâsibî and al-Ghazâlî.

[43] *Al-Munqiḏ min aḍ-ḍalâl*, text frequently printed; French trans. by Barbier de Meynard, *Journal asiatique*, IX (7th sér., 1877), 5–93. A most interesting analysis is offered by H. Frick, *Ghazâlîs Selbstbiographie: Ein Vergleich mit Augustins Konfessionen* (abridged ed.; Giessen, 1919); cf. also Rosenthal, *loc. cit.*, pp. 12–15.

tion and, above all, characterization of contemporaries. Their autobiographies, then, are little more than confessional monologues.

Where al-Ghazâlî stops and invokes the support of the reader's ecstatic experience, the mystical writers attempt to speak out the unspeakable. None of them shows greater boldness than Ibn al-Fâriḍ (d. 1235), in those verses of his *tâʾiyya* (poem rhyming in *t*) where he undertakes to propound the meaning of the oneness with God, to which, he feels, he has attained.

I was an apostle sent from myself to myself, and my essence was led to me by the evidence of my own signs.
And when I conveyed my soul, by purchase, from the possession of her own land to the kingdom of Paradise,
She soared with me, in consequence of my union, beyond everlasting life in her heaven. . . . .
No darkness covers me nor is there any harm to be feared, since the mercy of my light hath quenched the fire of my vengeance.[44]

In identifying himself with Mohammed conceived as manifesting himself to the senses as the created universe, Ibn al-Fâriḍ exclaims:

None lives but his life is from mine, and every willing soul is obedient to my will.
And there is no speaker but tells his tale with my words, nor any seer but sees with the sight of mine eyes;
And no silent (listener) but hears with my hearing, nor any one that grasps but with my strength and might;
And in the whole creation there is none save me that speaks or hears.[45]

At this point, meaning becomes meaningless.

III

It is probably fair to state that biography and, even more so, history arrived at a more comprehensive view of human character than poetry and autobiography, although the analytical finesse of these genres in presenting fleeting moods and especially in detailing the struggle of the conscience remains unexcelled.

[44] Vss. 460, 461, 463 (part), 497; trans. Nicholson, *Studies*, pp. 240, 241, 245.

[45] Vss. 639–42, trans. *ibid.*, p. 255; cf. Nicholson, *Personality*, p. 21.

The roots of the Muslim interest in biography are both favorable and unfavorable to the development of character drawing. When confronted with the task of describing the outstanding events of the Prophet's time, the only native technique to fall back on was the manner in which the *ayyâm* tales dealt with their subject, the "battle-days" of the pagan Arabs. In these stories, beautifully told in precise and colorful language, vividness of detail cannot obscure the powerful influence of literary patterns which compel the narrator to operate with stereotyped motives and almost as stereotyped episodes. The character of the protagonists transpires not infrequently through the incidents in which they appear,[46] but it is not the prime concern of the story-teller who confines his explicit statements to snapshot-like sketches of their looks. "A darkish-brown and vigorous man, with a head like a mown lawn."—"A man with small eyes, arched brows, strong moustachio; when he spoke his saliva flowed over his beard."[47]—His wife describes Zurâra to her captor. "He was and thou knowest it (well) of noble race, in manners kind to all / of tender skin, his frame is huge and tall / he eats what chance may bring, his barest need / for lack or loss he pays no heed / when danger comes at night he knows no rest / and does not eat his fill, a thrifty guest."[48]

A more disciplined treatment of personality the Arab biographers learned from two foreign sources. They became acquainted with Sassanian historiography, which grouped events around the individual kings.[49] And in the same direction pointed the *Lives* of the Christian saints, whose influence is tangible in the designation *maghâzî*, "fights," given the earliest biographies of Mohammed in accordance with the Christian usage of representing the holy personage as a combatant, his acts as fights.[50]

[46] Cf. W. Caskel, "Aiyâm al-ᶜArab," *Islamica*, III, Supplement (1931), 23–25; on p. 24 Caskel discusses the only hero who is distinguished by his "romantic" manner of action.

[47] *Ibid.*, p. 37; also *Wirklichkeitweite*, pp. 57–58.

[48] I. Lichtenstadter, *Women in the Aiyâm al-ᶜArab* (London, 1935), pp. 35–36, trans. from *Aghânî* (1st ed.), XIX, 129.

[49] Cf. Nöldeke, *Araber und Perser*, Introduction, pp. xiv–xviii.

[50] For detail cf. the writer, *JAOS*, LXII (1942), 291.

Thus, the *sîra*, "biography," of the Prophet, as it was evolved during the first century after his death, unified the three impulses of the pagan *ayyâm*, the Persian *siyar al-mulûk*, "Lives of the Kings," and the Christian *vita* of the soldier of God.[51] The form of the *sîra* is narrative *ḥadîṯ*, identical in structure with theological or eschatological tradition. The loquacity of the *qâṣṣ*, the professional teller of legends and stories, is reflected in the loosening of stylistic rigidity in many of the *sîra*'s episodes where the gain in vividness is paid for by the loss in accuracy.

The necessity of sifting the traditionists with regard to their reliability, of ascertaining their dates and their interdependence, gave rise to the gigantic collections of notices on persons who played some part in the preservation and promulgation of *ḥadîṯ*. However admirable the diligence of the collectors, whose biographical encyclopedias remained unparalleled in the West until very recently, the strictness with which they confined their interest to name, time, studies, writings, and a general estimate of orthodoxy and dependability, impoverished more than anything else the Muslim portrayal of man. Practical considerations doubtless justified the procedure, but from the historian's viewpoint this reduction of the individual to the tabulation of a few impersonal facts is an irreparable loss; and the narrowing of the biographical aspiration can be perceived for centuries.

Another type of biographical listings, the *ṭabaqât*, "classes," in which personalities were arranged not alphabetically but according to their generation, proved less but not much less destructive of the literary feeling for personality. Ibn Saᶜd's (d. 845) *Classes of the Companions* in many instances offers enlivening anecdote and, mostly by implication, keen characterization. But, like the *ṭabaqât* of poets that were compiled in the ninth century, the *Classes* never, except in the case of the Prophet and a very few of the earliest followers, purposes the presentation of character from the cradle to the grave, nor does it bother to maintain chronological sequence within the individual biography.

The Arab's fascination with curious incidents, *mirabilia*,

[51] G. L. Della Vida, in a masterly study of the *sîra*, *EI*, IV, 439–43, recognizes only the first two influences.

"striking sayings," did not stimulate but actually frustrated the development of a vision of the personality as a whole from which the several anecdotal items would receive their fitting perspective and for which, in turn, they would serve as illustrative evidence. Literary history, if this term is applicable at all, overcame the limitations of the *ṭabaqât* to some extent. The *Kitâb al-aghânî* ("Book of Songs"), compiled by Abû ʾl-Faraj al-Iṣfahânî (d. 967), attempts to round out the biographies of poets and singers by regularly beginning with their names and genealogies and ending with their deaths. But into this frame a farrago of stories, verse, and extraneous matter conjured up by association is crammed without any artistic planning being recognizable. We owe the most valuable data to this delight in miscellaneous information, and we are able more often than not to reconstruct the personalities Abû ʾl-Faraj discusses from the disconnected items which he brings to our attention. But hardly ever does he get beyond a generous offering of unco-ordinated material—a state of affairs which, it must be admitted, if unsatisfactory as an achievement of biographical art, much advances our chances at rebuilding an unbiased picture of the period. Yâqût's (d. 1229) *Dictionary of Learned Men,* a document of stupendous erudition, is better organized in its arrayal of facts, but almost everywhere the scholar is lost behind his accomplishments, and, with few exceptions, the personalities of the learned pale into indistinguishable dimness. The Arab writer excels in observation of detail; he is unsurpassed in the telling of poignantly characteristic anecdotes; but, for the most part, he is unable, or perhaps unwilling, to synthetize his impressions, which he prefers to string onto one another with little regard to the unity of the personality he depicts or of the literary composition in which he is engaged.

Description of physique or character when given explicitly is formulated under the influence of the Hellenistic pattern of the so-called *eikonismos,* first traceable in Ptolemaic papyri of the third century B.C. This pattern, using the terminology of the Greek physiognomists, provides for the asyndetic listing of a number of qualities after the fashion of the passport or the police warrant. Originally confined to fixing physical peculiarities, it is gradually extended to mental characteristics as well.[52]

Abû ʾl-Faraj has someone describe Umayya, the ancestor of the Umayyad dynasty, as "a short old man, of lean body, blind."[53] Ibn al-Maulà, a minor poet (*fl. ca.* 750), "was witty, continent, clean of dress, handsome of appearance."[54] The vizier al-Faḍl b. Sahl (d. 818 or 819) was "liberal, generous, harsh in punishment, easy to conciliate, civilized (forbearing, *ḥalîm*), eloquent, learned in the ways (*âdâb*) of the kings, resourceful, cautious, acquisitive."[55]

Ibn Ḫallikân (d. 1282) in his admirable collection of biographies, *The Deaths of the Prominent*, has much to say of the disposition of his heroes. But nowhere does he outgrow the stage in which character is explained by an enumeration, more or less complete and significant, of its component qualities. The limitations of this conception of personality become immediately evident when it is brought face to face with the Greek endeavor to explain the many aspects of a character by pointing to its principal motive force.

Ibn Ḫallikân says of Jaʿfar the Barmakid (d. 803), the favorite of Hârûn ar-Rashîd: "In the high rank which he attained and the great power which he wielded, in loftiness of spirit and in the esteem and favor shown him by the caliph, he stood without a rival. His disposition was generous, his looks encouraging, his demeanor kind; but his liberality and munificence, the richness and the prodigality of his donations, are too well known to require mention. He expressed his thoughts with great elegance, and was remarkable for his eloquence and command of language."[56] Nothing has been said that would not apply to many another courtier, nor have we been given the key to his personality. Plutarch, discussing Alcibiades, at once seizes upon the

[52] For the history of this pattern see the writer, *JAOS*, LXIV (1944), 62, and LXII (1942), 285–86, and n. 87 on p. 286. E. R. Curtius, *Deutsche Vierteljahrsschrift für Literaturwissenschaft und Geistesgeschichte*, XVI (1938), 468–69, points to parallel developments of the Ptolemaic *eikonismos* in Byzantine literature.

[53] *Aghânî* (3d ed.), I, 12.

[54] *Ibid.*, III, 286.

[55] Ibn aṭ-Ṭiqtaqà, *Kitâb al-faḫrî*, ed. W. Ahlwardt (Gotha, 1860), p. 265.

[56] Trans. De Slane (Paris, 1843–71), I, 301–2.

main trait of his hero and develops his life and his character from it. "His conduct displayed many great inconsistencies and variations, not unnaturally, in accordance with the many and wonderful vicissitudes of his fortunes; but among the many strong passions of his real character, the one most prevailing of all was his ambition and desire of superiority."[57]

It is difficult for the Arab biographer to trace a development in his hero, unless this development means his abnegation of this world. In Ibn Ḫallikân's *vita* of Ibn Ḥazm there is no inkling of his change from a statesman and littérateur to a theologian and historian of religion. His vast knowledge wins due praise; his humility and indifference to worldly advantages are remarked upon and contrasted with the high offices he, as his father before him, had held. But there is no unfolding, only a conspectus of his qualities and claims to fame.[58] Nowhere in this genre of scholarship do we find so much as an indication of a change in character and attitude as, to select an example at random, Plutarch provides when he states that, after he had broken up a dangerous opposition and obtained the banishment of Thucydides, Pericles "was no longer the same man he had been before, nor as tame and gentle and familiar with the populace, so as ready to yield to their pleasure. . . . . Quitting that loose, remiss, and, in some cases, licentious court of the popular will, he turned those soft and flowery modulations to the austerity of aristocratical and regal rule, etc."[59] Here we are shown cause and effect, development and motivation. The Muslim writer, on the other hand, freezes the fluid process and paints a keen but static portrait. What changes is not so much the individual but his station, and his actions are likely to affect his fate and the fate of nations rather than the core of his being, which is almost untouched by the drama of which he is the principal actor.

Curiously enough, historiography proper at times attains to greater adequacy and sophistication in the presentation of character. The tribal genealogy of the *ayyâm* tales, the stories told by transmitters to explain allusions in obscure poems, the en-

[57] *Lives*, trans. J. Dryden, revised by A. H. Clough (New York: Modern Library, n.d.), p. 234.

[58] Ibn Ḫallikân II, 267–68.

[59] *Lives*, p. 195.

deavors of the traditionists to motivate and localize precisely the origin of the *ḥadîṯ*, the records of individual conversion to Islam and of the manner in which any specific place surrendered to Muslim authority—all these stimuli of historiography made for the cultivation of accuracy in detail and for predilection for documentary, or at any rate contemporary, evidence.

Historiography did not set out to tell the saga of the evolution of society, nor did it wish to judge and interpret. Rather it meant to collect the accounts of the witnesses, marshaling them with the greatest possible completeness and with no concern for their contradictions. The reader was left to draw his own conclusions. The historian merely furnished the material. He took great pains to obtain reliable information and strictly accounted, in the style of the traditionists, for his authorities. On principle, anything that ever happened anywhere on earth was of interest and fit to be studied. Actually an author found himself compelled to limit his endeavors in time and space. Even the "Universal Histories"[60] of Ṭabarî (d. 923) or of Ibn al-Aṯîr (d. 1234) favor some areas to the detriment of others. For the sake of convenience the historian broke up his narrative into smaller units, covering single years or individual regions. Under the impact of literary standards of presentation, this neat but mechanical method of organization was discarded by some of the later historians who arranged their account, for instance, so as to deal with one reign in one chapter and have the smaller sections discuss a set of connected events rather than events falling within a certain unit of time.[61]

Standards of accuracy and conscientiousness are astoundingly high.* The juxtaposition of different reports on the same incident makes it comparatively easy to sense deliberate distortion

[60] The type of chronicles beginning with Creation or soon after goes back both in Byzantium and in Baghdad to Sextus Julius Africanus (d. after 240), *Chronographiai* (in five books), a history of the world from creation to A.D. 221 (or perhaps only 217/18). He influenced Eusebius, who wrote, probably before 303, *Chronikoi kanones kai epitome pantodapes historias Hellenon te kai barbaron.* He begins with the first year of Abraham, 2016/15 B.C. Cf. Schmid-Stählin, *Geschichte der griechischen Literatur* (6th ed.; Munich, 1924), II, 2, 1346–47, and 1366–67.

[61] On the development from annals to continuous history, see the writer, *WZKM*, XLIII (1936), 208–9.

through party or personal interest. One might almost venture to say that, measured by the unhappy standards of our propaganda-ridden generation, the partisan devices of the early historian are rather naïve and rather easily surprised.

The vividness of Arabic historiography is lost only toward the end of the period when history is likely to degenerate either into a dry summary of facts or into rhetorical verbiage in which those facts are all but drowned.[62] It is through inordinate praise of the patron on whose munificence he subsists that the historian upon occasion disfigures his report, even in the earlier and better period. What Lucian has to say concerning certain lesser writers of his day well applies to Arabic court poetry and historiography. "Eulogy, I need hardly say, may possibly please one person, the eulogized, but will disgust every one else; this is particularly so with the monstrous exaggerations which are in fashion; the authors are so intent on the patron-hunt that they cannot relinquish it without a full exhibition of servility; they have no idea of finesse, never mask their flattery, but blurt out their unconvincing tale anyhow."[63] The dependence of the littérateur on the powerful and wealthy made such degeneration of task well-nigh inevitable. But not everybody liked what he was compelled to do. Commissioned by ᶜAḍud ad-Daula (949–83) to compose a history of his family, the Bûyids, under his direct supervision Ibrâhîm b. Hilâl aṣ-Ṣâbiʾ (d. 994) intimated to a friend that he was but writing lies and trifles—a remark which very nearly cost him his neck.

The weakness of Arabic historiography is its concentration on personalities and on military incidents and court cabals. The works of war attract incomparably more attention than those of peace. For the most part happenings are explained as results of intrigues and ambitions of kings, generals, or politicians. The forces which these leaders represent frequently go unnoticed. The public came to be interested in the lesson history taught. But the lesson learned was merely one of morality, insight into

[62] This has been well stated by D. S. Margoliouth, *Lectures on Arabic Historians* (Calcutta, 1930), p. 155. The deterioration is, however, checked when the historian deals with his own time.

[63] *Quomodo historia sit conscribenda*, chap. 11; trans. H. W. and F. G. Fowler (Oxford, 1905), II, 115.

human character, and the vagaries of fate. Perhaps with the lone exception of Ibn Ḫaldûn, who, in addition to outlining principles of source criticism, essayed to grasp the underlying regularities, both social and psychological, the historians and their audience watched the pageant of events with rapture, sometimes reaching a certain understanding of the political and administrative mechanism which appeared to control their sequence; but they remained satisfied with accepting them at face value and did not bother about their economic, social, or cultural significance. Ibn Miskawaihi (d. 1030), who analyzes competently the long-range effect of political actions, stands almost alone.

The history of the Arab tribes is dominated by the genealogical outlook. Political relationships are seen in terms of kinship. Changes in political groupings are reflected in the pedigrees allotted to tribal ancestors. Allies are descended from common forebears. This is not to say that Arabic genealogy is fictitious—not only does it mirror actual conditions, but we have reason to assume that the Bedouin was to a certain extent conscious of the boundaries between fact and construction; and, then, the political life of the peninsula did show the feeling for kinship as a powerful force in the alignment of conflicting parties, although it often proved too weak to prevent internecine strife. With all this, it is clear that, with the Bedouin, genealogical construction takes the place held in less developed societies by the etiological myth invented to justify and antedate changes in the political relationship of their component groups.[64]

Partisanship and courtly flattery notwithstanding, the overall objectivity of Arabic historiography is remarkable. While the authors are not averse to displaying their stylistic abilities,

[64] For the Arabic genealogies cf. also E. Bräunlich, *Islamica*, VI (1934), 201–4 and 211–12;* on the political function of the myth see B. Malinowski, *Myth in Primitive Psychology* (London, 1926), esp., pp. 46–79. Cf. also Malinowski's observation, *Encyclopaedia of the Social Sciences*, IV, 644 (*s.v.* "Culture"): "Art and knowledge are strongly akin. . . . . The aesthetic drive integrates knowledge at low and at high levels. Proverbs, anagrams and tales, above all historical narrative, have been in primitive cultures and are in their developed forms very often a mixture of art and of science."

the rhetorical concept of history, that bane of classical historiography, wins ascendancy only toward the end of the period. The fourth century A.H. (tenth century A.D.), the greatest in the life of Muslim civilization, witnessed an amazing advance in interpretative subtlety and skill of presentation. Al-Masᶜûdî, Ibn Miskawaihi, and, in the field of the historical anecdote, al-Muḥassin at-Tanûḫî (d. 994) far outstrip their predecessors, if not in understanding of the human character, at any rate in describing and unfolding it. They are conscious of complexity and uniqueness of the individual, and they expend much effort in retracing the profile of the outstanding personality.

Historiography as a genre had never been subjected to the influence of the Christian hagiographical pattern nor had it had to cater to the practical needs of the traditionists. So its vista of man was not narrowed by a convention designed to stereotype rather than individualize. Development still escapes the Muslim writer, a fault this not of the genre but of his whole outlook on his human surroundings that would atomize the world and then view each atom as a stable monad, shifting only in its relation to its fellow-monads but unalterable in substance and even in form. But the intricacy and many-sidedness of man's soul had never in Muslim times been more keenly felt, more adequately rendered.

"(The caliph) Hishâm (724–43) had a squint," al-Masᶜûdî states; "he was untractable, rude in his manners and harsh. He amassed riches, stimulated agriculture and the improvement of horse strains. He organized horse-races assembling for them up to four thousand horses of his own and others. No one, in pagan or Islamic times, had been known to arrange anything of this kind and the poets spoke of the many horses he had gathered. He promoted the production of textiles and carpets. He made ready for war by preparing arms and drilling men, and he strengthened the border fortifications. He took care of conduits and reservoirs on the road to Mecca and of other public works of this kind which were to be destroyed by Dâᵓûd b. ᶜAlî in the beginning of ᶜAbbâsid rule. In his time silks of various colors and velvets were manufactured. People followed in his footsteps in guarding closely what they possessed. Generous action became rare, charity dried up. Never was there a time when people were harder."[65]

The finesse of this portrayal of a ruler and his effect on the attitudes of his subjects is matched by at-Tanûḫî's drawing, by means of an anecdote, of the character of al-Muᶜtaḍid (d. 902) and his vizier, al-Qâsim b. ᶜUbaidallâh (d. 904).

"Al-Qâsim b. ᶜUbaidallâh was in fear of Muᶜtaḍid and carried on his drinking and other amusements in secret, lest the caliph should regard him as a youth given up to frivolity and negligent of his duties, and so conceive a bad opinion of him. Still, being young and immature, he was fond of amusement, and when he could pursue it with extreme secrecy, he would steal a night or a day of his life, and drink. One night he wanted to have a drinking bout with roses and he contrived to amass a great quantity of the flowers, clandestinely, and he got together a great number of singing-girls, among them one to whom he was specially attached, and sat with them and no other company, drinking. With the roses he mingled light dirhems, and had a shower of these. . . . . He clothed himself in a woman's garment of dyed brocade, and owing to his extreme attachment to the singing-girl made the same garment cover both. The evening passed agreeably, and at midnight he stopped the drinking for fear of crapula, went to sleep, sailed to Muᶜtaḍid next morning and worked at his duties till the time for his departure arrived. When he wished to depart he went to Muᶜtaḍid's apartment to show himself to the caliph and take his leave. Muᶜtaḍid bade him approach till he was so near that no one else could hear what he said, and said to him: Qâsim, why did not you invite us yesterday . . . . ? I fancy you were ashamed of the fancy dress worn by you and your beloved.—Al-Qâsim almost died of chagrin. Muᶜtaḍid said to him: What is the matter with you, why are you so alarmed? What is there in this? Had we known that it would affect you so we should not have told you anything, or hurt your feelings. You may go, and God guard you."[66]

The appreciation of the vizier Abû ʾl-Faḍl b. al-ᶜAmîd (d.

[65] *Murûj*, V, 466–67.

[66] Trans. from manuscript of unprinted part of *Table Talk of a Mesopotamian Judge* by D. S. Margoliouth, *Islamic Culture*, VI (1932), 387–88.

970) by Ibn Miskawaihi is unsurpassed and rarely equaled in Arabic historiography for its maturity of personal and political judgment. Ibn Miskawaihi explains that the vizier outshone his contemporaries through a singular combination of qualities. He was the best *kâtib* of his time, "and possessed the greatest number of professional attainments, command of the Arabic language with its rarities, familiarity with grammar and prosody, felicity in etymology and metaphor, retention by memory of pre-Islamic and Islamic collections of poems." He also excelled in his literary compositions, both poetry and prose, both sportive and earnest. "In Koranic exegesis, ... and acquaintance with the different views of the jurists of the capitals he also reached the highest level. When, abandoning these studies, he took to mechanics and mathematics, there was no one to approach him in them." The same held good for logic and metaphysics. He was "sparing of words and disinclined to talk except when questions were asked him, and he found some one capable of understanding him. Then he would become vivacious, and things would be heard from him which were not to be had from any one else, with eloquent expressions, choice phraseology, and subtle sentiments, with no hesitation or difficulty. . . . . He was so courteous, good-natured and simple-minded that when any specialist in any study or science presented himself, he would quietly listen and express approval of all he heard from him" even though he would know more of the subject. In addition to his proficiency "in recognized studies and sciences . . . . he was sole master of the secrets of certain obscure sciences which no one professes, such as mechanics, acquiring the most abstruse knowledge of geometry and physics," etc.

On the battlefield "he was a lion for courage . . . . ; steadfast, resourceful, skilful at seizing opportunities, a prudent commander, an astute strategist." As an administrator he was in a class of his own. "The only thing that prevented him from establishing a reign of justice in his dominions and securing the prosperity of the provinces which he administered was the fact that his master, Rukn ad-Daula (d. 976), though superior to the contemporary Dailemite princes, was still on the level of the predatory soldier, who is in a hurry for plunder, and saw no occasion to consider the effects of his conduct or the future of his subjects." His way in managing the army, the subjects, and the sovereign was well-nigh miraculous. "Some reader of this section of my book who did not witness his career," Ibn Miskawaihi concludes, "may imagine that I have been gratuitously eulogizing, claiming for him more than the real extent of his attainments and height of his virtues. I swear by Him Who bade us utter the truth and forbade us to say anything else, that this is not so."[67]

IV

Arabic literary theory does not provide for fiction. The concepts of plot and action are lacking. It is a rather strange fact that Arabic literature, so rich in anecdotal material, so eager to seize upon the unusual word or deed, never did seriously turn toward the large-scale narrative or the drama. Except for parables and short stories, many of which are borrowings from foreign literatures or more or less accurate retracings of true incidents, the Arab Muslim disdained literary invention.

When Basil recommends limited perusal of classical authors, he especially warns to eschew such prose writings as contain stories invented for the pleasure of the listeners.[68] A like distrust of invention appears to have animated the Arab public. Pious legend was under suspicion, too, although for a different reason, and respectable poets did not occupy themselves too much with biblical or koranic subjects. In fact, standard literature, the literature of the educated, developed no more than two types of fiction; and these were destined to remain somewhat outside the main currents.

The sad adventures of romantic lovers were told, grouped around and interspersed with verse ascribed with varying justification to the protagonists. Novelettes of this kind can be traced as early as the sixth century, and they remain in vogue throughout the Middle Ages. But, while several littérateurs concerned themselves with collecting and retelling them, no one

[67] Selected from *Tajârib al-umam*, ed. and trans. H. F. Amedroz and D. S. Margoliouth (Oxford, 1920–21), text, II, 275–83; trans., V, 293–302.

[68] *Pros tous neous* . . . . , ed. and trans. F. Boulenger (Paris, 1935), chap. iv, ll. 28–30.

thought of choosing the anonymous reports and records as the basis of elaborate narrative. Arabic verse with its repetition of the same rhyme throughout a poem rendered prolongation beyond a certain point practically impossible, and the prose tale never found itself admitted to full literary distinction.

Nevertheless, it is exactly this prose tale, either of romantic incidents in bourgeois metropolitan life with the caliph's court in the background and the caliph or his vizier as ever ready *dei ex machina*, or else of the pranks of rogues, that represents the second type of prose fiction. These stories, the bourgeois intrigues predominantly of Baghdad, the picaresque of Cairene origin, are in large measure incorporated in the collection known as the *Arabian Nights*. Despite the superb quality of many of its stories, the *Arabian Nights* did not, until perhaps half a century ago, attain to full literary standing in Arab lands; and it seems that only once the attempt was made to "literarize" them. This attempt came to naught when its author, al-Jahshiyârî (d. 942), died before completing it.[69]

It is, however, in connection with the picaresque genre that Badî^c az-Zamân al-Hamaḏânî (d. 1008) created his famous Abû ᵓl-Fatḥ al-Iskandarî, the hero of his fifty-one *maqâmât*.[70] In these *maqâmât* (lit., lectures, *Standpredigten*)[71] the hero reappears and remains true to his character throughout. He is a man of easy conscience, given to deceive and defraud his fellow-men, sometimes well provided, but usually in straitened circumstances. He lives by his wit. His immense erudition and his astounding eloquence displayed in improvisations of rhymed prose and verse attract the lettered and the cultured to him. In miniature pieces of exquisite verbal art built around the most threadbare and trifling incidents, invention being almost always kept down to the indispensable minimum, Abû ᵓl-Fatḥ is given an opportunity to exhibit the many registers of his rhetorical abilities. Each *maqâma* is an independent unit and connects with the others only through the identity of the hero and the reporter ᶜÎsà b. Hishâm.

[69] Cf. *Fihrist*, p. 304.

[70] Trans. W. J. Prendergast (Madras, 1915).

[71] C. Brockelmann, *EI*, III, 162, states that in the third century A.H. the word came to denote "beggar's appeal" couched in careful language.

Al-Ḥarîrî (d. 1122) took over the pattern and replaced in his fifty *maqâmât* Abû ʾl-Fatḥ by the even more erudite and even more frivolous Abû Zaid of Sarûj, who in the end repents of his evil ways and spends the remainder of his days in prayer at the mosque of his home town, redeeming a morally worthless if artistically satisfactory life by tardy conversion.[72] Al-Ḥarîrî's popularity in the Arab world is immense. His consummate skill in handling language and imagery, the rich background of religious and literary learning, together with the genuine wit of the presentation and the ingenious character of some of the incidents, combine in making the *maqâmât* attractive reading, although they can be fully understood and appraised only with the aid of a detailed commentary that explains the many rare expressions as well as the recondite allusions that delighted the sophisticated contemporary. The *maqâmât*, the attenuated offspring of the classical *mimoi*, are perhaps the greatest triumph of the principle of art for art's sake. Every element from the flimsy incident to the moral graveness of many a passage is introduced for its oratorical potentialities and as a challenge to the author to display his control of the most subtle and most remote resources of the Arabic tongue. With all that, Abû Zaid is probably the most interesting character devised and presented by Arabic polite literature.[73]

Where the Arabs failed, the Persians succeeded. Persian literature, in addition to great lyrical accomplishments, attained to outstanding mastery of epical narrative. The Persian was interested in and knew how to present action. History, romance, and mysticism yielded subject matter for elaborate story-telling. The Arabs never felt the urge to poetize the grandeur and the glory of their conquests or of their rise to monotheism and power. When, finally, they accepted versified history, it was the Persian form of rhymed couplets they had to

[72] Trans. Th. Chenery and F. Steingass (London, 1867–98).

[73] Ḥayy b. Yaqẓân, the self-taught philosopher, who by the force of his reasoning arrives at the doctrine of the one God, is less a literary figure than a paradigm of philosophic teaching, or else, in a sense, an autobiography of the confessional type. But the influence on the West of Ibn Ṭufail (d. 1185), who built on an essay by Avicenna (d. 1037), is not to be underrated; cf. De Boer, *op. cit.*, pp. 143–44, and also H. A. R. Gibb in *The Legacy of Islam*, p. 201, n. 1.

use; and it is more than likely that not only the form but the inspiration goes back to a foreign impulse. Rhymed accounts of historical events, such as Ibn al-Muᶜtazz' description of the reign of al-Muᶜtaḍid or Ibn ᶜAbdrabbihi's of the exploits of the Spanish caliph ᶜAbdarraḥmân III (912–61; the poem carries to 934) are of considerable accuracy[74] but scant literary value.[75]

The renaissance of the Sâmânid age, on the other hand, gave the Persians a perfect literarization of their life as a nation. While subjected to simplification and, in many instances, to remotivation, history in the account of Firdausî's *Book of the Kings* is never hampered in its flow by the technical inadequacy of the poet. Firdausî lays stress, as poetry and popular imagination would, on personal exploits of heroized individuals; he is fond of legendary or novelistic interludes; he eagerly seizes upon any opportunity for description, be it a battle, a sunrise, or the physical beauty of a personage. Not all his figures are alive, and some of his kings and soldiers remain named shadows; but for the most part they are individualized, in keeping with popular or documentary recollection. The later historical epic was unable to equal the fulness and ease of Firdausî's narrative that combined the double advantage of as yet untapped and almost inexhaustible source materials and of the interpretative powers of a truly great writer delicately sensitive to the pictorial possibilities of incidents and characters. But, despite the shortcomings of the epigoni, the historical epic remained as an important vehicle of national self-expression.

The eleventh century added the romantic to the historical, and the twelfth the mystic-didactic epic to the two earlier genres. Persian literature admits action and rejoices in cleverly invented plots. At the height of the romantic development, Niẓâmî (d. 1203) in language of superb musicality, molded by the speculative erudition of centuries, succeeds in presenting ideas in terms of personal fate—the highest achievement perhaps to which literature may attain. In *Ḫusrav and Shîrîn* he had done no more than to lead the king, under the influence of

[74] Cf. Margoliouth, *Historians*, pp. 65–72 and 76–79.

[75] On the genre cf. the writer, *JNES*, III (1944), 8–13.

his love to Shîrîn, from youthful and irresponsible despotism to the relative maturity of manhood and conscientious kingship. History furnishes the substrate.[76] But it is Niẓâmî who draws the characters, envelops their emotions with luster and moral significance, and delineates in firm strokes the growth of these characters through their interaction—a procedure unparalleled in Arab writing. But in the *Haft Paikar*, the "Seven Portraits," a mosaic of seven tales told King Bahrâm Gûr by his seven brides, and one of the most sophisticated works of world literature, unrivaled in harmony of word and thought, of imagery and atmosphere, Niẓâmî presents the happenings on the earthly plane as metaphysically meaningful, as symbolizing events of a higher sphere to which man belongs, thanks to the longings of his soul, which remembers dimly its exalted origin far above this world of fleshly charm and corruption.

When hunting an onager, the king follows the prey into a cave in which he disappears.

Into the cave so deep the horseman rode: consigned the kingly treasure to the cave.
Behind the curtain which the cavern formed the king received the friend of the cave's embrace:[77]

The royal guards arrive and refuse to believe what they are told of their sovereign's end.

King Bahrâm with his calmness and good sense—how should he enter into this defile?[78]

But the answer given by the poet in cryptic language is that the king in obeisance to the yearning of his soul had returned to his spiritual home land and been united with the Divine One.

[76] On the subject matter of this epic cf. H. W. Duda, *Ferhâd und Schîrîn* (Prag, 1933).

[77] The Friend of the Cave is Abû Bakr, who shared with Mohammed a cave on their flight to Medina. In other words, the king reaches the same stature as Abû Bakr in closeness to the Prophet. C. E. Wilson, in his translation and commentary, II, 200, fails to see the allusion and translates: "The king became the Loved One's confidant." Cf. also H. Ritter, *Die Bildersprache Niẓâmîs* (Berlin and Leipzig, 1927), p. 67.

[78] The text of the edition by H. Ritter and J. Rypka (Prag, 1934), p. 292 (chap. 52, vs. 38), reads: "The elephant-bodied king, in the name of God," etc., thus preparing the way for the solution of the *aporia*.

The elephant, they knew not, dead asleep,[79] had had a dream and gone to Hindustân.

Though Fate had chained the king of mighty frame, Fate's check to king and castle he'd o'ercome.[80]

No people, it would seem, has been better able than the Persians to make tangible through optical imagery, through perfect co-ordination of carefully constructed yet immediately convincing pictorial intimation and of metaphysical concepts, and through personalization of universals, to poetize abstract speculation and to render understandable, by indirection and without rudely baring its innermost secrets, the strivings and failings of the God-loving soul.

"Listen to the reed how it tells a tale, complaining of separations," Jalâl ad-Dîn Rûmî (d. 1273) begins his monumental *Maṯnawî-yi maᶜnawî* (the spiritual *maṯnawî*, or epic in rhymed couplets), introducing the soul of the saint in the guise of the reed that moans its separation from the reedbed, "the spiritual world where it dwelt in the state of pre-existence."

Throughout this song of the reed two meanings attach to its lament. In terms of mundane emotion supramundane truth is enounced. Speculation, or doctrine, is conveyed as psychological experience.

Ever since I was parted from the reed-bed, my lament hath caused man and woman to moan.

I want a bosom torn by severance, that I may unfold (to such a one) the pain of love-desire.

My secret is not far from my plaint, but ear and eye lack the light (whereby it should be apprehended).

Body is not veiled from soul, nor soul from body, yet none is permitted to see the soul.

This noise of the reed is fire, it is not wind; whoso hath not this fire, may he be naught!

'Tis the fire of Love that is in the reed, 'tis the fervor of Love that is in the wine.[81]

[79] Ed. Ritter-Rypka, vs. 39*a:* "The elephant of that garden . . . ." ; for this type of phrasing cf. Ritter, *Bildersprache*, pp. 10 and 68.

[80] Ed. Ritter-Rypka, pp. 291–92 (52, 27.28.38.39.40); trans. Wilson (London, 1924), I, 277–78.

[81] *Maṯnawî*, ed. and trans. R. A. Nicholson (London, 1925–40), Book I, vss. 1–3.7–10, and his commentary, *ibid.*, VII, 8–10. On the development of the mystical epic cf. the stimulating paper by E. Berthels, *Islamica*, III (1927), 1–31.

The break between reality and symbol, sound and meaning, is overcome by projecting the experience of the soul onto both the planes on which, to the Persian poet, human life is lived. When Ḥâfiẓ (d. 1390) sings of wine and love, the question is not whether it is earthly wine and earthly love, or the intoxication with the One that inspires his verse—the two motives are inextricably joined. Earthly and heavenly longing are but aspects of the same aspiration. The ambiguity of the imagery exists only on the surface. The poet may be pleased to puzzle and mislead the ignorant; but ultimately the two-sidedness of his words reflects the two-sidedness of man's station in the universe. As long as he lives, he expresses himself in terms of his lower nature; but, stripped of his bodily chains, he belongs with the Eternal whence he issued and whither he is to return.

These are the words which Ḥafiẓ had written on his tombstone:

> Where are the tidings of union? that I may arise—
> Forth from the dust I will rise up to welcome thee!
> My soul, like a homing bird, yearning for Paradise,
> Shall arise and soar, from the snares of the world set free.
> When the voice of thy love shall call me to be thy slave,
> I shall rise to a greater far than mastery
> Of life and the living, time and the mortal span:
> Pour down, O Lord! from the clouds of thy guiding grace,
> The rain of a mercy that quickeneth on my grave,
> Before, like dust that the wind bears from place to place,
> I arise and flee beyond the knowledge of man.
> When to my grave thou turnest thy blessed feet,
> Wine and the lute thou shalt bring in thine hand to me,
> Thy voice shall sing through the folds of my winding-sheet,
> And I will arise and dance to thy ministrelsy.
> Though I be old, clasp me one night to thy breast,
> And I, when the dawn shall come to awaken me,
> With the flush of youth on my cheek from thy bosom will rise.
> Rise up! let mine eyes delight in thy stately grace!
> Thou art the goal to which all men's endeavor has pressed,
> And thou the idol of Hafiz' worship; thy face
> From the world and life shall bid him come forth and arise![82]

[82] Trans. G. L. Bell, *Poems from the Divan of Hafiz* (London, 1897), pp. 118–19.

CHAPTER NINE

CREATIVE BORROWING: GREECE IN THE *ARABIAN NIGHTS*

I

THAT huge collection of stories and fables, the *Arabian Nights*, developed in various sections of the Arabic-speaking world between about A.D. 900 and 1500. Language and local color effectively obscure the foreign origin of the greater part of the subject matter. The spirit of Islam has come to permeate tales of Jewish, Buddhist, or Hellenistic invention; and Muslim institutions, Muslim mores, and Muslim lore have quietly replaced the cultural conventions of the source material and lent to the corpus that unity of atmosphere which is so eminently characteristic of Islamic civilization and which will prevent the observer from noticing at first sight the motley array of heterogeneous elements of which it is composed.

The classical contribution to the formation of Islamic civilization in general has been freely recognized, but the survival of classical traditions in Arabic literature is only now beginning to be traced and appraised in its true importance. The all too strict separation between oriental and classical studies is as responsible for the relative backwardness of our knowledge in this field as is the character of the Greco-Roman contribution itself. While, for example, the Indian or the Jewish influence manifest themselves primarily in the transmission of narrative plots or motives, the influence of the ancients makes itself felt for the most part in less easily traceable elements such as "patterns of style, patterns of presentation and emotional conventions."[1] Perhaps even more elusive is the fact that the Arab's outlook on, and his expectations of, literature have been, to a remarkable degree, molded by the attitudes of the ancients as these developed from the Hellenistic period. The preference accorded

[1] The writer, *JAOS*, LXII (1942), 278.

by the Arab public to originality of presentation over originality of invention is a striking example;[2] and the theoretical discussion of literature, so popular with Arab scholars and writers, frequently resumes classical problems and is conducted with the aid of a terminology that could never have been devised without the precedent set by the rhetoricians of later and latest antiquity.

What goes for Arabic literature in general applies pointedly to the *Arabian Nights* in particular. Here, too, individual motives or plots, patterns of presentation, and conventional shades of emotion have been assimilated by the narrators and redactors to add to the dazzling colorfulness of the corpus. Here, too, the changed cultural background, and especially the different religious atmosphere, necessitated adaptation of the survivals that tended to obscure their provenance. The mythological bywork of ancient story-telling had to be discarded. Arab realism forced oriental names and oriental habits on the foreign characters. Classical patterns of emotion were superimposed on Persian and Indian plots. Typical personages of later Greek literature such as the foolish schoolmaster reappear in the same light but in a new narrative frame. And, finally, the more obvious borrowings, such as the plot of an action or a major part of it, are far outnumbered by the more subtle imprints left by Hellenistic ideas of life and love on the responsive minds of the Arab public.

Of the many vestiges of classical literature in the *Arabian Nights*, three kinds stand out so as to deserve special attention. These are a small but significant number of plots which the Arabs inherited; a somewhat greater amount of ethnological and geographical detail that goes back to ancient geographers' accounts or sailors' yarns; and, most important of all, the narrative pattern of the Greek novel and its concept of love are mirrored in many of the *Nights'* stories. The influence of the peculiar touch with which the Hellenistic age and its heirs treated love and the lover has been a major factor in the development of Arab ideas about love as shown in poetry and prose both within and outside of the *Arabian Nights*.

[2] Cf. the writer, *JNES*, III (1944), 234–53.

II

Pyrgopolynices, the braggart soldier of Plautus' *Miles Gloriosus*, has kidnaped Philocomasium, the lady-love of Pleusicles, a young Athenian gentleman. When Pleusicles discovers her whereabouts, he settles down in the house next to that of the soldier, and a tunnel dug secretly through the separating walls enables the lovers to meet at their pleasure. When a servant of the soldier sees the girl in the neighbor's house, he is told that her twin sister has arrived and that it is she and not Philocomasium whom he has watched in the arms of the young stranger. By hurrying back and forth through the tunnel, Philocomasium succeeds in making this story plausible. A further ruse rouses the soldier's desire to exchange Philocomasium for another woman, and he is persuaded to send her off and to bribe her with magnificent gifts that include her favorite slave (and helper in the intrigue) into leaving him quietly. Before his eyes and with his blessing the disguised Pleusicles takes her away.

The resemblance to the *Arabian Nights* story of "Qamar az-zamân and the Jeweler's Wife" is unmistakable. After Qamar az-zamân has won the affection of Ḥalîma, he rents the house next door to the jeweler's, a passageway is broken between the two houses, and Ḥalîma proceeds to transport her husband's riches into the home of her lover, who in the meantime has made friends with the luckless jeweler. On one occasion the jeweler notices a precious dagger of his in the hands of his new friend; on another he discovers his watch in Qamar az-zamân's apartment. In both cases his suspicions are allayed when, upon returning to his own house, he finds the objects in their customary place. A little later Ḥalîma, disguised as a slave-girl, is introduced to her husband in Qamar az-zamân's house. She is called by her true name, and the jeweler is asked to suggest a fitting sales price for her. Again his doubts are put to rest when he finds his wife waiting for him on his return. Finally, the lovers prepare their escape. The pair who have tucked away the jeweler's valuables bid him farewell in a moving scene. At the last moment Ḥalîma succeeds in obtaining for herself her favorite slave girl, and the elopers reach safely the Egyptian border.[3]

[3] Cf. *Arabian Nights*, trans. E. Littmann (Leipzig, 1921–28), VI, 451–532, and trans. E. Powys Mathers (New York, 1930), VI, 244–78.

The similarities are striking and go far beyond the identity of the outline of the plot: the farewell scene, the plundering of the victim, the assistance rendered the eloping lovers by their dupe, and the final gift of a slave—all these traits bespeak some relationship between the Roman play, or rather its Greek model or models, and the Cairene story. It is undeniable that the Arabic story excels the Plautine comedy in consistency. To mention only two details, "In the *Miles* the passage through the wall does not in any way serve to ensure the escape of Philocomasium; in the story it serves the manoeuvres of the lovers and helps in the mystification of the husband to the very end."[4] In the *Miles*, again, it is not the soldier whose suspicion is roused and allayed but a menial who never tells his master of his curious experience, whereas in the *Nights* it is the husband himself who allows the evidence of his own eyes to be discredited.

These and other circumstances make it evident that "Qamar az-zamân" does not directly reproduce or imitate the *Miles* but that both go back to a common source, which in all likelihood was an Ionic love story which either Plautus or the author of the Greek prototype of the *Miles* combined with episodes of a different origin, whereas the redactor of the Arabic novel stuck more closely to his model.[5]

Some recensions of the *Nights* contain another, though more remote, parallel to the *Miles* in the story of the "Butcher, His Wife, and the Soldier,"[6] in which once more a secret passage between two houses serves to dupe the husband. One day the husband is made drunk, his hair and beard are shorn, and he is given Turkish clothes and carried off to a remote district. When he awakes, he convinces himself of his changed identity as a Turk and makes off to Isfahan, leaving his wife and her lover undisturbed.[7]

[4] Ph. E. Legrand, *The New Greek Comedy* (London and New York, 1917), p. 225.

[5] Cf. E. Zarncke, *Rheinisches Museum*, XXXIX (1884), 22–25; Legrand, *op. cit.*, pp. 224–25. The Arabic writer surrounded his story with some colorful bywork and a moral ending but in no way allowed himself to tamper with the traditional plot. On the motif transfer cf. also F. Kuntze, *Neue Jbb. f. Wissenschaft und Jugendbildung*, I (1925), 717–28.

[6] *Arabian Nights*, ed. M. Habicht (Breslau, 1825–43), XI, 140–45; trans. by the same (Breslau, 1840 ff.), XIV, 60–64.

[7] Cf. Zarncke, *loc. cit.*, p. 1, and the writer, *JAOS*, LXII, 278–79, where further survivals of classical plots are listed.

III

Reminiscences of old travel tales and of fabulous ethnographical lore can be traced in many of the stories of the *Arabian Nights*. Nowhere are they as numerous as in the reports of Sindbad the Sailor on his seven perilous voyages. Although the Sindbad tales do not belong to the original core of the *Arabian Nights*,[8] they must have been in existence as an independent work no later than *ca.* A.D. 900.[9] It is hardly an exaggeration to say that every single ethnological or frankly legendary trait used by the unknown author or redactor can be amply paralleled from both Eastern and Western literatures.[10] Geographical lore seems to lend itself particularly well to being borrowed and reborrowed, and this fact reduces considerably the number of cases where we are able to assign a definite origin to a motive. The following instances, however, culled from the first four *Voyages* of the adventurous mariner can with certainty be assigned a Western, that is, a Greek source, at the very least in the sense that the motives, whatever the region of their invention, made their literary debut in Greek and were taken up and developed by the oriental narrator from the form they had been given by the classical author.

In the third book of his *Life of Alexander*, the Pseudo-Callisthenes inserts a letter alleged to have been written by the great king to his teacher Aristotle in order to keep him informed about the remarkable happenings on his Indian campaign. And there we read, right at the beginning of this curious collection of *mirabilia*, this sad incident.[11]

". . . . (Some barbarians at the coast of the Indian Ocean)

[8] Cf. J. Østrup, *Studien über 1001 Nacht*, trans. O. Rescher (Stuttgart, 1925), p. 35.

[9] Cf. M. J. de Goeje, *Actes du VIIIe Congrès international des orientalistes*, Part II (Leiden, 1893), p. 65. P. Casanova's arguments (*BIFAO*, XX [1922], 121) for dating the travels of Sindbad to the reign of Hârûn ar-Rashîd (786–809) are not convincing.

[10] E. Rohde, *Der griechische Roman und seine Vorläufer* (3d ed.; Leipzig, 1914), p. 192, n. 1, has assembled numerous parallels to the principal marvels reported by Sindbad.

[11] *Historia Alexandri Magni*, ed. W. Kroll (Berlin, 1926), iii. 17. 3–7. The editor dates this recension to about A.D. 300.

showed us an island which we all could see in the middle of the sea. They said it was the tomb of an ancient king in which much gold had been dedicated. (When we wished to sail to the island) the barbarians had disappeared leaving us twelve of their little boats. Pheidon, my closest friend, Hephaistion, Krateros and the other friends of mine did not suffer me to cross over (to the tomb in person). Pheidon said: Let me go first so that if anything should go wrong I would face the danger rather than you. If everything is alright I shall send the boat back for you. For if I, Pheidon, should perish, you will find other friends, but should you, Alexander, perish, the whole world would be steeped in grief. Convinced by his plea I gave them leave to cross over. But when they had gone ashore on what they thought was an island, after no more than an hour the animal suddenly dived down into the deep. We cried out loud while the animal disappeared and the men including my dearest friend came to a horrible end. Embittered I made a search for the barbarians but could not find them."

In this account the unexplained disappearance of some of Alexander's men near an ill-omened island as reported by Nearchos from his voyage in the Indian Ocean[12] and the legend of the tomb of King Erythres, the *heros eponymos* of the Erythrean Sea, supposed to be another island of the same ocean, are combined with the fable of the *aspidochelidone*, the giant tortoise, whose carapace the sailors mistake for an isle.[13] This intriguing animal reappears in St. Basil's (329–79) *Seventh Homily on the Hexaemeron* and, with some additional detail about its melodious voice with which it lures small fish to their death, in St. Eustathius' (a contemporary of Basil) *Commentary* on the same biblical text.[14]

In the ninth century this giant tortoise, probably an outgrowth of the imagination of the Persian Gulf population but introduced into literature by the Greeks, appears in an Arabic

[12] Arrian *Indica* 31. 1–3.

[13] A. Ausfeld, *Der griechische Alexanderroman* (Leipzig, 1907), pp. 178–79.

[14] In this passage the name *aspidochelidone* seems to appear for the first time. Both references are quoted by J. Zacher, *Pseudocallisthenes* (Halle, 1867), pp. 148–49.

work on animals. Al-Jâḥiẓ (d. 869), with creditable skepticism, sets out to destroy the belief in certain sea monsters and winds up his harangue by observing: "Of course, if we were to believe all that sailors tell . . . . for they claim that on occasion they have landed on certain islands having woods and valleys and fissures and have lit a great fire; and when the monster felt the fire on its back, it began to glide away with them and all the plants growing on it, so that only such as managed to flee were saved. This tale outdoes the most fabulous and preposterous of stories."[15]

The tone of al-Jâḥiẓ' note makes it plain that the motive was a familiar one in his time. So it was from an established tradition that the author of Sindbad's confabulations borrowed when he made his hero tell this episode of his first voyage.

"We continued our voyage until we arrived at an island like one of the gardens of Paradise, and at that island the master of the ship brought her to anchor with us. He cast the anchor, and put forth the landing-plank, and all who were in the ship landed upon that island. They had prepared for themselves fire-pots, and they lighted fires in them; and their occupations were various: some cooked; others washed, and others amused themselves. I was among those who were amusing themselves upon the shores of the island, and the passengers were assembled to eat and drink and play and sport.

"But while we were thus engaged, lo, the master of the ship, standing upon its side, called out with his loudest voice, O ye passengers, whom may God preserve! come up quickly into the ship, hasten to embark, and leave your merchandise, and flee with your lives, and save yourselves from destruction; for this apparent island, upon which ye are, is not really an island, but it is a great fish that hath become stationary in the midst of the sea, and the sand hath accumulated upon it, so that it hath become like an island, and trees have grown upon it since times of old; and when ye lighted upon it the fire, it felt the heat, and put itself in motion, and now it will descend with you into the sea,

[15] *Ḥayawân*, VII, 33–34; trans. M. Asín Palacios, *Islam and the Divine Comedy* (London, 1926), pp. 208–9; cf. also Casanova, *loc. cit.*, p. 137. Ibn Ḥauqal, too (*op. cit.*, p. 10[15]), lashes out at those travelers who do not aim at truthful reporting.

and ye will all be drowned: then seek for yourselves escape before destruction, and leave the merchandise!—The passengers, therefore, hearing the words of the master of the ship, hastened to go up into the vessel, leaving the merchandise, and their other goods, and their copper cooking-pots, and their fire-pots; and some reached the ship, and others reached it not. The island had moved, and descended to the bottom of the sea, with all that were upon it, and the roaring sea, agitated with waves, closed over it."[16]

Nothing could illustrate more strikingly the decline of critical scholarship in the following centuries than the readiness with which the learned al-Qazwînî (*ca.* 1203–83) accepts this piece of sailors' yarn in his *Cosmography*.[17] Quoting "a merchant" as his authority, he tells succinctly what Sindbad had reported at such comfortable length. Nothing is missing, neither the luscious vegetation on the animal's back nor the fire lighted by the visitors which causes it to move off into the depth. The only deviation consists in al-Qazwînî's replacing the fish of the Sindbad story by the tortoise of the older sources.[18]

On his second voyage Sindbad is left behind on a deserted island. When he explores the place, he perceives a white object which upon his approach turns out to be "a huge white dome, of great height and circumference." He walks around it—the circumference measures no less than fifty paces—finds its walls extremely smooth, but fails to discover an entrance. All of a sudden the sky becomes dark, and he imagines a cloud to have covered the sun, but he soon realizes that the darkness is due to a huge bird. He recalls stories told him by "travelers and voyagers" about a bird of enormous size, called the *ruḫ*,[19] and even

[16] *Arabian Nights*, trans. E. W. Lane (New York, 1944), p. 577. The idea that the animal is stirred by the heat of the fire kindled on its back seems to occur first in Eustathius, *op. cit.*, as quoted by Zacher, *op. cit.*, p. 148.

[17] Ed. F. Wüstenfeld (Göttingen, 1848–49), I, 136–37; trans. H. Ethé (Leipzig, 1868), I, 280; cf. also Lane, *op. cit.*, pp. 1186–87.

[18] For the spreading of the motive into the medieval West, cf. Zacher, *op. cit.*, p. 149, and De Goeje, *loc. cit.*, pp. 47–48.

[19] This bird recurs not infrequently in the *Arabian Nights;* for references cf. Littmann, *op. cit.*, VI, 750. For mention of the *ruḫ* in other literatures see J. K. Wright, *Geographical Lore*, p. 272.

before the bird alights on it he reaches the conclusion that the large white object he had been scrutinizing was its egg. This motive had accrued to the narrator's arsenal from Lucian's *True History*,[20] where the hero "ran aground on an enormous kingfisher's (*alkyon*) nest, really, it was sixty furlongs (*stadia*) in circumference." He then "cut open one of the eggs with axes and took from the shell a featherless chick fatter than twenty vultures."

As soon as the *ruḫ* had fallen asleep on the egg, Sindbad tied himself to its leg with his turban, and next morning the bird rose with him to the highest region of the sky and finally landed in some remote country, where Sindbad loosed his turban and continued his wanderings.[21]

In this story the author has made good use of an adventure ascribed to Alexander the Great in some manuscripts of Pseudo-Callisthenes.[22] Here the king has himself carried up into the highest dome of the sky by four hungry eagles that are tied to a chest in which Alexander has taken his seat and that are vainly attempting to reach a piece of horse liver fixed to the end of the pole to which they are harnessed.

This picturesque scene also affected Persian legend. The *Book of the Kings* ascribes the same procedure to King Kâʾûs when this monarch, succumbing to the devil's tempting, tries to ascend to heaven. Originally, the Persians had the king bid the demons build him a city floating between heaven and earth; but the impact of the Alexander saga effected the change.[23]

Here again, Sindbad's tall tale was accepted into respectable scientific literature. Al-Qazwînî opens the pages of his *Cosmography* to an amplified version of the strange event.[24]

The central episode of Sindbad's third voyage is a fairly ex-

20 ii. 40; trans. A. M. Harmon ("Loeb Classical Library" [London and New York, 1927 ff.]), I, 345–47.

21 Cf. Lane, *op. cit.*, pp. 584–85.

22 ii. 41; the manuscripts are L and C; cf. Zacher, *op. cit.*, p. 142.

23 Cf. Th. Nöldeke, "Beiträge zur Geschichte des Alexanderromans," *Denkschriften d. kais. Akademie der Wiss., phil.-hist. Kl.*, XXXVIII (1890), Abh. V, p. 26.

24 Arabic text, I, 117–19; trans., I, 240–42; cf. Lane, *op. cit.*, p. 1192.

act replica of Odysseus' adventure with Polyphemus.[25] The Arabic version, replete with lurid detail, omits the captured hero's ruse in claiming "No Man" to be his name, nor does he have any need to hide his companions and himself tied to the belly of thick-fleeced sheep to make good his escape from the monster's cave. On the other hand, the blinded giant's aim is luckier than Polyphemus': assisted by a female giant—an addition of the Arab narrator—he kills all but two of Sindbad's companions by throwing rocks at the small rafts in which they are struggling to reach the open sea. It is rather strange that the Sindbad story eliminated what would seem to us the most striking feature of the man-eating monster, viz., his one-eyedness. In all but one of the manuscripts the cannibal has two eyes, which, accordingly, Sindbad has to put out with two red-hot iron spits.[26]

This same change occurs in a doublet of the story, the account of Saᶜîd's adventures in the tale of "Saif al-mulûk and Badîᶜat az-zamân."[27] In one version of this account the murderous giant is called "Eli-Fanioun," an obvious echo of "Polyphemus." But the survival of the Cyclops' name did not entail the survival of the Greek idea of the one-eyed Cyclopes. Thus, the Arab rendering of this Greek motive is a telling symptom of that adaptation of the foreign subject matter to the thinking habits of the borrowing society which so frequently obscures the origin of a literary trait.

Although it is not necessary to cast about for a channel through which the Polyphemus story could have reached the Arabs, it may in this connection be recalled that educated Eastern circles kept up a certain interest in the Homeric poems to a relatively late date. Theophilus of Edessa (d. 785), a favorite of the caliph al-Mahdî (775–85) and a celebrated astrologer, translated "the two Books of Homer" into Syriac. This translation was, in all probability, not a complete version of the *Iliad* and *Odyssey*, but in addition there exist quotations from Homer in various other and later Syriac authors.[28] The influence of the

[25] *Odyssey* ix. 231–499.

[26] Cf. Lane, *op. cit.*, pp. 589–92, and p. 1195, n. 39.

[27] *Ibid.*, pp. 741–42, and p. 1245, n. 55; cf. also Østrup, *op. cit.*, p. 23.

[28] Cf. A. Baumstark, *Geschichte der syrischen Literatur* (Bonn, 1922), p. 341 and p. 341, n. 4.

Syriac writers and translators on Arab thought down to the middle of the tenth century is too well known to need more than a passing mention.

Before the *ghûl* slaughters his prisoners in the "Saif al-mulûk" story he gives them a drink of milk which immediately blinds them.[29] A similar device is practiced by the demon-ruled people into whose power Sindbad falls on his fourth voyage. They hand every new arrival to their town a drink of coconut oil and some unspecified food "in consequence of which his body becomes expanded, in order that he might eat largely, and his mind is stupefied, his faculty of reflection is destroyed, and he becomes like an idiot. Then they give him to eat and drink in abundance of that food and oil, until he becomes fat and stout, when they slaughter him and roast him, and serve him as meat to their king. But as to the companions of the king, they eat the flesh of men without roasting or otherwise cooking it."[30] Al-Qazwînî preserves another form of this motive in which the cannibals are represented as the dog-faced inhabitants of an island in the sea near Zanzibar.[31]

These stories remind one of the beginning of the *Acts of Andrew and Matthew*,[32] where we read: "At that time all the apostles were gathered together and divided the countries among themselves, casting lots. And it fell to Matthew to go to the land of the anthropophagi. Now the men of that city ate no bread nor drank wine, but ate the flesh and drank the blood of men; and every stranger who landed there they took and put out his eyes, and gave him a magic drink which took away his understanding."[33] Nobody can fail to recall the draught which Circe uses to transform Odysseus' companions into pigs.[34] Circe's magic technique is duplicated by Queen Lâb and her ad-

[29] Lane, *op. cit.*, p. 741.

[30] *Ibid.*, p. 598.

[31] Arabic text, I, 121–22; trans., I, 248–50; cf. Lane, *op. cit.*, pp. 1197–98.

[32] M. R. James, *The Apocryphal New Testament* (Oxford, 1926), p. 453 (chap. i).

[33] The parallel between this narrative and the "Fourth Voyage of Sindbad" was briefly indicated by A. von Gutschmid, *Rheinisches Museum*, XIX (1864), 395. On the preceding pages (pp. 390 ff.) von Gutschmid gives a detailed analysis of the *Acts* and tries to locate the country and the names of the cannibals.

[34] *Odyssey* x. 229–347.

versary in the story of "King Badr Bâsim,"[35] although it is not pigs but birds and a mule that result from their craftily employed foods and drinks.[36]

IV

The combination of travel adventures with a love action is held in common by certain of the *Arabian Nights* stories with the Greek novel. This Greek novel, traceable from *ca.* 100 B.C. to A.D. 300 with a curious revival in Byzantine literature in the twelfth century, builds its intricate plot around the basic scheme of accompanying a pair of beautiful and chaste lovers who are separated and tossed about by the whims of fate on their perilous wanderings until they are finally reunited in blissful happiness. One of the late Byzantine imitators, Nicetas Eugenianus, prefaced his work with a short *argumentum* that sums up aptly the content not only of his but of all Greek romance.

> Here read Drusilla's fate and Charicles'—
> Flight, wandering, capture, rescues, roaring seas,
> Robbers and prisons, pirates, hunger's grip,
> Dungeons so deep that never sun could dip
> His rays at noon-day to their dark recess,
> Chained hands and feet; and greater heaviness,
> Pitiful partings. Last the story tells
> Marriage, though late, and ends with wedding bells.[37]

The purpose of the trials to which the lovers are exposed is not the development of their characters. As a rule, the lovers remain what they started out to be.[38] What is more, the heroes resemble each other pretty much. The women usually are somewhat more elaborately drawn; they are more alive and better capable of taking the initiative when beset by difficulties. But it is clear that the public was interested in action and that any

[35] Lane, *op. cit.*, pp. 701–10.

[36] Cf. also the author, *JAOS*, LXII, 290.

[37] Nicetas Eugenianus, ed. J. F. Boissonade, in *Erotici scriptores Graeci*, ed. G. A. Hirschig (Paris, 1885), Argumentum totius operis; trans. S. Gaselee, "Appendix on the Greek Novel," in *Daphnis and Chloe* ("Loeb Classical Library" [New York and London, 1916]), pp. 410–11; Gaselee's translation is also quoted by E. H. Haight, *Essays on the Greek Romances* (New York, 1943), p. 1.

[38] Haight (*op. cit.*, p. 105) discusses the perhaps only exception, viz., Callisthenes in Achilles Tatius' novel, whom love very definitely changes for the better.

incident however improbable was welcome. Many of the lovers' troubles are brought on by their irresistible beauty and are again overcome by their passionate chastity.

In contemplating the transfer of the pattern from the Hellenistic to the Muslim milieu, we have to take into account the inevitable recrudescence of the popular character of the romances when they passed from the hands of the professional writer-rhetorician into those of the professional story-teller. The artistic level is bound to drop. The background of religion, so important in the novels, becomes meaningless. The Arab was not accustomed to that historical narrative in which some of the romances excel, and he had, on the whole, no experience in inventing and carrying through a complicated action, with many secondary actions to boot, stretching over hundreds of pages. These differences in literary tradition make for a loss of refinement, greater simplicity, or, perhaps, obviousness of the Arabic tales, but they leave the borrowed pattern unaltered.

Uns al-wujûd and al-Ward fî ᵓl-Akmâm[39] fall in love at first sight. The father of the girl takes her to a remote place where he has her strictly guarded in a mountain palace. Uns al-wujûd sets out to rejoin her, wandering in no particular direction. On his way he meets and soothes a fierce lion and ascends a mountain in the wilderness, where he encounters a wise and saintly recluse. On his advice Uns al-wujûd builds himself a raft of gourds on which he crosses the sea. By chance he lands near the palace where the girl is interned. In the courtyard he sees a number of cages with talking birds. In the meantime al-Ward fî ᵓl-Akmâm escapes from the castle and persuades a fisherman to take her back across the sea. This fisherman who is induced to help the girl by the remembrance of his own past love afflictions recalls the fisherman Aigialeus who, in Xenophon's *Ephesiaca*, assists the hero, Habrocomes, for the same reason.[40] A storm drives the fugitive off her course and to a foreign city. There she arouses the interest of the king, who is moved by the intensity of her love and tries to arrange for her marriage with Uns al-

[39] The girl is described as fond of stories (Lane, *op. cit.*, p. 541), even as Achilles Tatius considers the fair sex as *philomython* (v. 5).

[40] Xenophon *Ephesiaca* v. 1.

wujûd. After another series of adventures, which it is hardly necessary to recount, the lovers are united and live happily ever after.[41]

There are at least eight stories or major sections of long composite tales in the *Arabian Nights* in which the full novel pattern is used.[42] The structural identity is frequently punctuated by the recurrence of characteristic detail. Thus in the story of "Prince Saif al-mulûk"[43] the court astrologers predict at the time of his birth that the boy would leave his home and go abroad and that he would be shipwrecked and suffer want and captivity. Hard times are ahead of him, but finally he will reach his goal and be happy to the end of his days and rule his country in spite of his enemies.[44] This horoscope reflects the oracles which both in Heliodor's *Aethiopica*[45] and in Xenophon's *Ephesiaca*[46] forecast the fate of the loving couple. In Heliodor the words of the Pythia are too obscure to be properly understood except in retrospect, but in the *Ephesiaca* the Clarian Apollon expresses himself unequivocally, foretelling suffering, danger at sea, imprisonment, and other tribulations, but also final fulfilment and happiness.

In the story of "Ḫudâdad and His Brothers"[47] the hero is given a funeral, and a mausoleum is built for him while actually he is still alive.[48] There is little doubt that this curious motive stems from the novel, where it is employed rather frequently.

Another detail that survives in the *Arabian Nights*, the attempted but frustrated suicide of the easily discouraged hero, is particularly significant of the strength of the ancient pattern. For Islam condemns self-destruction. This attitude reduces but does not eliminate the suicide motive from the Arab love stories. In every Greek novel with the exception of Longus' *Daphnis and Chloe* one or both of the heroes at least plan to take their lives if

[41] Lane, *op. cit.*, pp. 541–48.

[42] They are enumerated by the author, *JAOS*, LXII, 282–83.

[43] Lane, *op. cit.*, pp. 712–53.

[44] Littmann, *op. cit.*, V, 251; Lane omits the passage (see his n. 14, *op. cit.*, p. 1243).

[45] ii. 35.

[46] i. 6.

[47] Littmann, *op. cit.*, VI, 314–53.

[48] *Ibid.*, pp. 347–49.

they do not actually attempt to; but nowhere do they succeed.[49] When overtaken by shipwreck while voyaging in quest for his beloved, Saif al-mulûk is ready at once to drown himself, but his servants forcibly prevent him from throwing away his life.[50] In another tale the young squanderer who is compelled to sell his beloved slave girl throws himself into the Tigris but is saved by the bystanders.[51] The close connection in the lovers' minds of love and death is the supreme expression of that peculiar type of emotion with which both the Greek and the Arab authors animate their protagonists.

This emotion is extremely sentimental and self-indulging, emotion for emotion's sake. It even seems somewhat impersonal in its indiscriminate ecstasies. He who falls prey to this passion very nearly loses his individuality; he becomes a lover, thus entering the ranks of what could almost be called a profession. The public takes an interest in his doings and expects certain actions and reactions of him as it would *mutatis mutandis* of a king, a priest, or a soldier. In this capacity the lover enjoys great liberties; he is forgiven everything except disloyalty. His mood vacillates between delirious joy and deadening dejection. On the whole, suffering outweighs pleasure. He is given to weeping, he cannot find rest or sleep, he becomes emaciated, he will fall ill, and he may die when hopelessness overtakes him. Both in happiness and in despair he is likely to swoon; before he acts he has to pass through a stage of protracted moaning. And with all his impetuous passion and despite the predominantly sensual coloring of his feelings, his love is chaste—so much so at times in the Arab tales that the reader cannot help wondering whether the self-conscious lover is enamored of his alleged beloved or of his own luxuriant sensibility.

49 K. Kerényi, *Die griechisch-orientalische Romanliteratur in religionsgeschichtlicher Beleuchtung* (Tübingen, 1927), pp. 142 ff., has references and interesting comments. The idea of suicide for unrequited or otherwise frustrated love is by no means confined to the novel. For instances from other literary genres see R. Hirzel's ample collection, *Archiv für Religionswissenschaft*, XI (1908), 424–32. On suicide in Islam cf. F. Rosenthal, *JAOS*, LXVI (1946), 239–59.

50 Lane, *op. cit.*, p. 726.

51 Littmann, *op. cit.*, V, 807. In some other Arabic stories self-destruction is actually achieved; cf., e.g., the brief love tales recorded by Masʿûdî, *Murûj*, VII, 223–28.*

In Chariton's *Chaereas and Callirhoe,* Dionysius, one of the more interesting and engaging characters of the Greek novel, "disappointed in his love for Callirhoe, and no longer able to carry on, had determined to starve himself to death and was writing his last will with directions for his burial. In the document he begged Callirhoe to visit him even after he was dead." In this moment he receives the news that the girl had changed her mind and agreed to marry him. "At this unexpected announcement Dionysius suffered a great shock. A dark cloud settled down over his eyes and in his weakened condition he collapsed and presented the appearance of a dead man."[52]

The Arab author is less discreet in picturing Ḥasan of Baṣra's state when he has lost his lady-love. "Ḥasan . . . . despaired . . . . and he desired to rise and descend from his place, but he could not rise. His tears ran down upon his cheek, and his desire became violent, and he recited these verses:

May Allah deny me the accomplishment of my vow, if after your absence I know pleasant sleep,
And may my eyes not be closed after your separation, nor rest delight me after your departure!
It would seem to me as though I saw you in sleep: and would that the visions of sleep might be real!
I love sleep, though without requiring it; for perhaps a sight of you might be granted in a dream. . . . ."

Finally, Ḥasan dragged himself to his chamber, "and he lay upon his side, sick, neither eating nor drinking . . . . he wept violently, till he fainted, and fell prostrate upon the ground. . . . . The night had come and the whole world was strait unto him, and he ceased not to weep and lament for himself all the night until the morning came and the sun rose over the hills and the lowlands. He ate not nor drank nor slept, nor had he any rest: during the day he was perplexed, and during the night sleepless, confounded, intoxicated by his solicitude, expressing the violence of his desire in some verses of a distracted poet."[53]

Those verses in which some other slave of love had once spoken his sorrow, and which Ḥasan and his fellow-sufferers re-

[52] iii. 1; trans. W. E. Blake (Ann Arbor and London, 1939), p. 37.

[53] Lane, *op. cit.,* pp. 770–71.

cite profusely at the slightest provocation, point to the fact that love as portrayed by the Greek novel and by the *Arabian Nights* had permeated other literary genres as well, both on Greek and on Arabic territory.

Literary recognition—which, however, does not imply moral approval—to this turbulent and unrestrained type of emotion was first extended by Plato, who, in the *Symposium*, has Pausanias discourse on the peculiar attitude the world takes toward a lover. "Consider, too, how great is the encouragement which all the world gives to the lover; . . . . And in the pursuit of his love the custom of mankind allows him to do many strange things, which philosophy would bitterly censure if they were done from any motive of interest, or wish for office or power. He may pray, and entreat, and supplicate, and swear, and be a servant of servants, and lie on a mat at the door (of his beloved). . . . . The actions of a lover have a grace which ennobles them; and custom has decided that they are highly commendable."[54]

All of the pattern's significant topics can be traced backward from the *Arabian Nights*, whose poetical parts mostly stem from poets living between A.D. 850 and 1350,[55] through earlier Arabic poetry to Hellenistic verse. And even before the Hellenistic age popular poetry seems to have moved in this direction. Aristophanes inserts in his *Ecclesiazusae* (first performance in 392 or 389 B.C.) a love song of unmistakably popular hue in which the swain implores the lass in these words:

Hither, O hither, my love,
This way, this way!
Run, run down from above,
Open the wicket, I pray:
Else I shall swoon, I shall die![56]

[54] *Symposium* 183A; trans. B. Jowett. A very different attitude is voiced by the Xenophontic Socrates: "When he [Socrates] found that Critias loved Euthydemus and wanted to lead him astray, he tried to restrain him by saying that it was mean and unbecoming in a gentleman to sue like a beggar to the object of his affection whose good opinion he coveted, stooping to ask a favor that it was wrong to grant" (Xenophon *Memorabilia* i. ii. 29 [trans. E. C. Marchant ("Loeb Classical Library")]). This criticism, however, but illustrates accepted practice.

[55] Cf. J. Horovitz, *Sachau-Festschrift* (Berlin, 1915), pp. 375–79.

[56] *Ecclesiazusae*, vss. 960–63; trans. B. B. Rogers (London, 1917), p. 147; the decisive words are (vs. 963): εἰ δὲ μή, καταπεσὼν κείσομαι.

Theocritus elevated the phrase to full literary dignity in his *Third Idyll*.[57] His (probably spurious) *Twenty-third Idyll*[58] makes the spurned lover who prepares to hang himself at her door ask his beloved to write upon his grave: "This man love slew. . . . ." Dying by one's own hand on account of unrequited love or dying of one's luckless passion as of a mortal disease has ever since been a frequent *topos* in ancient poetry. But not only in poetry. A Greek inscription from the Ḥaurân (Syria), composed perhaps some six centuries after Theocritus sang, tells of one Aurelius Wahbân, son of Alexander, a Hellenized Arab, whose death was caused by love.[59]

When Musâfir b. abî ᶜAmr b. Umayya learns that Abû Sufyân (d. *ca.* 652) had married Hind (d. probably between 640 and 650), his disappointed love made him fall into that illness from which he was to die.[60] The poet Yazîd b. aṭ-Ṭaṯriyya (d. *ca.* 744) narrowly escaped the same fate when separated from his beloved Waḥshiyya. But the lovers are reunited in time, and Yazîd recovers.[61] It remains for a pedestrian critic like the Sayyid Murtaḍà (d. 1044) to explain that the phrase, "somebody was killed by his love for someone else," was nothing but poetical hyperbole.[62]

An occasional protest of this kind did not, however, affect the popularity of this stylized sentimentality among those who boasted a polite education. In laying down the requirements of such education, al-Washshâʾ (d. 936) defines in detail and with complete seriousness the symptoms of love à la mode.

"Know that the first signs of love in the man of polite behavior (*ḏû adab*) are the emaciation of his body, long sickness, the paling of his color, and sleeplessness. His eyes are cast down, he

[57] iii. 53. Cf. also Tibullus iii. ii. 29–30.

[58] xxiii. 47–48. Cf. Seneca *Ad Lucilium* iv. 4: "alius ante amicae foras laqueo pependit" ("one hangs himself before the door of his mistress"). Dio of Prusa (*Or.* xxxii. 50) rebukes the Alexandrines for similar occurrences in their town.*

[59] Cf. the writer, *JAOS*, LXII, 284–85, for references.

[60] *Aghânî* (3d ed.), IX, 50.

[61] *Ibid.*, VIII, 160–62. Another happy recovery is made when the father of an Edessan youth who is pining away for love of a beautiful statue representing Hailâna (i.e., Helena) strikes off the sculptured woman's head (*BGA*, V, 134).

[62] *Amâlî* (Cairo, 1325/1907), IV, 13.

worries unceasingly, his tears are quick to flow. He carries himself with humility, moans a great deal, and shows openly his yearning. There is no end to his shedding of tears and his heaving of deep sighs. A lover will not remain hidden even if he conceal himself, nor will his passion remain secret even if he control himself. His claim to have joined the ranks of the addicts to love and passion cannot but become public knowledge, for the signs of passion are glowing and the symptoms of the claim are manifest."[63]

This love is conducted by the fashionable in obeisance to an established code exacting different behavior from men and women. Dress, perfume, gifts, food, and drinks of the elegant lover are, so to speak, standardized. Any infringement on this polite convention removes the impetuous from the circle of the cultured.[64] It is obvious, and al-Washshâʾ states it expressly, that this type of love is a matter for the well-to-do. It took copious resources to defray the obligation of flooding the beloved with exquisite presents. To love in style you had to live in style, too.[65]

The elaborate mannerisms of polite passion provoked gentle satire. "The Caliph Mutawakkil (847–861) said to Abû ʾl-ʿAnbas: 'Tell me about your ass and his death and the poetry which he recited to you in a dream.' 'Yes, O Prince of the Faithful: my ass had more sense than all the *qâḍîs* together; 'twas not in him to run away or stumble. Suddenly he fell ill and died. Afterwards I saw him in a dream and said to him, "O my ass, did not I make thy water cool and thy barley clean, and show thee the utmost kindness? Why didst thou die so suddenly? What was the matter with thee?" "True," he answered, "but the day you stopped to converse with so-and-so the perfumer about such-and-such an affair, a beautiful she-ass passed by: I saw her and lost my heart and loved so passionately that I died of grief,

[63] *Kitâb al-muwashshà*, p. 48.*

[64] Cf. *ibid.*, pp. 123–24.

[65] Cf. *ibid.*, p. 110. Cf. also the line of Muṭîʿ b. Iyâs (d. 785): "I am surprised he has become a lover even though he does not have in his home as much as a shroud and a bedstead!" (*Aghânî*, XII, 84[17]; Frag. XLV, 2 of the writer's edition, *Orientalia*, N.S., XVII [1948], 193).

pining for her." "O my ass," said I, "didst thou make a poem on the subject?" "Yes," he said; then he chanted:

I was frenzied by a she-ass
  at the door of a perfumer.
She enthralled me, smiling coyly,
  showing me her lovely side-teeth,
Charmed me with a pair of soft cheeks
  colored like the *shaiqurânî*.
For her sake I died; and had I
  lived, then great were my dishonor!

I said: "O my ass, what is the *shaiqurânî?*" "This," he replied, "is one of the strange and uncommon words in the language of the asses." ' Mutawakkil was delighted and ordered the minstrels to set the poem of the ass to music and sing it on that day. No one had ever seen him so gay and joyous before. He redoubled his marks of favor to Abû ʾl-ʿAnbas and loaded him with gifts."[66]

The influence on Arabic civilization exerted by Greek literature and thought during the ninth and tenth centuries is well recognized. It is less widely realized, however, that even the earliest Arabic poetry shows definite traces of Hellenistic tradition. As early as *ca.* A.D. 500 the poet al-Muraqqish the Elder died of love.[67] Before his demise he addressed his beloved cousin Asmâʾ in these words:

And whenever thou hearest, whereso it reaches thee, of a lover who's dead of love or is dying,
Know that that wretch is I without doubt, and weep for one whom Love chained and slew with none to avenge.[68]

By the middle of the sixth century al-Muraqqish's story had become a common theme. Ṭarafa (d. *ca.* 565) illustrates his own passion for Salmà by a reference to the older poet's fate and expressly states that al-Muraqqish met his death through love.[69]

[66] *Murûj*, VII, 204–6; trans. R. A. Nicholson, *Translations of Eastern Poetry and Prose* (Cambridge, 1922), pp. 72–73. *Aghânî*, III, 64, connects a briefer version of the story with the poet Bashshâr b. Burd (d. 783).

[67] The story is told in detail by C. J. Lyall, *Mufaḍḍaliyyât*, II, 167–68.

[68] Trans. Lyall, *ibid.*, Appendix, III, 7–8 (II, 366).

[69] Ed. W. Ahlwardt (London, 1870), XIII, 14–23.

Not much later, al-Aᶜshà (*ca.* 565–629) calls his beloved "a slayer of men."[70]

This same poet introduced another Hellenistic motive to Arabic literature. In his *Fifth Fragment* Moschos (*ca.* 150 B.C.) thus draws the picture of an exasperating tangle of emotions: "Pan loved his neighbor Echo; Echo loved a frisking Satyr; and Satyr, he was head over ears for Lyde. As Echo was Pan's flame, so was Satyr Echo's, and Lyde master Satyr's. 'Twas love reciprocal; for by just course, even as each of those hearts did scorn its lover, so was it also scorned being such a lover itself."[71]

Horace's imitation of the passage is familiar.[72] In al-Aᶜshà's verse the mythological names are, of course, discarded.

I fell in love accidentally, but she was attached to another man who in turn was in love with another girl.
This man again was loved by a young lady who was unapproachable for a kinsman, who was dying from longing, delirious about her, a madman.
But I myself was loved by a little woman who did not suit me—so with all of us love was odious in each case.
Each of us yearned deliriously for his companion in suffering, remote and close at the same time, entangled and entangling.[73]

Literary patterns are by no means the only contribution of the Greeks to Arab life in that early age. Arab drinking etiquette, to select an illustration from an entirely different section of social activity, follows Greek etiquette very closely.[74] The Greeks, to mention just a few characteristic details, drank their toasts only from left to right.[75] The Arabs circulated the cup in

[70] Ed. R. Geyer (London, 1928), XI, 1; it would be easy to add a great many more examples.

[71] Frag. v. 1–6; trans. J. M. Edmonds ("Loeb Classical Library" [London and New York, 1938]).

[72] *Odes* i. 33; cf. G. Pasquali, *Orazio lirico* (Florence, 1920), pp. 495–97.

[73] VI, 17–20. The motive found much favor with later poets; cf. the examples collected by R. Geyer, *SBAW* (Phil.-hist. Kl.), CXCII (1919), Abh. III, 93–95.

[74] R. Geyer, *SBAW* (Phil.-hist. Kl.), CIL (1905), Abh. VI, 218, notes the existence of such agreement without, however, mentioning any detail.

[75] Cf., e.g., Athenaeus, *Deipnosophistae*, trans. C. B. Gulick (London and New York, 1927–41), II, 193–95.

the same sense.[76] Both peoples were fond of perfumed wines.[77] Both the Arab and the Greek reveler trailed his skirt behind him on the ground as an expression of his frivolously high spirits.[78] Arabs as well as Greeks strewed the banquet room with flowers[79] and crowned themselves with wreaths.[80] Even the pious custom of dedicating a few drops of the wine to the gods as a libation survived at least into the eleventh century, although there was nothing in the Islamic milieu to encourage it.[81]

No sooner had the Arabs set foot on and conquered territories formerly held by the Eastern Empire and Greek civilization than a second wave of Hellenistic influence swept into love poetry.

The first personality of note in whose verse this new element manifests itself seems to be Abû Ḏuʾaib, who spent the last years of his life in Egypt (d. *ca.* 650). It is more than likely that it was in this former Byzantine province that he got the inspiration for the markedly sentimental poems of his later period.[82] Toward the end of the century the "new" style had become the vogue, particularly among the so-called Medinese group of poets.

[76] Cf., e.g., ʿAmr b. Kulṯûm (*fl. ca.* 570), *Muʿallaqa*, vs. 5, with Th. Nöldeke's remarks, *SBAW* (Phil.-hist. Kl.), CXL (1899), Abh. VII, 34, and G. Jacob, *Altarab. Beduinenleben* (2d ed.), p. 100; also al-Walîd b. Yazîd (d. 744), ed. F. Gabrieli, Frag. 49.1, in *RSO*, XV (1935), 47.

[77] Cf. Jacob, *op. cit.*, pp. 102 and 250, and Legrand, *op. cit.*, p. 57.

[78] Cf. Geyer, *SBAW* (Phil.-hist. Kl.), CXCII (1919), Abh. III, 259, where Plutarch *Alcibiades* i and xvi and Horace *Satires* i. 2. 25 are referred to.

[79] Mez, *op. cit.*, p. 399; for earlier Arabic references cf., e.g., Aʿshà, XXII, 20, and LV, 8–10.

[80] Cf. Mez, *op. cit.*, p. 399; an earlier instance, Muṭîʿ b. Iyâs (*fl. ca.* 750), *Aghânî* (1st ed.), XII, 92[b].

[81] U. M. Daudpota, *The Influence of Arabic Poetry on the Development of Persian Poetry* (Bombay, 1934), pp. 141–42, lists both Arabic and Persian instances. In this connection it might be mentioned that Abû Miḥjan's (d. *ca.* 637) famous verses (ed. C. Landberg [Leiden, 1886], pp. 61–62; ed. L. Abel [Leiden, 1887], XV, 1–2) in which the poet asks to be buried under vines—vs. 2 has also been ascribed to Aʿshà, Frag. 172.1—closely resemble classical lines such as *Anthologia Palatina* vii. 28 (an anonymous sepulchral epigram for Anacreon) and Leaena's dictum in Plautus, *Curculio*, vs. 104. In their form, Abû Miḥjan's verses appear to parody ash-Shanfarà's forceful line in which he expresses the wish to remain unburied, a prey for the hyena (cf. *Ḥamâsa*, ed. G. W. Freytag [Bonn, 1828–51], I, 242).*

[82] Cf. J. Hell, *Abû Ḏuʾaib* (Hanover, 1926), Introduction, p. 3.

While in pre-Islamic days sentimental love of the kind described above is met with on comparatively rare occasions, it becomes the accepted emotional pattern during the second part of the seventh century, and, with it, the love-death topic comes to be employed by every poet of rank. Famous are the lines of Jamîl al-ᶜUḏrî (d. 701) in which he awakens his sleeping comrades in the dead of night to ask them, "Does love kill a man?" "Yes," they replied, "it breaks his bones, leaves him perplexed, chased out of his wits."[83]

The real contribution of this age to the love-death concept is, however, the idea that the chaste lover who dies of his love is a martyr and thus as sure of Paradise as the martyr of the Holy War. The Prophet Mohammed himself is represented as pronouncing this verdict and thereby conferring "official" standing on this type of lover. A considerable number of stories are told featuring the pure love and usually resulting in the death of one or both of the lovers.[84] The sad story of "Majnûn and Lailà" became a favorite, never again to disappear from Arabic or from Persian and Turkish literature. It is significant that the historicity of Majnûn was doubted at a very early date. Nonetheless, a collection of his melancholy and somewhat spineless poetry has reached us.[85]

The suggestion may be ventured that the concept of the martyr of love constitutes an original contribution of Arabic poetry. In it are fused two earlier developments: the originally Greek notion of the victim of love and that other Greek idea of the lover as fighter or soldier.[86] It is well known that Christian martyrology made extensive use of erotical phraseology, and

[83] Ed. F. Gabrieli, Frag. 2.1–2, in *RSO*, XVII (1937–38), 62; trans. by the writer, *The Arab Heritage*, ed. N. A. Faris (Princeton, 1944), p. 138.

[84] Cf. R. Paret, *Früharabische Liebesgeschichten* (Bern, 1927), pp. 9 ff. for samples.

[85] Cf. *GAL*, I, 48, and Suppl. I, 81; R. A. Nicholson, *EI*, III, 96, refers to the main sources. Another sentimental hero of this period is the ᶜUḏrite ᶜUrwa, the *qatîl al-ḥubb*, "the victim of love"; cf. G. L. Della Vida, *EI*, IV, 989, on this personage, and L. Massignon, *ibid.*, IV, 990, on ᶜUḏrite (=Platonic) love.

[86] Cf. the author, *JAOS*, LXII, 285, n. 83*a*, and the literature there quoted; examples are too frequent to require special listing.

there is no doubt that the Arabs had, by that time, become familiar with Christian martyrology. The transfer of the fighter-martyr concept to the battles of love appears as a rather bold and perhaps somewhat frivolous, at any rate, a highly original, innovation of the later seventh century. The trend of the times toward using religious topics in love poetry and love phraseology in religious verse strongly supports this assumption.[87]

Either Jamîl or his contemporary, Ibn Qais ar-Ruqayyât, was the first to call love madness, *junûn*[88]—another testimony to the increasing effectiveness of Greek ideas. Perhaps a hundred years later, when a theoretical interest in the nature of love began to show, the Platonic definition of love as a sort of divine madness[89] is brought forward by one of the disputants of that famous conference on love held by the learned circle of the Barmakid vizier, Yaḥyà b. H̲âlid (disgraced in 803).[90] Plato's definition recurs many times. It may suffice here to refer to Ibn Dâʾûd's (d. 909) *Kitâb az-zahra*[91] and the *Rasâʾil* of the Pure Brethren of Baṣra.[92] It is interesting that in this case the poets were ahead of the philosophers in making use of Greek inspiration.

There is no need to trace the models of every major *topos* of this "Medinese" love poetry (as easily could be done), nor is it necessary to follow any further the fascinating development of Arabic love poetry destined to reach a new peak in the lyrics of

[87] For this trend cf. above, chap. iv, and P. Schwarz, *ʿUmar b. abî Rebîʿa*, IV (Leipzig, 1909), 28–29.

[88] Ibn Qais ar-Ruqayyât, X, 8, and Appen., XXX, 1; Jamîl, Frag. 58.6. With Ibn Qais another Hellenistic motive, that of the heart divided between two loves, appears in Arabic verse; cf. Ibn Qais, VIII, 3, 5; XIII, 5–11; XXIV, 1–3; LIII, 5; in Greek, cf., e.g., *Anthologia Palatina* xii. 88–91, 93, and 94.

[89] *Phaedros* 244A; cf. also 245C.

[90] *Murûj*, VI, 385; for an analysis of the ideas offered during this séance cf. the writer, *JNES*, XI (1952), 233–38. Still earlier discussions of love may be reflected in verses by ʿUlayya (d. 825), sister of Hârûn ar-Rashîd, quoted by Goldziher, *Ẓâhiriten*, p. 228.

[91] P. 15.

[92] III, 63. Nykl's Introduction to his translation of Ibn Ḥazm, *The Dove's Neck-Ring*, and H. Ritter, *Islam*, XXI (1933), 84–109, should be consulted for further preliminary information. It should be emphasized that the dependence of Arabic on Greek love theory is very far-reaching.

al-ᶜAbbâs b. al-Aḥnaf in order to understand the spiritual kinship of the lyrical passages of the *Arabian Nights* with Hellenistic poetry. At least one section of the Arab public and the Arab littérateurs took over the erotic conventions of the Hellenistic epoch; for the most part, we will have to assume, without realizing the true source of outlook or phraseology.

How perfectly the Arabic poet entered into the spirit of his predecessors will be perceived through an analysis of these verses culled again from the larmoyant story of Ḥasan of Baṣra.

You made a covenant with me that you would remain faithful; but when you had gained possession of my heart you deceived me.
I conjure you by Allah, if I die, that you write upon my tombstone, This was a slave of love:[93]
That perchance some mourner who hath felt the same flame may pass by the lover's grave and pity him.

Nearly every conceit employed in these lines could be matched from Meleager of Gadara (first century B.C.):

We swore, he to love me, and I never to leave him; but now he says that such vows are in running water.
When I am dead, I pray thee lay me under earth and write above, Love's gift to Death.
I will leave letters uttering this voice, Look, stranger, on Love's murdered man.
Even myself I carry the wounds of Love and shed tears over thy tears.[94]

Thus fully has the Arab lover and poet responded to the tune of the love-lorn Greek.

V

Indian and Persian, Jewish and Greek, Babylonian and Egyptian, together with genuinely Arabian elements, have been welded into one by the unknown masters responsible for the overwhelming richness of the corpus of the *Arabian Nights*. Outwardly, the Arabic language, inwardly, the spirit of Islam unite those manifold threads into one dazzling tapestry. In this syn-

[93] This verse is quoted in Arabic, *JAOS*, LXII, 285, n. 82.

[94] *Anthologia Palatina*, v. 8, xii. 74, v. 215, xii. 72; slightly abridged trans. J. W. Mackail, *Lectures on Poetry* (London, 1914), p. 102; for the Arabic verses, cf. Lane, *op. cit.*, pp. 813–14. The motive of *Anthologia* v. 8 was taken up by Catullus, Frag. LXX.

thesis of the disparate the *Arabian Nights* present a likeness on a small scale of Islamic civilization as a whole.

With a certain shift in emphasis, away from the Indian,[95] Babylonian, and Egyptian, and toward the Persian, the Greek, and the Judeo-Christian, and, of course, with much greater stress on the genuinely Arabic, the structure of Islamic civilization repeats the structure of the *Nights*. Islamic civilization is thoroughly syncretistic, and it proves its vitality by coating each and every borrowing with its own inimitable patina.

[95] It is worth noting that al-Bêrûnî (d. 1048), the greatest Muslim expert on India, was perfectly aware of the relative insignificance of the Indian influence on his civilization. Both the statement of fact and the reasons accounting for this situation are found in an unpublished passage of Bêrûnî's *Kitâb aṣ-Ṣaidana* ("Book of Drugs"), translated from the unique Brussa manuscript by M. Meyerhof, *Islamic Culture*, XI (1937), 27. Barhebraeus *Chronography* I. 92 avers the Greeks and only the Greeks to have provided the foundations of Arab philosophy, mathematics, and medicine, three branches of learning in which the Arabs came to surpass "the ancient [sages] in the exactness of their knowledge."

CHAPTER TEN

CONCLUSION

I

THE casual onlooker is struck by the picturesque uniformity of Islamic civilization. Individual objects as well as entire cities appear to speak the same *Formensprache*, most clearly symbolized by the sinuous intricacies of the Arabic script, the foreignness of it all being emphasized and protected by a difficult and puzzling language. Gradually, the student becomes aware of the inexhaustible diversity hiding behind the colorful veil, and he perceives the national and the regional elements. Further analysis reveals the alien provenience of much that looked indigenous; still, in the end, the most careful investigation will have to testify to that unity in the spiritual structure and that amazing power of adaptation that will present the foreign borrowing, hardly recognizable, in native garb. More and more we have come to discover non-Arab or non-Islamic elements in the framework of this civilization; the Christian, the Jewish, and, increasingly prominent, the Hellenistic and the Persian contributions stand out clearly to the trained eye, the early Muslim scholars themselves being alive to some extent to their dependence on non-Muslim erudition. The evolution of Mohammed's preaching, with its comparatively poor background of Arabian civilization, into the cultural system of Islam, with its claim to universal validity, forcefully coloring with its own and unmistakable luster every single object appropriated and every single thought accepted, is one of the most fascinating spectacles history presents.[1]

Islamic civilization seems omnivorous but actually is highly selective. It has admitted, even searched for, such contributions from outside as would help it to keep its identity under

[1] In striving for uniformity of style as a first step toward full political and cultural integration, Islam continues the policy of imperial Rome in its Eastern provinces.

changed conditions. So it welcomed Greek dialectics, the method of allegorical interpretation, the psychology of Christian asceticism, as means of broadening its base beyond the limitations inherent in the koranic text. It cultivated the "mental habits" that had supported Greek research, viz., "the ability to discuss problems according to the categories of formal logic, the appreciation of purely theoretical speculation, and, above all, the acknowledgment of a 'secular' science, fully independent of any religious sectarianism."[2] It encouraged foreign skills: the Christian physician, the Indian mathematician, and the Persian administrator and musician could count on appreciation and reward. It tried, and not infrequently preserved, alien forms of organization; the guilds of the ancient world, the financial system of the Sassanian treasury, and the age-old oriental idea of religious despotism remained live forces. Islam even took over some of the prejudices and abuses of the civilizations it meant to supersede; the dislike for pictorial representation of living beings and the worship of the saints, and, on the other hand, the system of the harem with its paraphernalia of eunuchs and homosexuality were allowed to survive although not necessarily approved. But while Islam for many a century continued liberal in accepting information, techniques, objects, and customs from all quarters, it was careful to eliminate or neutralize any element endangering its religious foundation, and it endeavored consistently to obscure the foreign character of important borrowings and to reject what could not be thus adjusted to its style of thinking and feeling.

Through emphasis on religion as the principal bond between people, Islam was capable, to a considerable extent, of maintaining the intellectual unity of its area long after political disintegration had set the various sections apart and against one another. The educated Muslim was acceptable everywhere on Muslim territory. The faith, learning based on this faith—although not always in harmony with it—and Arabic as the language of both kept united what the changing fortunes of princes and generals had ripped asunder and constantly regrouped. Ibn Baṭṭûṭa, the famous traveler (d. 1377), a native

[2] G. L. Della Vida, *Crozer Quarterly*, XXI (1944), 212–13.

of Tangier, was made a judge first in Delhi, India, and later in the Maldive Islands when he happened to pass through those countries. That great historian and statesman, Ibn Ḫaldûn, born in Tunis, served various princes in North Africa and finally sat as Chief Judge in Cairo. The number of non-Turks who on the basis of their Muslim faith rose to high and highest office in the Ottoman Empire is legion.[3] The renowned physician and vizier of the Mongols, Rashîd ad-Dîn (d. 1318), in a letter instructs "one of his agents in Asia Minor as to the adequate remuneration in money and presents of the learned men in the Maghrib . . . . who had written books in his honor. Of these ten, six were resident in Cordova, Sevilla and other parts of Andalusia, and four in Tunis, Tripolis and Qayrawân."[4] Political disunity had as yet left communication of ideas and the travels of the learned unaffected.

Conservatism expressing itself as the determination never to let go of past achievement and thus unduly accentuating the crudeness of its origins, and the tendency natural to despotism and orthodoxy to discourage revision and reform, combined with Islam's catholic curiosity and receptiveness, are responsible for that lack of integration of the component elements which makes Islamic civilization look like a torso. Arrested in its growth during the eleventh century, it has remained an unfulfilled promise. It lost the power of subjecting the innumerable elements to an organizing idea more comprehensive than the desire for individual salvation. It stagnated in self-inflicted sterility. And expecting renascence from return to its beginnings Islam, in the last centuries of the Middle Ages, weeded out whatever remnants of Hellenism could still be isolated from its structure.

It is fairly obvious that five cultural strains determined the Islamic development. Mohammed welded Judeo-Christian and Arabic ideas and values in his teaching. Speaking for Arabs, he

[3] Comparable instances from predemocratic Europe suggest the prevalence of absolutism as a contributory factor in rendering possible the holding of political office in different states by the same individual.

[4] Quoted from manuscript by E. G. Browne, *Arabian Medicine* (Cambridge, 1921), p. 106.*

canonized as much as feasible of the pagan tradition. He combated and disciplined but never fundamentally changed Arab mentality. The religion of the Koran meant a huge advance for his people, but it was backward compared with the spiritual stage reached elsewhere in Hither Asia. The insistence on the Arabic background assured Mohammed's originality, but the relative backwardness of Islam was never quite to be eliminated, owing to the understandable reluctance of the later generations to part with the associations of the hallowed origins. Jewish and Christian inspiration went into the formation of the early revelation. No other influence ever reached down as deeply to the very roots of Islam.

Mohammed met neither Christianity nor Judaism at their best. But it may be doubted if the theology of the Fathers and the ethics of the rabbis would have proved stronger stimuli to the Prophet than the somewhat vague concoction of a humanitarian monotheism from which he gleaned a variety of concepts, wise sayings, and narrative matter. Later, the church presented itself in its armor of Greek dogmatics and side by side with unalloyed Greek philosophy. But, here again, Islam was not too fortunate in the representatives of Hellenic thought whom it encountered: Instead of Plato, Neo-Platonism, instead of Plotinus, Porphyry and Proclus, and Aristotle mostly as seen through the commentaries of the epigoni. Moreover, the Greek view of the world was received through translations, more often than not made from a Syriac version of the original, which, while admirable accomplishments, were inadequate, as the Arabs themselves were inclined to realize.[5] Still, it was under the impact of Hellenism on every area of thought, be it philosophy, the sciences, or literary theory, and under that of the Persian tradition that Islamic civilization passed through that glorious era of the ninth and tenth centuries whose colorful intensity and diversity will always astound and enchant the spectator.

The Persian tradition, itself strongly affected by an earlier influx of Hellenism, showed its power in molding the forms and ethics of civic life. It was sympathetic to speculation but also to

[5] Cf. *Ḥayawân*, I, 38–40.

ritualism, and it furnished the Muslim mind with a great deal of imaginative and moralistic subject matter, part of which it had absorbed from Indian sources. The world of the ancient Orient, of which, in a sense, pre-Islamic Arabia had been part and survival, makes itself felt most forcefully below the surface of standard Islam, in popular beliefs, that is, and in sectarian theology. It should be remembered in this context that much "ancient Oriental" material was communicated indirectly, for example, through the Persian tradition to whose formation earlier cultural strata had made significant contributions. What other elements can be traced in Islamic civilization are hardly relevant for the understanding of its structure. Indian medicine and pharmacology, Indian mathematics, possibly Indian mystical as well as literary theory were known, to some extent, and influenced the development of certain compartments of Muslim learning. They did not, however, add any decisive trait to the cultural profile of Islam.*

The tolerant attitude of Islam to the foreign material and its powers of assimilation are likely to create the impression of lacking originality. But Islam's originality consists exactly in the capacity of adapting the alien inspiration to its needs, of re-creating it in its own garb, and of rejecting the unadaptable. Islam can hardly be called creative in the sense that the Greeks were creative in the fifth and fourth centuries B.C. or the Western world since the Renaissance, but its flavor is unmistakable on whatever it touched; and, while very little of its conceptual and not too much of its emotional contribution is new or unique, its style of thought and range of feelings are without a real precedent.

Consequently, to understand both the mechanics and the spirit of Islamic civilization, it is necessary not only to trace foreign borrowings but to appraise their effectiveness. This effectiveness can be measured, so to speak, only by the extent to which the borrowing is absorbed into a "native" train of thought or is made a steppingstone in its further development. And it is evident that effectiveness and conspicuousness are unlikely always to coincide.

The representatives of the *kalâm* operated with Greek tools.

Greek terms, Greek methods, and Greek problems directed their endeavors. But they were content to accept the basic Islamic premises which the *falâsifa*, the philosophers proper, refused.* There can be no doubt that men like al-Kindî (d. 873) or al-Fârâbî (d. 950) were both greater minds and greater Hellenists than their Muᶜtazilite contemporaries. Nevertheless, it was these Muᶜtazilites who forced a measure of the Greek approach into orthodox thought, whereas the Aristotelian speculation of the *falâsifa* remained the esoteric and relatively ineffective property of a small group. This group is of the highest importance for the history of philosophy but of doubtful repute within the community of the faithful.

In the field of literary theory, borrowings from the classics remained ineffective whenever it was intended to introduce Greek poetics. Al-Fârâbî's *Canons of Poetry*[6] and the interpretations of Aristotle's *Poetics* by Avicenna (d. 1037) and Averroes (d. 1198)[7] will have to be regarded as nothing but curios by the historian of Arabic theory. It is not the misunderstandings of their Greek model or the clumsy terminology to which they had to resort but the utter unrelatedness of the material from which Aristotle deduced his views with that at the disposal of the Arabs which caused failure of their efforts to influence the Arab littérateurs. Philological error aggravated but did not condition this lack of response.

Another, infinitely more subtle, attempt at instilling Greek method into Arabic literary theory was made by Qudâma b. Jaᶜfar (d. 922). In his *Criticism of Poetry* Qudâma did not use Aristotle's *Poetics*, but he must have been familiar with his *Rhetoric* and his logical writings.[8] Qudâma, a Christian convert to Islam and a government official who wrote a book on taxation, divided poetics into five parts, treating of meter, rhyme, lexicological means, subject matter, and criticism. To make

[6] Ed. and trans. A. J. Arberry, *RSO*, XVII (1936–37), 266–78.

[7] On these interpretations cf. F. Gabrieli, *RSO*, XII (1929–30), 291–331.

[8] Qudâma may, however, have used the *Poetics* in preparing the material that later went into the *Naqd an-naṯr*. Cf. *Naqd an-naṯr*, chaps. 8–11, with *Poetics*, chaps. 20–21, and see Ṭaha Ḥusain's Introduction to the edition (Cairo, 1933), p. 17.

Arabic poetry fit the Aristotelian concept of the epideictic genre (oratory of display), Qudâma arranges the poetical kinds not very satisfactorily under the categories of praise and satire. Despite occasional loss of contact with the realities of Arabic poetry, his treatment of poetics is an accomplishment of considerable value and undoubtedly the most intelligent attempt ever made to construct an Arabic poetics on Greek lines. His terminology is fairly independent and none too artificial. He might have succeeded but for the foreign flavor of his classifications and definitions, too obviously based on Aristotelian logic.[9] While al-Fârâbî met with no response whatever when he outlined the Greek *Canons of Poetry*, Qudâma was quoted frequently and with respect by the theorists of the next hundred and fifty years. Thus al-ᶜAskarî (d. 1005) and Ibn Rashîq (d. 1064 or 1070) never fail to register his opinion when it deviates from their own. But after the eleventh century his influence, never strong enough to secure him more than an honorable mention, is completely overcome, although his definitions continue to be listed as a matter of form.[10]

The main stream of Arabic theory is believed by the Arabs themselves to emanate from the "native" poetics of Ibn al-Muᶜtazz (d. 908). Ibn al-Muᶜtazz proposes to show that the figures of speech which the public considers the distinctive quality of the "modern" poetry (supposed to begin with Muslim b. al-Walîd [d. 823] and represented especially by Abû Tammâm [d. 846] and al-Buḥturî [d. 897]) are not really modern inventions but occur in ancient poetry and prose as well as in the Koran. His every statement is based on Arabic material. He offers a somewhat gauche terminology which, on the surface, appears genuinely Arabic. The very inadequacy of his approach—he merely establishes five figures of speech to which he adds thirteen excellencies, or beauties, of style without so much as trying to explain his reasons for distinguishing between the two categories—would bear witness to the "Arabic"

[9] Cf. also I. Kratchkovsky, *Le Monde oriental*, XXIII (1929), 36–38.

[10] They are carried over into the final presentation of Arabic theory in the works of as-Sakkâkî (d. 1229) and his commentators, al-Qazwînî (d. 1338) and at-Taftazânî (d. 1389).*

origin of his disquisition.[11] Ibn al-Muᶜtazz well avoids that foreign atmosphere of formal logic which made Qudâma's work at the same time a better and, to the Arab critics, a less attractive book.

Nonetheless, the *Kitâb al-badîᶜ*, the "Book of the New Style," is unthinkable without Greek antecedents. The five figures which, in Ibn al-Muᶜtazz' view, make up the *badîᶜ* are all of Greek origin. They are metaphor, antithesis, paronomasy, *ploke* (*radd al-ᶜajz ᶜalà ᵓṣ-ṣadr*), and, through a curious misunderstanding, the syllogism, or more exactly, the *enthymema*, *al-maḏhab al-kalâmî*, an error quickly eliminated by his successors.[12] Among the excellencies Ibn al-Muᶜtazz includes the simile, which the Arabs continued to distinguish from the metaphor in accord with Aristotle's definition of the two terms, even to the extent of using his example, only replacing Achilles with that stand-by of the grammatical example, Zaid. So they declare, with the Stagirite,[13] "Zaid is like a lion in courage" to be a simile, while "Zaid, a lion," constitutes a metaphor.

Thus, here again, the disguised and "obscured" borrowing proved the more effective. Subsequent developments tended to strengthen the Greek influence while concealing it. In purely Arabic garb such basic ideas of Greek theory were introduced as the distinction between figures of speech and figures of thought,[14]

[11] It is possible that the division between *maḥâsin* and *badîᶜ* is based on the observation, ascribed by W. Caskel (*OLZ*, 1938, col. 147) to Ibn al-Muᶜtazz, that it is only the five figures of the *badîᶜ* that are more frequently used by the "modern" poets, whereas the categories of the *maḥâsin* are no more prevalent in modern than in ancient style. Unfortunately, the text of the *Kitâb al-badîᶜ* neither supports nor refutes this explanation. This writer is inclined to doubt the factual correctness of Caskel's opinion that the *maḥâsin* recur with the same frequency in old and new poetry. Still, Caskel may have adequately retraced Ibn al-Muᶜtazz' line of thought.*

[12] The same type of misunderstanding occurred when al-Bâqillânî, *Iᶜjâz al-Qurᵓân*, p. 27 of trans., treated *musâwât*, accurate correspondence between wording and idea, as a figure of speech. Better authorities place it correctly with *iṭnâb* and *îjâz*, prolixity and concision; the terms reproduce Aristotle's distinction, *Rhetoric* iii. 12. 6 (1414*a*), of *saphes lexis*, *adoleschia*, *syntomia*. Cf. also al-Fârâbî's *shâᶜir musaljis*, the "syllogistic poet," *op. cit.*, p. 272[3].

[13] *Rhetoric* iii. 4. 3 (1406*b*).

[14] "Schemata lexeos, schemata dianoias/al-badîᶜiyyât al-lafẓiyya, al-badîᶜiyyât al-maᶜnawiyya."

or the concept of literary theory as an "art."[15] And very considerable is the number of Greek terms of critical appreciation that, in the course of this movement, made their way into Arabic criticism without being suspected of foreign origin. The very word *maḥâsin*, excellencies, which Ibn al-Muᶜtazz employs, *bârid*, "frigid," and *maṣnûᶜ*, artificial or faked, are three instances selected at random as illustrations from three separate branches of the critic's vocabulary.[16]

More than anything else does this hiding of the foreign influence and the concomitant increase in its power of stimulation contribute to the apparent uniformity and roundedness of Muslim civilization.

II

It is fair but somewhat misleading to judge Muslim scientific achievement by the outstanding accomplishments of a handful of exceptional men. It is fair because the unusual contribution remains to influence remote generations, misleading with respect to the attitude toward his work of the average Muslim investigator. To him, the sciences were fundamentally a stable system of formal and material truths communicated to man for safekeeping in what we should call prehistoric times. Ibn al-Qifṭî (d. 1248) points out:

"The learned of the nations are at variance about who was the first to discourse on Wisdom, *ḥikma*, and its pillars, propaedeutics, *riyâḍa*, logic, *manṭiq*, natural and theological (physical and metaphysical) sciences (*ṭabîᶜî, ilâhî*), each group finding him amongst their own people. But he would not be the first in reality. But when the investigators had looked into the matter thoroughly they saw that this (beginning of scientific knowledge) was prophetic information sent down upon Idrîs (Henoch). All those originators (*awâʾil*) mentioned in every part of the world just gathered up this knowledge (vouchsafed Idrîs) from the reports of his pupils or the pupils of his pupils."[17]

In the same vein, Ibn Ḥazm had explained two centuries

[15] *Techne, ṣinâᶜa;* another "art" is *kitâba*, the accomplishment of the scribe.

[16] The Greek counterparts are *kalle, psychros, pepoiemenon;* for the first cf. the writer, *Bâqillânî*, Part II, n. 12; for the last, Isocrates, ed. Benseler-Blass, II, 275.

[17] Ibn al-Qifṭî, *Taʾrîḫ al-ḥukamâʾ*, ed. J. Lippert (Leipzig, 1903), p. 1.

earlier: "We know with certainty that never could man have acquired the sciences and arts by himself guided only by his natural abilities and without benefit of instruction. (This applies, e.g., to) medicine, the knowledge of the physiological temperaments, the diseases and their causes, in all their numerous varieties, and the invention of adequate treatment and cure of each of them by means of drugs or preparations, which could never have been actually tried out. For how could anyone test every prescription on every disease since this would take tens of thousands of years and necessitate the examination of every sick person in the world?" And what goes for medicine goes for astronomy, too, etc.[18]

The purpose for which the Lord bestowed this knowledge on mankind was to make them realize his glory in the wonders of nature.[19] So the ultimate result of investigation was predetermined. Studies carried out in the wrong spirit or leading to unexpected metaphysical conclusions were tainted with heresy. The devotees of the Greek ideal of research for the sake of truth alone could not be numerous in an order whose stability, or rather whose survival, depended on the perpetual vindication of revealed verities.

The psalmist had proclaimed: "The heavens relate the glory of God, and the expanse telleth of the work of his hands."[20] The Syrian, Barḥadbshabbâ of Ḥalwân (*fl. ca.* 600), had explained: "Three things impede the nature of beings endowed with reason and created to accomplish the good: evil, ignorance, and weakness."[21] Knowledge is justified by its ethical or educational value. It begins and ends with admiration of the Creator and understanding of his laws.

On the strength of such considerations Ibn al-Qifṭî classifies the savants interested in the nature of things created and their

[18] *Kitâb al-fiṣal fî ʾl-milal*, I, 72; a fuller extract in Spanish by M. Asín Palacios, *Al-Andalus*, IV (1936–39), 253–55.

[19] Cf. Levy, *Sociology*, II, 346.

[20] Ps. 19:12. Levy, *loc. cit.*, refers to this verse.

[21] *Cause de la fondation des écoles*, ed. and trans. A. Scher, *Patrologia orientalis*, IV (Paris, 1908), 329. Scher erroneously identified the author with Barḥadbshabbâ ʿArbâyâ; cf. A. Baumstark, *Geschichte der syrischen Literatur* (Bonn, 1922), p. 136.

Creator in three groups. The first of these are the materialists, *dahriyyûn*, who deny the existence of a Maker and have the world subsist, as it were, on its own. There has been no beginning to the world's rotation, and plant sprang from grain and grain from plant in an infinite sequence without a fixed starting-point. Thales of Miletus was the first to develop this doctrine. Those who adhere to it are called *zanâdiqa*, heretics.

The second group are the *Naturphilosophen*, *ṭabî'iyyûn*. They are interested in the active and passive qualities of natural phenomena, in plants and animals, their structure and anatomy. "They glorify God and exalt Him and verify through His creatures that He is Maker in accord with His own choosing and planning, powerful, wise, and knowing. (They realize that) He issues the created beings from His wisdom and assigns to them their fate in keeping with His knowledge and His will." They infer, however, from the decay visible in all created beings when they near the end of their course that man, even as the animals, passes away into nothingness. They do not accept the belief in man's afterlife in Paradise. They feel that the soul perishes with the body. Whatever the prophets and saints saw fit to state on this subject had no other purpose but to safeguard order and civilization by restraining people from misdeeds through hope and fear of a future life. "But they err and lead into error. They, too, are heretics, *zanâdiqa*. For only those are believers who believe in God, the Last Day, the resurrection and the quickening of the dead, even as the Books record it."

The third group are the metaphysicians, *ilâhiyyûn*, the greatest of them Aristotle, whose praises Ibn al-Qifṭî sings with remarkable eloquence. But even he, relying as he did on his own reasoning and deprived of the guidance of revelation, went astray on some important points, and so did al-Fârâbî and Ibn Sînâ (Avicenna), his foremost expositors and followers. Their work falls into three categories; one of these brands them as unbelievers, the next as innovators, but the third is acceptable.

This third category is made up of the propaedeutic sciences, such as arithmetic and geometry, and of formal logic. These have nothing to do with matters of the faith but only with demonstrable propositions and the methods of demonstration.

Their results cannot be denied. Their danger consists in suggesting that every subject could be treated with their methods, and this assumption would, of course, lead into religious error. The dangers of false inference inherent in the natural sciences were set forth in dealing with the natural philosophers. Metaphysics, *ilâhiyyât*, the most controversial of all sciences, causes the adherents of Aristotle to fall into unbelief when they trust demonstrative reasoning beyond its true range and allow themselves to deny bodily resurrection, God's knowledge of particulars, and the beginning of the world through a definite act of God at a definite point of time. The acceptance of seventeen other tenets, referred to but not listed by Ibn al-Qifṭî, classes the followers of Aristotle as innovators.[22]

We are inclined to admire medieval scholars who broke the limitations that theology as the highest of sciences imposed on the rational investigation of the universe. With due respect to their intellectual boldness, the question cannot always be brushed aside whether those innovators had any right to their departure from the established system. In the absence of a theory of knowledge the criteria deciding upon the acceptability of any particular item were of the vaguest. The habit of speculation encouraged the putting-forward of opinions which might be true but could neither be proved as facts nor integrated in a system which would assign them their proper significance.

When al-Jâḥiẓ, al-Masᶜûdî, and the *Iḫwân aṣ-ṣafâ* express their belief in evolution, envisaging a gradual ascent of life "from mineral to plant, from plant to animal, from animal to man,"[23] they were conjecturing or else restating what Greek opinion had surmised from the days of Anaximander. But they had no chance, nor did they attempt, to prove their case. Niẓâmî ᶜArûḍî (wrote 1156) is in no position to substantiate his vision of the upward development from the inorganic to the organic world. The grandeur of the vision is as astounding as the irresponsibility with which it is propounded.

"So this kingdom (of the organic world) rose superior to the

[22] Ibn al-Qifṭî, pp. 49–53.

[23] G. Sarton, *Introduction to the History of Science* (Baltimore, 1927 ff.), I, 638, speaking of al-Masᶜûdî.

inorganic world . . . . , and the far-reaching Wisdom of the Creator so ordained that these kingdoms should be connected one with another successively and continuously, so that in the inorganic world the first material, which was clay, underwent a process of evolution and became higher in organization until it grew to coral, which is the ultimate term of the inorganic world and is connected with the most primitive stage of plant-life. And the most primitive thing in the vegetable kingdom is the thorn, and the most highly developed the date-palm and the grape, which resemble the animal kingdom in that the former needs the male to fertilize it so that it may bear fruit, while the latter flees from its foe. For the vine flees from the bind-weed, a plant which, when it twists round the vine, causes it to shrivel up, wherefore the vine flees from it. In the vegetable kingdom, therefore, there is nothing higher than the date-palm and the vine, inasmuch as they have assimilated themselves to that which is superior to their own kingdom, and have subtly overstepped the limits of their own world, and evolved themselves in a higher direction."[24]

Arabic research continued what might be called an authoritarian tradition. What with credulity rampant, standards of credibility not consciously evolved, most of the work stimulated by foreign impulses, and revealed theology setting the style, the abortive recognition of observational and experimental methods of truth-finding appears little short of miraculous. To appreciate the outlook of the times, both in the East and in the West, it must be realized that "in those days the art of observation was so undeveloped (let alone the art of experimentation) that the facts which it revealed seemed very changeable and shaky; whatever positive knowledge they had was not very reliable; any one of their scientific statements could easily be challenged. Compared with that, the theological constructions seemed unshakable; they were not based upon observation, hence no amount of observation could destroy them; they were not based upon deduction, hence no amount of logic could

[24] *Chahâr Maqâla*, trans. E. G. Browne (London, 1921), p. 6; cf. p. 9 for similar remarks about the animal kingdom. The question is discussed briefly by Browne, *Arabian Medicine*, pp. 118–19.*

impugn them. They stood apart and above the world of experience."[25]

The same Jâḥiẓ who refutes by experiment the superstition that snakes are unable to stand the scent of the rue and who asks a butcher to show him testicles and faucial bag of a camel so as to disprove the popular idea that these organs disappear when the animal is slaughtered,[26] does not hesitate to accept the report that the period of gestation for the rhinoceros is seven years and that during this time the young occasionally leaves the womb of his mother to graze awhile, afterward to return until he is finally given birth for good. Al-Masᶜûdî, puzzled by this piece of information, inquired among the natives of the rhinoceros' habitat, who assured him emphatically that it was incorrect.[27] Al-Jâḥiẓ, as well as, later, ad-Damîrî (d. 1405), when discussing animals or processes of nature subscribed to what authoritative writers of the past had affirmed so that, in many instances, their exactitude depends entirely on the accuracy of their sources.[28]

The great physicians of the ninth and tenth centuries, above all, ar-Râzî (d. *ca.* 925), whose writings exercised considerable influence on Western medical thinking, developed great precision in the observation and description of symptoms. "The outbreak of small-pox is preceded by continuous fever, aching in the back, itching in the nose and shivering during sleep. The main symptoms of its presence are: back-ache with fever, stinging pain in the whole body, congestion of the face, sometimes

[25] Sarton, *op. cit.*, I, 5.*

[26] Brockelmann, *GAL*, Suppl., I, 240. This appeal to observation reminds of Augustine's keeping a slice of peacock meat to test (and, as it turned out, confirm) the general belief that this bird's flesh was exempt from corruption (cf. *De civitate dei* xxi. 4). Similarly Dicuil (wrote 825), who has seen Abû Lubâba, the elephant (d. 810) given to Charlemagne by Hârûn ar-Rashîd, rebukes Solinus (third cent.) for asserting that no elephant was able to lie down (cf. Beazley, *op. cit.*, I, 318 and 325).

[27] Carra de Vaux, *Penseurs de l'Islam*, I, 102; cf. *Murûj*, I, 387–88, where Masᶜûdî has reference to Jâḥiẓ, *Hayawân*, VII, 40.**

[28] Cf. al-Jâḥiẓ' assertion that "when the ant stores corn for food it mutilates each grain in such a way as to prevent it from germinating." This observation is correct, but al-Jâḥiẓ just took it over sight unseen from Pliny. See Browne, *Literary History of Persia*, IV, 440–41.

shrinkage, violent redness of the cheeks and eyes, a sense of pressure in the body, creeping of the flesh, pain in the throat and breast accompanied by difficulty of respiration and coughing, dryness of the mouth, thick salivation, hoarseness of the voice, headache and pressure in the head, excitement, anxiety, nausea and unrest. Excitement, nausea and unrest are more pronounced in measles than in small-pox whilst the aching in the back is more severe in small-pox than in measles."[29] Ar-Râzî's approach was truly scientific, and he went so far as to write a tract "On the Fact That Even Skilful Physicians Cannot Heal All Diseases."

ᶜAlî b. al-ᶜAbbâs al-Majûsî (*fl. ca.* 970–80) expressly enjoins observation and empirical study of diseases on the future physician. "And of those things which are incumbent on the student of this art (i.e., medicine) are that he should constantly attend the hospitals and sick-houses; pay unremitting attention to the conditions and circumstances of their inmates, in company with the most acute professors of Medicine; and enquire frequently as to the state of the patients and the symptoms apparent in them, bearing in mind what he has read about these variations, and what they indicate of good or evil. If he does this he will reach a high degree in this Art."[30]

Advances of the clinical spirit did not by themselves reduce reliance on well-established literary authorities. As a matter of fact, it was not before late in the eleventh century that collections of experimental data came to be published, without, of course, displacing the systematic works of the old style. It is interesting to note that the authors of such treatises, entitled *mujarrabât*, *experimenta*, hailed from very different parts of the Islamic world. The earliest seems to have been Abû ʾl-ᶜAlâʾ Zuhr of Cordova (d. 1077/78), the father of the more celebrated physician Avenzoar (Ibn Zuhr; d. 1161/62); he was followed by the Christian Ibn at-Tilmîḏ of Baghdad (d. 1164/65) and the Egyptian Jews, Ibn al-Mudawwar (d. 1184/85), Ibn an-Nâqid (d.

[29] M. Meyerhof, in *Legacy of Islam*, pp. 323–24, from ar-Râzî, *On Small-Pox and Measles;* cf. the admirable case history, Browne, *Medicine*, pp. 51–53.

[30] Browne, *Medicine*, p. 56.

1188/89), and Abû ʾl-Maʿâlî, who was perhaps Maimonides' brother-in-law (d. 1222).[31]

The range and value of these *mujarrabât* must not be overrated. "The experimental spirit was exceedingly slow in finding itself."[32] Nevertheless, their importance as signs of a reorientation of the investigating mind is very considerable. They were necessarily crude but apparently less so than the experiments of the West which soon followed suit. Frederick II (d. 1250) no longer hesitates to correct Aristotle where experience proves him wrong. But the methods devised for experimental truth-finding and some of the problems they were supposed to solve still are somewhat barbaric and ill-chosen—if our tradition can be trusted. "There is the story of the man whom Frederick shut up in a wine-cask to prove that the soul died with the body, and the two men whom he disembowelled to show the respective effects of sleep and exercise on digestion." Imitating, perhaps unwittingly, an experiment reported by Herodotus (ii. 2), Frederick caused children to be brought up in silence in order to discover "whether they would speak Hebrew, which was the first language, or Greek or Latin or Arabic or at least the language of their parents; but he labored in vain, for the children all died."[33] This particular experiment deserves attention because it shows the struggle between accepting problems deriving from traditional philosophy and the "modern" impulse to accept truth only on controlled evidence.

It would seem that in Islam inductive methods were in actual practice most widely received in medicine. Long after Arabian medicine had fallen into a state of torpor—incidentally, it is only after this time, *ca.* 1100, that it began to influence Western medicine most strongly—Ibn al-H̱aṭîb of Granada (d. 1374), famed as statesman, historian, stylist, and physician, braved

[31] Cf. Sarton, *op. cit.*, II, 1, 433. Masʿûdî, *Tanbîh*, p. 63, records an experiment undertaken by the Caliph al-Mahdî (775–85) to test the relative warmth of various animal pelts. For further material on Muslim experiments cf. R. Paret, *Islam*, XXV (1939), 228–33, and F. Rosenthal, *Technique*, pp. 65–66.

[32] *Ibid.*, II, 1, 94.

[33] C. H. Haskins, *Studies in the History of Mediaeval Science* (Cambridge, Mass., 1927), p. 262.

orthodoxy in his study on plague by stating: "The existence of contagion is established by experience, study, and the evidence of the senses, by trustworthy reports on transmission by garments, vessels, ear-rings; by the spread of it by persons from one house, by infection of a healthy sea-port by an arrival from an infected land . . . . by the immunity of isolated individuals and . . . . nomadic Bedouin tribes of Africa." To appreciate the boldness of this thesis, it must be remembered that the Prophet had expressly denied the existence of contagion. Ibn al-Ḫaṭîb proceeds to enunciate this daring principle. "A proof taken from the traditions has to undergo modification when in manifest contradiction with the evidence of the perception of the senses."[34]

But this insight came too late, for by this time the urge of scientific advance had almost died down throughout the Muslim world.

With all the keenness of observation displayed in the study of the sciences, it is quite obvious that, on the whole, Muslim scholarship was superior in what is now called the humanities. There is infinitely more mental initiative in Muslim historiography and philology than in their obsequious refurbishing of ancient science. One cannot help the impression that the Muslim savant's mastery of the facts was less solid, and his presentation more conventional when he dealt with the natural sciences. He was prepared to register the minutest detail when it came to describe philosophical opinion, and he controlled a superb machinery of concepts and terms to help him organize his results. Research in the humanities not being as manifestly impeded by the acceptance of authority as work in the natural sciences, he could proceed with complete self-assurance: the technique was tested, and his sensitivity to shades of thought as well as his perspicacity regarding the implications of speculative positions most delicately developed.

Theological bias might distort conclusions, but hardly ever would it affect the conscientious accuracy with which he would outline the very weirdest errors of heresy. In their books on sects, or comparative religion, the research acumen of the

[34] Meyerhof, *Legacy*, p. 340.

Muslims shows at its best. The inspiration came from Christian heresiography—the literary structure of the Muslim works allows little doubt about the stimulus received from books like John of Damascus' *On Heresies*. But while the Christians would neglect this kind of studies, the Muslims developed it most impressively. When al-Ashᶜarî in his *Maqâlât* discusses the opinions of the several Muslim schools and sects, he does so with a view to vindicate the truth of what to him was orthodoxy. But ash-Shahrastânî (d. 1153), and before him al-Baghdâdî (d. 1037), and even the irritable and somewhat intolerant Ibn Ḥazm (d. 1064) are moved for the most part by the intrinsic interest of the subject. They have their own theological standpoints to defend, but they readily allow themselves to succumb to the fascination of their theme, which they investigate with as much thoroughness as sympathy—the obligatory blasts at the dissenter and miscreant notwithstanding.[35]

III

To appraise the effect of Muslim civilization on the development of the Occident, three sets of facts must be taken into consideration.

1. During the better part of the Middle Ages Muslim scientific and material superiority was undeniable and widely acknowledged. Toward the end of the period this superiority decreases, as the East stagnates intellectually and declines economically, while Europe revives and catches up, stimulated, in large measure, by progressive acquaintance with Muslim learning. The sixteenth century witnesses the end of "Arabism" in European studies, although stray survivals linger on as late as the first part of the nineteenth century.[36] Some modern apolo-

[35] Masᶜûdî, *BGA*, VIII, 93, clearly distinguishes between writers who set out to refute Zoroastrian doctrines and such who merely wish to discuss them. The passage proves the existence of "comparative religion" more than half a century before al-Baghdâdî. *Ibid.*, pp. 395–96, Masᶜûdî lists no less than sixteen authors who had dealt with this subject. The earliest work on religious history in Persian is Abû ʾl-Maᶜâlî Muḥammad's *Bayân al-adyân*, written in 1092, which deserves the same praise; for the Persian treatment of the subject cf. Ethé in Geiger-Kuhn, *Grundriss*, II, 360.

[36] Cf. Meyerhof, *Legacy*, p. 353.

gists for the Middle Ages have tried to convince themselves that Western man lost less ground in the collapse of ancient civilization than is commonly assumed. The startling difference between East and West in outlook and factual knowledge, owing to the partial salvaging in the East of the heritage which the West had almost totally forgotten, belies their efforts and underlines the shocking retrogression of a barbarized world which it took perhaps four centuries to halt and two more to reverse. The realization that that difference was due not so much to Muslim addition to the classical legacy but merely to its preservation, and this none too complete, serves to emphasize both the greatness of the ancient world and the extent to which the West had let go of its accomplishments.

The present state of our knowledge regarding ancient and Muslim sciences does not permit a final judgment on the Muslim contribution to each individual branch of learning. It can, however, be asserted with a fair degree of certainty that, by and large, and with the express exception of optics, in which the Arabs clearly surpassed their Greek masters, the Arab scholars did not alter the theoretical background of the material they took over and that it was only in medicine and astronomy that they added important observations of fact. In mathematics, Indian influence was strong, and it proved especially helpful in supplanting the clumsy classical system of numbers by that which at long last was to become ours through the efforts of Lionardo Fibonacci (first half of thirteenth century), who had enjoyed the instruction of Muslim teachers in North Africa.

Reverence for authority lay as a heavy cloud over Muslim research. Its shadow did not always cover the humanities, but the natural sciences, in which the interest of the general public was not so intense as in theology, poetics, or linguistics, never were treated with a degree of self-confidence sufficient to overhaul the theoretical structure imposed on them by the ancients. The keenest observers among the Muslim physicians accepted "Greek anatomy, physiology, and pathology," content to correct an occasional detail from their personal experience. The desire to start investigations on one's own, to re-examine a traditional system of learning, apparently was as good as unknown.

The physician ᶜAbdallaṭîf (d. after 1228), while traveling through Egypt, "discovered a great collection of skeletons, accumulated during a pestilence, on the hill at Maks, and was there able by the evidence of his own eyes to correct Galen's description of the structure of the human mandible." But "it had never occurred to him . . . . previously to examine a subject for himself in order to discover the truth."[37]

The Spanish Muslim, Ibn Ṭumlûs (d. 1223), evaluating the scientific attainments of his coreligionists, arrives at this conclusion. "In the sciences of geometry, arithmetic, astronomy, and music the scholars of Islam have surpassed their ancient predecessors. Still, although it can be said with great probability that men nowadays have access to fuller knowledge than the ancients, it is only fair to remember that it is likely that a good many of the works of the ancients have perished."[38] It would seem that this estimate, admirable in its detached and scholarly spirit, is somewhat severe on the Muslim contribution.

When Ibn Ṭumlûs wrote, the productive age of Muslim research had come to a close. Ibn Ḫaldûn was keenly conscious of the cultural decline of the period. He explains that, with the extinction of scientific knowledge, civilization had perished throughout the Muslim West. Only faint traces of scientific erudition remain, and its representatives are forced to evade the surveillance of the orthodox doctors. In southern Persia and Transoxiana, also in Egypt, the situation is slightly more encouraging.* Ibn Ḫaldûn understands that in the land of the Franks, that is, in Rome and "its dependencies" on the northern shore of the Mediterranean, the philosophical studies are flourishing. Scientific work has been revived in these parts, and great numbers of teachers and students are engaged in its promotion. But only God knows what actually goes on in those countries![39]

37 Levy, *op. cit.*, II, 404.

38 Quoted by A. Guillaume, in *Legacy of Islam*, p. 271.

39 *Prolegomena*, III, 92–93 (trans., III, 128–29). Ibn Ḫaldûn's sociological studies, antedating modern European sociology by more than four centuries, came too late to arouse any response in his own civilization. The influence of milieu on thought was realized before him by as-Sakkâkî (cf. the writer, *JAOS*, LXV [1945], 62), but Ibn Ḫaldûn's pioneering work took him far beyond his predecessor.

It has been overlooked so far that the basic problems that occupied Ibn Ḫaldûn's

2. Arabic scholarship as transmitter of ancient thought has been a powerful inspiration for the medieval West. And at times the West not only accepted avidly the material offered by the Muslims and rendered accessible by extensive translations, first organized on a considerable scale, and with the aid of Jewish savants, in Toledo early in the twelfth century, but adopted as well the interpretation given this material by the Arab thinkers. In the fourteenth century the University of Paris admitted Aristotle only as explained in Averroes' commentary.[40] Leading Muslim scholars were regarded with awe and might acquire unchallenged authority. It must be noted, however, that in a number of cases the most important stimuli reached the West, more or less simultaneously, through two channels. Greek thought was rediscovered either directly from Byzantium or indirectly from Arabic versions. Thus Aristotle's *Metaphysics* came to Paris from Constantinople about 1220, but only a few years later an Arabic translation arrived.[41] Arab philosophy had aroused Western interest in philosophy as such and in Greek philosophy in particular, but the source material was recovered both with and without benefit of Arabic mediation.

A somewhat similar situation obtains in the development of Western *Minnesang*. There can be little doubt as to the influence of Arabic poetry on the songs of the troubadours. Spanish-Arabic lyrics and, before them, the verses addressed by al-ᶜAbbâs b. al-Aḥnaf (d. 806) to his fair lady, Fauz, unmistakably show the seeds, and more than the seeds, of the peculiar

---

attention were studied by at least one Muslim author more than four centuries before his time. Masᶜûdî, *Tanbîh*, pp. 3–4, avers having discussed in earlier works of his not only the various systems of government, but specifically the support lent by religion, *dîn*, to royal power, *mulk*, and vice versa, and the causes of political and religious decline. In another passage of the same book (p. 84), Masᶜûdî notes the dependence of a nation's laws on these four factors: its religion, its economy, its innate character, and the influence of neighboring peoples. Unfortunately, we do not know Masᶜûdî's solutions. Nor do we know if Ibn Ḫaldûn was acquainted with Masᶜûdî's studies. The evidence available at present does not allow any inference as to Masᶜûdî's sources. But his reference, *Tanbîh*, p. 78, to Aristotle's *Politeia*, may have some significance in this connection, at least so far as the discussion of the forms of government is concerned.

[40] Cf. Guillaume, *Legacy*, p. 276, n. 1.

[41] Guillaume, *Legacy*, p. 246. Incidentally, both versions were incomplete.*

love attitude that characterizes the minnesinger.[42] And it is not merely the spirit that crossed the Pyrenees. The Provençal poets adopted many of the complicated prosodical forms of the Spanish Muslims, just as the French prose writer took over the prosimetric form of the Arab narrator when he composed *Aucassin and Nicolette*, the Arab inspiration disguised by the very perfection of its assimilation.

Much in the sentiment animating the Arab popular romance and the love poetry of both learned and untutored minstrels perpetuates a feeling first made vocal in the Hellenistic age. The direct heirs of Hellenistic poetry, the Romans of the Augustan period, had preserved that same sentiment, although it may perhaps be said that on its way through Arab lands it had become more varied, subtilized, and attenuated. Somewhere on the way a good part of the frivolousness of Ovidian verse had been replaced by sentimentality. So when European, and especially southern European, society looked out for a medium in which to express the newly won sensibility, the finest flower of courtly refinement, they found the pattern more or less readied in the style of their most civilized contemporaries; and they found it again, not as delicately diversified perhaps, but imbedded in an alluring array of mythological action, in their Latin heritage. Both the Arabic and the Latin verse were solidified, so to speak, by an elaborate theory of love.

It is important to realize that, however incisive the Arab influence on Western word and thought after 1100, the Occident was prepared to keep only such gifts as were in tune with and, in a sense, derived from older strains of the European development that had been cut short and obliterated by an unkindly fate many a century before. Not infrequently, thus, it was the Arabic borrowing that restored the continuity of the European evolution which the barbarians had interrupted.

3. When Western civilization as it crystallized through Middle Ages and Renaissance is analyzed for its main components, the limited effect of its prolonged but somewhat superficial contacts with the Muslim world is clearly felt. Islamic civilization, one might say, contributed a good deal of detail

[42] Cf. J. Hell, *Islamica*, II (1926–27), 271–307.*

and acted as a catalyzer, but it did not influence the fundamental structure of the West. It may be debatable to what extent modern occidental civilization can be explained as the continuation of classical civilization—but it would be preposterous so much as to ask whether any of its essentials are of Muslim inspiration. Medieval East and West had at least two roots in common: the cultural legacy of the heathen world around the Mediterranean and Judeo-Christian monotheism. The East proved the more conscientious heir until a repentant West turned back to its origins greatly aided by Eastern guidance. But, except for Averroism, it would seem that never did original Muslim thought influence Western thought so as to remain a live force over a prolonged period of time completely integrated and indispensable to its further growth.

There is hardly an area of human experience where Islam has not enriched the Western tradition. Foods and drinks, drugs and medicaments, armor and heraldry, industrial, commercial, and maritime techniques, and again artistic tastes and motives, not to speak of the many terms of astronomy or mathematics—a list indicative of the full measure of the Islamic contribution would take up many a page without being even remotely complete. The very existence of the Muslim world has done much to mold European history and European civilization. The Crusades were, in many ways, the greatest and most consequential adventure on which medieval man embarked. Muslim narrative and poetical imagery, Muslim eschatology and the boldness of Muslim mysticism, all have left their traces on the medieval West. The greatest theologian and the greatest poet of the European Middle Ages are deeply indebted to Islam for inspiration as well as material. Thomas Aquinas uses Maimonides (d. 1204) and Averroes (d. 1198), and he employs a manner of argumentation familiar from Muslim scholasticism. Dante's debt to Muslim visionaries, to whose ideas translations had given a certain vogue, can hardly be doubted.* Parallel effort in alchemy and astrology, with Islam as teacher and Christendom a self-willed student, introduced more concepts and associations to be held in common.

And yet, although intimately allied with the East in truth and error, the West retained its spiritual independence. From the fourteenth century onward the two civilizations grew more and more apart. The political and commercial ties with the heartlands of Islam slackened. Europe concentrated on itself, regaining its classical past in the process. Intellectual contact with the East, so long a need, became a luxury. From being the teacher Islamic civilization gradually changed into an object of study, and in this capacity its contribution to Western self-interpretation has been invaluable. But the profound resemblances between medieval Islam and medieval Christendom, both Latin and Greek, while heightened by political contacts and an intensive exchange of ideas, are due to community of origin rather than to adjustment of any one unit to the impact of outside influence.*

IV

Mastery of nature, public morality, and the condition of the common man have been suggested as measures of backwardness or achievement of a civilization.[43] It does not require elaborate demonstration that, by these standards, the Islamic world has but a small contribution to make. There has never been a concerted effort in Islam to put natural resources to such use as would insure progressive control of the physical conditions of life. Inventions, discoveries, and improvements might be accepted but hardly ever were searched for. Despotism, foreign rule, a certain lack of organizational stamina, and otherworldliness prevented the perpetual verbal attacks on corruption from taking effect and never allowed the concept of the opposition as a constructive political force to take root. The misery of the lowly is made permanent by the contempt of the squalid masses that has animated the leading castes throughout Islam, individual charity and religious equality notwithstanding. The finest accomplishments of Muslim civilization remained confined to a relatively small circle, and even al-Ghazâlî deemed it necessary to withhold a part of his teachings from the untutored ears of the crowd. Social consciousness never grew sufficiently strong to raise the value of human life not protected by

[43] By W. E. Hocking, *The Spirit of World Politics* (New York, 1932), pp. 12–17.

any claim to special consideration, such as power, wealth, or education.

Islam has never shown that overflowing abundance of ideas, that boundless fertility that is the greatness of the Greeks, nor did it spend itself in exuberant advance to unknown shores regardless of the havoc such advance might wreak on the present possession, as is the way of the West. Islam does not reach to the stars—it is realistic, which is only a euphemism for being timid. And this timidity comes from the realization that the combination of the many disparate elements which make up Muslim civilization might split under the impact of the unknown. So traditionalism is erected like a wall to shield the gathered harvest and assure next year's returns. The mental effort is directed toward ever subtler understanding of the ancestral heritage, and toward ever more perfect expression of the familiar. Expansion of the range of control would entail the relinquishing of proved verities and procedures. There is no authoritative guide to progress, and human wisdom is not to be trusted. The awareness of man's frailty and the futility of his works stunts that undaunted self-confidence which is the basis of the will to progress.

When aṣ-Ṣûlî (d. 946) tells of the beginnings of the Arabic script, there is no doubt in his mind that the Arabs learned the art of writing from the people of Ḥîra in Mesopotamia. But he does not have the courage to discard an etiological story whose inanity he could not possibly have failed to notice. Six foreigners settled among the ᶜAdnân, and their names, Abjad, Safᶜaḍ, etc., were split up into what came to be the letters of the Arabic alphabet. A few missing signs were then invented by the immigrants to meet the needs of their hosts' language. On second thought, these foreigners are described as kings of Midian and said to have perished together with those who disbelieved in the mission of the prophet Shuᶜaib.[44]

Since religion was the fortress under whose protection Islamic life unfolded, extreme caution was required not to let corroding skepticism enter through what would to the heedless eye seem a very minor breach in the wall. From very early times the

[44] Ṣûlî, *Adab al-kuttâb*, pp. 28–30.

presence of foreign words in the "Arabic Koran" had puzzled the pious. In the beginning there was no hesitation to acknowledge the fact. An "Arabic Koran" was a Koran easily understandable to the Arabs but not necessarily composed of none but genuinely Arabic words. Only a little later, however, the philologist, Abû ᶜUbaida (d. 825), said: "Whoever pretends that there is in the Koran anything other than the Arabic tongue has made a serious charge against God." His motive apparently was a feeling that "the existence of foreign words in the Book would be a reflection on the sufficiency of Arabic as a medium for the divine revelation." Aṭ-Ṭabarî declared that the so-called "foreign" words were cases of coincidence where Arabic and a foreign tongue happened to use the same expression for the same thing. Others went so far as to claim that those controversial words were of Arabic origin and had been borrowed by the neighboring peoples. As-Suyûṭî suggests a compromise solution to the effect that the "foreign" words had been adopted by the pagan Arabs on their travels in Syria and Abyssinia. Some of them had been Arabicized, some had retained their foreign sound and form. These words had been used in prose and poetry and, finally, in the Koran. Thus, the words are Arabic, although, in the last analysis, of non-Arabic provenience.[45] It is evident that nonscientific considerations inspired by the "higher interest" of preserving a point of faith prevented the Muslim scholars from speaking their minds on this subject or possibly even from acknowledging to themselves the obvious facts of the case.

From the viewpoint of what it set out to do, Islam failed to make good its universalist claim, but it succeeded in providing the believer with a civilized and dignified form of life. Islam has not conquered the world. Muslim civilization grew through its tolerance of alien elements, but their variety defied complete integration and the intellectual basis of its Arab roots proved too slim to carry and unify the legacies of the many pasts which

[45] For this question cf. A. Jeffery, *The Foreign Vocabulary of the Qur'ân* pp. 5–10, from which the above instances are taken. Almost three centuries before as-Suyûṭî, as-Sakkâkî (d. 1229), had made the sensible observation that despite a certain proportion of foreign words in the text the Koran was called "Arabic" a fortiori (cf. *Miftâḥ al-ᶜulûm* [Cairo, n.d.; *ca.* 1317/1898], p. 308).

Islam found itself called upon to administer. In the light of the crudeness of its origin[46] its achievement is extraordinary, and the tenacious vitality of this civilization, whose answers to the elemental questions besetting the human mind still satisfy about one-eighth of mankind, is indeed a cause for wonder.

The strength of Islam is in the roundedness of personality which at its best it is able to produce. This does not mean universality, nor does it imply that immediacy in relation to the worlds of thought and perception which lends so much color to the personality of the Greek. But the Muslim possesses a quality of repose, of dignity and poise, which could develop only as the result of a static conception of the ideal world and the ideal society. The West is ready to sacrifice the present for the future. We crave not the good life for ourselves but the better life for our posterity. We recognize the supreme value of change, because we are afraid of stagnation; and stagnation to us not only signifies death but means betrayal of our one and only task, which is the advancement of the race. Such a concept of life requires constant adaptation to new conditions. While the ultimate ideal of perfection remains unaltered, the auxiliary ideals of the day, that are means rather than final ends-in-themselves, compel continuous reorientation. We strive without letup, and the effort of our uphill fight which we feel we shall be winning if only we keep at it long enough is the true satisfaction of our lives.

The Muslim's world is at rest, and he is at rest within it. His immediacy to God and his acceptance of the divine order were never, during the Middle Ages, seriously disturbed. Resignation and submission to the inevitable and abdication of searching reason before the inscrutable were rewarded by the consciousness of fitting perfectly and naturally into the great preordained scheme of things that embraces mankind as it embraces the genii, the angels, and the stars. The Muslim knows and accepts man's limitations. In fact, he is inclined to underrate man's capabilities. He finds happiness in attuning himself to the will of the Lord as it is revealed in the wondrous world around him. God has vouchsafed him enough of the truth to understand

[46] For this judgment cf. Della Vida, *Crozer Quarterly*, XXI, 215.

what needs understanding and to trust divine wisdom where understanding ends.

Know, al-Ghazâlî says, man has not been created for jest or without a purpose, but his value is high and great his dignity. He is not from eternity, but he is destined for eternity. His body is earthly and of this lower world, but his mind belongs to the upper world and is divine. From the deepest depths to the highest heights everything low and everything sublime is within his range.[47]

At the end of his path, Ḥayy b. Yaqẓân, "the Self-taught Philosopher," knew that "all Wisdom, Direction and good Success, consisted in what the Messengers of God had spoken, and the divine Law deliver'd; and that there was no other way besides this, and that there could be nothing added to it; and that there were Men appointed to every Work, and that every one was best capable of doing that unto which he was appointed by nature; that 'this was God's way of dealing with those which were gone before, and thou shalt find no Change in his way.' "[48]

In exchange for the self-enjoyment of the advancing mind, the Muslim has been given peace and repose. He stands secure in the center of a wisely ordained world. He knows his duties and his rewards. He is safe as long as he obeys. Paradise is his birthright, and patient composure will preserve it in the hustle and bustle of this world with its specious beauty and vain allurements. Empires rise and fall, but he knows the lesson of their passing vainglory. His soul is in wait for the hour the Lord has appointed for the final encounter. It is for him to liberate himself from defilement and mean desire, to defy temptation, and to subdue the passions. He trembles as he thinks of his shortcomings; but the Prophet will intercede for him, and Allah's mercy is without bounds. He will be saved.

[47] H. Ritter, *Al-Ghasali, Das Elixir der Glückseligkeit* (Jena, 1923), p. 16; this passage is missing in *Kîmiyâʾ as-saʿâda* (2d ed.; Cairo, 1343). Masʿûdî, *Tanbîh*, p. 76, seems to stand alone with his belief in unlimited scientific progress. He interprets the line, Koran 12:76, "above everyone who has knowledge is One Who Knows"—intended in the context to emphasize God's omniscience—as referring to the superior knowledge of each subsequent writer who profits by the experience of his predecessors.

[48] The last phrase recalls Koran 48:23. *The History of Hayy ibn Yaqzan* by Abu Bakr Ibn Tufail, trans. Simon Ockley (1708), revised by A. S. Fulton (New York, n.d.; after 1928), p. 175.

ADDENDA

P. 10, n. 4. C. Erdmann, *Die Entstehung des Kreuzzugsgedankens* (Stuttgart, 1935), esp. pp. 1–29, studies the Western concept of "Holy War," pointing out that the Christian *jihâd* was primarily directed against heretics and only later against the unbelievers in general. The Augustinian concept of the *bellum iustum* (against the enemies of God) came to be fairly universally accepted throughout Western but not in Eastern Christianity. Nicephoros' attitude is thus a rather isolated phenomenon. Cf. M. Canard, *Revue africaine*, LXXIX (1936), 605–23. Generally speaking, the Muslim was satisfied with expanding Allah's political dominion, whereas the Christian conquest for God implied the conversion of the conquered.

P. 26, n. 63. For details on Sallâm's expedition to the Rampart cf. C. E. Wilson, *Asia Major, Introductory Volume* (*Hirth Anniversary Volume*) (London, 1923), pp. 575–612, esp. pp. 592–97, the translation from Ibn Ḫurdâḏbih, and pp. 609–11, the actual itinerary of the expedition. The public interest in the area is reflected in a verse of Abû ʾsh-Shamaqmaq (d. *ca.* 796), Frag. XLVI, 2, of the edition prepared by this writer.

P. 33, n. 4. R. Menéndez Pidal, *La España del Cid* (Madrid, 1929), I, 64, independently reached the same conclusion as Pirenne with regard to Islam breaking up the *unidad antigua* and bringing about the Middle Ages, which to him are essentially *una época latino-árabe*. E. R. Curtius, *Zs. f. roman. Philologie*, LVIII (1938), 132, n. 4, appears to indorse Menéndez's view. On the whole, however, scholarly opinion has tended to veer away from Pirenne's theories; cf., e.g., R. S. Lopez, *Speculum*, XVIII (1943), 14–39, M. Lombard, *Annales: économies, sociétés, civilisations*, III (1948), 196–98, and C. M. Cipolla, *Annales: économies, sociétés, civilisations*, IV (1949), 5–9.

P. 40. The name goes back to a passage in *Kalîla wa-Dimna* as demonstrated by I. Goldziher, *Islam*, I (1910), 22 ff. For its significance in terms of the tendencies represented by the Iḫwân cf. G. Richter, *Studien zur Geschichte der älteren arabischen Fürstenspiegel* (Leipzig, 1932), p. 31. The name may perhaps be compared with that of the Iḫwân aṣ-ṣidq (of Balḫ ?), referred to by Qushairî; cf. R. Hartmann, *Islam*, VI (1916), 47. The Ḥanbalite Ibn Taimiyya (d. 1328), interpreting the designation Iḫwân aṣ-Ṣafâ as "Brethren of Purity," speaks of them tauntingly as Iḫwân al-Kadar, "Brethren of Turbidness"; *Kitâb minhâj as-sunna an-nabawiyya* . . . . (Cairo, 1321–22), IV, 146^{11-22}.

P. 45, n. 56. H. Beck, *Vorsehung und Vorherbestimmung in der theologischen Literatur der Byzantiner* (Rome, 1937), pp. 46–47, dates Bartholomew to *ca.* 900.

P. 50, n. 69. On Ricoldus and his work cf. U. Monneret de Villard, *Orientalia Christiana periodica*, X (1944), 227–74, and the same author's *Lo Studio dell'Islam in Europa nel XII e nel XIII secolo* (Citta del Vaticano, 1944), *passim*.

P. 52. For anti-Islamic polemics in the Middle Ages cf. also G. Hölscher, *Zs. f. philosophische Forschung*, II (1947/48), 259–74.

P. 54, n. 88. For the problems which the translators had to face cf. Rosenthal, *Technique*, pp. 27–29.

P. 56, n. 95. V. Minorsky, '*Ḥudûd al-ᶜâlam*' (London, 1937), pp. 418–25, lists the major passages dealing with Byzantium that are to be found in Arabic writers. For additional information cf. M. Izzeddin, *Revue des études islamiques, 1941–46* (1947), pp. 41–62, and Minorsky, *Annuaire de l'Institut de Philologie et d'Histoire Orientales et Slaves*, X (1950), 455 ff.

P. 59, n. 102. Rabîᶜa b. Umayya b. Ḫalaf al-Jumaḥî leaves the Muslims for Byzantium because of a conflict with Abû Bakr, the first caliph; cf. R. A. Nicholson, *JRAS*, 1902, pp. 340 and 827.

P. 59, n. 103. An immigrant from the *dâr al-islâm*, Bishr by name, is alleged to have instigated the first proceedings against the images; cf. L. Caetani, *Chronographia* (Paris, 1912–23), *s.a.* 104. E. Montet, *Revue de l'histoire des religions*, LIII (1906), 145–63, has published a "rituel d'abjuration des Musulmans dans l'Église grecque," dating from the period of Photios (d. 891; patriarch of Constantinople, 858–67 and 878–86).

P. 71. The pre-Islamic Allah belongs with the early high-gods that tend to fade from actual cult but who will not infrequently be revived by "prophets" bent on eliminating what to them is the degenerate paganism of their contemporaries. In this sense Mohammed is in line with Moses and again the later Israelite Prophets who uphold the heavenly *Hochgott* Yahwe against the *baᶜlîm* of their day. Cf. M. Éliade, *Traité d'histoire des religions* (Paris, 1949), pp. 75 and 102. C. Brockelmann, *Archiv f. Religionswissenschaft*, XXI (1922), 118, considers the idea of Allah as a *Hochgott* the possession of certain esoteric circles.

P. 81, n. 25. Similarly Ḥamd b. Muḥammad al-Ḫaṭṭâbî (d. 996 or 998), *Kitâb bayân iᶜjâz al-Qurᵓân*, MS Leiden 1654, fol. 30*a*–*b*. Ibn Taimiyya, on the other hand, insists that the several versions of the same story in the Book always have their particular significance; cf. H. Laoust, *Essai sur les doctrines sociales et politiques de Taḳî-d-Dîn Aḥmed b. Taimîya* (Cairo, 1939), p. 231.

P. 91, n. 63. R. Blachère, *Histoire de la littérature arabe*, Vol. I (Paris, 1952), pronounces against the authenticity of the poem on the ground of its style being so much simpler than that of the rest of al-Aᶜshâ's verse. But it would seem that this simplicity would be accounted for by the newness of the theme and its independence from the recognized kinds.

P. 96, n. 79. B. Snell, *Die Entdeckung des Geistes* (Hamburg, 1946), p. 43, refers to Gideon's demand that God break the "laws" of nature as a sign of support (Judg. 6:36–40) and observes that the signs which the Greeks ask of their gods are always in keeping with natural process, their portentous character being due to their timing. He goes on to note that "im Gegensatz zu den Griechen, die aus dem geordneten Kosmos auf die Existenz Gottes schliessen, offenbart sich dieser den Christen gerade aus dem Paradoxen. . . . ." It is obvious that in this regard Muslim piety is firmly rooted in the Judeo-Christian tradition.

P. 98, n. 89. Faḍl b. Sahl (d. as vizier of al-Maʾmûn in 818 or 819), when only recently converted to Islam, was found, *ca.* 806, by his physician reading the Koran. When the physician asked him (in Persian): How do you find the Koran? Faḍl replied: Nice; and like (the animal fables of) Kalîla and Dimna (Ibn al-Qifṭî, *Taʾrîḫ al-ḥukamâʾ*, ed. J. Lippert [Leipzig, 1903], p. 140; quoted by J. Fück, "Arabiya. Untersuchungen zur arab. Sprach- und Stilgeschichte," *Abh. Sächs. AW, philologisch-hist. Kl.*, XLV/1 [1950], 47).

P. 101. But Ashʿarî tries to safeguard man's responsibility by presenting him as "acquiring" (but not causing) his actions through assenting to them. The notion of this *kasb*, or acquisition, corresponds to the *sygkatathesis* of the Stoics; whether influence must be assumed is debated; cf. S. Horovitz, *Ueber den Einfluss der griech. Philosophie auf die Entwicklung des Kalam* (Breslau, 1909), p. 41, n. 1, and the same, *Der Einfluss der griech. Skepsis auf die Entwicklung der Philosophie bei den Arabern* (Breslau, 1915), pp. 32–33. W. M. Watt, *Free Will and Predestination in Early Islam* (London, 1948), p. 1, characterizes the Muslim "debate about Predestination and Free Will" as "a discussion of the respective share of God and man in determining the course of events in the present," which, as he rightly observes, is "far removed from the modern discussion of Free Will and Scientific Determinism."

P. 101, n. 98. Cf. Girolamo Cardano (d. 1576), *De vita propria*, trans. Jean Stoner (New York, 1930), p. 265: "I know that the souls of men are immortal; the manner I know not."

P. 102, n. 99. For the doctrines of the Muʿtazila cf. H. S. Nyberg, *EI*, III, 787–93; German translation in *Handwörterbuch des Islam*, ed. A. J. Wensinck and J. H. Kramers (Leiden, 1941), pp. 556–62.

P. 109, n. 4. Later the idea gained ground that the *sunna* had been revealed to Mohammed by Gabriel at the same time as the Koran; cf. Laoust, *Essai*, p. 234.

P. 111, n. 9. So also St. Ambrose: "Omne verum a quocumque dicatur, a Spiritu

Sancto est" (quoted by E. Gilson, *The Spirit of Mediaeval Philosophy* [New York, 1936], p. 428).

P. 112, n. 11. The dislike of innovation, the authority of tradition as such, and the consequent necessity to present reforms in terms of a restoration of the conditions prevailing at the period of the founder Islam has in common with medieval Christianity.

P. 133. The *ḫirqa* of the Ṣûfî, which is originally blue (the color of mourning), is made up of patches sometimes hailing from the cloak of a fellow-mystic. The mantles of the Syriac saints such as Ephraim Syrus, Jacob Bardeᶜânâ, or Mar Babai "consisted of rags of many colors"; cf. Wensinck, *Verhandelingen d. Kon. Ak. van Wetenschappen*, Afd. Letterkunde, N.R., XVIII (1918), No. 1, pp. 54–55.

P. 135, n. 108. The concept of the *scala mentis*, the rungs of the ladder on which the mystic nears God, goes back to Plato *Symposium* 211*C*, where the rise to the unicity of the Forms is described as occurring in upward stages; cf. A. J. Festugière, *Contemplation et vie contemplative selon Platon* (Paris, 1936), p. 165, n. 1.

P. 135, n. 111. It is perhaps worth noting that Plotinus, according to Porphyry's *Vita*, chap. 23, attained to ecstasy only four times during Porphyry's stay with him. In general, ecstasy was rare among the Neo-Platonists but comparatively frequent in the circles of the medieval mystics. (But cf. Bernard of Clairvaux *Sermo in Canticum*, 23:15, who complains of the rareness and brevity of ecstasy: "Heu rara hora et parva mora!") The passage in which Plotinus describes his supreme experience was known to the Arabs through the so-called *Theology of Aristotle*, ed. F. Dieterici (Leipzig, 1882), p. 8 (trans. [Leipzig, 1883], pp. 8–9); cf. G. Vajda, *Journal asiatique*, CCXXXVI (1948), 325.

P. 137. Other mystics, too, worked in this direction; thus, e.g., Hujwîrî and Anṣârî of Herat (d. 1088/89).

P. 139, n. 121. These remarks are attributed to Bâyazîd Bisṭâmî (d. *ca.* 875) by Qushairî, *Risâla* (Cairo, 1330), p. 164^{15-16}. M. Smith, *Râbiᶜa*, p. 31, records another saying of Bâyazîd's according to which he did not attach high value to the miracles of saints because even the Satans were on occasion granted such "answering of prayers."

P. 145, n. 5. The Roman definition of *jurisprudentia* is derived from the Stoic concept of philosophy as the knowledge, *episteme*, of things human and divine; cf. H. von Arnim, *Stoicorum veterum fragmenta* (Leipzig and Berlin, 1921–24), II, 35 and 36.

P. 151. Andrae, *Person*, p. 229, points out that, in the beginning at least, the doctrine of the *ᶜiṣma* aimed at safeguarding the authenticity of Revelation rather than at exalting the Prophet.

P. 153. For an analysis of the Muslim state in its relation to its function in terms of the Muslim outlook on life cf. the writer's study, "Government in Islam," in *Freedom and Authority in Our Time: Proceedings of the 12th Conference on Science, Philosophy and Religion* (New York, 1953), pp. 701–16.

P. 154. Ghazâlî, *Iḥyâ ᶜulûm ad-dîn* (Bûlâq, 1289/1872), II, 129[22], describes the relation of *dîn*, religion, and *mulk*, state, as that of twins who are dependent on each other (the same expression is used by his contemporary, Niẓâm al-Mulk, *Siyâsat Nâmah*, p. 55 [p. 83 of trans.], where it occurs in a saying ascribed to the Prophet); the Persian tradition reinforced this concept (cf. A. Christensen, *Les Gestes des rois dans les traditions de l'Iran antique* [Paris, 1936], p. 92). The Ḥanafite *qâḍî*, Ibn Jamâᶜa (d. 1333), *Taḥrîr al-aḥkâm*, ed. H. Kofler, *Islamica*, VI (1934), 357, appears to have conceived of the ruler's office as "contractually assumed" (cf. also H. A. R. Gibb and H. Bowen, *Islamic Society and the West*, I, i [London, etc., 1950], 32).

P. 159, n. 34. In assessing Mâwardî's theories, it must not be forgotten that he is pleading the cause of the caliphate eager to shake off the tutelage of the Bûyid princes; cf. H. A. R. Gibb, *Islamic Culture*, XI (1937), 291–302, and *Archives d'histoire du droit oriental*, III (1948), 401–10.

P. 168, n. 58. The conviction that bad government is preferable to revolt and anarchy expresses itself in early Islam in the affirmative answer given to the question whether prayer behind an unrighteous *imâm* is valid. Ghazâlî's contemporary, Aᶜmaq (*ca.* 1100), also expresses himself strongly in favor of royal injustice as against the possibility of revolutionary disorders (H. Massé, *Anthologie persane* [Paris, 1950], p. 54).

P. 171, n. 5. Characteristic of Persian rank and caste consciousness is the much-quoted story of the Sassanian king Ḫusrav Anôsharvân and the shoemaker who, in return for a loan of four million *dirham*, wishes to have his son included among the scribes—the king indignantly refuses the request on the ground that low birth could not be repaired; cf. Firdausî, *Shâh-Nâmah* (Calcutta, 1829), pp. 1777–79 (trans. A. G. and E. Warner [London, 1905–25], VIII, 48–50).

P. 179. For *ḏimma* in the sense of "citizenship" of the Muslim subject of the empire cf. F. Løkkegaard, *Islamic Taxation in the Classic Period* (Copenhagen, 1950), p. 84.

P. 179. In analogy to the *jizya*, or poll tax, exacted from the *ḏimmî*, the Byzantines levied a capitation tax, *kephalition*, on Jews and Muslims (cf. N. H. Baynes and H. St. L. B. Moss, *Byzantium* [Oxford, 1948], p. 82, n. 3).

P. 182, n. 26. Cf. also E. Strauss, *P. Hirschler Memorial Book* (Budapest, 1949), pp. 73–94.

P. 191, n. 45. W. Thomson, *The Macdonald Presentation Volume* (Princeton, 1933), p. 384, points to the connection of the concepts of *quᶜûd*, neutrality (in civic-religious conflicts), and *taqiyya*. The idea of *taqiyya* (as a religious injunction) antedates Islam; it can be traced, for instance, among Elkesaites and Mandaeans (cf. H. Waitz, *Harnack-Ehrung* [Leipzig, 1921], p. 96; E. S. Drower, *The Mandaeans of Iraq and Iran* [Oxford, 1937], p. 15). *Taqiyya* was practiced also among Manichaeans in Christian areas and by Zoroastrians in Muslim; cf. B. Spuler, *Iran in früh-islamischer Zeit* (Wiesbaden, 1952), p. 181.

P. 193, n. 49. The passion play has been considered in an anthropological context by E. Doutté, *Magie et religion dans l'Afrique du Nord* (*Algiers*, 1909), pp. 537–40.

P. 205, n. 79. Yazîd b. abî Unaisa (*fl.* after 744), the founder of the Yazîdiyya, denies the universal character of Mohammed's mission and expects a Persian prophet with a new revelation which would cancel the koranic law; cf. R. Strothmann, *Islam*, IV (1913), 72 ff.

P. 206. In Islam, as in Western Christendom, cultural renaissances are apt to develop at the expense of political unity.

P. 208, n. 88. The interest in national psychology was to continue. The Iḫwân aṣ-Ṣafâ tried their hand on the problem, and Tauḥîdî, *Imtâᶜ*, I, 70 ff., even analyzes the problem of a comparison of nations *qua* problem; cf. also *ibid.*, pp. 211–13.

P. 210, n. 100. The "Companion" Abû Ḏarr (d. 653) marries a Negro woman to be lowered in the eyes of his fellows (A. S. Tritton, *Muslim Theology* [London, 1947], p. 13); the *imâm* Ḥasan (d. 669), in return for a service, by the force of his prayer miraculously changes a Negro into a white (Donaldson, *op. cit.*, p. 75).

P. 213, n. 105. Similarly, Niẓâm al-Mulk, *Siyâsat Nâmah*, p. 131 (trans., pp. 192–93). Cf. also Ibn al-Qalânisî (d. 1160), *History of Damascus*, ed. H. F. Amedroz (Leiden, 1908), pp 283–84 (trans. R. Le Tourneau, *Damas de 1075 à 1154* [Damascus, 1952], pp. 272–74).

P. 215. Similarly Qudâma b. Jaᶜfar (d. 922), *Naqd ash-shiᶜr* (Cairo, 1934), pp. 51–52, who includes artisans as well as robbers among the *sûqa*, the common people.

P. 215. The *Qâbûs Nâmah* (trans. Levy), p. 18, correlates social position and personal value. "God had power, truth to tell, to make all men rich; but in his wisdom He decided that some should be rich and others poor, that the rank and honor due to different men might be clearly shown and the more noble of them be distinguished." The passage in

Tauḥîdî's "Risâla fî ᵓl-ᶜulûm" (in *Risâlatân* [Constantinople, 1301]), pp. 205–6, bespeaks a revival of the classic prejudice against the technician. The problem of merit and education versus descent as giving title to social position remains alive throughout the Middle Ages; cf. ᶜAbdarraḥmân b. Muḥammad al-Bisṭâmî (d. 1454), *Manâhij at-tawassul* (Constantinople, 1299), p. 137.

P. 218, n. 122. G. Vajda, *Journal asiatique*, CCXXXVI (1948), 325, points out that the *muḥtasib* is, so to speak, the successor of the Hellenistic *agoranomos*. In the life of St. John the Almsgiver (d. 619) there occurs an overseer of the market in Alexandria who has the right to scourge and parade publicly an offending shopkeeper; cf. E. Dawes and N. H. Baynes, *Three Byzantine Saints* (Oxford, 1948), p. 227.

P. 236, n. 29. A portrait of the "ideal layman" was drawn by ᶜAbdalqâdir al-Jîlânî (d. 1166) in his *Futûḥ al-ghaib*, trans. W. Braune (Berlin and Leipzig, 1933), *maqâla* 78, pp. 156–60.

P. 240. The wearing of a soldier's uniform constitutes a presumption of bad character, Ghazâlî, *Iḥyâ'*, II, 107^{32} (cf. also *ibid.*, p. $109^{15, 29}$). The Ṣûfî, Aḥmad b. Ḫiḍrûya (late ninth cent.), dons soldier's clothes to invite public contempt, Hujwîrî, p. 119 (quoted by R. Hartmann, *Islam*, VIII [1918], 198).

P. 243, n. 50. A. J. Wensinck, *The Muslim Creed* (Cambridge, 1932), p. 110, quotes a tradition from Muslim to the effect that "it is a proof of a man's *fiqh* (= insight) that he says *Allâh aᶜlam* (God knows best) in matters of which he has no knowledge." The *Qâbûs Nâmah*, p. 23 (trans., pp. 32–33), adduces Socrates and Buzurjmihr as instances of illustrious men who would readily avow their ignorance.

P. 246. Niẓâm al-Mulk speaks of God as choosing one model ruler in each *ᶜaṣr*, or century, *Siyâsat Nâmah*, p. 5 (trans., p. 5).

P. 247, n. 62. The disputation in which Mattà finds himself involved concerns a problem that was much on the minds of his contemporaries, viz., the relation of grammar and logic; P. Kraus, *Jābir ibn Ḥayyān: Contribution à l'histoire des idées scientifiques dans l'Islam* (Cairo, 1942–43), II, 251, n. 2, offers a rich collection of pertinent material. A. Abel, *Byzantinoslavica*, X (1949), 229–32, analyzes the literary pattern of the *Religionsgespräch*.

P. 248, n. 63. For additional instances cf. B. Spuler, *Iran in früh-islamischer Zeit* (Wiesbaden, 1952), p. 153, n. 3. The disputation was equally popular in the West and retained its vogue into the seventeenth century.

P. 250. The basis for a history of the term was laid by C. A. Nallino, *Raccolta di scritti editi e inediti* (Rome, 1939–48),

VI, 1–17 (French trans. by C. Pellat, *La Littérature arabe des origines à l'époque de la dynastie Umayyade* [Paris, 1950], pp. 7–28). Richter, *Studien*, p. 41, and Christensen, *Gestes*, p. 102, have pointed out that in the early translation literature *adab* renders the Pahlavi *âyên*, "rules" (of behavior, etiquette, etc.). A brief characterization of *adab* was attempted by F. Rosenthal, *Orientalia*, N.S., XI (1942), 263–68.

P. 250, n. 67. A variant of Maʾmûn's saying is ascribed to Alexander the Great by al-Bisṭâmî, *Manâhij*, p. 100; Tauḥîdî, *Imtâᶜ*, II, 62, quotes contemporary opinion to the same effect; the *Qâbûs Nâmah*, p. 30[6] (trans., p. 45), quotes Anôshirvân as telling his son: "How can a man who has acquaintance with kings lay himself down to sleep free of care?" Ghazâlî, *Iḥyâʾ*, II, 124–42 (trans. H. Bauer, *Islamische Ethik* [Halle a/Saale, 1922], III, 147–200), well illustrates the Muslim's attitude to his rulers. The *Siyâsat Nâmah* has, pp. 5–8 (trans., pp. 5–9), a description of the ideal ruler and his functions, which it is useful to compare with the Persian concept of the model king; cf. Christensen, *Gestes*, pp. 75–106 and 141.

P. 255, n. 80. For history as an essential part of Muslim education cf. F. Rosenthal, *A History of Muslim Historiography* (Leiden, 1952), pp. 28–48.

P. 255, n. 82. The relation of *adab* and *sunna* was seen as a problem; cf., e.g., Tauḥîdî, *Imtâᶜ*, II, 76, where Manṣûr is criticized for putting *adab* above *sunna*.

P. 256, n. 85. The same spirit animates Saladin's (d. 1193) saying as reported by Ibn Jubair, p. 298 (trans. R. J. C. Broadhurst [London, 1952], p. 311): ". . . . and if I emptied to him all that is in my treasury . . . . it would not console him for the hot blush on his cheek as he asked of me." Ghazâlî, *Iḥyâ*,ʾ II, 162[11-13], describes "giving without being asked" as the lowest degree in the execution of that right which your friend has over your property.

P. 274. The pattern is adumbrated in Lucian's (d. after A.D. 180) *Menippos* iv (I, 193, Jacobitz) and Justin Martyr (d. betw. 163 and 167), *Dialogue with Tryphon* ii–viii. 2 (where A. von Harnack, *Mission und Ausbreitung des Christentums* [Leipzig, 1924], p. 405, discerns a fixed scheme which Justin follows). Muḥâsibî's influence on Ghazâlî is indicated by Massignon, *Lexique*, p. 216, and discussed at some length by M. Smith, *JRAS*, 1936, pp. 65–78. H. H. Schaeder, *Orientalistische Literaturzeitung*, XXIX (1926), 54–55, observes the closeness of Ghazâlî's *Munqiḏ* to Nâṣir-i Ḫusrav's autobiographical *qaṣîda*, ᶜUmar Ḫayyâm's *Silsilat at-tartîb* (about which cf. H. Ritter, *Oriens*, I [1948], 362), and the ideas of the Iḫwân aṣ-Ṣafâ.

P. 281. In a famous passage, Bêrûnî, *India*, ed. E. Sachau

(London, 1887), p. 207 (trans. [London, 1888], II, 10–11), notes the disinterest of the Hindu in historical matters and contrasts their outlook by implication with the very different attitude of the Muslims.

P. 283, n. 64. H. S. Nyberg, *Die Religionen des alten Iran* (Leipzig, 1938), p. 403, characterizes the function of genealogy. "Die Genealogie ist im Orient, ja fast überall auser bei uns Modernen, keine Wissenschaft, und sie ist es nie gewesen; sie ist eine praktische Angelegenheit, eine Rechtsnorm und ein Mittel in der Hand geschickter Politiker, ungefähr so, wie es die Etikettefragen an den europäischen Höfen des 17. Jh. waren."

P. 308, n. 51. Jâmî (d. 1492) gives the motif of the love suicide a mystical turn; cf. Massé, *Anthologie*, pp. 176–77.

P. 311, n. 58. Already Aristotle *Eth. Nic.* iii. vii. 13 observes: "But to seek death in order to escape from poverty, or the pangs of love, or from pain or sorrow, is not the act of a courageous man" (trans. H. Rackham, "Loeb Classical Library").

P. 312, n. 63. On love as sickness cf. V. Hoelzer, *De poesi amatoria a comicis atticis exculta* . . . . (diss., Marburg, 1899), esp. pp. 43 ff. (reference owed to Professor E. R. Curtius), and H. Crohns, *Archiv für Kulturgeschichte*, III (1905), 66–86.

P. 315, n. 81. The *Qâbûs Nâmah*, p. 40^{17-19} (trans., p. 62) observes: ". . . . wine-drinking is a transgression; if you wish to commit a transgression, it should at least not be a flavorless one. If you drink wine, let it be the finest; if you listen to music, let it be the sweetest, and if you commit a forbidden act, let it be with a beautiful partner, so that even though you may be convicted of sin in the next world, you will at any rate not be branded a fool in this."

P. 322, n. 4. The internationalism of the Muslim scholar brings to mind Vitruvius' words (*De architectura* vi, Introduction): "Alone, of all mankind, the scholar is no stranger in foreign lands; . . . . he is a citizen in every state . . . ." (trans. F. Granger, "Loeb Classical Library" [London and New York, 1931–34]).

P. 324. For the relationship of Indian and Muslim civilization cf. Massignon, *Lexique*, pp. 63–80; S. Pines, *Beiträge zur islamischen Atomenlehre* (Berlin, 1936), pp. 118–23; and M. M. Moreno, "Mistica musulmana e mistica indiana," *Annali lateranensi*, X (1946), 103–212.

P. 325. For the problems of the theological scholasticism of the Muᶜtazila and the philosophical scholasticism of the *falâsifa* cf. L. Gauthier, *Revue d'histoire de la philosophie*, II (1928), 348 ff. Abû Sulaimân al-Manṭiqî (d. shortly after 981), as quoted by Tauḥîdî (d. 1023), *Muqâbasât* (Cairo, 1347/1929), pp. 223–24, describes the Muᶜtazilites as dialecticians and sophists and the *falâsifa* as those who are concerned with essential problems.

P. 326, n. 10. Abû Ṭâhir al-Baghdâdî (d. 1123), *Qânûn al-balâgha*, ed. M. Kurd ᶜAlî, *Rasâᵓil al-bulaghâᵓ* (3d ed.; Cairo, 1946), pp. 408–68, seems to have been influenced by Qudâma.

P. 327, n. 11. It is perhaps relevant in this connection to quote A. B. Keith, *The Sanskrit Drama* (Oxford, 1924), pp. 329–30, who feels that the division stipulated by the Indian theorists between "dramatic ornaments" and "characteristics" (or "beauties") cannot be justified on any conceivable theory—both are modes of exposition, figures of thought and diction.

P. 332, n. 24. Nâṣir-i Ḫusrav sketches his own intellectual and philosophical development in terms of his growth from the vegetable to the animal state, etc.; cf. Massé, *Anthologie*, pp. 90–91.

P. 333, n. 25. Sarton, *op. cit.*, II, 61–62, discusses the interrelation of theological and scientific endeavor. Muslim interest in zoölogy is based on this problem: "How did all the creatures of God come into being? Was the act of divine creation a continuous or an instantaneous performance, and in the second case, to what extent did it involve the future? It is not probable that they were acquainted with St. Augustine's theory of potential creation, but some of their philosophers developed a very similar one. . . . . For example al-Naẓẓâm (d. 845) . . . . explained the idea of a creation which was largely hidden; only a part of it appears at a time, generation after generation, though the creation was complete from the outset. This is truly a theory of evolution. . . . Other speculations on fundamental biological problems—such as the struggle for existence and adaptation—are found in [Jâḥiẓ' *Ḥayawân*]. The idea that all objects of nature could be arranged in a progressive series 'from mineral to plant, from plant to animal and from animal to man' was a commonplace in Islam . . . . but that arrangement should not be confused with our modern idea of gradual transformation of one species into another." Snell, *Entdeckung*, p. 44, quotes U. von Wilamowitz for the view that the belief in a created world precludes the development of a true science of nature.

P. 333, n. 27. In discussing the statement that the Prophet saw the world in the East as well as in the West, Faḫr ad-Dîn ar-Râzî (d. 1209), *Mafâtîḥ al-ghaib* (Cairo, 1324/1906), II, 433^{14-19}, asks why this should be impossible, considering that a giraffe is able to see at a distance of a three days' journey; cf. Andrae, *Person*, pp. 365–66.

P. 339. In fact, Egyptian scholarship, especially in the historical sciences, rises to a considerable level of originality during the fourteenth and fifteenth centuries. But the feeling that, on the whole, science is declining was voiced already by Bêrûnî and ᶜUmar Ḫayyâm; cf. M. Krause, *Islam*, XXVI (1942), 2 and 6–7.

P. 340, n. 41. Similarly the *Almagest* was translated into Latin in the twelfth century both from the Greek original and from its Arabic version; cf. L. Thorndike, *A History of Magic and Experimental Science* (New York, 1923), I, 109–10.

P. 341, n. 42. For the transfer from Baghdad to Spain cf. the writer, *JNES*, XI (1952), 237.

P. 342. For the present status of the problem cf. M. Rodinson, *Revue d'histoire des religions,* CXL (1951), 203–36 (with bibliography).

P. 343. Common origin as the cause of many a parallel development in Muslim and Western medieval civilization has been suggested by F. Taeschner, in *Beiträge zur Arabistik, Semitistik und Islamwissenschaft,* ed. R. Hartmann and H. Scheel (Leipzig, 1944), pp. 340–41. Taeschner is concerned primarily with parallelisms between *futuwwa* and chivalry. Th. Silverstein, *Modern Philology,* XLVII (1949), 117–26, furnishes materials permitting the more precise tracing of another such parallelism in the growth of the intellectual background of Courtly Love.

INDEX

[This Index includes proper names, adjectives derived from proper names, Arabic and other foreign technical terms, and titles of books referred to in the text. Foreign terms and book titles (except for Bible, Koran, and similar works) appear in italics. ᵓ represents a glottal stop, ᶜ a guttural not found in any Indo-European language; ḫ corresponds to *ch* in Scottish *loch* or German *ach*. Dots below a consonant indicate emphatic pronunciation.]

PRINTED IN U·S·A